Odense University Studies in History and Social Sciences vol. 225

Elites, Parties and Democracy

Elites, Parties and Democracy

Festschrift for Professor Mogens N. Pedersen

Edited by

Erik Beukel,
Kurt Klaudi Klausen
and
Poul Erik Mouritzen

Odense University Press

Publication of this book was made possible thanks to the cooperation
and generous support from
University of Southern Denmark
Ingeniør N. M. Knudsens Fond

© The authors and Odense University Press 1999
Cover design and typographical layout by Fyens Medie Center A/S
Printed by Fyens Medie Center A/S
Cover illustration by Helle Baslund

ISBN 87-7838-506-7
ISSN 0078-3307

Odense University Press
Campusvej 55
5230 Odense M
Denmark

Phone + 45 66 15 79 99
Fax + 45 66 15 81 26

E-mail: Press@forlag.sdu.dk
www-location:http//www.oup.dk

Customers in the United States and Canada please contact:

International Specialized Book Services
5804 NE Hassalo St, Portland, OR 97213, USA
Phone: + 1-800-944-6190
E-mail: info@isbs.com

Contents

Tabula Gratulatoria VII

Preface 1

Still a Young Man in a Hurry:
Mogens N. Pedersen's Works and Career 3
Gunnar Sjöblom

Democracy Pacific Style:
Between Custom and Modernity 11
Dag Anckar

A Note on Danish Parliamentary Research 31
Erik Damgaard

Institutions and Networks: A Comparison of European
and Southeast Asian Integration 49
Kjell A. Eliassen & Catherine Børve Monsen

What Was the Problem
If a First Divisor of 1.4 Was the Solution? 75
Jørgen Elklit

On Bias and Disclosure: A Personal Pathways
Perspective in Legislative Research 103
Heinz Eulau

European Union Regional Policy – Not So Inclusive? ... 119
Mike Goldsmith

Opinion Structures in Political Parties - The Law of
Increasing Polarization 137
Roger Buch Jensen

Saturation Without Parity: The Stagnating Number of
Female Councillors in Denmark 149
Ulrik Kjær

Bringing the Politics Back in:
The Public Accountability of Regulators 169
Michael Laver

When Should a Minority Government Resign? 181
Leif Lewin

Types of Democracy and Generosity with Foreign Aid:
An Indirect Test of the Democratic Peace Proposition ... 193
Arend Lijphart and Peter J. Bowman

New Political Parties in Established Party Systems:
How Successful Are They? 207
Peter Mair

To Hell with Athens' Agora 225
Jørn Henrik Petersen

The Danes and Direct Democracy 247
Palle Svensson

The European Participation Crisis:
The Problem of Democracy 265
Curt Sørensen

Immigrants at the Polls: Immigrant and Refugee
Participation in Danish Local Elections 297
Lise Togeby

Elites and the Management of Ethnoterritorial
Conflict in Western Democracies 321
Derek W. Urwin

Mogens N. Pedersen's Bibliography 333

Contributors 341

Tabula Gratulatoria

Jørn Ahlburg,
Albertslund

**Akademikernes
Centralorganisation,**
Copenhagen

Erik Allardt,
Helsinki

Dag Anckar,
Åbo

Stefan Birkebjerg Andersen,
Odense

Mads Bryde Andersen,
Copenhagen

Vibeke Normann Andersen,
Odense

Lene Anderson,
Lyngby

Hanne og Carl Bache,
Odense

Carsten Bengt-Pedersen,
Copenhagen

Rikke Berg,
Odense

Dirk Berg-Schlosser,
Marburg

Jacob Bertramsen,
Aalborg

Birgit Beukel,
Odense

Erik Beukel,
Odense

Lars Bille,
Copenhagen

Ivar Bleiklie,
Bergen

Peter Bowman,
Oceanside

Per Boye,
Odense

Michael Brochmann,
Odense

Tom Bryder,
Lund

Dag Arne Christensen,
Bergen

John Christensen,
Odense

Tom Christensen,
Oslo

Flemming Juul Christiansen,
Roskilde

Nils Christiansen,
Ringe

Vibeke og Mogens Christiansen,
Rynkeby

Copy-Dan,
Copenhagen

Peter Dahler-Larsen,
Odense

Drude Dahlerup,
Stockholm

Erik Damgaard,
Aarhus

Dansk Data Arkiv,
Odense

Wilfried Dewachter,
Leuven

K.L.L.M Dittrich,
Maastricht

Morten Egeberg,
Oslo

Niels Ejersbo,
Odense

Kjell A. Eliassen,
Sandvika

Tove og Jørgen Elklit,
Odder

Per Eriksen,
Copenhagen

Heinz Eulau,
Stanford

Egil Fivelsdal,
Holte

Annie Gaardsted Frandsen,
Aarup

Marianne Frost,
Odense

Bestyrelsen og direktionen for Fyens Stiftstidende A/S

Michael Goldsmith,
Salford

Gunnel Gustafsson,
Umeå

Sverker Gustavsson,
Uppsala

Kasper Møller Hansen,
Odense

Litten Hansen,
Copenhagen

Morten Balle Hansen,
Odense

Tore Hansen,
Oslo

Knut Heidar,
Oslo

Lars Heltoft,
Vedbæk

Sören Holmberg,
Göteborg

Uffe Jakobsen,
Copenhagen

Roger Buch Jensen,
Odense

Anders Møller Jensen,
Odense

Magnus Jerneck,
Lund

Hans Chr. Johansen,
Odense

Sune Johansson,
Odense

Bo Hakon Jørgensen,
Copenhagen

Lauri Karvonen,
Åbo

Ulrik Kjær,
Odense

Kurt Klaudi Klausen,
Odense

Erik Knudsen,
Odense

Oddbjørn Knutsen,
Oslo

Gustav Kristensen,
Odense

Stein Kuhnle,
Bergen

Søs Kaarsted,
Odense

Thomas Kaarsted,
Odense

Helge O. Larsen,
Tromsø

Helge Muhle Larsen,
Odense

Henrik Larsen,
Odense

Knud Larsen,
Holte

Finn Laursen,
Morud

Michael Laver,
Dublin

Klaus H. Levinsen,
Odense

Leif Lewin,
Uppsala

Aase Lindahl,
Odense

Wolf Linder,
Bern

Arend Lijphart,
La Jolla

Peter Porse Madsen,
Randers

Tomas Bech Madsen,
Odense

Peter Mair,
Leiden

Gerald R. McDaniel,
Faaborg

Johannes Michelsen,
Ribe

Knut Midgaard,
Oslo

Catherine Børve Monsen,
Sandvika

Anne Charlotte Mouret,
Odense

Poul Erik Mouritzen,
Odense

Wolfgang C. Müller,
Vienna

Peter Mår,
Bloemendaal

Jesper Maarbjerg,
Copenhagen

Hanne Marthe Narud,
Oslo

Ann Nielsen,
Odense

Jens Oddershede,
Munkebo

Audun Offerdal,
Fyllingsdalen

Christian Oldenburg,
Ålsgårde

Henrik Pedersen,
Odense

Inger Pedersen,
Odense

Jørgen Flindt Pedersen,
Kerteminde

Søren Hviid Pedersen,
Odense

Jørn Henrik Petersen,
Odense

Steffen Petersen,
Odense

Vibeke Pierson,
Odense

Karen Prehn,
Aarhus

Rune Premfors,
Stockholm

Hilmar Rommetvedt,
Stavanger

Karsten Ronit,
Copenhagen

Larry Rose,
Oslo

Bo Rothstein,
Göteborg

Olof Ruin,
Stockholm

Bjørn K. Sagdahl,
Bodø

Diane Sainsbury,
Stockholm

Hermann Schmitt,
Mannheim

Jens Schovsbo,
Copenhagen

Christian og Fritze Siersted,
Odense

Gunnar Sjöblom,
Copenhagen

Nils Stjernquist,
Lund

Randall Strahan,
Atlanta

Jan Sundberg,
Helsinki

Palle Svensson,
Copenhagen

Bjarne Graabech Sørensen,
Odense

Curt Sørensen,
Aarhus

Lene Bøgh Sørensen,
Odense

Syddansk Universitetsbibliotek,
Odense

Niels Thomsen,
Klampenborg

Tove Thorsfelt,
Odense

Carsten Toft,
Odense

Lise Togeby,
Aarhus

Peder og Nana Tuborgh,
Højbjerg

Henrik Tvarnø,
Odense

Margrethe Udesen,
Vedbæk

Arild Underdal,
Oslo

Derek W. Urwin,
Aberdeen

Henry Valen,
Oslo

Torbjörn Vallinder,
Lund

Evert Vedung,
Gävle

Martin Westergaard,
Odense

Jörgen Westerståhl,
Göteborg

Torben Worre,
Espergærde

Jacob Aars,
Bergen

Preface

On December 14, 1999, our colleague Professor Mogens N. Pedersen completes his sixtieth year. We would like to celebrate the day by publishing this *Festschrift* to a good colleague and friend. As described more detailed in Gunnar Sjöblom's introductory article, Mogens is not only one of the very first political scientists in Denmark, but has also for many years held a prominent position in European political science, as editor of the European Journal of Political Research and as chairman of the ECPR. His notable contributions to the discipline may conveniently be subsumed under the heading »Elites, Parties and Democracy«, the title we have chosen as the theme of this *Festschrift*.

We have asked colleagues from several countries to contribute to this *Festschrift*, primarily political scientists who have cooperated closely with Mogens at some time during his career. Gunnar Sjöblom from Copenhagen University has prepared the introductory contribution on Mogens' works and career, and hereafter the contributions follow in alphabetical order.

Vibeke Pierson has finalized and adjusted the manuscripts so that they follow the stylesheet of Odense University Press. That job has often demanded patience and we owe Vibeke our sincere thanks. We also wish to thank Steven Sampson for his valuable work on correcting linguistic errors in the manuscripts. The list of publications has been prepared by Kasper Møller Hansen. Steffen Petersen and Søren Mølgård have also performed various jobs in finalizing the manuscripts. We thank all for their help.

Erik Beukel *Kurt Klaudi Klausen* *Poul Erik Mouritzen*

Still a Young Man in a Hurry: Notes on Mogens N. Pedersen's Works and Career

Gunnar Sjöblom

Introduction

The year 1997 saw the appearance of *Comparative European Politics: The Story of a Profession,* a collection edited by Hans Daalder. The book, based mainly on an ECPR workshop held in Leiden in 1993 on the topic of »The Intellectual Autobiography of Comparative European Politics«, is an invaluable source for those interested in the development of comparative politics. How inspiring it must have been for the authors to concentrate – legitimately for once – on their favorite subjects. Ego-trips? Partly, but in most cases quite enjoyable and always very instructive. A close reading gives us adequate grounds to assess what is new (or not so new) in the development of political science during the postwar period.

Mogens N. Pedersen is one of the contributors to Daalder's anthology with the article entitled »Present at the Creation« (a slightly longer and different version was published in Scandinavian Political Studies in 1996 under the title »Young Man in a Hurry: Recollections of a Soldier of Fortune«). Treating roughly the period between 1958 and 1970 Pedersen gives us a picture of »the interplay between an emergent Danish political science and a young scholar who just happened to graduate as the first professionally trained political scientist in Denmark«. As he makes clear, political science as a discipline was a late-comer at Danish universities and institutionalized at Aarhus University only in the early 1960s, at the university of Copenhagen only in the mid-1960s and in Odense not until the early 1970s (Mogens N. Pedersen became the first political science professor in Odense in 1973). Hence, there was ample room for pioneer work.

Pedersen's article provides a personal account of political science in Denmark in these early years. He also draws an interesting picture of the optimistic mood among political scientists in the late 1950s and 1960s: a feeling of innovation and, perhaps, breakthrough, in comparative politics, where the traditional institutional approach was combined (and sometimes superseded by) a behavioural approach, and when international political science cooperation was gradually institutionalized – in Europe above all by the creation of the European Consortium for Political Research with Stein Rokkan, Jean Blondel, Hans Daalder and Rudolf Wildenmann as the founders. Mogens N. Pedersen was particularly close to Rokkan and Daalder, both deeply erudite men in comparative politics, both scholarly entrepreneurs and both with great scholarly ambitions for the development of the discipline. In a visit to Stanford University in the early 1970s Pedersen also studied with Gabriel Almond, a leader of the comparative movement (but Mogens has always been sceptical about the functionalist approach), and with Heinz Eulau, a student of legislative behaviour and a sharp methodologist, and possessed by a rather sardonic wit (which probably also influenced Mogens, one of his other favorites being Machiavelli).

His Career

Let us have a look at Mogens N. Pedersen's career. As mentioned, in 1973, at the tender age of 33, he became the first professor of political science at the newly founded Odense University (now University of Southern Denmark). He soon became a member of The Danish Social Science Research Council and also served on a number of government committees. In 1980 he was appointed editor of the *European Journal of Political Research*, a post he held until 1994. In the mid-1980s Mogens started an eight-year-long tenure as dean of Odense University's Social Science Faculty. In 1995, he became member and chairman of the ECPR's Executive Committee. He has been initiator and chairman of several ECPR Workshops, and has arranged a number of scholarly conferences. He has been a member of evaluation committees of political science (e.g. concerning Swedish political science). He has participated in a large number of selection committees for chairs (and other posts) in political science in all the Scandinavian countries. Mogens N. Pedersen is the co-editor of *Nordic Political Facts*, the *Dictionary in Political Science*, and several bibliographies. He has been chairman of the Danish Society of Political Science and member of the executive committees of both the Nordic Political Science Association (NOPSA) and the International Political Science Association (IPSA). He has taken part in many debates concerning conditions in the universities and in political science e.g., in the discussion of the intricate balance between academic freedom and political steering of research.

This list, while far from complete, nevertheless demonstrates, that Mogens N. Pedersen is widely trusted and respected by both his Danish and international colleagues. This respect is based on his deep concern for scholarly quality, his good judgement and his efficiency. He is also difficult to deceive. Early on he realized as did Hamlet, »that one may smile, and smile, and be a villain; at least I am sure it may be so in Denmark.«

All these activities, of course, have had their price in form of a heavy workload, taking time from scholarly research. It is no wonder that his article »Present at the Creation« ends with a postscript »with a bit of jeremiads« (a genre that Mogens masters) about the *onera*, but he also declares that, »I have returned to the calm and free life of an ordinary professor,« (a point I will return to later on).

His Scholarship

Mogens N. Pedersen's list of publications (until early 1998) includes 90 items. As all such lists, this one is a mixture of large and small, but it testifies to a great (and enviable) productivity and also to a wide area of interests. While I have certainly not read all 90 items, I will try to make a brief characterisation of some of his more important works. I will then concentrate on what I regard as his main contribution to political science, research on parties and party system (conceived, however, in a very broad way). This review will include some work from another of his research specialities: elites and elite recruitment.

Even with this limitation, the overview should give a picture of Mogens N. Pedersen's key contributions to a wide area of subjects. This exposition is divided into the following parts: political recruitment, parliamentary studies, the use of the right/left continuum, the Danish party system, the role of small parties, party systems analyzed in terms of volatility, and finally, some brief remarks on works on pure methodology and on the role of political scientists as consultants. The classification is not strict: the chronology is free. In those cases where full titles are not given and the reference numbers refer to his list of publications.

Undeniably, political recruitment is one of the major topics of political science research. Many people see political recruitment as a boring subject, which may often be the case. However, if you want to read an example to the opposite, read Pedersen's »Political Development and Elite Transformations in Denmark« (No. 16, 1976). The introduction reads:

Still a Young Man in a Hurry

> This paper contains a description of how various Danish political elites have changed their composition during the 120 years which have elapsed since the introduction of democratic institutions in Denmark. Secondly, it tries to relate inter-elite differences, the changes in elite composition and changes in the social and political structures of the Danish society, the main assumption being that the transformation of political leadership is determined by the transition from mainly traditional to a modern society. Thirdly, it discusses the relationship between changes in elite composition and changes in public policy. Thus, the composition of the elites is seen as a component in a society on the move; the elite can be treated as dependent or independent variables in a dynamic analysis (p. 6).

»Potz Donnerwetter, hat er das alles getan?« In my view Mogens is very successful and the long article is fascinating reading. His analysis is convincing in all aspects: problem formulation, the search for and control of data, conceptualization, modelling variables, relations between political mobilization and institutional threshold on the input side and coalition potentials, coalition propensity and institutional threshold on the output side (decisions and policies). It is an excellent example of a dynamic analysis, not only in his analysis of the transformations taking place but also for understanding the historical background for many persistent features of the contemporary Danish political system.

Another article by Mogens N. Pedersen on political recruitment is the highly succinct »The Geographical Matrix of Parliamentary Representation: a Spatial Model of Political Recruitment« (No. 13, 1975).

> In political systems that do not require the legislator to have his residence in the constituency which elects him, a data matrix can be created by juxtaposing the two variables of constituency affiliation and residence affiliations of legislators... [this] simple axiomatic model of political recruitment... is based on the assumptions that rational office-seekers and agents of selection will make their decisions with regard to nomination in such a way that the costs of communication between the representative and his constituency is minimized. This decisional premise is operationalized by means of the three spatial distances between residence, constituency and the site of the legislature [from Abstract, p. 1].

A number of hypotheses are formulated and tested in the article. While the substantive result may not be very surprising, the article is a model of distinctiveness.

Other works by Mogens N. Pedersen on political recruitment treat preferential voting (No. 2), the relation between electoral volatility and recruitment (No. 39), the advantages of incumbent candidates over non-incumbents (No. 72), the circulation of personnel in a legislature (No. 19), and (with another author) »Professionalization of Legislatures: Long Term Change in Political Recruitment in Denmark and Norway« (No. 22, 1978).

Mogens N. Pedersen has written extensively on parliaments. Some pioneer works include: »Conflict and Consensus in the Danish Folketing 1956-65« (No. 4, 1967) and »Party Distances in the Danish Folketing« (No. 8, 1971 with two other authors). He has written on parliamentary role-call analysis (No. 20, 1977) and a highly instructive overview of »Research on European Parliaments: A Review Article on Scholarly and Institutional Variety« (No. 44, 1984). He has also contributed to the old discussion on the use and misuse of the left-right political continuum (No. 58, 1989, No. 85, 1997).

A large part of Mogens' production is about Danish party politics: its historical development (No. 57, 1989), about the condition for and effects of the famous Danish earthquake election of 1973 with the entrance of new parties (No. 50, 1987, No. 54, 1988, No. 35, 1983 – the last one a very eloquent expression of bad temper), about party finance (No. 65, 1991, one co-author) and about the Danish parties' reaction to their new roles in the European Union (No. 81, 1995). In a lecture about the future of the Danish political parties (No. 60, 1990) Mogens demonstrates his scepticism towards the common jeremiads, crisis-mongering, doomsday-prophecies and complaints about party government: »If we look at the Danish parties, not the single party but the politics as a whole, the party system I really think, if you excuse me, that we have a rather well-functioning party system in this kingdom« (ibid., p. 80) – voter turnouts are high, governments are formed fairly easily, it has incorporated and tamed anti-system parties, etc.

In this connection, mention should be made of some innovative articles about small parties: »Towards a New Typology of Party Lifespans and Minor Parties« (No. 31, 1982) and »The Birth, the Life and the Death of Small Parties in Danish Politics« (No. 63, 1991).

Mogens' most famous and most quoted articles are »The Dynamics of European Party Systems: Changing Patterns of Electoral Volatility« (No. 24, 1979) and a later version (No. 34, 1983) »Changing Patterns of Electoral Volatility in European Party Systems 1948-1977: Explorations in Explanation«.

When the *European Journal of Political Research* celebrated its 25th anniversary, the editors asked all members of the Editorial Board »to look over the past 25 years of the journal's output and nominate an article from this that they felt had made a special contribution to political science«. The nominators wrote a comment in retrospect (EJPR, Vol. 31, Nos. 1-2, 1997). Mogens N. Pedersen's classic 1979 article was an obvious choice. (For the comments of the two nominators, see ibid.: 83-93, for Mogens N. Pedersen's Reflections, see ibid.: 93-97). Connected to this area of research is also the important article »On Measuring Party System Change: A Methodological Critique and a Suggestion« (No. 27, 1980).

Speaking of methodology, we should also mention »On the Proper Use of Historical Material in Political Science« (in Danish, No. 17, 1977), published in the Festschrift to one of Mogens' teachers in Århus, Erik Rasmussen. It mirrors Mogens' longstanding interest in the use of case studies and in dynamic analysis. Another illustration of the problem of relations between history and political science is the article on a leading trade union leader from the beginning of the 20th century: »Lyngsie as Tactician« (in Danish, No. 53, 1988) in which a historical case is explained by the use of bargaining theory.

In this brief illustration of MNP's works, let me finally mention his plenary lecture at the Nordic Political Science Association's (NOPSA's) conference in Reykjavik in 1990, »The Political Scientist as Consultant: Reflections on a Developing Role« (in Danish, No. 62, 1990). Properly enough, he starts with the old favorite Machiavelli (and continues, e.g., with Heinz Eulau). Can the political scientist in a consulting role learn something from the roles of engineers, doctors, and lawyers, or even try to develop a competence in »political risk analysis«? Mogens is rather sceptical. Evidently, the political scientist can learn a lot about politics and about the limitations of political science as a »practical discipline« by working close to political actors, but the dangers should not be underestimated. Political scientists may be good at overview analyses and of mapping problems and their general connections but rarely at giving precise prescriptions.

Mogens N. Pedersen's Scholarly Production: Some Characteristics

How should Mogens N. Pedersen's production be characterized in more general terms? Let me try to formulate some of its properties (which, by the way, are often also the subjects of his own discussions and analyses).

1. He writes with *enthusiasm* – it is clear that he regards his themes as

interesting and important, and he conveys this feeling to his readers (I am sure of this, even if I recognize the risks of drawing conclusions from »the context of justification« to »the context of discovery«). This is no mean achievement at a time of an overproduction of texts, in which blood, sweat and tears ooze from the lines and between them.

2. He writes *concisely* and only when he has something to say – again a notable achievement at a time when life gets shorter day by day for all of us, but when too many texts have low specific weight, i.e., a disproportion between weight and volume.

3. He has a sophisticated view of *the balance between »theoretical parsimony« and »realism«*. The starting point of an analysis is a problem – if a problem becomes unrecognizable after having been translated into theoretical terms, something has gone wrong. On the other hand, the solution of substantial problems should contribute to our theoretical understanding. As is well known, this is often difficult in comparative politics. For instance, Mogens N. Pedersen has given much thought to the use of case studies in political science.

4. (close to 3.) He is a very *sober* scholar, who does not fall victim to whims and fashions. Theories are there to help explanation and understanding – to be used – and not to form glittering generalities at the beginning of the text.

5. He has a very keen sense of the validity and reliability of *data*, how they can be collected, transformed, used, how much they can say and what they cannot say.

6. He is attentive to the differences between *static* vs. *dynamic* analyses. When do we need a historical perspective? Are series of data just a collection of snapshots between different points of time (t, t+1, etc.) or are they so constructed that they by themselves express changes over time?

7. Mogens N. Pedersen's production shows a great concern for the relation between different *levels of analyses*, e.g. between explanations in the form of actor-analyses vs. explanation in systemic forms. He demonstrates great skill in systemic analyses, as shown clearly from his analyses of party systems in terms of volatility.

8. Through his production, he often returns to the question of *the relation between innovation and cumulation* (a question which also greatly inte-

rested Stein Rokkan). This relation is highly pertinent in comparative politics (but relevant for all sorts of science) and underlies many discussions concerning the steering of research. Is an innovation only terminological, or does it also refer to concepts and theories? Under what conditions (if any) can we promote a much-needed cumulation in political science?

One might say that all the terms and problems listed here are general and apply to all scholars. Nevertheless, it is rare to find in one scholar such high consciousness of all of them simultaneously, as is the case with our Festschrift-recipient.

Epilogue

Dear Mogens, congratulations on your 60th birthday. You have used your time well: an impressive scholarly production and an equally impressive organizational and editorial work for Danish and for European political science.

My personal thanks for 30 years of good cooperation and comradeship.

All this may sound like an obituary. Since I regard you as still a »young man in a hurry«, let me end more in an »ex-ante-«mood (you may not wish to hear it, but, as you know, such considerations have rarely stopped me). There is a need for a thorough book on Danish Politics in Comparative Perspective. I know of a person who (in his own words, earlier quoted) has »returned to the calm and free life of an ordinary professor« and who combines deep knowledge of Danish politics, of comparative politics and of comparative methodology to make such a book an international standard text.

Democracy Pacific Style: Between Custom and Modernity

Dag Anckar

Abstract

Processes of decolonization involve imposition of the political and moral norms of the metropolitan power upon the values, political traditions and cultures of other nations. Where the value systems of the sender and the receiver are basically the same, the transplantation of ideas and institutions from one context to another may proceed smoothly and may in fact resemble a transfer; when norms and values differ, however, the procedure becomes complicated and acquires features of transformation. The Pacific small island states which gained independence during the last decades have clearly faced the dilemmas of transformation. Although differences certainly exist among these states, democracy having been present in some cultures but very little in others, none of the islands have escaped a collision between modernity and tradition. In most cases, Britain being the metropolitan power, the clash was between a majoritarian Westminster government system and a traditional system based on hierarchical structures and a consensual form of decision-making. To reconcile custom with modernity, different strategies were applied. Assemblies of chiefs were in several cases set up parallel to the legislature and other bodies, and the erosion of custom was prevented by requiring custom to be made the basis of national law. The emergence of national ideologies and a commitment to national institutions were clearly hampered by the clash between modernity and tradition, as cultural factors are inconsistent with and promote resistance to the open divisiveness of party politics, elections and majority rule.

Introduction

Whereas most Third World countries have been unable to establish durable forms of democracy (Pinkney 1993, 61-82), some countries have today a record of continuous pluralist democracy. Among these countries are a handful of small Pacific island states; however, the introduction of democracy in these islands during decolonization was not an altogether smooth and easy undertaking. This was because the Pacific islands, in contrast to the Caribbean region for instance, have long-standing indigenous cultures and traditions (Horner 1992) which permeate many facets of life, are a source of national pride and are not easily reconciled with democratic ideals. In his introductory chapter to a volume on *Law, Politics and Government in the Pacific Island States,* Yash Ghai (1988a, 39) emphasizes that in the making of constitutions for the newly independent countries in the region »the incorporation of customary values and practices and the accommodation of traditional authorities in the constitution was the most difficult and complex intellectual and technical problem in the whole exercise«. Ghai points out that the constitution-making process involved consultation and that traditional authorities were often members of committees and conventions; the role of custom and chiefs therefore became more of an issue than if the process had been more elitist or political parties better and nationally organized. Furthermore, custom achieved prominence due to a general desire for the constitution to be related to the social and economic conditions of the country and based on its values. Ghai also notes that the imminence of independence led to a renaissance of pride in the past and the contemporary culture of the people, as evidenced in the many constitutional preambles (1988a, 39).

Several Pacific constitutions indeed emphasize the survival of custom and tradition in the new state. The preamble to the Constitution of Vanuatu cherishes »our ethnic, linguistic and cultural diversity« and proclaims »the establishment of the united and free Republic of Vanuatu founded on traditional Melanesian values, faith in God, and Christian principles« (*Pacific Constitutions*). The preamble to the Constitution of Kiribati declares that »we shall continue to cherish and uphold the customs and traditions of Kiribati«, and in the preamble to the Constitution of the Solomon Islands the people, »proud of the wisdom and the worthy customs of our ancestors« explain that they »cherish and promote the different cultural traditions within Solomon Islands« (ibid.). The Constitution of Papua New Guinea pays »homage to the memory of our ancestors« and acknowledges »the worthy customs and traditional wisdoms of our people« (ibid.). Some constitutions declare even stronger commitments to custom and tradition. For instance, the preamble to the Constitution of Tuvalu states that the guiding principles of Tuvalu in government and social affairs are »agreement, courtesy and the search for consensus in accordance with traditional Tuvaluan procedures, rather than alien ideas of confrontation and divisiveness« (ibid.). The Constitution of Western Samoa declares that »whereas the leaders of Western Samoa have declared that Western Samoa should be an Independent State based on Christian principles and Samoan custom and tradition« (Lawson 1996, 138).

Since Britain has been the major metropolitan power in the Pacific, the immediate task for the new nations was to adopt the British Westminster model and then integrate it with local conditions and cultural values. A writer representing Kiribati states, in a slightly melancholy fashion, that »we have the Westminster system because we had no realistic alternatives« (Neemia 1992, 8). The same writer, however, takes care to emphasize that in accepting the model, »we have modified it to suit our egalitarian ethos« (ibid.). The resulting patterns of modification are different and varied: from a chapter on the future of democracy in the Pacific islands we learn that »Although the current political systems in Western Samoa, Fiji, Kiribati, Tuvalu, Vanuatu, Solomon Islands, Papua New Guinea, the Cook Islands and others all incorporate various aspects of the Westminster system, each of them is very different from the other« (Crocombe 1992, 10). The phrasing »very different« may be an exaggeration, as the several derivatives of the Westminster model that we find in the Pacific still derive from fairly similar basic conceptions and assumptions. It is true, however, that identical solutions are in scarce supply and that the Pacific nations' efforts to incorporate various traits of culture and tradition into their political structures have produced an assemblage of political systems.

The Problem

The magnitude of the problem of reconciling modernity and tradition is not always fully recognized. Some observers belittle the clash between modern and ancient, arguing that the new arrangements were in fact not much different from the old ones. For instance, about the success of democracy in Papua New Guinea it has been said that it lies in »a somewhat coincidental marriage between the crucial democratic values and their equivalents inherent in PNG cultures« (Deklin 1992, 47). In a like manner, in an interview some years ago, Tuilaepa Sailele Malielegaoi, Deputy Prime Minister of Western Samoa, emphasized that the introduction in 1990 of universal suffrage in his country was quite in accordance with Samoan customs: it was to apply »something that had always been there in any case. Samoans have always taken part in the process of choosing their leaders, and voting is simply another way of doing this. The only difference is that we would arrive at a decision by getting together through our village structures and talking, whereas your system involves marking a ballot« (*The Courier*, No. 159, 1996, p. 37).

Such opinions, however, are in a minority and also appear to be exaggerated. In fact, democracy has a precedent in some Pacific Islands cultures but very little in others. Concerning the specific cases of Papua New Guinea and Western Samoa, we learn from one author that »representative democracy is a foreign import and as such has nothing to do with the original political traditions anywhere in Papua New Guinea« (Jacobsen 1995, 231); let it also be said that Papua New Guinea has in fact a less convincing democratic record than many other small Pacific island states (Hadenius 1992, 62). In the voting system in Samoa, where the right to run for parliament remains restricted to bearers of traditional *matai* chief titles, is certainly less than convincing evidence of a harmony between modern democratic forms and local custom. Most observations of the interplay between modernity and tradition reveal controversies and imbalances. A voice from the Solomon Islands explains that »this system of election and voting and forming political parties is new and foreign to us« (Alasia 1989, 137); a voice from Fiji declares that democratic concepts »will have to be refashioned to our needs and circumstances if they are to take root and flourish in Fiji« (Ravuvu 1992, 65). Commenting on the case of Vanuatu, one author emphasizes that in this country »traditional politics and democratic parliamentary politics are two very different systems« (Molisa 1995, 432); an exposition of politics in Tonga describes the present as »a transitional era in which the indigenous and the foreign are unequally and unevenly blended« (Campbell 1992, 228). The opinion has been voiced in the Marshall Islands that there is a fundamental incompatibility of the traditional *Iroij* (hereditary chief) system and the modern democratic system (Crocombe *et al.* 1992, 242), and an informed observer has noted that the Marshall Islands constitutes a society that is straddling a fine line between traditional and Western democracy, the people »having their feet firmly planted in both the Western and traditional power structures« (Johnson 1988, 82-83). A description of political and social life in Belau underlines that most Belauans still follow family and clan leadership in economic and political choices, including the selection and support of candidates for office (Quimby 1988, 114).

The view that tradition and democracy in important respects collide is much in the foreground in Stephanie Lawson's authoritative and penetrating study of Fiji, Tonga and Western Samoa (1996). Lawson argues that many efforts to reclaim and defend tradition in fact protect the power and privileges of indigenous elites. Her argument has been voiced by other authors as well, who have maintained that appeals to tradition and custom at times »provide a convenient rationale for the protection of vested interests« (Henningham 1995, 6), and stated that »if the culture of a people is bound up with its traditional patterns of authority, then the right of a people to maintain its culture could imply curtailing the rights of the same members of that people compared with the rights they could expect to exercise in a Western-style democracy« (Mulgan 1991, 127). Lawson maintains that her study has shown that the chief elites have not hesitated to use invented tradition to sanctify their own dominance and to exclude others from a meaningful share of political power (1996, 171); she also suggests that it is useful to consider traditionalism »in terms of a self-contained discourse that functions to unify a particular field of thought in such a way as to exclude alternative modes of thinking« (1996, 173). The observations by Lawson highlight another dimension to the problem of integrating two very different political and social doctrines. The problem not only intrudes on ways of thinking which are considered by many to constitute almost a natural order, it also entails going against established systems of power and interests of power. The problem has been further accentuated by the fact that there is not one Pacific islands culture but many cultures. Whereas tradition in Micronesia and Polynesia embraces a hierarchical social structure, authority being vested in hereditary chiefs, Melanesian societies have generally been more egalitarian with wide dispersal of political authority (e.g., Ghai 1988a, 2-3; Mulgan 1991, 127). Furthermore, although some countries are homogeneous in terms of culture, others are not. Some countries have several traditional systems, others, like Fiji, have immigrant communities with different traditions.

This essay focuses on two aspects of the foundation of tradition in the Pacific political sphere. The first involves strategies for the accommodation of modernity and tradition. One method entails allowing the introduced political ideas to coexist with indigenous forms of political organization on an equal footing. Another method, working by assimilation, would have customary values being incorporated into and leaving their mark on democratic practices and processes. The second focus of the essay involves a specific political feature which is a consequence of political practice rather than a rational choice outcome. This feature finds expression in the fact that modernity and tradition thrive side by side, although on different levels of political life: whereas national politics is conducted much in terms of modern rules and institutions, the day-to-day village life of ordinary people is still framed within traditional norms and patterns. Hence, the question arises as to the extent and type of influence the two contexts have on each other.

The Council of Chiefs

Many descriptions of Pacific political life observe that democratic institutions cohabit the region with traditionalist ones, as traditional leaders have positions in national institutions set up in parallel to the legislature (e.g., Chehabi 1995). The by far most important of these bodies is Fiji's *Bose Levu Vakaturaga* (Great Council of Chiefs), which was created as a part of the Native Administration in colonial Fiji and which is therefore not a traditional institution in a strict sense of the word (Lawson 1991, 69). The council consists of some 70 hereditary chiefs of a Fijian clan. Following the military coup in Fiji in 1987, the council initiated the formation of a political party, the Fijian Political Party, as a voice of ethnic Fijians. The party has since then been a dominant force in Fijian political life. According to the 1990 Fijian Constitution, the Great Council of Chiefs fulfilled important functions when the Council nominated ethnic Fijians to 24 of the 34 seats in the Senate and appointed the President of the Republic, who has executive authority. The new 1997 Constitution of Fiji is a move towards multiethnic government and a decreased dominance of ethnic Fijians (Hussein 1997). It abolishes the Senate, revises the electoral system, and reduces the role of the *Bose Levu Vakaturaga*. Still, however, the council appoints the President, and thereby retains a power signifying that the country is essentially an ethnically Fijian state and the president a symbol of Fijian supremacy (Ghai & Cottrell 1990, 226).

Likewise, the Federated States of Micronesia provide a powerful position of traditional authority, as the constitution permits a Chamber of Chiefs to be created as the Second House. However, so far such a second house has not yet been established, and it seems unlikely that the option will ever be used (Burdick 1988, 266). Senators in Micronesia are elected every four years and Representatives every two years. Each of the four states of the federation may set aside one of its two-year seats for a traditional leader; again, none of them have chosen to do so (Burdick 1988, 265-266). In other cases of councils of chiefs, the regulations concerning these bodies provide only for consultation or rights of recommendation, and these provisions may be easily circumvented (Larmour 1988, 165). In Vanuatu, a National Council of Chiefs, called *Malvatumauri* and elected by its peers, advises on matters relating to custom and tradition and may make recommendations to Parliament for the preservation and promotion of the culture and languages of Vanuatu. The Council may also be consulted on any question in connection with any bill before Parliament. Furthermore, each region may elect a regional council, and the Constitution lays particular emphasis on the representation of custom chiefs within each region. In Belau (Palau) a Council of Chiefs shall advise the President on matters concerning traditional laws, customs and their relationship to the Constitution and laws of Belau; no person shall be a member of this council unless he has been appointed and accepted as a chief in a traditional manner and is recognized as such by the traditional council of chiefs in his state. In the Marshall Islands, the *House of Iroij* may consider any matter of concern to the Marshall Islands and can on matters of custom or land refer the case to the *Nitijela,* the Parliament.

From the point of view of safeguarding custom and tradition, and in view of the fact that many Pacific countries are fragmented by ethnic and racial divisions, one would perhaps expect many nations to have a second parliamentary chamber to accommodate the representation of distinct interests. This, however, is not the case. Instead, functions of second chambers are carried out by other mechanisms, including the councils of chiefs institution, which provides representation on a different basis from that of the legislature and makes possible some form of expertise or specialized interest to influence national issues (Ghai 1988b, 64-65). It is doubtful, however, if such functions are really served. Very little, if anything, is in fact known in terms of systematic research about the real functioning and impact of these institutions. Rather, the scattered information that exists suggests that their overall political significance is marginal and that they have no important political or legislative role (Ghai 1988 b, 65). In the Cook Islands, the *House of Ariki* is viewed as not having produced any significant contribution to a greater understanding or documentation of Cook Islands custom. According to the same source, although Parliament has submitted several issues to the House for consideration, the House has submitted few recommendations only to Parliament, which has not taken these seriously (Takiora Ingram 1992, 162-163). It is also quite significant that an extensive and fairly recent volume on politics in Vanuatu (van Trease 1995) provides no evidence for the importance and impact of the *Malvatumauri.*

One reason for the modest impact of the councils may simply be that the new government leaders have come to see chieftaincy as a rival order, to be clearly subordinated to formal state institutions; another and related reason may be that the important and most influential chiefs have chosen to move to the legislature and the executive (Ghai 1988b, 65). There are probably differences between countries in this last respect; it would appear, for instance, that the chief establishment in Belau does not often stand for office (Anckar *et al.* 1998; Quimby 1988, 113-114). From the point of view of democratic theory, the councils, while recognizing chiefhood and its ceremonial role in the community, are certainly misnomers (Anckar & Anckar 1998, 14-15). It is one of many democratic requirements that elections must be efficient, meaning that elected organs shall not be limited in their decision-making by instances which lack democratic support (Hadenius 1992, 49); in theory, although in most cases not in practice, the chief councils constitute limitations and thereby deviations from democratic standards. Establishment of the council of chiefs institution was one of several concessions to traditional authority in the decolonization processes; however, practice has proven this concession to be rather insignificant. The councils have symbolic functions which should not be disparaged. In the long term, however, the limited policy role of the councils may lead to an erosion of traditional authority.

Intersecting Areas of Jurisdiction

The parallelism discussed in the previous section finds many equivalents in efforts to prevent the erosion of custom by requiring custom to be made the basis of national law. Of course, the rule is that the law and government of a country should be conducted in accordance with the constitution of that country. In his review of Pacific islands constitutions Peter Bayne (1988, 107) cites the Constitution of Kiribati which declares that »This Constitution is the supreme law of Kiribati and if any other law is inconsistent with this Constitution, that other law shall, to the extent of the inconsistency, be void.« However, whereas this principle is clear enough, problems arise if and when accommodation to custom is made part and parcel of the constitution itself. Since custom almost as a rule embraces norms and beliefs that may only with great difficulty, if at all, be brought into line with the frames of reference of modernity, a conflict between the two sets of norms becomes almost inevitable. The obvious method for handling such conflicts is to establish a pattern of subordination. The very intention behind the parallelism would then be watered down however. Hence, the method has rather been to resort to phrasing that makes it unclear if and when a constitutional provision is subject to or overrides custom. »Statute and custom, the modern and the ancient, co-exist uneasily, helped by deliberate ambiguities«, Yash Ghai writes in a penetrating review of this method (1988a, 42). A few examples may shed light on the problem.

In the case of Belau, the prescription is that statutes and traditional law shall be equally authoritative, statutes prevailing in case of conflict only to the extent they are not in conflict with the underlying principles of the traditional law. Furthermore, it is proclaimed that the government shall take no action to prohibit or revoke the role and function of a traditional leader as recognized by custom and tradition not inconsistent with the Constitution (Article V, Sections 1 & 2; Ghai 1988a, 41). To be sure, the full legal and empirical meaning of these prescriptions remains vague, but in terms of culture and tradition, they certainly express restrictions on the competence of the Belau Parliament, the *Olbiil Era Kelulau*. Similar statements also appear in the Constitution of the Federated States of Micronesia, proclaiming that nothing in the Constitution shall take away a role or a function of a traditional leader as recognized by custom and tradition (Article V, 51), and that the traditions of the people of the country may be protected by statute and, if such statute shall be challenged as violative of fundamental rights, then the protection of Micronesian tradition shall be considered a compelling social purpose warranting such governmental action (Article V, Section 2; Ghai 1988a, 41-42). The actual meaning of these vague prescriptions is difficult to grasp. The same is certainly true for a similar clause in the Solomon Islands Constitution, providing for »the establishment of the underlying law, based on the customary law and concepts of the Solomon Islands people«.

It is inevitable that operating with double standards sometimes entails disruptive consequences. One telling example is provided by the Village Fono Act, enacted in Western Samoa in 1990, mostly for the purpose of compensating Samoan tradition for the introduction of universal suffrage in the country at that time (earlier, since independence in 1962, the franchise was restricted to bearers of traditional *matai* chief titles). According to this act, the village *fono* (council) was formally empowered, as formal law now recognized a wide range of traditional powers and allowed every village *fono* to exercise any power or authority in accordance with the customs and usage of that village. As a consequence, in several cases, a reversion to old traditional punishments has taken place involving acts of brutality and arbitrariness. As reported by Lawson (1996, 155-156), a Western Samoan villager was shot dead in September 1993 in front of his family, after first having his house and other property destroyed. Following disputes between the victim and the village *matai*, including a refusal by the victim to pay fines imposed by the village *fono* and an ensuing ban on the victim's shop and bus service, a large crowd of villagers gathered in the final confrontation, where the victim was killed by two young men acting on the instructions of a senior *matai*. Under the Village Fono Act, this execution was apparently justified as it was performed in accordance with custom and usage. Lawson also reports (1996, 156) an incident where a *matai* was banished from his home village by its *fono* for a period of one hundred years after having assisted in the campaign of a candidate from another village in a local by-election. This action was likewise justified under the Village Fono Act.

One must agree with Bayne when he asserts that: »The general question of the role of custom in the legal systems of the Pacific Island states has not yet received a very clear answer in any of them« (1988, 129). Yet it remains an undisputable fact that the parallel application of old and new principles may open possibilities for a systematic violation of such freedoms and rights which are and should be characteristic of modern democracies. The extent to which such possibilities have been and are utilized in the Pacific has not been thoroughly investigated, but it is probably a justified assumption that the violations are less than frequent and that they do not seriously damage the quality of Pacific democratic life. It should be noted that classifications of the Pacific nations in terms of adherence to human and civil rights are as a rule quite positive; for instance, most of the nations receive high ratings in the *Freedom House* survey of civil liberties, comparing favourably with Western democracies like Germany or United Kingdom. It should likewise be noted that the introduction of chapters on Bills of Rights in the Pacific constitutions almost nowhere encountered difficulties or dissent (Ghai 1988a, 42). Still, the question of how custom should be reconciled with other laws, and in particular with the constitution, forms a singular, peculiar and certainly confusing component of Democracy Pacific Style.

Majority versus Consensus

The best term to describe Pacific political culture is probably »consensus«. From an exposition of Samoan politics we learn that the *fa'amatai* (the social organization) insists on making decisions on a consultative basis, the ideal being that the decision-making processes include and involve all relevant people. This consultative process is viewed as efficient because it makes the appropriately involved individual feel important by being consulted (Tagaloa 1992, 122-123). Similar descriptions of the belief systems that guide Pacific political life are discernible in the constitutional preambles cited in the opening section of this essay, and the literature abounds with them. Indeed, the name of the Belau Parliament, *Olbiil Era Kelulau,* means »The Place of Whispers«, and refers to a tradition of making decisions by quiet consultation in local and other councils within a consensus system (Quimby 1988, 116). From field research in Vanuatu one observes that although there are differences, animosities and scores to be settled, conflicts are suppressed as people attempt to portray their community as a cohesive and coherent whole. The same research also suggests that because of its oppositional structure, modern politics appears to many people as »a largely useless, often destructive enterprise characterized by heated argument, efforts to deceive, and even incitement to violence of members of one party against those of another« (Facey 1995, 214). Further observations suggest that in the Nauruan society there is a relative absence of aggression and an emphasis on harmony (Crocombe 1988, 54), and that discontent is rarely voiced in the Marshall Islands which reflects the influence of the traditional system on modern day politics (Johnson 1988, 82). In Kiribati, society leadership is characterized as »ideally consensual« as it avoids confrontation, public criticism or the embarrassment of others (Macdonald 1996, 6). Regarding the *maneaba* system in Kiribati, which »combines theory, institution and process and has been in Kiribati since the beginning of time« (Tabokai 1993, 23) it has been said that it fosters a consensus spirit as well as embraces a social order which likewise fuels a consensual view of life:

> Furthermore, the *maneaba* teaches something which cannot be learned anywhere else - an oratory system. Sometimes people argue on very serious topics, but in the end they shake hands. It is a mature approach in a discussion of vital issues, not to rationalise them so that in the end the majority wins, but to debate and argue issues to the very limit so that consensus is achieved and everyone enjoys the feeling of having reached an agreement accepted by all ....Moreover, a debate in the *maneaba* is not polarised. One explanation could be the Kiribati tradition of distant marriage. In some societies, people try to marry as closely as possible in order to avoid dispersion of their land and their powers. In Kiribati the tradition is just the opposite. Close marriage is not permitted, probably because of the small island populations, instead, distant marriage is encouraged. The effect of this tradition widens the individual's loyalties, and politically it reduces the possibility of a polarisation within society. With this in mind, it is easier to understand why consensus politics is the norm, rather than rule by majority (Tabokai 1993, 26-27).

Admittedly, in important respects, this emphasis on consensus and consultation may be questioned. According to Stephanie Lawson (1996, 166), the emphasis is »quite misleading« as inspections of traditional practices would in several cases reveal that consensus in fact comes close to the issuing of orders and is certainly not reached in an atmosphere of free and frank discussion. Lawson also takes care to underscore that consensus is a key feature of authoritarian rule (1996, 166). However, to the extent that consensus is conceived as a cultural resistance against ideas and institutions which promote and maintain divisions and conflicts, the Pacific region is undeniably imbued by consensual traits, which, to be sure, have deviated from metropolitan models and have thereby moulded and cultivated Democracy Pacific Style. Perhaps the most obvious deviation is represented by the Marshall Islands, who rejected the U.S. presidential system for a Westminster style of government, justifying their decision by arguing that a parliamentary system was more in line with the participatory and consensual Micronesian societies (Anckar 1997, 21). Another former American territory, the Federated States of Micronesia, while opting for presidentialism, provides yet another example. The President, it should be noted, is not elected by the people but by Congress from among the four-year members of Congress. This method was chosen to diminish the possibility that a President is elected solely because the largest state has overwhelming electoral power (Burdick 1988, 266-267).

As explained earlier, however, most modifications pertain to the Westminster model. In 1984, Arend Lijphart expanded his earlier thoughts on the promises held by a consociational democracy for Third World Countries (1977), and formulated principles and mechanisms for a consensual form of democracy, which was to be a logical opposite to the majoritarian view of democracy. This consensual democracy was based on the principle of sharing, dispersing and limiting power. In several respects, the clash between modernity and tradition runs parallel to Lijphart's distinction between majoritarian and consensual forms of democracy. Since most Pacific island states are former British colonies, or have a colonial past marked by a British presence (e.g., Nauru, which before independence in 1968 was a Trust Territory governed by Britain, Australia and New Zealand), the mark left by the metropolitan power upon her withdrawal from the colonies was the Westminster model. As suggested by Lijphart (1984), this is a sort of prototype for a majoritarian democracy. The clash between modernity and tradition therefore came to involve a clash between schools of thought about democracy: in the processes of decolonization, countries that were culturally inclined towards a consensual form of democracy were encouraged and manipulated if not forced to adopt a system which represented the very opposite of consensus and consensualism. The outcome of this clash has in many cases been a watered-down version of the Westminster model: although the main characteristics of this model are present (such as a plurality electoral method), other characteristics are not (Anckar 1999). The scope of this essay does not permit a discussion of the many peculiarities that exist, one of which is a fairly extensive use of selective allocation and apportionment strategies in legislative recruitment which advance consensual rather than majoritarian goals (Anckar 1996). One observation about the general position of the legislature must suffice.

Although a repudiation of majoritarianism would really imply deviations from the principle that ministers are usually members of parliament, which has been said to be basic to parliamentary government (Verney 1992, 35-36), most Pacific systems support this principle (Anckar 1997, 19-22). Instead, the modifications to the Westminster system concern other aspects of the executive-legislative relationship. The fusion of executive and legislative authority characteristic of the Westminster system usually means executive predominance, as the system prescribes cabinet control of parliament (e.g., McRae 1997, 283). Most Pacific systems, however, depart from this pattern, having chosen to strengthen the position of the legislature. In particular, the challenges to the Westminster model concern the appointment and dismissal of the prime minister and the dissolution of the legislature (Ghai 1988c, 82-88). The principle that the Head of State appoints the prime minister is thus largely disregarded, as the prime minister is elected by the legislature and also removed from office by the legislature, given that certain conditions are met. Furthermore, in most cases, the Head of State or Governor-General owes his office to the legislature and not to the executive. Moreover, dissolution of parliament is not usually at the discretion of the executive, as under the Westminster model. Although control is less than exclusive, Parliament as a rule decides on its own dissolution.

The emphasis on the role of the legislature is in fact linked to custom and tradition in several ways. By tilting the balance in favour of the legislature, one step, although moderate, is taken in the direction of a separation of powers, and the implication of this step is therefore an advancement of consensualism to the disadvantage of majoritarianism. Furthermore, the accentuation recognizes that party systems remain rather undeveloped in the Pacific states, due to the culturally tuned distaste for divisions and conflicts. One consequence of this is that the right of the executive to dissolve Parliament would not serve such ends, this right is generally supposed to serve. Since most parliamentarians are elected in their individual rather than party capacity, no guarantee exists that dissolutions break deadlocks; furthermore, for the same reason, general elections in the Pacific are seldom elections for a government (Ghai 1988c, 84). Restrictions on the power of the executive to seek early dissolution are therefore indirect if not even direct consequences of the Pacific tendency toward consensus. The weaknesses of the party systems and the shapelessness of Pacific party politics can also explain why the prime minister is elected by the legislature, as this method determines the member with the widest support.

Village versus Nation

The clash between modernity and tradition has several manifestations and ensuing consequences for everyday political life. An essential question, of course, is the extent to which the two cultures influence each other and which culture holds the upper hand. Does living in two different mental contexts imply that people are gradually socialized in their village life to a democratic way of thinking, or does it imply the opposite, i.e., an encroachment of village norms and patterns upon political life on the national level? On the one hand, there is much evidence that national politics is influenced by custom. On Kiribati it is reported that informal island councils of *unimane*, i.e., the old men who are the traditional leaders of the *I-Kiribati* society, still have significant influence in the election of Members of the *Maneaba ni Maungatabu* (House of Assembly) and the President, and also remain a powerful force in local government (Macdonald 1996, 5-6). In Belau, although respect for and compliance with traditional laws is waning in some policy fields (Johannes 1991), official sources tell us that the traditional chief system and traditional governing structure retain a strong, though largely undefined role within the Western government system (*Republic of Palau. National Environmental Management Strategy* 1994, 13). In Micronesia, it has been said, there exists a structural handicap for formulating a development strategy which requires society-wide mobilization and reduction of imports as politicians tend to come from the ranks of the customary leadership, the status of which is based on clients' tribute from below and patron donation from above rather than active leadership in production activities (Cameron 1992, 165-166). In some instances, the incongruity between bureaucratic and traditional relationships may even have amusing effects: »The director of health may be placed in charge of his uncle, who he must obey according to traditional lore« (Taylor 1990, 103).

There is, on the other hand, less evidence that local politics is influenced by modernity and departure from custom. Displaying indignation even at the thought that modernity would have an impact on village life, a Samoan scholar asserts that it would be »unrealistic to expect the Samoans to throw away their system through which they derive the basics of life, and adopt a new set of rules which would make less sense or be less attractive in the day-to-day village routine, and which would contradict so many of the norms and practices which have developed out of necessity and practical experience during the last two thousand years or so« (Meleisea 1987, 231). Besides expressing a normative point of view, this statement provides a fairly accurate factual description of the way village relates to nation and *vice versa*. To understand this bias in the two-way traffic between modernity and tradition, we need to consider the interplay between custom and several other factors, the most important of which are probably geography and fragmentation. The archipelagic nature of most Pacific island states in itself implies divisions and differences. As most parts of the Pacific archipelagos have a distinct history, certain unique cultural characteristics, and their own language or dialect (Hamilton-Jones 1992, 200), these geographical distances are frequently matched and accentuated by differences in terms of mental distance. Although there certainly are dissimilarities between individual states in this respect, the observed fragmentation is no doubt valid for most cases. This, of course, creates all sorts of problems for the emergence of nationhood and national identities. In some cases, Micronesia perhaps being the most obvious example, the problem emerged in the very formation of the new nation, as entities were created that represented mixed varieties in terms of race, language and religion. The concept of »nation-destroying« has even been introduced to describe decolonization outcomes (Connor 1972), and there are analysts who believe that the Federated States of Micronesia may well in the future disintegrate into a series of microstates (Petersen 1994, 366-367). Michael Jacobsen's description of Papua New Guinea can certainly illustrate the interplay between local and national affairs among other Pacific nations:

> In discussing the national and provincial government as the political representatives of modern society, local leaders and people in general distinguish rather sharply between these institutions and their own local community. This distinction is based on a principle of priority: the local community occupies the all-important place in the lives of every individual. Here their identity is formed through different processes of socialization into their respective subclan, and here people are born, marry, and die. This, then, is the center of their life cycles. »The nation«, and all it stands for, is something »out there« which only becomes reality on specific occasions, for instance, at national election time (Jacobsen 1995, 240).

With regard to this emphasis on local affairs and the local community, we may, in fact, speak of a sort of vicious circle (Anckar 2000). On the one hand, the voters expect politicians to take care of local matters. Politicians are elected because as local »bigwigs« they have proved their capability and because of expectations that they are able to provide for the local community and its specific needs. This, in turn, motivates politicians to give local affairs their best attention. Close ties are thus created between politicians and constituencies, ties which serve to distance politicians as well as voters from the sphere of non-local party politics. One consequence of this is that politicians are not strongly attached to parties and national party platforms. This, in turn, weakens the position of the political parties and hardly inspires popular confidence in parties as institutions. For students of party politics, the clash between modernity and tradition may open perspectives that challenge the conventional belief in the necessity of political parties for the working of democracies. One observation from the Solomon Islands is that most people do not vote for candidates according to party policies or philosophies. They vote instead for candidates on the basis of performance and achievement, performance being measured by how well the candidate has fared as initiator and overseer of community projects in the area he hopes to represent in parliament (Alasia 1989, 137). Likewise, studies of political life in Kiribati suggest that politicians are elected on the basis of personal achievement rather than as representatives of any party, organization, policy, class or ideology (Macdonald 1996, 6). In Tuvalu, politics are also based on personalities and island affiliations rather than ideologies (Rowe 1995, 19). Similar observations can in fact be made for most Pacific islands, and even in places where party politics has gained a foothold, the impact of the political parties is less than decisive. For instance, in the 1997 general elections in Papua New Guinea, twenty parties were registered for the election, but only 700 of the 2.300 candidates were endorsed by a party (Derek Ingram 1997, 469). A relevant observation on the impact of tradition on party politics is that those countries more culturally resistant than others to manifestations of political cleavages and divisions comprise a small group of Pacific democracies which manage without political parties (Anckar & Anckar 2000). A quotation from a chapter on politics in Vanuatu and the position of the leading party in the Southern Islands part of that country summarizes many of the culturally and geographically defined peculiarities and singularities embracing Democracy Pacific Style, and thereby forms an appropriate conclusion to this essay:

> While there is little doubt that the Vanua'aku Pati has a strong core of supporters based on its Presbyterian and anglophone links, we cannot assume the trend will continue. On each island, there are issues capable of splitting existing blocks of votes. New personalities can appear who may, due to their educational background and family ties, influence people to change their allegiance. Furthermore, the Southern Islands' constituency has the inherent problem of being composed of four separate islands, each of which has a strong sense of its own identity and would like to see one of their own representing them in Parliament. Until now, the Vanua'aku Pati has been able to overcome

this potentially divisive issue and hold a solid majority. There are indications, however, that this may be changing and that politics in the Southern Islands will become much less predictable in the future (Fakamuria *et al.* 1995, 399).

References

Alasia, Sam (1989). »Politics«, pp. 137-151, in Hugh Laracy (ed.), *Ples Blong Iumi. Solomon Islands, The Past Four Thousand Years,* Suva: Institute of Pacific Studies, University of the South Pacific.

Anckar, Dag (1996). »Noncontiguity and Political Architecture: The Parliaments of Small Island States«, *Political Geography,* Vol. 15, No. 8, pp. 697-713.

Anckar, Dag (1997). »Montesquieu in the Pacific. Cabinet Recruitment Patterns in Eleven Small Island States«, pp. 3-24, in Voitto Helander & Siv Sandberg (eds.), *Festskrift till Krister Ståhlberg. 50 år den 31 maj 1997,* Åbo: Åbo Akademi Förlag.

Anckar, Dag (1999). »Westminster Democracy: Small Island States Varieties«, unpublished manuscript.

Anckar, Dag (2000). »Party Systems and Voter Alignments in Small Island States«, in Lauri Karvonen & Stein Kuhnle (eds.), *Party Systems and Voter Alignments: Revisited* (forthcoming).

Anckar, Dag & Carsten Anckar (1998). *Cultural Heritage and Electoral Systems: The Case of Small Island States,* Åbo: Department of Political Science, Åbo Akademi University, Occasional Papers Series, No 2.

Anckar, Dag & Carsten Anckar (2000). »Democracies Without Parties«, *Comparative Political Studies* (forthcoming).

Anckar, Dag, Carsten Anckar & Lars Nilsson (1998). »Constitutional and Political Life in the Republic of Belau«, *Scandinavian Journal of Development Alternatives and Area Studies,* Vol. 17, No. 2 & 3, pp. 75-97.

Bayne, Peter (1988). »Judicial Review and Pacific Islands Constitutions«, pp. 106-134, in Yash Ghai (ed.), *Law, Politics and Government in the Pacific Island States,* Suva: Institute of Pacific Studies, University of the South Pacific.

Burdick, A. B. (1988). »The Constitution of the Federated States of Micronesia«, pp. 252-283, in Yash Ghai (ed.), *Law, Politics and Government in the Pacific Island States,* Suva: Institute of Pacific Studies, University of the South Pacific.

Cameron, John (1992). »The Federated States of Micronesia: Is there a Pacific Way to Avoid a *Mirab* Society?«, pp. 150-179, inode, Helen M. Hintjens & Malyn D. D. Newitt (eds.), *The Political Economy of Small Tropical Islands,* Exeter: University of Exeter Press.

Campbell, I. C. (1992). *Island Kingdom: Tonga Ancient & Modern,* Christchurch: Canterbury University Press.

Chehabi, H.E. (1995). »Small Island States«, pp. 1134-1137, in Seymour Martin Lipset (ed.), *The Encyclopedia of Democracy,* Vol. 4, London: Routledge.

Connor, Walker (1972). »Nation-Building or Nation-Destroying?«, *World Politics,* Vol. 24, No. 2, pp. 319-355.

Crocombe, Ron (1988). »Nauru. The Politics of Phosphate«, pp. 40-66, in *Micronesian Politics,* Suva: Institute of Pacific Studies, University of the South Pacific.

Crocombe, Ron (1992). »The Future of Democracy in the Pacific Islands«, pp. 9-27, in Ron Crocombe *et al.* (eds.), *Culture & Democracy in the South Pacific,* Suva: Institute of Pacific Studies, University of the South Pacific.

Crocombe, Ron, Uentamo Neemia, Asesela Ravuvu & Werner von Busch (1992). »Achievements and Directions«, pp. 239-261, in Ron Crocombe *et al.* (eds.), *Culture & Democracy in the South Pacific,* Suva: Institute of Pacific Studies, University of the South Pacific.

The Courier, No 159, September-October, 1996.

Deklin, Tony (1992). »Culture and Democracy in Papua New Guinea: Marit Tru or Giaman Marit ?«, pp. 35-48, in Ron Crocombe *et al.* (eds.), *Culture & Democracy in the South Pacific,* Suva: Institute of Pacific Studies, University of the South Pacific.

Facey, Ellen E. (1995). »*Kastom* and Nation-Making: The Politicization of Tradition on Nguna, Vanuatu«, pp. 207-225, in Robert J. Foster (ed.), *Nation-Making: Emergent Identities in Postcolonial Melanesia,* Ann Arbor: The University of Michigan Press.

Fakamuria, K., J. Keitadi, J. Kilu, T. Kailo, A. Nafuki & J. Naupa (1995). »Futuna, Aneityum, Aniwa, Erromango«, pp. 377-399, in Howard van Trease (ed.), *Melanesian Politics: Stael Blong Vanuatu,* Christchurch: Macmillan Brown Centre for Pacific Studies, University of Canterbury.

Freedom House (1999) Table of Independent Countries: Comparative Measure of Freedom. Internet: http://www.freedomhouse.org/political/frtablel.htm.

Ghai, Yash (1988a). »Constitution Making and Decolonisation«, pp. 1-53, in Yash Ghai (ed.), *Law, Politics and Government in the Pacific Island States,* Suva: Institute of Pacific Studies, University of the South Pacific.

Ghai, Yash (1988b). »Systems of Government I«, pp. 54-75 in Yash Ghai (ed.), *Law, Politics and Government in the Pacific Island States,* Suva: Institute of Pacific Studies, University of the South Pacific.

Ghai, Yash (1988c). »Systems of Government II«, pp. 76-105, in Yash Ghai (ed.), *Law, Politics and Government in the Pacific Island States,* Suva: Institute of Pacific Studies, University of the South Pacific.

Ghai, Yash & Jill Cottrell (1990). *Heads of State in the Pacific: A Legal and Constitutional Analysis,* Suva: Institute of Pacific Studies, University of the South Pacific.

Hadenius, Axel (1992). *Democracy and Development,* Cambridge: Cambridge University Press.

Hamilton-Jones, David (1992). »Problems of Inter-Island Shipping in Archipelagic Small Island Countries: Fiji and Cook Islands«, pp. 200-222, in Helen Hintjens & Malyn Newitt (eds.), *The Political Economy of Small Tropical Islands,* Exeter: University of Exeter Press.

Henningham, Stephen (1995). *The Pacific Island States,* London: Macmillan Press.

Horner, Simon (1992). »Political Systems Shaped by Many Influences«, *The Courier,* No 135 (September-October), pp. 72-75.

Hussein, Bernadette (1997). »A Time of Change«, *Pacific Islands Monthly,* Vol. 67, No 9, pp. 16-18.

Ingram, Derek (1997). »Commonwealth Update«, *The Round Table. The Commonwealth Journal of International Affairs,* Issue 344, pp. 459-471.

Ingram, Takiora (1992). »The Culture of Politics and the Politicization of Culture in the Cook Islands«, pp. 153-170, in Ron Crocombe et al (eds.), *Culture & Democracy in the South Pacific,* Suva: Institute of Pacific Studies, University of the South Pacific.

Jacobsen, Michael (1995). »Vanishing Nations and the Infiltration of Nationalism: The Case of Papua New Guinea«, pp. 227-249, in Robert J. Foster (ed.), *Nation-Making: Emergent Identities in Postcolonial Melanesia,* Ann Arbor: The University of Michigan Press.

Johannes, R. E. (1991). *Report for the Division of Marine Resources of the Republic of Palau,* Koror: Bureau of National Resources and Development, Republic of Palau.

Johnson, Giff (1988). »Marshall Islands: Politics in the Marshall Islands«, pp. 69-83, in *Micronesian Politics,* Suva: Institute of Pacific Studies, University of the South Pacific.

Larmour, Peter (1988). »Land Tenure Provisions of Pacific Islands Constitutions«, pp. 163-173 in Yash Ghai (ed.), *Law, Politics and Government in the Pacific Island States,* Suva: Institute of Pacific Studies, University of the South Pacific.

Lawson, Stephanie (1991). *The Failure of Democratic Politics in Fiji.* Oxford: Clarendon Press.

Lawson, Stephanic (1 996). *Tradition Versus Democracy in the South Pacific: Fiji, Tonga and Western Samoa,* Cambridge: Cambridge University Press.

Lijphart, Arend (1977). *Democraci, in Plural Societies. A Comparative Exploration,* New Haven: Yale University Press.

Lijphart. Arend (1984). *Democracies. Patterns of Majoritarian and Consensus Government in Twenty-One Countries,* New Haven: Yale University Press.

Macdonald, Barrie (1996). *Governance and Political Process i Kiribati,* Canberra: Working papers Nr 2, Research School of Pacific and Asian Studies, The Australian National University.

McRae, Kenneth (1997). »Contrasting Styles of Democratic Decision-Making: Adversial Versus Consensual Politics«, *International Political Science Review,* 18, No 3, pp. 279-295.

Meleisea, Malama (1987). *The Making of Modcrn Samoa,* Suva: Institute of Pacific Studies, University of the South Pacific.

Molisa, Grace Mera (1995). »A Crisis of Leadership«, pp. 427-433 in Howard van Trease (ed.), *Melanesian Politics.Stael Blong Vanuatu,* Christchurch: Maemillan Brown Centre for Pacific Studies, University of Canterbury.

Mulgan, Richard G. (1991). »Peoples of the South Pacific and Their Rights«", pp. 117-131 in Ramesh Thakur (ed.), *The South Pacific. Problems, Issues an Prospecty,* London: Macmillan.

Neemia, Uentabo (1992). »Decolonization and Democracy in the South Pacific«, pp. 1-8, in Ron Crocombe *et al.* (eds.), *Culture & Democracy in the South Pacific,* Suva: Institute of Pacific Studies, University of the South Pacific.

Pacific Constitutions. Vol. 2, Port Vila: Pacific Law Unit, University of the South Pacific.

Petersen, Glenn (1994). »The Federated States of Micronesia's 1990 Constitutional Convention: Calm Before the Storm ?«, *Contemporary Pacific,* Vol. 6, No. 2, pp. 337-369.

Pinkney, Robert (1993). *Democracy in the Third World,* Buckingham: Open University Press.

Quimby, Frank (1988). »The Yin and Yang of Belau: A Nuclear Free Movement Struggles with the Quest for Economic Development«, pp. 109-144, in *Micronesian Politics,* Suva: Institute of Pacific Studies, University of the South Pacific.

Ravuvu, Asesela (1992). »Culture and Traditions: Implications for Modern Nation Building«, pp. 57-65, in Ron Crocombe *et al.* (eds.), *Culture & Democracy in the South Pacific,* Suva: Institute of Pacific Studies, University of the South Pacific.

Republic of Palau. National Environmental Management Strategy (1994), Apia: South Pacific Regional Environment Programme.

Rowe, Robert (1995). »Tuvalu«, *The Courier,* No. 149 (January-February) pp. 19-21.

Tabokai, Nakibae (1993). »The *Maneaba* System«, pp. 23-29, in Howard van Trease (ed.), *Atoll Politics. The Republic of Kiribati,* Christchurch: Macmillan Brown Centre for Pacific Studies, University of Canterbury.

Tagaloa, Dr. Aiono Fanaafi Le (1992). »The Samoan Culture and Government«, pp. 117-138, in Ron Crocombe *et al* (eds.), *Culture & Democracy in the South Pacific,* Suva: Institute of Pacific Studies, University of the South Pacific.

Taylor, Richard (1990). »Problems of Health Administration in Small States: Some Observations from the Pacific«, pp. 60-114, in Yash Ghai (ed.), *Public Administration and Management in Small States,* Suva: The Commonwealth Secretariat and the University of the South Pacific.

van Trease, Howard (ed.) (1995). *Melanesian Politics. Stael Blong Vanuatu,* Christchurch: Macmillan Brown Centre for Pacific Studies, University of Canterbury.

Verney, Douglas V. (1992). »Parliamentary Government and Presidential Government«, pp. 31-47, in Arend Lijphart (ed.), *Parliamentary Versus Presidential Government,* Oxford: Oxford University Press.

A Note on Danish Parliamentary Research

Erik Damgaard

Abstract

A brief review of Danish parliamentary research since the 1960s shows that much new knowledge has been accumulated on legislative recruitment, parliamentary organisation (committees, party groups), legislative behaviour (party cohesion and co-operation, activities and roles) and government formation; that the repertoire of research methods has subsequently been expanded; and that Danish scholars have become increasingly integrated in comparative research projects and international research teams. However, more research is needed on topics such as recruitment, representation, party groups, committees and the »life« of governments.

Introduction

In a small country with very few legislative scholars, the literature on parliament and parliamentary government is bound to be both restricted and closely related to the research interests of those scholars. This was certainly the case in the 1960s and 1970s. However, even in the 1980s and 1990s, when the number of political scientists had increased considerably, the number of scholars researching Danish parliamentary government, remained limited, including a small number of foreign scholars with an interest in Danish politics such as Kenneth E. Miller (1968; 1996), John Fitzmaurice (1981; 1996), Alastair Thomas (1973; 1982) and David Arter (1984; 1995).

This article deals with Danish research on parliament and government. It does not include studies of the electoral system (e.g., Elklit 1997), electoral behaviour (e.g., Borre & Andersen 1997) and studies on extra-parliamentary party organisations (e.g., Bille 1997) although such topics, and indeed several others (public administration, interest groups, mass media), are necessary for an understanding of parliamentary life in Denmark. We shall examine research published since the mid-1960s, that is, the period during which one may reasonably talk about modern political science research in Denmark (cf. Nannestad 1977). Focus will be on the Danish parliament (Folketinget), its parties, its members and its relations to the government.

First, we shall review the literature on legislative (or parliamentary, the two terms will be used interchangeably in this article) recruitment. Next, studies on legislative organisation in terms of parties and committees will be surveyed. This is followed by an examination of studies on legislative behaviour, with an emphasis on internal party cohesion and inter-party cooperation as well as on the individual activities and roles of MPs. Finally, we shall consider the formation, life and termination of Danish governments, in the processes of which parliamentary parties play crucial roles.

It should be emphasised that, although parliamentary research in Denmark is limited compared to that of many other consolidated democracies, the ambition is not to provide a complete listing of the maximum number of possibly relevant publications, but rather, to mention those studies which the author views as especially important or interesting.

Recruitment and Members

In retrospect one may legitimately claim that the 1970s saw a surprisingly high number of publications on Danish legislative recruitment, mainly because Mogens N. Pedersen had become interested in that topic. Except for a few of Pedersen's students (e.g., Foverskov 1978; 1979; Johansen & Kristensen 1979) who tended to leave academia at a relatively young age, other scholars rarely touched the topic in the two subsequent decades. Apparently, many members of the Danish political science profession at that time felt that legislative recruitment was not only rather dull as a research topic but also somewhat irrelevant. Originally employed as the most senior junior member of the Aarhus political science department (1964-73), Pedersen, had become inspired by the American legislative behaviour approach to politics. He has recounted his career in two articles (Pedersen 1997; 1996) on his own early work (with other observations on the political science profession as it developed at home and abroad).

One might say that until recently, Danish legislative recruitment research has been mainly conducted by Pedersen. He originally organised a major data collection enterprise (Pedersen 1972a) and sometimes worked in collaboration with Kjell Eliassen (who worked »temporarily« at the Aarhus department from 1972 to 1980). In a longitudinal study of the 1849-1968 period, Pedersen (1977) showed that Danish parliamentarians changed from relatively closed to a more open elite. The change occurred primarily at the turn of the century and seems to be closely associated with the consolidation of the Danish party system of that period (on the »old« Danish party system and its development, see Pedersen 1987; Elklit 1984; Damgaard 1974). Pedersen (1976) further showed that the original »incumbents« were gradually replaced by »challengers«, first of the »rural« and then of the »urban« variety, in the same grand historical process. In a comparative Danish-Norwegian analysis, Eliassen and Pedersen (1978) also described a pattern of political professionalisation in which the basic criterion for legislative recruitment gradually changed from social to political status.

Pedersen authored at least two other important articles on legislative recruitment in the 1970s that deserve mention. The first is an impressive comparison of U.S. and Danish legislators (Pedersen 1972b) focusing on lawyers in politics. It compares two equally »deviant« cases: the U.S. with a very high proportion of lawyers in the House of Representatives and Denmark with a very low proportion in Folketinget. Pedersen suggests that one must pay attention to the barriers as well as the opportunities for jurists to enter parliament in order to really understand the recruitment process.

The second important contribution of the 1970s (Pedersen 1975) is an analysis of what he called the »geographical matrix of representation« in legislative recruitment. The author assumed that MPs would act according to rational choice calculations (a term which had hardly entered the Danish scholarly explanatory vocabulary at the time, cf. Nannestad 1993), in order to minimise (the costs of) the aggregated geographical and travelling distances between their home, their constituency (where they are not obliged to live), and the site of parliament in Copenhagen. From this axiom, Pedersen derived a number of testable hypotheses that received considerable support in the empirical analyses.

As indicated, these recruitment studies were not really followed up by other scholars in the 1980s, although this period saw the appearance of some studies on (increasing) female representation and activity in parliament (e.g., Haavio-Mannila *et al.* 1985; Dahlerup 1988). Although Pedersen (1984a) sketched some relationships between electoral volatility and legislative recruitment, there was nevertheless a lacuna in Danish legislative recruitment research. In the 1990s, however, a few new analyses appeared. On the basis of newly available data, Henrik Christoffersen (1992) demonstrated that the professionalisation of MPs continued to increase in several ways in the 1966-1988 period. Pedersen (1994a) also came with an analysis of incumbency success and failure in the 1945-1990 period, showing that there was a higher turnover rate in the 1970s (including the »critical election« of 1973) than either before or after. Furthermore, Torben Jensen (1999a) using new biographical and questionnaire data demonstrated that contemporary Danish MPs have become »professionals in every sense of the word«. There is every reason to believe that additional Danish studies will appear in the not so distant future on the effects of changes in the recruitment patterns.

Legislative Organisation

The general development of legislative organisation in Denmark was analysed in Damgaard (1977). The book described the organisational adjustments to changing societal conditions and a steadily increasing workload for MPs. Procedural innovations were emphasised, as were reforms of the committee system and the increasing importance of specialisation in legislative work, all designed to alleviate the increasing pressure of a heavy work load. Damgaard also noted a gradual expansion of the parliamentary staff. The focus of the study was very much on the new system of specialised committees, but it paid insufficient attention to the parliamentary party groups. Such neglect was neither incidental nor particular to Danish research, however. Thus, some years later, in a comparative essay on governments, parliaments and the structure of power in political parties, Klaus von Beyme (1983, 341) noted that »the parliamentary group have been neglected as a unit of research«. This certainly applied to Denmark, notwithstanding party groups were mentioned in a couple of early textbooks (Meyer 1965; Rasmussen 1968).

Parliamentary Parties. Even today, party groups in parliament have not been sufficiently researched, perhaps because the internal affairs of parliamentary parties are much more difficult to access, and certainly to measure, than are other aspects of parliamentary organisation and activity. In Denmark, note was made of the introduction (Damgaard 1977) and later increases of public financing of MPs and parliamentary parties (Bille 1997; Pedersen & Bille 1991), while Buksti (1989) provided an account of the increasing staff support and professionalisation of the party groups.

In the most general terms, Torben Worre (1970) claimed, with good reason, that the party groups were perhaps the most important power centres in the political system. Worre described a number of aspects related to party groups in terms of recruitment, organisation, cohesion, work and external relations as of the late 1960s, but his interesting journal article was not really followed up upon by other scholars. Some aspects of parliamentary parties, emphasising patterns of intra-party specialisation and co-ordination, were studied in the late 1970s and early 1980s (Damgaard *et al.* 1979; 1982a), and the legislative voting studies mentioned below are clearly also relevant in this context. While a full-scale study of the party groups remains to be conducted, certain small steps have recently been taken in that direction. Thus, a few chapters in the comparative analysis of the Nordic parliaments, based on parallel questionnaires in all five Nordic countries clearly demonstrate the central importance of parliamentary parties (Heidar & Esaiasson 1999). The importance of party groups to individual MPs is also evident in Torben K. Jensen's (1993) study of the political culture of Danish MPs', in Henrik Jensen's (1995) study of the parliamentary committees, and in a comparative analysis of party control of committee members (Damgaard 1995). While other studies could be mentioned, one must nevertheless conclude that party groups remain insufficiently studied in Danish parliamentary research, especially considering the obvious role that parties play in governance (Sjöblom 1987). New research projects are likely to improve this situation within the next few years, and Henrik Jensen's forthcoming article (1999) is possibly a first confirmation of this conjecture.

Parliamentary Committees. The reorganisation of the Danish committee system in 1972, which introduced a system of some 20 permanent, specialised committees, has attracted considerable scholarly interest (e.g., Larsen *et al.* 1977; Damgaard 1977; Hansen 1985; Henrik Jensen 1995; Damgaard 1998). The literature shows that MPs indeed specialise, and that they are very often assigned to committees in areas with which they are familiar from their private life, job or education. Some authors, notably Hansen (1985), tend to think that the committees are rather autonomous unitary actors, whereas others (notably H. Jensen 1995) argue that the committees are best understood as arenas for the activities of members who are basically party representatives. The latter argument seems to be more convincing, even if in some rare instances committees act as autonomous non-party players (cf. Damgaard 1987; 1999; H. Jensen 1995). Within a rational choice perspective, it has also been suggested that the sectoral specialisation of MPs may create a serious problem of overall co-ordination of national policy-making (Damgaard 1980a).

Henrik Jensen's work (1995) is the most comprehensive study of parliamentary committees to date. Utilising a variety of data and information sources, some of which consulted only after having been granted privileged access, the author updates earlier findings from the 1970s on sectoral specialisation. Jensen concludes that committee work is still a domain for experts within the parties; he adds new information on how individual MPs (overwhelmingly members of opposition parties) use the committees to ask questions of ministers (cf. also H. Jensen 1994). He shows that committee meetings can be best understood if the members are regarded as party representatives, and that the party groups have developed internal structures to handle co-ordination issues, although apparently not yet quite successfully with respect to EU policies that interfere with the jurisdictions of »domestic« committees.

Since Denmark joined the EC/EU in 1973, one permanent committee (now called the European Affairs Committee, EAC) has played a crucially important role in the parliamentary control of Danish governments with respect to their EU policies. The Danish EAC is arguably the strongest of this type of committee in the member states (cf. Bergman 1997) and has been described in several articles (e.g., Auken *et al.* 1974 provide an early account; Arter 1995, Laursen 1995, Fitzmaurice 1996, Sidenius *et al.* 1997, Damgaard & Nørgaard 1998 give more recent treatments; and Torben Jensen (1995) compares EAC members to other MPs on a number of attitudinal dimensions and in terms of their international involvement). The EAC must grant the minister in charge a bargaining mandate before he or she can commit the country in the EU Council of Ministers, and the committee has gradually managed to increase its level of information on upcoming EU proposals and initiatives. New initiatives to be taken in 1999 include ways of improving the integration of various specialised committees in the decision-making processes.

As with the party groups, however, more research is still needed on committees. Henrik Jensen's (1995) general study ought ideally to be followed up by more detailed analyses on how the various committees work, in order to reveal important similarities and differences.

Legislative Behaviour

When Mogens N. Pedersen introduced recruitment research in Denmark, he had already published articles on the voting behaviour of individual legislators and party groups, inspired by the American legislative voting research tradition going back to Stuart Rice (1928). That strand of research has been followed up by several scholars. Some of them have also done other work within the area of individual legislator behaviour and attitudes, using a variety of approaches and methods. It is possible to distinguish between studies of party cohesion and co-operation, on the one hand, and studies of parliamentary activities and roles, on the other, though there is a certain amount of overlap of the two categories.

Party Cohesion and Co-operation. In two early articles, Pedersen (1967a, 1967b) analysed the cohesion of parliamentary parties and the »distances« between the parties, both measured by using the voting records of individual party group members. After tediously coding and analysing thousands of votes at a time when computers were not available for such operations, Pedersen found a very high degree of party cohesion in the 1945-1966 period. He also mapped the main patterns of inter-party co-operation and conflict in law-making.

Since that time, cohesion has been dealt with by other researchers who basically confirmed the earlier message of a very high, and even increasing, level of party discipline in Danish legislative voting. Party discipline or cohesion is usually explained in terms that draw upon cultural-sociological factors relating to party and legislative socialisation, a heavy work load on MPs, and rational choice calculations by individual MPs. The studies include Damgaard (1973), Svensson (1982), Damgaard and Svensson (1989), Mikkelsen (1994), Torben Jensen (1999b) and Skjæveland (1997). The latter author is further able to demonstrate that the level of party cohesion, even if it is very high, nonetheless follows a distinct electoral cycle. Thus, party cohesion is highest immediately before and after an election. Such findings have rarely been discovered elsewhere (Skjæveland 1999).

With respect to inter-party co-operation, Mogens N. Pedersen has published data that, at least in a quantitative sense, showed much more co-operation than conflict, especially among the four »old« parties in Danish politics (Liberals, Conservatives, Social Democrats, Radical Liberals). That result was perhaps in accordance with the wisdom received of competent observers of Danish politics, but the hard data were not available at the time. An analysis of the same theme, for the 1982-1992 period, is to be found in Wittrup (1994).

Together with collaborators, Pedersen also suggested that the relations among parliamentary parties could be mapped in a one-dimensional or two-dimensional space (Pedersen *et al.* 1971). The same topic was analysed in a coalition study of Danish lawmaking 1953-70 (Damgaard 1973), which (also) found a left-right dimension to be the most important one. Such dimensional analyses, ultimately based on legislative voting behaviour, were later carried out by Damgaard and Rusk (1976), who tried to include the notions of representational linkages and issue-area variation in decision-making, and by Peter Nannestad (1989), who used more sophisticated multidimensional scaling techniques in comparing the spatial locations of (rational) voters and MPs.

From a somewhat different and broader perspective, inter-party cooperation in Danish law-making was studied by Damgaard and Eliassen in a number of articles (e.g., 1978; 1979; 1980). They reported on variations in terms of the representation of external sectoral interests, levels of party conflicts and stages of the legislative process.

Activities and Roles. Whereas parliamentary research in the 1960s and 1970s was almost exclusively based on documentary or »process generated« data, research in the ensuing two decades included other sources and methods of data collection and analysis. To be sure, publicly available parliamentary records are still in use. For example, it has been shown that questions in parliament, which Pedersen (1997; 1996) found difficult to analyse in the mid-1960s, can indeed be subjected to rigorous investigation if the right, though not too ambitious, questions are asked (Damgaard 1994a). Much of Henrik Jensen's (1995) study of committees was also based on documentary data, as was Refsgaard's (1990) article on the committee assignments of female MPs. The women's assignments still differ from those of male MPs, although the difference has been reduced since the 1970s (Damgaard 1997a).

New types of data have been introduced since the late 1970s, however. Thus, a modest »spectator observation« and qualitative interview investigation of the activities and perceptions of 14 Danish MPs was reported in 1979. The survey dealt with a number of topics, such as the time spent by MPs on various activities, their work in committees and party groups, relations with the media, as well as their varying role orientations (Damgaard *et al.* 1979, cf. Damgaard 1980b). Hans J. Nielsen (1992) used loosely structured personal interviews to map the activities and role orientations of MPs. Torben Jensen (1993; 1994) published results from in-depth personal interviews with 18 (current and former) MPs focusing on their »political style«. Jensen claims that MPs employ three strategies to acquire information and secure influence, terming them »networks«, »media«, and »matter-of-factness«. These strategies can be empirically combined in a number of ways.

The repertoire of legislative research methods was further expanded in the 1980s with mail questionnaires to MPs. Such surveys turned out to be quite difficult to carry out in Denmark compared to other countries, such as The Netherlands and Sweden (cf. Pedersen 1984b). The first Danish questionnaire was administered in 1980, and some of its main results were reported in Damgaard (1982a, 1982b; 1984a, 1984b; 1986, 1997a), and Damgaard and Kristensen (1982). Among the several topics dealt with were

MPs' contacts to social groups and interest organisations, MPs' perceptions of power relations, MPs' individual role orientation in terms of focus and style of representation, information sources, reasons for specialisation, problems of co-ordination and patterns of sectoral policy-making.

A second mail questionnaire was conducted by Torben Jensen in 1995 (Jensen 1996) as the Danish component of a five country Nordic comparative project, covering a wide variety of topics. The main publication of the Nordic research group is that of Heidar and Esaiasson, eds., (1999), but parts of the material have also been reported by Torben Jensen (1995; 1997; 1999b). Finally, mention should be made of parts of Henrik Jensen's (1995) book on committees, based on a questionnaire survey. The response rate was very high, perhaps in part because Jensen asked fewer questions than in the two previous questionnaires.

Government Formation and Termination

Arguably, the formation, support and termination of governments are the most important functions of parliamentary parties. Traditionally, this area of politics has attracted considerable interest in Denmark. There are several studies on historically important »government crises« (e.g., Rasmussen 1957; Kaarsted 1968) and on more normal and recent government formation situations (e.g., Kaarsted 1964; 1969; 1988; 1992). The most systematic early treatment of Danish parliamentary government and its development over time has been that of Erik Rasmussen (1972), originally published in 1969. Valuable information may also be found in Meyer (1984) and Rasmussen (1985). Quite comprehensive and useful accounts have also been provided by Thomas (1982) and recently by Miller (1996). Some peculiar Danish innovations in parliamentary government since the early 1980s have been outlined in Damgaard (1992; 1999a) and Andersen (1994).

In the 1960s, coalition theory emerged within political science, not least because of William Riker's (1962) book on political coalitions. Riker's elegant rational choice theory on coalitions inspired Damgaard to analyse Danish government formations in the 20th century in order to test the »size principle«, which was not without difficulties (Damgaard 1969). As Riker and Ordeshook (1973) remarked a few years later, this study showed »not only that grand coalitions break up immediately, but that, if we interpret the members of coalitions as parties (rather than individual parliamentarians), every coalition formed from 1906 onward is a minimal winning one.« Fortunately they hastened to add: »Since, however, these minimal winning coalitions were also invariably composed of ideologically adjacent parties, this evidence is not as strong as one might wish« (Riker & Ordeshook 1973, 193). In addition, the Danish experience especially called for explanations of minority cabinets.

Coalition theory, as applied to government formation in multiparty systems, has come a long way since Riker published his now classic study. There are various »office«- and »policy«- seeking theories, studies of pay-off, cabinet duration and termination, coalition agreements, etc. Many of these topics are included in the volume edited by Müller and Strøm (1997) which also contains a chapter on Denmark. Müller and Strøm's project not only includes the »birth« of governments, but also their »life«, durability, »death« and electoral performance. Further studies are in preparation for publication.

Studies on the life of Danish governments, as opposed to their birth and death, hardly exist (Damgaard 1997b), although Grønnegaard Christensen (1985) has analysed the importance and functions of cabinet committees. There are, however, some studies on executive-legislative relations. A few of these (notably Damgaard & Svensson 1989; Damgaard 1992) attempt to describe the peculiar new Danish model of parliamentary government, in which the government may not actually govern, but rather, oppose a ruling »alternative majority« in parliament, whereas it was previously assumed that a government could and should not tolerate defeat in matters of even minor importance (Worre 1982). Other studies (e.g., Damgaard 1999; Torben Jensen 1999b) compare aspects of Danish executive-legislative relations to the experiences of the four other Nordic countries, departing from the seminal ideas of Anthony King (1976) on various modes of executive-legislative relations. Damgaard (1994c) claims that the parliaments of Denmark, Norway and Sweden have become stronger in recent years relative to their (minority) governments.

An exploratory mapping of the causes of Danish government termination was carried out by Damgaard (1994b). The article demonstrates that majority coalitions in the post-war period always lose their majority in the first upcoming election. It also indicates that party strategic calculations basically explain why specific governments are formed and terminated. Parties in the centre of the political spectrum are usually decisive in both respects. This topic, as well as problems related to the life of governments, deserves further attention.

Conclusion

Looking back at the end of the 20th century, we may conclude that Danish parliamentary research made a modest but promising beginning in the late 1960s; that it gained momentum during the 1970s, some of which was apparently lost in the 1980s; and, finally, that new momentum has been achieved in the 1990s.

More than 30 years of research has provided us with new knowledge about legislative recruitment, development of parliamentary organisation (notably committees and party groups), legislative behaviour (party cohesion and co-operation, activities and roles), and government formation. One may also note a development towards expanding the repertoire of research methods employed. Furthermore, Danish scholars have become increasingly integrated into comparative research projects and international research teams, not least at the Nordic and European levels.

All this sounds positive and comforting. However, we have also noted a need for more research on recruitment, political representation, parliamentary party groups, committees and government operations. Not to be forgotten are the challenges emanating from the ongoing process of European integration. As the 21st century begins, there is plenty of work to do for parliamentary scholars.

References

Andersen, Louise (1994). »Dansk parlamentarisme: Politiske og retlige normer under opbrud?«, *Politica*, No. 1, pp. 12-24.

Arter, David (1984). *The Nordic Parliaments: A Comparative Analysis*, London: C. Hurst.

Arter, David (1995). »The Folketing and Denmark's 'European Policy': The Case of an 'Authorising Assembly'?«, *The Journal of Legislative Studies*, Vol. 1, No. 3, pp. 110-123.

Auken, Svend, Jacob Buksti & Carsten Lehmann Sørensen (1974). »Danmark i EF: Tilpasningsmønstre i danske politiske og administrative processer som følge af EF-medlemskabet«, *Nordisk Administrativt Tidsskrift*, pp. 239-286.

Bergman, Torbjörn (1997). »National Parliaments and EU Affairs Committees: Notes on Empirical Variation and Competing Explanations«, *Journal of European Public Policy*, Vol. 4, No. 3, pp. 373-387.

Bille, Lars (1997). *Partier i forandring*, Odense: Odense Universitetsforlag.

Borre, Ole & Jørgen Goul Andersen (1997). *Voting and Political Attitudes in Denmark*, Aarhus: Aarhus University Press.

Buksti, Jacob A. (1989). »Partiapparaternes rolle og udvikling«, *Politica*, pp. 279-287.

Christensen, Jørgen Grønnegaard (1985). »In search of unity: cabinet committees in Denmark«, pp. 114-137, in Thomas T. Mackie & Brian W. Hogwood (eds.), *Unlocking the Cabinet*, London: Sage Publications.

Christoffersen, Henrik (1992). »Udviklingen i selektionen af Folketingspolitikere 1966 til 1988«, pp. 342-380, in Jørgen Goul Andersen et al. (red.), *Vi og vore politikere*, Copenhagen: Spektrum.

Dahlerup, Drude (1988). »From a Small to a Large Minority: Women in Scandinavian Politics«, *Scandinavian Political Studies*, Vol. 11, No. 4, pp. 275-298.

Damgaard, Erik (1969). »The Parliamentary Basis of Danish Governments: The Patterns of Coalition Formation«, *Scandinavian Political Studies*, Yearbook 4, pp. 30-57.

Damgaard, Erik (1973). »Party Coalitions in Danish Law-Making 1953-1970«, *European Journal of Political Research*, Vol. 1, No. 1, pp. 35-66.

Damgaard, Erik (1974). »Stability and Change in the Danish Party System Over Half a Century«, *Scandinavian Political Studies*, Yearbook 9, pp. 104-125.

Damgaard, Erik (1977). *Folketinget under forandring*, Copenhagen: Samfundsvidenskabeligt Forlag.

Damgaard, Erik (1980a). »The Dilemma of Rational Legislative Action: Some Danish Evidence«, pp. 217-236, in Leif Lewin & Evert Vedung, (eds.), *Politics as Rational Action*, Dordrecht: D. Reidel.

Damgaard, Erik (1980b). »The Function of Parliament in the Danish Political System: Results of Recent Research«, *Legislative Studies Quarterly*, Vol. V, No, 1, pp. 101-121.

Damgaard, Erik (1982a). *Partigrupper, repræsentation og styring*, Copenhagen: Schultz.

Damgaard, Erik (1982b). »The Public Sector in a Democratic Order: Problems and Non-Solutions in the Danish Case«, *Scandinavian Political Studies*, Vol. 5, No. 4, pp. 337-358.

Damgaard, Erik (1984a). »The Importance and Limits of Party Government: Problems of Governance in Denmark«, *Scandinavian Political Studies*, Vol. 7, No. 2, pp. 97-110.

Damgaard, Erik (1984b). »Partier og demokratisk styring«, pp. 80-103, in Erik Damgaard et al., *Dansk demokrati under forandring*, Copenhagen: Schultz.

Damgaard, Erik (1986). »Causes, Forms, and Consequences of Sectoral Policy-Making: Some Danish Evidence«, *European Journal of Political Research*, Vol. 14, No. 3, pp. 273-287.

Damgaard, Erik (1987). »Ændringer i den parlamentariske kultur«, *Politica*, Vol. 19, No. 3, pp. 280-289.

Damgaard, Erik (1992). »Denmark: Experiments in Parliamentary Government«, pp. 19-49, in Erik Damgaard (ed.), *Parliamentary Change in the Nordic Countries*, Oslo: Scandinavian University Press.

Damgaard, Erik (1994a). »Parliamentary Questions and Control in Denmark«, pp. 44-76, in Matti Wiberg, (ed.), *Parliamentary Control in the Nordic Countries*, Helsinki: The Finnish Political Science Association.

Damgaard, Erik (1994b). »Termination of Danish Government Coalitions: Theoretical and Empirical Aspects«, *Scandinavian Political Studies*, Vol. 17, No. 3, pp. 193-211.

Damgaard, Erik (1994c). »The Strong Parliaments of Scandinavia: Continuity and Change of Scandinavian Parliaments«, pp. 85-103, in Gary W. Copeland & Samuel C. Patterson (eds.), *Parliaments in the Modern World*, Ann Arbor: University of Michigan Press.

Damgaard, Erik (1995). »How Parties Control Committee Members«, pp. 308-325, in Herbert Döring (ed.), *Parliaments and Majority Rule in Western Europe*, Frankfurt: Campus Verlag.

Damgaard, Erik (1997a). »The Political Roles of Danish MPs«, *The Journal of Legislative Studies*, Vol. 3, No. 1, pp. 79-80.

Damgaard, Erik (1997b). »Dänemark: Das Leben und Sterben von Koalitionsregierungen«, pp. 289-326, in Wolfgang C. Müller & Kaare Strøm (eds.), *Koalitionsregierungen in Westeuropa*, Vienna: Signum. Revised version to be published as *Coalition Governments in Western Europe* by Oxford University Press, 2000.

Damgaard, Erik (1998). »Denmark«, pp. 205-210, in George T. Kurian (ed.), *World Encyclopedia of Parliaments and Legislatures*, Washington, D. C.: Congressional Quarterly.

Damgaard, Erik (1999a). »Parlamentarismens udvikling« *(chapter contribution, forthcoming)*.

Damgaard, Erik (1999b). »Parliaments and Governments: Executive-Legislative Relations«, in Knut Heidar & Peter Esaiasson (eds.), *Beyond Congress and Westminster— The Nordic Experience*, Columbus: Ohio State University Press (forthcoming).

Damgaard, Erik et al. (1979). *Folketingsmedlemmer på arbejde*, Aarhus: Politica.

Damgaard, Erik & Kjell Eliassen (1978). »Corporate Pluralism in Danish Law-Making«, *Scandinavian Political Studies*, Vol. 1, No. 4, pp. 285-314.

Damgaard, Erik & Kjell Eliassen (1979). »Lovgivning, interesseområder og politisk segmentering«, pp. 289-319, in Mogens N. Pedersen (ed.), *Dansk politik i 1970'erne*, Copenhagen: Samfundsvidenskabeligt Forlag.

Damgaard, Erik & Kjell Eliassen (1980). »Reduction of Party Conflict through Corporate Participation in Danish Law-Making«, *Scandinavian Political Studies*, Vol. 3, No. 2, pp. 105-121.

Damgaard, Erik & Ole P. Kristensen (1982). »Party Government under Pressure«, pp. 33-56, in Dag Anckar et al. (eds.), *Partier, ideologier, väljare*, Åbo: Åbo Akademi.

Damgaard, Erik & Asbjørn Sonne Nørgaard (1998).*The European Union and Danish Parliamentary Democracy*, paper for workshop on Nordic Parliaments and the European Union, Aarhus: Department of Political Science.

Damgaard, Erik & Jerrold G. Rusk (1976). »Cleavage Structures and Representational Linkages: A Longitudinal Analysis of Danish Legislative Voting Behaviour«, pp. 163-188, in Ian Budge et al. (eds.), *Party Identification and Beyond*, London: Wiley.

Damgaard, Erik & Palle Svensson (1989). »Who Governs? Parties and Policies in Denmark«, *European Journal of Political Research*, Vol. 17, No. 6, pp. 731-745.

Eliassen, Kjell & Mogens N. Pedersen (1978). »Professionalization of Legislatures: Long-Term Change in Political Recruitment in Denmark and Norway«, *Comparative Studies in Society and History*, Vol. 20, No. 2, pp. 286-318.

Elklit, Jørgen (1984). »Det klassiske danske partisystem bliver til«, pp. 21-38, in Jørgen Elklit & Ole Tonsgaard (eds.), *Valg og vælgeradfærd*, Aarhus: Politica.

Elklit, Jørgen (1997). *The Politics of Electoral System Development and Change: The Danish Case*, paper for UCI conference on Party and Electoral Systems in Scandinavia, Aarhus: Department of Political Science.

Fitzmaurice, John (1981). *Politics in Denmark*, London: Hurst.

Fitzmaurice, John (1996). »Denmark«, pp. 236-258, in Roger Morgan & Clare Tame (eds.), *Parliaments and Parties*, London: Macmillan.

Foverskov, Peter (1978). »Women in Parliament: The Causes of Underrepresentation Exemplified by Denmark and Norway in the 1960s«, *European Journal of Political Research*, Vol. 6, No. 1, pp. 53-69.

Foverskov, Peter (1979). »Den politiske rekrutteringsproces omkring folketingsvalget

1973«, pp. 206-222, in Mogens N. Pedersen (ed.), *Dansk politik i 1970'erne*, Copenhagen: Samfundsvidenskabelig Forlag.

Haavio-Mannila, Elina et al. (1985). *Unfinished Democracy. Women in Nordic Politics*, Oxford: Pergamon Press.

Hansen, Holger (1985). *Folketingets stående udvalg*, Copenhagen: Jurist- og Økonomforbundets Forlag.

Heidar, Knut & Peter Esaiasson (eds.) (1999). *Beyond Congress and Westminster—The Nordic Experience*, Columbus: Ohio State University Press (forthcoming).

Jensen, Henrik (1994).»Committees as Actors or Arenas?«, pp. 77-102, in Matti Wiberg (ed.), *Parliamentary Control in the Nordic Countries*, Helsinki: The Finnish Political Science Association.

Jensen, Henrik (1995). *Arenaer eller aktører? En analyse af Folketingets stående udvalg*, Frederiksberg: Samfundslitteratur.

Jensen, Henrik (1999).»Folketingets partigrupper« *(chapter contribution, forthcoming)*.

Jensen, Torben (1993). *Politik i praxis. Aspekter af danske folketingsmedlemmers politiske kultur og livsverden*, Frederiksberg: Samfundslitteratur.

Jensen, Torben (1994). *Knowledge, Strategy or Prudence*, paper for XV IPSA World Congress, Berlin, August 1994.

Jensen, Torben (1995).»Partierne, Europaudvalget og europæiseringen», *Politica*, Vol. 27, No. 4, pp. 464-479.

Jensen, Torben (1996). *Rapport vedrørende data og dataindsamling i forbindelse med spørgeskemaundersøgelsen i Folketinget i forsommeren 1995*, Aarhus: Department of Political Science.

Jensen, Torben (1997).»Ways of Life, Myths of Nature and Risk Perceptions Among Danish MPs«, paper for ECPR Joint Sessions of Workshops, Bern, 1997.

Jensen, Torben (1999a).»Denmark: Professional Politicians in an Egalitarian Political Culture«, in Jens Bochart (ed.), *Politics as a Vocation: The Political Class in Western Democracies* (forthcoming).

Jensen, Torben (1999b).»Party Cohesion and Co-operation Across Party Lines in Nordic Parliamentary Parties«, in Knut Heidar & Peter Esaiasson (eds.), *Beyond Congress and Westminster—The Nordic Experience*, Columbus: Ohio State University Press (forthcoming).

Johansen, Lars N. & Ole P. Kristensen (1979).»Sikre kredse og personlig stemmeafgivning ved folketingsvalgene i 1960'erne og 1970'erne«, pp. 151-205, in Mogens N. Pedersen (ed.), *Dansk politik i 1970'erne*. Copenhagen: Samfundsvidenskabeligt Forlag.

Kaarsted, Tage (1964). *Regeringskrisen 1957*, Aarhus: Universitetsforlaget.

Kaarsted, Tage (1968). *Påskekrisen 1920*, Aarhus: Universitetsforlaget.

Kaarsted, Tage (1969). *Dansk politik i 1960'erne*, Copenhagen: Gyldendal.

Kaarsted, Tage (1988). *Regeringen, vi aldrig fik. Regeringsdannelsen i 1975 og dens baggrund*, Odense: Odense Universitetsforlag.

Kaarsted, Tage (1992). *De danske ministerier 1953-1972*, Copenhagen: PFA Pension.

Larsen, Dan et al. (1977). *Folketingets udvalg 1950-1975*, Aarhus: Danmarks Journalisthøjskole.

Laursen, Finn (1995).»Parliamentary Bodies Specialising in European Union Affairs: Denmark and the Europe Committee of the Folketing«, pp. 43-60, in Finn Laursen &

Spyros A. Pappas (eds.), *The Changing Role of Parliaments in the European Union*, Maastricht: European Institute of Public Administration.

Meyer, Poul (1965). *Politiske partier*, Copenhagen: Arnold Busck.

Meyer, Poul (1984). *Dansk politik*, Copenhagen: G.E.C. Gads Forlag.

Mikkelsen, Hans C. (1994). »Udviklingen af partisammenholdet«, *Politica*, Vol. 26, No. 1, pp. 25-45.

Miller, Kenneth E. (1968). *Government and Politics in Denmark*, Boston: Houghton Mifflin.

Miller, Kenneth E. (1996). *Friends and Rivals. Coalition Politics in Denmark*, New York: University Press of America.

Müller, Wolfgang C. & Kaare Strøm (eds.) (1997). *Koalitionsregierungen in Westeuropa*, Vienna: Signum. Revised version to be published in 1999 as *Coalition Governments in Western Europe* by Oxford University Press.

Nannestad, Peter (1977). »Political Science Research in Denmark: Trends of Research 1960-1975«, *Scandinavian Political Studies*, Yearbook 12, pp. 85-104.

Nannestad, Peter (1989). *Reactive Voting in Danish General Elections 1971-1979*, Aarhus: Aarhus University Press.

Nannestad, Peter (1993). »Paradigm, School, or Sect? Some Reflections on the Status of Rational Choice Theory in Contemporary Scandinavian Political Science«, *Scandinavian Political Studies*, Vol. 16, No. 2, pp. 127-147.

Nielsen, Hans J. (1992). »Politikersamtalerne«, pp. 203-271, in Gunnar V. Mogensen (ed.), *Vi og vore politikere*, Copenhagen: Spektrum.

Pedersen, Mogens N. (1967a). »Consensus and Conflict in the Danish Folketing 1945-1965«, *Scandinavian Political Studies*, Yearbook 2, pp. 143-166.

Pedersen, Mogens N. (1967b). »Partiernes holdning ved vedtagelsen af regeringens lovforslag 1945-1966«, *Historie, Jyske samlinger*, ny række VII, 3, pp. 404-435.

Pedersen, Mogens N. (1972a). *Danske Politiker-Arkiver (Archives on Danish Politicians 1848-1971)*, Aarhus: Department of Political Science.

Pedersen, Mogens N. (1972b). »Lawyers in Politics: The Danish Folketing and United States Legislatures«, pp. 25-63, in Samuel C. Patterson & John C. Wahlke (eds.), *Comparative Legislative Behavior: Frontiers of Research*, New York: Wiley.

Pedersen, Mogens N. (1975). »The Geographical Matrix of Parliamentary Representation: A Spatial Model of Parliamentary Representation«, *European Journal of Political Research*, Vol. 3, No. 1, pp. 1-19.

Pedersen, Mogens N. (1976). *Political Development and Elite Transformation in Denmark*, London: Sage Publications.

Pedersen, Mogens N. (1977). »The Personal Circulation of a Legislature: The Danish Folketing 1849-1968«, pp. 63-101, in W. O. Aydelotte (ed.), *The History of Parliamentary Behavior*, Princeton: Princeton University Press.

Pedersen, Mogens N. (1984a). »Vælgerbevægelighed og politisk rekruttering: nogle spekulationer og nogle foreløbige resultater«, pp. 60-85, in Ole Berg & Arild Underdal (eds.), *Fra valg til vedtak*, Oslo: Aschehoug.

Pedersen, Mogens N. (1984b). »Research on European Parliaments: A Review Article on Scholarly and Institutional Variety«, *Legislative Studies Quarterly*, Vol. IX, No. 3, pp. 505-529.

Pedersen, Mogens N. (1987). »The Danish 'Working Multiparty System': Breakdown or Adaptation?«, pp. 1-60, in Hans Daalder (ed.), *Party Systems in Denmark, Austria, Switzerland, The Netherlands, and Belgium*, London: Frances Pinter.

Pedersen, Mogens N. (1994). »Incumbency Success and Defeat in Times of Electoral Turbulences: Patterns of Legislative Recruitment in Denmark 1945-1990«, pp. 218-250, in A. Somit et al. (eds.), *The Victorious Incumbent: A Threat to Democracy?*, Aldershot: Dartmouth.

Pedersen, Mogens N. (1996). »Young Man in a Hurry: Recollections of a Soldier of Fortune«, *Scandinavian Political Studies*, Vol. 19, No. 3, pp. 181-204.

Pedersen, Mogens N. (1997). »Present at the Creation«, pp. 253-266, in Hans Daalder (ed.), *Comparative European Politics: The Story of a Profession*, London: Pinter.

Pedersen, Mogens N., Erik Damgaard & Peter Nannestad (1971). »Party Distances in the Danish Folketing 1945-1968«, *Scandinavian Political Studies*, Yearbook 6, pp. 87-106.

Pedersen, Mogens N. & Lars Bille (1991). »Public Financing and Public Control of Political Parties in Denmark«, pp. 147-172, in Matti Wiberg (ed.), *The Public Purse and Political Parties*, Helsinki: The Finnish Political Science Association.

Rasmussen, Erik (1957). *Statslånskrisen 1919*, Aarhus: Universitetsforlaget.

Rasmussen, Erik (1968). *Komparativ Politik 1* (1st ed.), Copenhagen: Gyldendal.

Rasmussen, Erik (1972). *Komparativ Politik 2* (2nd ed.), Copenhagen: Gyldendal.

Rasmussen, Erik (1985). »Finanslovsforkastelse i dansk parlamentarisme: normer og konsekvenser«, *Historie, Jyske Samlinger*, Ny række, Vol. 16, No. 1, pp. 56-118.

Refsgaard, Elisabeth (1990). »Tæt ved toppen. Kvinders placering i Folketingets arbejds- og magtdeling«, pp. 106-140, in Drude Dahlerup & Kr. Hvidt (eds.), *Kvinder på Tinge*, Copenhagen: Rosinante.

Rice, Stuart (1928). *Quantitative Methods in Politics*, New York: Alfred Knopf.

Riker, William H. (1962). *The Theory of Political Coalitions*, New Haven: Yale University Press.

Riker, William H. & Peter C. Ordeshook (1973). *An Introduction to Positive Political Theory*, Englewood Cliffs: Prentice-Hall.

Sidenius, Niels Chr., Bjørn Einersen & Jens Adser Sørensen (1977), »The European Affairs Committee and Danish European Union Politics«, pp. 9-28, in Matti Wiber (ed.), *Trying to Make Democracy Work*, Stockholm: The Bank of Sweden Tercentenary Foundation.

Sjöblom, Gunnar (1987). »The Role of Political Parties in Denmark and Sweden, 1970-1984«, pp. 155-201, in Richard S. Katz, *Party Governments: European and American Experiences*, Berlin: Walter de Gruyter.

Skjæveland, Asbjørn (1997). *Ydre partisamstemmighed i Folketinget*, unpublished thesis, Aarhus: Department of Political Science.

Skjæveland, Asbjørn (1999). »A Danish Party Cohesion Cycle«, *Scandinavian Political Studies* (forthcoming).

Svensson, Palle (1982). »Party Cohesion in the Danish Parliament during the 1970s«, *Scandinavian Political Studies*, Vol. 5, No. 1, pp. 17-42.

Thomas, Alastair H. (1973). *Parliamentary Parties in Denmark, 1945-1972*, Glasgow: University of Strathclyde, Survey Research Centre.

Thomas, Alastair H. (1982). »Denmark: Coalitions and Minority Governments«, pp. 109-141, in Eric C. Browne & John Dreijmanis (eds.), *Government Coalitions in Western Democracies*, New York: Longman.

von Beyme, Klaus (1983). »Governments, Parliaments, and the Structure of Power in Political Parties«, pp. 341-367, in Hans Daalder & Peter Mair (eds.), *Western European Party Systems*, London: Sage.

Wittrup, Jesper (1994). »Konflikt og konsensus i det danske Folketing«, *Politica*, Vol. 26, No. 1, pp. 46-56.

Worre, Torben (1970). »Partigrupperne i Folketinget. Et magtcentrum i dansk politik«, *Økonomi & Politik*, Vol. 44, No. 2, pp. 143-188.

Worre, Torben (1982). *Det politiske system i Danmark*, Copenhagen: Akademisk Forlag.

Institutions and Networks: A Comparison of European and Southeast Asian Integration

Kjell A. Eliassen & Catherine Børve Monsen

Abstract

This chapter addresses differences in the mechanisms and processes of regional integration. It focuses on two successful examples of organisations for regional cooperation, the European Union (EU) and the Association of Southeast Asian Nations (ASEAN). We will describe both the organisational structure and the integrating mechanisms of the two cases and explain differences in the emphasis on law-based institutional arrangements versus network co-operation. The two main questions asked in the paper are: why do two regions of the world develop so different models of increased integration and co-operation? Second, to what extent and how are these differences linked to historical, cultural and economic structures and variations in business patterns in Europe and Southeast Asia?

Introduction

The main aim of this chapter is to discuss how and why regional organisational structures and integrating mechanisms differ between various regions of the world.[1] While there are numerous studies of European integration, there has also emerged a substantial literature on regional integration in other parts of the world, including Pacific Asia. However, there are few studies comparing the European and Asian models of regional integration (for exceptions, see Holland 1994; Higgot 1995; Milner 1995; Spindler 1997). This theme is touched upon more generally in the analyses of regional integration (e.g., Katzenstein 1996).

Over the past two years, several studies of the Asian currency crisis have appeared (Gill 1998; Henderson 1998; Montes 1998; Pape 1998). Most of these studies focus on the rationale behind, as well as on the possible effects of the Asian crisis. In their assessment of impact, however, few scholars focus explicitly on the future of regional integration despite the difficult situation in which most Southeast Asian countries now find themselves. Recent developments indicate that the crisis has a profound effect on regional co-operation, including the nature of relations between the countries and degree of institutionalisation. One of the main questions to be addressed in this chapter is whether the crisis will in fact lead to greater integration and to new forms of multilateral co-operation. In examining this question, the answers may vary according to time-perspective. Based on the last year's developments, for example, certain short- and medium term trends can be distinguished, while any assessment of long-term implications must remain a vague prediction.

This chapter examines differences in organisational structure and integrating mechanisms by comparing the development of the European Union (EU) with the Association of Southeast Asian Nation-States (ASEAN). An important characteristic of the new regionalism (e.g., ASEAN) is the wide variation in levels of institutionalisation, with many regional groupings consciously avoiding the institutional and bureaucratic structures of traditional international organisations and of the regionalist model represented by the EU (Garnaut & Drysdale 1994).[2]

Gills (1997) and others have argued that both the European and the Asian economic model are not so different, neither historically nor presently. We also find institutional elements in the Asian model and a substantial element of networks (e.g., lobbying) in the European model of regional integration. Thus, there is a tendency to overstate the differences between regionalisms in these two parts of the world.

As this chapter focuses on variations in regional responses by comparing the EU with ASEAN, we will first discuss the revival of regional integration. The second part of the chapter focuses on the various mechanisms of regional integration and types of institutional arrangements in Europe and Asia. The EU and ASEAN will be analysed as examples of two quite successful regional co-operating organisations with different organisational structures and integration mechanisms. After a comparison of the EU French inspired law and institutional integration within the ASEAN pattern of network co-operation, it is a natural next step to investigate why they differ. In trying to explain the differences, we will investigate the main factors behind regional integration and the different types of integration logic in the two regions.

Furthermore, we will investigate whether varying historical, political, economic and cultural patterns have an impact on the differences in the two regional organisations. As previously mentioned, we will emphasise the economic crisis in Asia, which arguably has had a profound impact on the political, social and even cultural patterns in the Southeast Asian countries. The present crisis in the region creates both opportunities for and obstacles to greater regional integration. Our analysis will emphasise the trends that seem to prevail in the current situation, and these will be explained with reference to, among others, aspects of state-making in Asia.

Why should we compare ASEAN and the EU and not other organisations? ASEAN is one of the regional organisations most similar to that of the EU when it comes to the scope and range of activities covered. We feel that an analysis of similarities and differences between these two institutions of regional co-operation would help us understand the role of intergovernmental institutions in various regional responses to the globalisation process. Furthermore, regional integration in Europe, it emerges, has been subregional integration: the construction of institutional structures to combine the interests of a group of countries within a wider region (Wallace 1995). Seen from this perspective, the European Community could more accurately be compared with ASEAN rather than APEC.

Before beginning our analysis, we find it necessary to address the revival of regional integration and the principal varieties of regionalism.

The Revival of Regional Integration

The period since the late 1980s has witnessed a renaissance of regionalism in world politics. Old regionalist organisations have been revived, new organisations formed, and a call for strengthened regionalist arrangements has been central to many of the debates about the nature of the post-Cold War international order. The revival of political and academic interest in regionalism has been linked to: the end of the Cold War and the erosion of the Cold War alliance systems, the recurrent fears of the stability of the GATT and the multilateral trading order during the prolonged negotiations of the Uruguay Round, the impact of increasing economic integration and globalisation, changed attitudes towards economic development in many parts of the developing world, and the impact of democracy and democratisation (Fawcett & Hurrell 1995,1).

The political salience of regionalism increased significantly as a result of developments within Europe, the successful negotiation and ratification of the North American Free Trade Agreement (NAFTA), the increased momentum of co-operative efforts within the Association of Southeast Asian

Nation-States (ASEAN), and the continuing discussions within the Asia-Pacific region over new economic and security agreements (APEC, PECC, ARF) (Garnaut & Drysdale 1994).[3] We even have witnessed the development of inter regional co-operation, e.g., the EU-ASEAN co-operation program and ASEM (Cho & Chung 1997).

We are now witnessing fundamental changes in the functioning of the world economy and in the way multinational companies run their business. Increased trade and a global liberalisation have been characteristic features of this change, not only within the blocks but also on a world scale. At the same time, rapid technological development has made the world smaller and altered the conditions for operation. This development has often resulted in increased regional integration. One explanation may be that globalisation and liberalisation have led to reduced national control over the economy. This will result, at least for the industrialised countries, in an attempt to compensate by demanding some regional control. The next step will be not only to assert control within their own region but also across different regions in order to regain the political control which they had lost (Oman 1994).

The revival of regionalism and regionalist projects must be seen in a global perspective (Fawcett & Hurrell 1995, 3; Higgot 1997). The emergence of regionalist projects in so many parts of the world, suggests that broad international forces may be at work and that a single-region focus is misleading. While the return of regionalism to the international agenda has produced mixed reactions, both regional optimists and pessimists agree that regionalism is on the increase. The end of the Cold War had an important impact on global economic change and the transformation of the international system, and, together with the passing of the Single European Act in 1986, marked the turning-point in the fortunes of regionalism (Fawcett & Hurrell 1995, 9). These and other factors have resulted in the proliferation of new regional groupings and a revitalization of older regional bodies. What distinguishes this regional wave special from others is the truly global nature of the regionalism.

Recent debates suggest that the broad term »regionalism« is used to cover a variety of distinct phenomena. Rather than to try to work with a single, overarching concept, it is more useful to divide the notion of regionalism into five categories: regionalisation, regional awareness and identity, regional interstate co-operation, state-promoted regional integration and regional cohesion (Hurrell 1995, 39). Let us briefly address these five categories.

First, regionalisation refers to the growth of societal integration within a region and to the often undirected processes of social and economic interaction. Furthermore, »regional awareness« and »regional identity« are inherently imprecise and diffuse concepts. Yet it is impossible to ignore them since regional awareness and identity have become more central to the analysis of contemporary regionalism.

Regional interstate co-operation can be of a formal or informal nature, although a high level of institutionalisation is no guarantee of either effectiveness or political importance. Regional co-operation can entail the creation of formal institutions, but it is often based on a much looser structure, involving patterns of regular meetings with some rules attached, together with mechanisms for preparation and follow-up.

Regional integration involves specific policy decisions by governments aimed at reducing or removing barriers for the mutual exchange of goods, services, capital and people. These policies have received considerable attention with regard to the processes of integration, the paths that it might take, and the objectives that it might fulfil. Regional cohesion refers to the possibility that a combination of the first four categories just mentioned might lead to the emergence of a cohesive and consolidated regional unit. It is this cohesion that makes regionalism important to the study of international relations.

These five categories are key aspects of this chapter and will be used as a general framework for our analysis. Let us first describe, however, the two main regional entities the European Union (EU) and the Association of Southeast Asian Nation-States (ASEAN).

EU: Institution-Based Integration

There exist various descriptions of the EU, its history, construction, functioning, decision-making process etc. Since its birth in the 1950s, however, the European Community (EC) has been analysed mainly as an example of *supranational integration* of, or *intergovernmental co-operation* between, (former) sovereign nation-states (Hix 1994). Analyses of European integration have been dominated by two general, interpretative approaches: neo-functionalism and intergovernmentalism (Rhodes & Mazey 1995). Neo-functionalism and liberal intergovernmentalism are two contrasting theoretical perspectives on the nature of politics and the process of change within the European Community.

Many scholars see genuine movement in the direction of a polity, as individuals, corporations, and government actors increasingly identify with and act according to European-level institutions and processes (Rhodes & Mazey 1995). Others view the European Union as an ongoing struggle of give and take between member states, where no real European polity has emerged.

Most descriptions focus on the EU's legal and institutional aspects. Recent analyses reveal a marked shift from the traditional emphasis on national governments as the key actors in EU policy-making towards a broader examination of other actors involved in the EU policy process. The impact of lobbying by organised interests has come under scrutiny (Andersen & Eliassen 1993; Mazey & Richardson 1993; Greenwood 1997) and increasing attention has been paid to the role of policy networks at the European level (Bomberg 1994; Peterson 1992; 1995). Furthermore, increased attention has been paid to the role played by the European institutions themselves as an «institutional-matter» perspective on EU policy-making (Bulmer 1994a; Peterson 1992; 1995). Neo-institutionalism views actors in European integration as centralised institutions. Integration within neo-institutionalism is driven by an internal institutional logic characterised by elite predominance.

The important new element in regional integration introduced in the Treaty of Rome was the supranational institutions, best illustrated by the European Commission, the European Parliament and the European Court of Justice. The supranational element gave the EU the possibility of initiative unlike any other regional organisation since the 1950s and onwards.

The European Commission acts independently of the national governments and solely in the interest of the Union, while with very few exceptions the Commission is responsible for initiating legislation (Edwards & Spence 1995). The main responsibilities of the European Parliament are budget, legislation and control authority. Direct contacts between the European Commission and the Parliament are growing, thus creating a basis for more autonomous EU decision-making, independent of national interests. Furthermore, the European Court of Justice, with a central position in the whole EU system, is intended to safeguard the enforcement of the Directives in the member countries. Legal interpretations and final decisions are left with the Court of Justice (Andersen & Eliassen 1993, 26).

There may be several reasons for maintaining the priority of supranationalism. A key element is the model of strong nation states in Europe who themselves have experienced state- and nation-building processes. Another reason could be the influence of federal models from the United States. Finally, the six initial member countries of the European Community can also be characterised as relatively homogenous, both politically and economically. However, the existence of supranational institutions has not been without problems and inertia in the development of the EU. The dynamism of the 1980s appeared with another kind of »supranationality« through majority voting in the European Council, which, in addition to the strong supranational institutions, points to the other predominant feature of the development in Europe.

The considerable role of nation states and governments, both in the further development of regional integration and in current policy shaping in the EU also contrasts with other attempts at regional integration. The EEC was established in 1957 as a result of an intergovernmental conference in Rome, and its legal foundation has continuously been changed as a result of new intergovernmental conferences. Simultaneously, the European Council is the EU's most important executive and legislative authority. Thus, economic and political integration is primarily a result of nation-state politics.

The Single European Act (SEA), signed in 1986, was the first major revision of the Treaty of Rome, and it entered into force in 1987. The SEA helped complete the internal market and introduced majority voting and is widely considered a turning point in the integration process in Western Europe. The SEA provided the EC with a legal basis for the internal market, rules for majority voting, an outspoken commitment to promote social and economic cohesion, a framework for further development of concerted action in the area of foreign policy and a new role for the European Parliament through the co-decision procedure.

The Treaty on the European Union (TEU) signed at Maastricht on 7 February 1992, created a new European Union based on the European Community, which »marks a new stage in the process of creating an ever closer union among the peoples of Europe« (Duff 1994). The Maastricht Treaty (1993) has further expanded the scope of the EU to include education, culture, public health, industry and some other policy areas. Much of the Treaty built on past EC treaties and on the corpus of law policy made by the common institutions over forty years. The Maastricht Treaty divides policy areas into three »pillars«. The first amends the EEC, ECSE, and Euratom Treaties and is formally named the European Community (governed on a supranational level). The second pillar concerns foreign and security policy and is based upon existing intergovernmental procedures of European political co-operation. The third pillar covers justice and home affairs. Other provisions of Maastricht are intended to respond to new external challenges of the Community, including enlargement.

Five years after the signing of the Maastricht Treaty, following the Amsterdam Treaty, we have seen that European co-operation has again progressed in a range of areas. After a few setbacks, the internal market was put into effect as planned. The Schengen Agreement, which deals with the abolishment of border controls, will be implemented in more countries than originally planned. And since January 1999, the EMU has progressed according to schedule. This represents perhaps the most important input to a further deepening of the integration process in the years to come.

Although there are examples of difficult policy areas in the EU, such as employment, energy policy, and the second and third pillars, the competence of the Commission has increased within areas such as: education, culture, telecommunications, banking, transport, small and medium sized companies and the environment (Andersen & Eliassen 1993, 22). The SEA, the Maastricht Treaty in particular, and to a certain degree also the Amsterdam Treaty, all broaden the scope and variety of policy issues which will be influenced by the EU. In the future almost all national policy areas will have an EU dimension (Andersen & Eliassen 1993, 12), based on a strong EU secretariat in each country. How, then, does this European situation compare to the development in Asia?

ASEAN: Network-Based Integration

Compared to Europe, economic integration in the Asia-Pacific region is developing in its own distinct way. Unlike in Europe, where governments have played a key role in forging regional frameworks for regional business activity, in the Asia-Pacific region it is the business community which has forced governments to consider ways of regulating regional relations.

Economic integration in Southeast Asia is a result of trade- and business operations, which has led to a minimum of regional economic integration arrangements (Gallant & Stubbs 1996).

The most progressive attempt to build a formalised regional integration organisation in Southeast Asia is the Association of Southeast Asian Nations (ASEAN).[4] ASEAN was established on 8 August 1967 with the signing of the Bangkok Declaration. When representatives from Indonesia, Malaysia, the Philippines, Singapore and Thailand established the Association, they held out a bold vision of all countries in Southeast Asia co-operating actively towards peace, stability, progress and prosperity in the region. The ASEAN nations came together with the aim to promote the region's economic, social and cultural development through co-operative programmes, safeguarding the region's political and economic stability against Big Power rivalry, and serving as a forum for the resolution of intra-regional differences (COM (96) 314 final). However, the Vietnam War and the threat of Communist expansion to other parts of the Pacific are regarded as the actual reasons for the establishment of the organisation. ASEAN is thus a good example of how economic regionalism can become a mechanism by which broader security and political goals can be pursued, stressing these goals more than specific questions of economic integration, as was the case in the European example (Fawcett & Hurrell 1995, 4). Political aspects completely dominated the first 15 years of ASEAN's activities.

Thus, the progress of economic co-operation was more of a symbolic character. An example of the symbolic character of such economic co-operation is that the 16.000 products listed under the PTA agreement accounted for only 1 percent of total intra-ASEAN trade (Bernard & Ravenhill 1995).

After the end of the Cold War and the changes in Indochina, ASEAN leaders began increasingly to realize that improving and strengthening the group's cooperation was vital for the viability and relevance of ASEAN (Soesastro 1995). At the Fourth ASEAN Summit in Singapore in 1992, the heads of government signed a »Framework Agreement on Enhancing ASEAN Economic Co-operation«, committing the six to establish ASEAN Free-Trade Area (AFTA). The purpose of this agreement was to reduce all tariff rates for intra-ASEAN trade in industry and agricultural products within fifteen years.

ASEAN also established the ASEAN Regional Forum (ARF) which, apart from the ASEAN countries, includes several other Asian countries, Russia, the EU, USA, Canada, Australia and New Zealand.[5] ARF has been assigned the major task of maintaining peace and stability in the region, a task the Association has striven to ensure since its inception. In addition, it is contributing to ease China's integration into international and regional structures.

After the foreign ministers' meeting in Jakarta on April 30, 1999, ASEAN admitted Cambodia as its tenth member, thus fulfilling its vision to establish an organisation for all Southeast Asian countries.[6]

Unlike the EU, ASEAN has no supranational authority. New members are expected to blend into the membership and adopt the so-called »ASEAN way« of defence, positive attitude, quiet diplomacy and goodwill in consultations to achieve consensus and strengthen solidarity (Chalermpalanupap 1997). ASEAN membership increases the importance of the regional dimension in the policy-making process of the new members. However, political co-operation in ASEAN, involves little or no internal adjustments. Each member still develops its own political system and its own government structure. The reality is that national interests and preferences remain a major determinant on possibilities of economic co-operation within ASEAN (Acharaya 1997).

One major difference between integration in Europe and Southeast Asia can be found between formal and informal integration. Formal integration involves the establishment of institutions and common regulations in order to control the relationship between nation states, as is the case with APEC in Asia and the EU in Europe. Although there exist examples of formal integration in Asia, the informal integration is a comprehensive form of regional co-operation in Asia.[7] It is mainly the informal character that distinguishes the Southeast Asian pattern from that of other regions (Peng 1997) and this feature should therefore be given more attention. The informal aspects include the production networks, sub-regional economic zones (SREZs) and ethnic business networks.

What then, are the reasons for the great differences in the integration patterns between Europe and Southeast Asia?

Explaining Different Patterns of Regional Integration

Having described how the EU and ASEAN differ and having focused on variations in organisational structure and institutional mechanisms, we need to raise an important issue: the difference between a political and a chronological time perspective when comparing EU and ASEAN. To what extent is it fair to compare ASEAN today with the EU today? Obviously, the EU has had a longer life and a much more rapid development than ASEAN. Perhaps a more reasonable comparison would be to try to find comparable political time periods and compare, for example, the EU in the 1970s with ASEAN today. The differences between the two organisations with respect to supranationality and organisational development would still be important, but the conclusions regarding a successful versus a slow development of regional co-operation would not be so obvious.

Regional integration can be explained using both political and economic reasoning. According to Katzenstein (1996) regional integration is attractive on several economic grounds. First, relations to neighbouring countries stimulate increased trade and investment relations. Second, economic relations do not demand the kind of reciprocity that the World Trade Organisation (WTO) usually does. Third, efficiency and ability to compete at a regional level is usually strengthened through a global liberalisation. Finally, the effects of the regional economies of scale and saving in transport costs may create dynamic effects which also reinforce economic growth.

We find good examples of the role and importance of these arguments for regional integration in the European case. The revitalising of the EU through the single market was a direct consequence of a desire to make Europe competitive compared to the United States and Asia. The aim was to diminish the obstacles towards trade and to create a large domestic market large enough so that global companies with a base in the EU could be developed. The aim of the internal market was to establish market integration and, hence, develop stronger competition. This would entail restructuring industry and the companies based on comparative advantages and economies of scale.

The factors behind and the success of the Single European Act and the

Internal Market can be explained in economic terms (Balassa 1962; Kindleberger 1973; Cooper 1976; Summers 1991; Bhagwati 1993; Krugman 1993; Young 1993; Baldwin & Venables 1995), but the success can also be accounted for in terms of political integration theory. The great success of the Internal Market was seen as a firm indication of the relevance of neo-functionalist theory. From a neo-functionalistic perspective, the Maastricht Treaty represents an integrationist impulse likely to strengthen the supranational institutions and responsibilities of the Community. The Maastricht Treaty (TEU) followed the earlier logic of the 1986 Single European Act (SEA), i.e., the TEU was made possible because of the SEA. The neo-functionalists, therefore, maintain that Maastricht was a spillover from the Single European Act (SEA). However, intergovernmentalism has also frequently been used to explain the success of the Internal Market. From an intergovernmental perspective, the Community remains. Despite the 1993 initiative, the creation and instrument of national politics and national interests will continue to constrain integrationist impulses within the Community.

ASEAN was created in 1967, mainly as a political co-operation organisation. The aim was to halt the further expansion of communism in the region. From the very beginning, however, economic co-operation was believed to be an important part of this defence against revolutionary movements. Gradually, ASEAN's focus has turned toward economic and societal co-operation. Thus, the economic theories of regional integration can well explain the development of ASEAN. One important difference between the EU and ASEAN is the lack of supranational institutions in Asian organisations. At the same time, ASEAN does not cover the same policy areas as the EU and has only limited free trade among its members. Thus, it is difficult to apply the same type of political integration theories to explain the development of ASEAN.

The formation of the ASEAN Free Trade Area (AFTA) is seen as an important achievement in enhancing regional economic integration within ASEAN. The Common Effective Preferential Tariff (CEPT) is the main implementing mechanism of AFTA. Under the CEPT, the member countries gradually lower tariffs on each other's imports. The ultimate aim is to turn ASEAN into a truly free trade area, and this should be achieved over a 15-year period. AFTA also involves several other areas of co-operation, including harmonisation of standards, reciprocal recognition of tests and certification, removal of barriers to foreign investments, macro-economic consultations, rules for fair competition, and promotion of venture capital. Still, ASEAN will continue to lack the supranational institutions, and its ambiguous legislative program makes AFTA more like EFTA.

In order to try to utilise theories of political integration in explaining ASEAN's development, an intergovernmental perspective may be useful. The liberal intergovernmentalist approach assumes that the member states of the European Union remain the key actors in determining outcomes in European integration issues. The driving forces for these actors are interstate bargaining, dealing with national interests, member states capabilities, and state-to-state negotiations. The reality is that national interests and preferences remain a major determinant of the possibilities of economic co-operation within ASEAN. As Kusuma Snitwongse (1990) notes, in order for economic co-operation to progress, a model is required that can be acceptable to all because it promises equal benefit; at the same time, greater political will is needed to sacrifice at least some national interests for the welfare of the whole is necessary. In the case of ASEAN, national interests have priority over regional interests.

In the Asian region, we witness a kind of regional integration based on trade patterns, business operations and investments, sub-regional co-operation patterns, and informal personal contacts. An important form of non-institutional economic co-operation is Asian business networks. As used here, business networks refer to international business systems formed along ethnic and/or cultural lines, as found in Katzenstein's definition (Katzenstein 1996, 35).

Peng (1997) notes this even more precisely. He examines three forms of informal co-operation in Asia: 1) production networks based on a multi-tier economic division of labour, i.e., co-operation along the line of industrial production; 2) sub-regional economic zones in which co-operation is based on geographical proximity; 3) ethnic business networks comprising co-operation along ethnic and cultural lines. These three forms of informal co-operation, Peng claims, are usually overlooked as important instruments of regional co-operation, although they actually drive trade and investment within the region in the absence of formal economic institutions. Their importance apparently exceeds that of formal co-operation (Peng 1997, 13). The theory of (business) networks in regional integration, however, is not very well developed. One exception is Bressand & Nicolaidis (1990).

In addition to Peng's three types of informal co-operation in Southeast Asia, we will also include the development of policy communities within ASEAN. If we look at the development of ASEAN in the last 30 years, there has been continuous growth of both formal and particularly informal policy networks or communities. The total number of official ASEAN meetings now approaches 300 (Chalermpalanupap 1997, 7) and the number of informal contacts and meetings obviously much higher. We assume that this development of more and more arenas for co-operation and higher frequency is an important source of a future higher level of political and economic integration within this region.

Within the study of European policy-making, we have found the same tendency for a multi-level, multi-channel, multi-actor informal and formal type of policy-making. In order to impose some kind of order into this description, several authors have introduced the concept of »policy networks« to describe the linkages between different interests and EU policy-makers (Heclo 1978; Richardson 1995; Richardson 1996). Policy communities have also been used to underline the informal aspects of this (Richardson & Jordan 1979) and that there is some kind of continuum of different degrees of formalisation of these networks.

We assume that in addition to more economically based network theory this idea of policy communities could add some further understanding to the nature and functioning of the decision-making process within the Southeast Asian community. We believe that these emerging policy communities in the region have to be more closely examined in order to reach a fuller understanding of the Southeast Asian development. Perhaps this line of reasoning also could give a clue to the question of how to compare the two models of regional integration.

A Comparison of European and Southeast Asian Integration

The second element in our attempt to explain how organisational structure and integration mechanisms differ between the EU and ASEAN, is an examination of historical, political, economic, and cultural patterns. In comparison with Europe or North America, the Pacific region as a whole is much more heterogeneous. In examining varying historical patterns between the EU and ASEAN we will focus on two determinants of Asian regionalism, as suggested by Katzenstein (1996). In trying to account for the relative weakness of formal political institutions of Asian regionalism in comparison with Europe, Katzenstein proposes two explanations: 1) power and norms in the international system and 2) the character of domestic state structures.

Measured in relative terms, American power in post-1945 Asia was much greater than in Europe, and the United States' foreign policy established the principle of multilateralism in Europe but not in Asia (Katzenstein 1996). American diplomacy in Pacific Asia has overwhelmingly been bilateral and not multilateral. This has made it much more difficult for Asian states to develop the kind of broad, interlocking and institutionalised political arrangements that have characterised the European integration process. However, it is argued (Acharya 1997) that it is the Asia Pacific region's very diversity, rather than American hegemony, which may have inhibited the emergence of multilateral institutions in the early post-war period. The Asia-Pacific nations are remarkably different in terms of their political systems, cultural heritage and historical experience.

Katzenstein (1996) also notes that the comparative weakness in the institutionalisation of Asian regionalism is due to the character of Asian state structures. Some state structures are better suited to deal with public law and formal institutions as the preferred vehicle for regional integration. Asia, or any of its sub-regions, lacks equivalents of the European-wide institutions, the foremost one being the European Union. In the establishment of formal institutions, Asian regionalism during the last decades has experienced a series of very slow, or even false, starts. An argument made in regard to the slow development of Asian regionalism is that »only the more developed countries appear to accept deeper forms of integration« (Wijkman & Sundkvist Lindstroem 1989).

Furthermore, Southeast Asia has been greatly influenced by British, Dutch, French, Spanish, and American colonialism. Social forces deeply penetrate these post-colonial states and thus create multiple political connections in intricate network structures. These states have inherited the colonial tradition of »the rule by law« rather than the West European tradition of »the rule of law« (Katzenstein 1996). Southeast Asian countries are constituted legally, but the relation between state and society is governed by social rather than legal norms.

Our discussion of political heterogeneity between the EU and ASEAN examining the *political systems* in the region, is related to the definition in most dictionaries. As defined by Hanks, »Politics refers to the study of the ways in which a country is governed and power is acquired« (Hanks 1986). Politically, there is a high degree of heterogeneity in the Pacific region. The most appropriate description of the political systems in the ASEAN countries would be that they are all composed of some form of authoritarian capitalist or semi-democratic system, but that the differences between the ASEAN countries are considerable. All the EU member countries are democratic countries, and it could be claimed that the differentiation in political systems among the ASEAN countries is greater than that among EC members. The difference of political systems is obviously a major barrier to institutional economic co-operation. So far, all the free trade agreements have been reached among countries of similar political systems. This can be explained by the fact that political systems are closely associated with systems of production.

An economy is the system according to which the money, industry and trade of a country or region are organised (Hanks 1986). Here we will examine the *degree of liberalisation of economy* and *differences in per capita income*. The high heterogeneity in the Pacific region makes formal economic co-operation difficult, because it greatly increases the transaction costs of institution- building. One explanation for Asian non-institutional economic co-operation lies in the process by which the Southeast Asian countries, since the 1960s, have successively liberalised their economies, especially their trade and investment. Liberalisation has accelerated since the 1980s. The major characteristics of non-institutional economic co-operation are informality, gradualness and flexibility. Hence, informal approaches are a very effective way to open up while minimising the outside shock accompanying the liberalisation (Peng 1997, 14).

Economic disparity is the most important barrier to formal regional co-operation in the Asia Pacific region. The region has extensive differences in industrialisation, technology, labour costs, export capacity and several other key indices. Within ASEAN there are enormous differences in per capita income/GNP, ranging at the end of the 1990s from $1086 in Indonesia to $20,400 in Brunei (Poh 1997). There is no precedent of a successful free trade agreement among countries with great economic disparity (Peng 1997, 15).[8] The closest example is the General Agreement on Tariffs and Trade (GATT), but GATT is a regulatory organisation rather than a real, free trade area.

Cultural heterogeneity can also raise transaction costs. A definition of culture (though difficult to define) is that it is a particular society or civilisation, especially one considered in relation to its ideas, its art, its customs or its way of life (Hanks 1986). When we investigate varying cultural aspects, *religion* and *language* are compared in the EU and ASEAN.

The ASEAN countries contain 6 major religions: Buddhism, Taoism, Hinduism, Christianity, Islam and Confucianism, while all the EU countries are Christian. One may argue that within Christianity there are several branches, but they remain within a single religious creed. Moreover, language diversity in the Asia-Pacific region is much greater than in Europe. All the EC countries except Finland belong to the Indo-European family of languages. In contrast, there is a larger diversity between the ASEAN countries, where Thailand and Singapore belong to the Chinese-Tibetan family, and Malaysia, Indonesia, Philippines and Brunei belong to the Malay-Polynesian. Cultural heterogeneity not only includes language diversity, but also extends to much broader categories like consumption behaviour, business practices, methods of management, and so on.

The formation of Asian business networks has to do with strong East Asian cultural traditions (Katzenstein 1996). Confucianism, which has a strong influence in all the major Northeast Asian societies, Vietnam and the Overseas Chinese societies, has always placed great emphasis on human relations and personal ties. In fact, extensive use of personal networks is an effective way to get around barriers to business in many Southeast Asian countries, both domestically and internationally.

Impact of the Asian Crisis on the Development of Regional Integration

In a number of recent articles and books about the Asian currency crisis, it is noted that the two Chinese characters for the word »crisis«, literally translated, mean »danger« and »opportunity« (Henderson 1998; Heim 1998; Montes 1998). This is a point of departure to examine the short-, medium-, and long-term impacts of the Asian crisis. In each scenario, one can identify a set of dangers in terms of negative economic, social and political consequences, along with a window of opportunity for reform, and renewed, sustainable growth. Most authors point to the unique opportunity for increased regional economic co-operation a situation where a large number of countries face similar problems. However, few studies had focused in depth on the dangers and opportunities resulting from the crisis in relation to the future development of regional integration.[9] In this section, we will address this issue in the light of recent events by pointing to the specific features of the ASEAN countries and the organisations likely to represent opportunities for and dangers to regional integration.

A first point to be highlighted is the expectation among at least a number of Western observers regarding the possibility for reform in the wake of the crisis. As with the aftermath of the breakdown of the communist system in 1989, there is a perceived opportunity, albeit on a smaller scale, to redress all the inadequacies and the obvious shortcomings of what has been termed Asian »crony capitalism«.[10] Although each ASEAN country, like the former Communist countries in Central and Eastern Europe, has its specific constellation of problems and differing abilities to handle the situation, the region as a whole is presented with similar policy-recommendations: e.g., liberalisation of financial markets, transparency in transactions, establishment of new regulatory frameworks, and increase in intra-regional trade. The global nature of financial transactions, business and trade makes unilateral action inefficient, if not impossible. States that tried to cut interest rates unilaterally would face the risk of renewed currency depreciation. The logic of the markets, coupled with the need for reform, thus create »push« and »pull« mechanisms leading toward greater regional integration. An international panel of experts which reports regularly to the APEC forum has recently urged Asian leaders to adopt concerted fiscal and monetary stimulus measures (Montagnon 1998). Institutionalised co-operation in these areas, barely conceivable before the crisis, is now viewed as a necessity.

Second, as analysts of the EU integration process have noted, it is sometimes easier to carry out reform when a certain degree of power is delegated to an institution operating outside the national framework. If internal pressure can be counter-weighted by external commitments, national elites will have more incentive and leeway to carry out unpopular reforms. We need not necessarily talk about supra-nationalism. Greater regional integration in the form of an intergovernmental board of experts, a regional watchdog charged with monitoring the national economies, would make it easier for other countries to be informed and to exert pressure.

The creation of preventive measures were at the core of the discussion between the ASEAN finance ministers in December 1997. It was these discussions that resulted in the establishment of the »Manila framework«, whereby member states would partake in mutual surveillance of each other's economies (Higgot 1998, 26).

In October 1998, the ASEAN countries announced the creation of another joint surveillance system to provide early warning for future economic problems in the region. The system will be based on peer review and information exchange in areas such as interest rates, exchange rates and capital flows, and it is more ASEAN-focused than the Manila Framework (ASEAN Secretariat).

On the one hand, this activity may be viewed as a sign that the drive towards institutionalisation of co-operation takes place in various fora simultaneously. On the other hand, it might indicate that the former initiative has run into problems and needs to be replaced. Even in the new framework, it remains unclear whether the countries are actually ready to delegate power, and to allow interference in each other's affairs. In the enthusiasm over new regional initiatives, it should not be forgotten that IMF-based monitoring functioned before the crises (Henderson 1998), but that the warnings issued were conveniently ignored by Thailand. Future crises can only be averted or anticipated if there is willingness to co-operate with and to follow recommendations from the regional watchdog.

One advantage of regional institutions over the IMF watchdog mechanism is that the work of the former might be facilitated by a growing sense of regional identity, the »cognitive regionalism«, stemming from the »all in the same boat« logic. A number of ASEAN countries, notably Indonesia, Malaysia and to some extent the Philippines, by rejecting certain stipulations in the IMF packages, have focused on the importance of Asian alternatives to what is perceived as Western interventions. Thus, the crisis might be viewed as a blessing in disguise if it indeed leads to reform of a system with inherent flaws under the auspices of a dynamic regional association, based on a stronger sense of a common regional identity. To this end, even the search for a scapegoat such as the IMF or the anonymous »speculators« might prove useful, as it could rally the populations around certain policies that in the long run have positive effects. One of the stated objectives of ASEAN is to create an »ASEAN Awareness« that the political leaders hope will contribute to social cohesion and political solidarity (Chalermpalanupap 1997).

However, a constructed regional identity has no meaning in itself if not backed by either an »imagined (regional) community« (Anderson 1989), or a successful institutionalisation of cohesive forces. The success of the latter has so far been modest in terms of concrete actions. The idea of an Asian bail-out fund, launched by Dr. Mahathir of Malaysia, has proven extremely difficult to realise at this stage of the process. More realistic projects include regional clearing-houses for domestic and foreign-currency denominated bond markets, an ASEAN Central Bank forum and an ASEAN free trade zone.[11]

In Asia, the strong economic growth over the last 20 years, as noted above, has not produced a high degree of formal, institutionalised co-operation. This can be partly explained by 1) the nature of ASEAN, linked to its original *raison d'etre,* i.e., the desire to create stability in the region, 2) by forcing Indonesia into a co-operative framework, and 3) by constituting a pole to maintain power balance. Stability has always been at the core of ASEAN regional co-operation, and although economic issues have arguably been higher up on the agenda since the mid-1970s, it would be misleading to speak of a functional spill-over and thus a genuine strengthening and deepening of integration. Differences in political structure and economic conditions persist among the countries, and these have not been diminished by the crisis.

These differences have in fact reemerged in the context of increasing instability. Tony Tan, Singapore's Defense Minister, stated in early 1998 that »if there is instability in Indonesia, it will destabilise the whole region« (Montagnon 1998). Destabilisation of the region is both translated into and confronted by the inability of ASEAN to act, as exemplified by the huge environmental problems, in particular the destruction of the forests in Indonesia in the summer of 1998; the refugee-problem, which created tensions between Malaysia and Indonesia (and the Philippines); Indonesia's acute economic problems, which in addition to creating serious internal turmoil, also affect relations between Indonesia, Singapore and Malaysia.[12]

To fully understand the source of tensions among the countries, and the importance of external stability, we must look beyond efforts aimed at a greater regional integration, to the internal structure of the Asian states.

One proposed framework for analysis is the Security-Development-Participation scheme (Ayoob & Chai-Anan 1989), which emphasises the importance of external stability to enable political leaders to focus on the more serious internal threats usually emanating from grievances of an ethnic, social, economic or political character. The economic development over the last 20 years in Asia is based on external stability and has in turn been used to calm internal tensions. Certain groups have been rewarded economically for accepting the absence of (or for the military, decrease in) political participation and influence. In most cases, participation is thus overshadowed by security and development, and an inversion of the equation has traditionally only taken place through serious internal conflicts and bloodshed. In a situation following economic crisis, political leaders have less ability to »purchase« the loyalty of the population, which in turn may result in popular explosions, as witnessed in Indonesia. The balance between external and internal politics is extremely delicate in Asia, and quite different than what we observe in the countries of the European Union.

In relation to this is the empirical evidence found regarding the behaviour of states in the international system in the wake of an economic recession, or crisis. Ever since the Great Depression more than 50 years ago, economic turmoil has created a tendency for states to slow the pace of liberalisation and turn to protectionist policies. Integration in the European Union slowed down in the difficult 1960s and 1970s, and was fuelled by the economic upturn in the 1980s. In the beginning of the 1990s (1992/1993), domestic recession (and the need to use monetary policy as instrument to alleviate it) led the UK to pull out of the ERM-band, thus slowing the pace of complete monetary integration. In Asia, according to Thailand's Foreign Minister Surin Pitsuwan the same trend can be observed: the countries are turning inward, trying to fend for themselves, and they are suspicious of outsiders (*Time Asia* 1998).

This trend comes on top of a long-standing cardinal principle of non-interference, which has shaped the work of ASEAN and the relations between the countries. The current problem is that certain »isolationist« policies favoured by some countries affect the others negatively.[13] The political leaders in Asia disagree on the tactics chosen and policies to be pursued, and they have become increasingly outspoken as they realise that the actions of one have an impact on the stability of the region, and thereby, on the economic situation of all the countries.

Greater regional integration thus presupposes new forms of co-operation, which in fact signifies changes in the political culture governing the relations between the political elites in the region. Thailand's Foreign Minister has proposed a new policy of »flexible engagement« within ASEAN which would allow member states more leeway in interfering in each other's internal affairs, and not only in strictly economic issues (*Time Asia* 1998). It remains to be seen what form the engagement should take, but it is certain that a new form of co-operation is required. Only a greater ability to interfere in »internal affairs« would reverse the trend of ASEAN's waning influence.

Conclusions

To complete our analysis, let us address the question of whether the aforementioned changes in ASEAN and within ASEAN countries lead us to conclude that on a long-term basis the association will become more similar to the EU.

In recent years we have witnessed several tendencies towards a more comparable development in the two regions. First of all, the general tendency described earlier to develop policy networks or communities in nearly all sectors of society in Southeast Asia, and the increase in the number of summits and formal ministerial conferences, makes ASEAN more like the intergovernmental aspects of the EU. Still, however, ASEAN is not a supranational body, nor does it possess a formal legal identity.

ASEAN involvement in new policy issues, such as free trade through AFTA, will strengthen the tendency towards more organised co-operation. One possible hypothesis could be that further development of free trade agreements between countries and regions in order to be effective, creates a need for rules and controlling institutions. If AFTA becomes a success, we could predict the development of a more institutionalised organisation (Westerlund 1997). ASEAN has already attempted to develop new institutional structures along these lines. In November 1996, for instance, it created a protocol on a dispute settlement mechanism based on majority voting procedure.

The financial crisis, the fires across parts of the region and the expansion of ASEAN to ten has strengthened organisational co-operation. Several new meetings, working groups and procedures are being institutionalised. ASEAN's decision-making procedures are coming to resemble the European Union, having developed elements of majority voting and flexible consensus.

The present economic, political and social crises in the region have both unifying and divisive implications. Our earlier analysis emphasised the divisions that seem to dominate in the current situation, partly because national elites have difficulties in striking the right balance in coping with internal pressure and external instability. Evidently, most ASEAN countries have been turning inwards, in several cases to try to calm mounting social pressure due to the relative deprivation experienced by their populations. The current problem is that certain isolationist policies favoured by some countries have a negative impact on others. Political leaders have become increasingly outspoken as they realise that the actions of one affect all the others. In this context, proposals for a »flexible engagement« policy have emerged. We see this as the most constructive proposal for reinforcing and strengthening regional integration and regional identity in the post-crisis ASEAN. The crisis has also reinforced rather than impeded ASEAN's free trade plans as seen from the re-affirmation and acceleration of regional economic integration by the ASEAN heads of government at the December 1998 Hanoi Summit.

From the comparative study of the EU and ASEAN, there are significant distinctions which are likely to lead to the emergence of a unique Asian regional model. As Paul Evans (1994) has argued, institution-building in the Asia-Pacific region, rather than following the pattern established in Europe and North America, is instead »emerging from unique historical circumstances and will likely evolve in its own particular way«. The crisis has given immediacy to the need to re-examine certain traditions rooted in the state-making process of the Asian countries. And although the picture today remains chaotic, the transition unleashed by the crisis might prove essential for greater integration in the future.

Notes

1. An earlier version of this chapter was presented at the conference on Non-State Actors and Authority in the Global System, University of Warwick, 31st October - 1st November 1997.
   We would like to thank Solgunn Hoff, Anne Caroline Tveøy, and Alice Chamrernnusit who have participated in preparing part of this manuscript, and also Pinar Tank for their help in the final editing of the paper, all working at the Centre for European and Asian Studies at Norwegian School of Management, BI in Oslo.
2. The term »new regionalism« has been used by several scholars, including Norman D. Palmer, *The New Regionalism in Asia and the Pacific* (Lexington, Mass.: Lexington Books, 1991).

3. Asia-Pacific Economic Co-operation Forum (APEC), Pacific Economic Co-operation Council (PECC), ASEAN Regional Forum (ARF).
4. ASEAN is composed of Brunei, Darussalam, Cambodia, Indonesia, Laos, Malaysia, Myanmar, the Philippines, Singapore, Thailand and Vietnam.
5. The other Asian countries are China, Japan, South Korea, Cambodia, Papua New-Guinea and India.
6. The ten member countries are Brunei, Darussalam, Cambodia, Indonesia, Laos, Malaysia, Myanmar, the Philippines, Singapore, Thailand and Vietnam
7. Examples of formal integration include co-operation through regional institutions such as APEC, PECC, EAEC (East Asia Economic Caucus) and sub-regional free trade areas such as NAFTA, the ASEAN Free Trade Area and the Australia-New Zealand free trade area.
8. This is also evident in the present enlargement process of the EU where member states are unwilling to take in new members if they do not have a certain economic development level.
9. One exception is Pinar Tank (1998).
10. In a number of articles published in leading newspapers and magazines, scholars like Jeffery Sachs and Joseph Stiglitz have repeated that the Asian crisis does not bear witness to the triumph of Marxist logic and a coming breakdown of an exhausted capitalist system, but rather, shows the need to create an ideal, full-fledged, and consequently more Western-style, capitalist system.
11. AFTA is now to be officially completed in 2002 instead of 2003 for Brunei, Darussalam, Indonesia, Malaysia, the Philippines, Singapore and Thailand, and three years later for Vietnam. Cambodia, Laos and Myanmar will also have 10 years to complete AFTA, i.e., from 1998 to 2007 (ASEAN Secretariat).
12. Singaporean banks are heavily exposed in Indonesia, and Indonesian refugees constitute a burden on the neighbouring countries.
13. Some of the declarations made by Dr. Mahathir, for instance, those regarding a ban on foreign trading and investment restrictions, are telling examples.

References

Acharaya, Amitav (1997). »Ideas, identity and institution-building: from the »ASEAN way« to the »Asia-Pacific way««, *The Pacific Review*, Vol. 10, No. 3, pp. 319-346.
Aggarwal, Vinod (1994). »Comparing regional co-operation efforts in the Asia-Pacific and North America«, in Andrew Mack & John Ravenhill (eds.), *Pacific Co-operation: Building Economic and Security Regimes in the Asia-Pacific Region*, St. Leonards, New South Wales: Allen and Unwin.
Andersen, Svein S. & Eliassen Kjell. A. (1993). »Complex Policy-Making: Lobbying in the EC«, pp. 35-54, in S.S. Andersen & K.A. Eliassen (eds.) *Making Policy in Europe*, London: Sage Publications Ltd.
Andersen, Svein S. & Kjell A. Eliassen (eds.) (1993). *Making Policy in Europe – the Europeification of National Policy-Making,* London: Sage Publications Ltd.

Andersen, Svein S. (1996). *Europeisering av politikk: Petrolium, indre marked og miljø,* Oslo: Fagbokforlaget.

Anderson, M. (1989). *Policing the World: Interpol and the Politics of International Police Co-operation,* New York: Oxford University Press.

ASEAN Secretariat. ASEAN website: http://www.asean.or.id.

Ayoob, Mohammed & Samudavanija Chai-Anan, (1989). »Leadership and Security in Southeast Asia: Exploring General Propositions«, in M. Ayoob & Samudavanija Chai-Anan, *Leadership Perceptions and National Security: The Southeast Asian Experience,* London: Routledge.

Balassa, Bela (1962). *The Theory of Economic Integration,* London: Greenwood Press.

Baldwin, Richard E. & Anthony J. Venables (1995). »Regional Economic Integration«, pp. 1597-1644, in Gene M. Grossman & Kenneth Rogoff (eds.), *Handbook of International Economics,* Vol. 3, Amsterdam: North-Holland.

Bernard, Mitchell & John Ravenhill (1995). »Beyond Product Cycles and Flying Geese: Regionalization, Hierarchy and the Industrialisation of East Asia«, *World Politics,* Vol. 47, No. 2, pp. 171-209.

Bhagwati, Jagdish (1993). »Regionalism and Multilateralism: an overview«, pp. 145-167, in Ross Garnaut & Peter Drysdale (eds.), *Asia Pacific Regionalism: Readings in International Economic Relations,* Pymble: Harper Publishers.

Bomberg, E. (1994). »Policy Networks on the Periphery: EU Environmental Policy and Scotland«, *Regional Politics and Policy,* Vol. 4, pp. 45-61.

Bressand, A. & Kalypso Nicolaidis (1990). »Regional Integration in a Networked World Economy«, pp. 27-50, in William Wallace (ed.), *The Dynamics of European Integration,* London: Pinter Publishers.

Bulmer, S. (1994a). »The Governance of the European Union: A New Institutionalist Approach«, *Journal of Public Policy,* Vol. 13, No. 4, pp. 351-380.

Bulmer, S. (1994b). »Institutions and Policy Change in the European Communities: The Case of Merger Control«, *Public Administration,* Vol. 72, pp. 423-444.

Cai, Penghong (1992). »The Fourth ASEAN Summit Talk and its Influence Over Regional Economic Co-operation«, *Asia-Pacific Economic Review,* No. 2, pp. 16-18.

Chalermpalanupap, Termsak (1997). *Enlargement of ASEAN: Prospects for Closer Regional Cooperation,* paper presented at the Malaysian Institute of Economic Research's Conference on ASEAN at the Crossroads: Opportunities and Challenges, Kuala Lumpur, November, 1997.

Cho, Yong-sang & Chong-tae Chung (1997). *ASEM's Hopes and Apprehensions: an Inter-Regional Organisation in the 21st Century,* paper presented for the International Political Science Association at the 17th World Congress, Seoul, August 1997.

Commission of the European Community (1996). *Creating a new dynamic in EU-ASEAN relations,* report from the Commission of the European Communities.

Cooper, Richard (1994). »World-wide regional integration: is there an optimal size of the integrated area?«, pp. 11-19, in Ross Garnaut & Peter Drysdale (eds.), *Asia Pacific Regionalism – Readings in International Economic Relations,* The Australian National University: Harper Educational.

Duff, A. (1994). »The main reforms«, in A. Duff, J. Pinder, & R. Pryce (eds.), *Maastricht and Beyond: Building the European Union,* London: Routledge.

Duff, A., J. Pinder, & R. Pryce (eds.) (1994). *Maastricht and Beyond: Building the European Union.* London: Routledge.

Edwards, G. & D. Spence (1995). *The European Commission,* London: Longman Group Ltd.

Evans, Paul M. (1994). »The dialogue process on Asia Pacific security issues: inventory and analyses«, in Paul M. Evans (ed.), *Studying Asia Pacific Security*, Toronto and Jakarta: University of Toronto-York University Joint Centre for Asia Pacific Studies and Centre for Strategic and International Studies.

Fawcett, Louise & Andrew Hurrell (1995). *Regionalism in World Politics: Regional Organisation and International Order*, Oxford: Oxford University Press.

Gallant, Nicole & Richard Stubbs (1996). »Asia-Pacific Business Activity and Regional Institution-Building«, in J. Greenwood & H. Jacek (eds.), *Organised Business and the New Global Order,* London: Macmillian.

Garnaut, Ross & Peter Drysdale (eds.) (1994). *Asia Pacific Regionalism: Readings in International Economic Relations*, Pymble: Harper Publishers.

Gill, Ranjit (1998). *Asia under Siege: How the Asian Miracle Went Wrong,* Singapore: Epic Management Services Pte Ltd.

Gills, Barry K. (1997). *East Asian Development in World Historical Perspective: Ascent, Descent, Ascent*, paper presented at the 17th World Congress of the International Political Science Association, Seoul, August 1997.

Greenwood, J. (1997). *Representing Interests in the European Union.* London: Macmillan Press Ltd.

Hanks, P. (1986). *Collins English Dictionary* (second edition), Glasgow: William Collins Sons & Co. Ltd.

Heclo, Hugh (1978). »Issue Networks and the Executive Establishment«, in A. King (ed.), *The New American Political System*, Washington D.C.: American Enterprise Institute.

Heim, Celine (1998). *L'UE et L'ASEAN: Hétérogénéités et analogies entre deux processus d'intégration*, unpublished paper.

Henderson, Callum (1998). *Asia Falling? Making Sense of the Asian Currency Crisis and Its Aftermath,* Singapore: McGraw-Hill.

Hernandez, Carolina G. (1996). »Controlling Asia's armed forces», in L. Diamond & M. Plattner (eds.), *Civil-Military Relations and Democracy.*

Higgot, Richard (1997).*Globalisation, Regionalisation and Localisation: Political Economy, the State and Levels of Governance*, paper presented at the 25th Joint Sessions of Workshops of the European Consortium for Political Research, Bern, February-March 1997.

Higgot, Richard (1995). »Economic Co-operation in the Asia Pacific: a Theoretical Comparison with the European Union«, *Journal of European Public Policy,* Vol. 2, No. 3, pp. 361-383.

Higgot, R. & S. Reich (1998). »Globalisation and Sites of Conflict: Towards Definition and Taxonomy«, *GSGR Working Paper,* 3.

Hix, S. (1994). »The Study of European Community: the Challenges of Comparative Politics« *West European Politics*, Vol. 17, No. 1, pp. 1-30.

Holland, K.M. (1994). »NAFTA and the Single European Act« in T.D. Mason & A.M.

Turay (eds.), *Japan, NAFTA and Europe. Trilateral Cooperation or Confrontation?*, New York: St. Martin's Press.

Hurrell, Adrew (1995). »Regionalism in theoretical perspective«, in Louise Fawcett & Andrew Hurrell (eds.), *Regionalism in World Politics: Regional Organisation and International Order*, Oxford: Oxford University Press.

Katzenstein, Peter (1996). »Regionalism in Comparative Perspective«, *ARENA working paper* No. 1.

Kindleberger, Charles P. (1973). »Economic Integration«, *International Economics*, Illinois: Richard D. Irwin, Inc.

Krugman, Paul (1993). »Regionalism versus Multilateralism: analytic notes«, in R. Garnaut & P. Drysdale (eds.), *Asia Pacific Regionalism: Readings in International Economic Relations*, Pymble: Harper Publishers.

Larimer, Tim (1998a). »Fightin' Words«, *Asia Week*, Nov. 2nd, Vol. 152, No. 17.

Larimer, Tim (1998b). »Surin: 'Because of the crisis, we are prone to conflict'«, *Asia Week*, Nov. 2nd, Vol. 152, No. 17.

Lim, Robyn (1998). »The ASEAN Regional Forum: Building on Sand«, *Contemporary Southeast Asia,* Vol. 20, No. 2, pp. 115-136.

Lorenz, Ditlev (1992). »Economic geography and the political economy of regionalization: the example of Western Europe«, *The American Economic Review*, Vol. 82, No. 2, pp. 84-87.

Mazey, S. & J. Richardson (eds.) (1993). *Lobbying in the European Community*, Oxford: Oxford University Press.

Milner, H. (1995). »Regional Economic Cooperation, Global Markets and Domestic Politics: A Comparison of NAFTA and the Maastricht Treaty«, *Journal of European Public Policy,* Vol. 2, No 3, pp. 337-360.

Montagon, Peter (1998). »Recovery: Reflation, Reform and Refinancing«, *The Financial Times*, January 16th.

Montagon, Peter & Gwen Robinson (1998). »Asian crisis: APEC urged to spur growth«, *The Financial Times*, November 6th.

Montes, Manual F. (1998), *The Currency Crisis in Southeast Asia,* Singapore: Institute of Southeast Asian Studies.

Nelsen, B.F. & A. C-G. Stubb (eds.) (1994). *The European Union: Readings on the Theory and Practice of European Integration*, Boulder: Lynne Rienner.

Oman, Charles (1994). *Globalisation and Regionalisation: The Challenge for Developing Countries,* Paris: OECD Development Centre.

Pape, Wolfgang (ed.) (1998). *East Asia by the Year 2000 and Beyond: Shaping Factors: A Study for the European Commission*, Surrey: Curzon Press.

Peng, Dajin (1997). *An East Asian Model of Regional Economic Co-operation*, Centre for European and Asian Studies, Norwegian School of Management, CEAS RI.05.97.

Peterson, J. (1992). »The European Technology Community: Policy Networks in a Supranational Setting«, in D. Marsh & R. Rhodes (eds.), *Policy Networks in British Government*. Oxford: Oxford University Press.

Peterson, J. (1995). »Decision-Making in the European Union: Towards a Framework for Analysis«, *Journal of European Public Policy*, Vol. 2, No. 1, pp. 69-93.

Poh, Steven K.C. (1997). »Just don't expect a feast«, *Asia Week*, April 25th.

Regelsberger, E. (1988). »EPC in the 1980s: Reaching Another Plateau?«, in A. Pijpers, E. Regelsberger & W. Wessels (eds.), *European Political Cooperation in the 1980s – A Common Foreign Policy for Western Europe?*, Dordrecht: Martinus Nijhoff Publishers.

Rhodes, C. & S. Mazey (1995). *The State of the European Union: Building a European Polity?*, Colorado: Lynne Rienner Publishers Inc.

Richardson, Jeremy R. (ed.) (1996). *European Union: Power and Policy-making*, London: Routledge.

Richardson, Jeremy R. (1995). » Actor Based Models of National and EU Policy-making: Policy Communities, Issue Networks and Epistemic Communities«, in A. Menon & H. Kassim (eds.), *The EU and National Industrial Policy*, London: Routledge.

Richardson, Jeremy R. & Grant Jordan (1979). *Governing under Pressure: The Policy Process in a Post-Parliamentary Democracy*, Oxford: Martin Robertson.

Roney, Alex (1995). *EC/EU Fact book – a complete question and answer guide,* London: Chamber of Commerce & Industry.

Soesastro, H. (1995). »ASEAN Economic Cooperation: The Long Journey to AFTA«, *The Indonesian Quarterly*, Vol. 23, No. 1, pp. 25-38.

Snitwongse, K. (1990). »Meeting the challenges of changing Southeast Asia«, in R. Scalapino (ed.), *Regional Dynamics: Security, Political, Economic Issues in the Asia-Pacific Region*, Jakarta: Centre for Strategic and International Studies.

Spindler, Manuela (1997). »The Role of Ideas in Regime Building: the EU and APEC compared«, *Occasional Paper* No. 8, Research Institute for European Studies, November 1997.

Summers, Lawrence H. (1991). »Regionalism and the world trading system«, in R. Garnaut & P. Drysdale (eds.), *Asia Pacific Regionalism: Readings in International Economic Relations*, Pymble: Harper Publishers.

Suite101.com (1997). »Cambodia and ASEAN: A Separation of Economics and Politics«, July 25th.

Tassell, Tony (1998a). »ASEAN: Agreement to speed up regional tariff cuts«, *The Financial Times*, Oct. 7th.

Tassell, Tony (1998b). »Regional risk monitoring planned«, *The Financial Times*, Oct. 8th.

The Economist (1998). »The Limits of Politeness«, Feb. 28th.

The Economist Intelligence Unit (1997). »European policy analyst – key issues and developments for business«, *Regional Monitor* 1st quarter 1997.

Time Asia (1998). November.

Wallace, William (1995). »Regionalism in Europe: Model or Exception?«, in Louise Fawcett & Andrew Hurrell (eds.), *Regionalism in World Politics: Regional Organisation and International Order*, Oxford: Oxford University Press.

Westerlund, Percy (1997). »Kan ASEM stärka den svaga länken i triangeln EU-Ostasien-Nordamerika?«, Brussels: Directorate General I, European Commission.

Wijkman, Per Magnus & Eva Sundkvist Lindstroem (1989). »Pacific basin integration as a step towards freer trade«, pp. 144-62, in John Nieuwenhuysen (ed.), *Towards Freer Trade between Nations,* Melbourne: Oxford University Press.

Young, Soogil (1993). »Globalism and regionalism: complements or competitors?«, pp. 179-183, in R. Garnaut & P. Drysdale (eds.), *Asia Pacific Regionalism: Readings in International Economic Relations*, Pymble: Harper Publishers.

What Was the Problem If a First Divisor of 1.4 Was the Solution?

Jørgen Elklit*

Abstract

Why did Sweden, followed by Denmark and Norway, all in 1952, introduce the same completely new (and untested) system for proportional allocation of seats in national elections, the so-called modified Sainte-Laguë system? Modification of the well-known (but also not much used) Sainte-Laguë divisor system to increased the formula's first divisor from 1 to 1.4, but this was an arbitrary number, without theoretical foundation. One aim – but not in all three countries – was to decrease the possibility for small parties to gain seats in the multimember constituencies. Another (at least in Norway and Sweden) was to increase the chances that medium-sized parties would not be continuously underrepresented in parliament. The justifications behind the changes differed, and the chapter demonstrates how this seat allocation system was subsequently introduced in the three Scandinavian countries as an institutional solution to problems which, however, were not identical.

Students of electoral systems often ask why the first divisor of the modified Sainte-Laguë seat allocation formula is 1.4. The question is well put because 1.4 *is* a rather odd figure, lacking any equivalent in other electoral systems and with no theoretical basis whatsoever (Laakso 1979).

Why was this odd electoral law element introduced in Denmark in the early 1950s, suggested in 1952 and enacted in 1953? What were the problems to which this institutional change was seen as the solution? And how could such a change in the electoral system be enacted and implemented without major differences of opinion among the political parties?

At about the same time as Denmark, Sweden and Norway also changed their electoral systems to the modified Sainte-Laguë system. Studies explaining theses changes are already available (von Sydow 1989; Aardal forthcoming; Rokkan 1970. Särlvik 1983 and Eide 1998 are also useful).

However, we have no equivalent account of the introduction of this system into Danish electoral politics which might allow us to draw some tentative conclusions about certain kinds of institutional change in specific polities. The basic approach here is in line with other studies of electoral system change and development in which a rational choice approach has been instrumental in explaining the political actors' motivations (see, for example, Bawn 1993; Geddes, 1998; von Sydow 1989; Elklit 1988).

Our goal here, however, is not only to examine the Danish case and its peculiarities. The almost simultaneous introduction of the modified Sainte-Laguë system in all three Scandinavian countries often gives rise to a comparative approach – even though a comparative analysis might suffer from the cases not being independent and the variation in the dependent variable being too small.

Swedish electoral law was the first to combine the introduction of the Sainte-Laguë electoral system with 1.4 as the first divisor. It is, therefore, only natural to start by looking at why the Swedes opted for that route.

It All Started in Sweden ...

The electoral law problem in Sweden can only be understood if we familiarise ourselves with the country's party and electoral system of the late 1940s and early 1950s. The electoral system for the lower house of parliament was a straightforward one-tier system of proportional representation, in which all 230 seats were allocated in multimember constituencies (average magnitude: 8.2), using the d'Hondt highest average allocation formula.

This seat allocation system is slightly biased in favour of the larger parties, which might therefore occasionally win slightly more seats than their share of the votes would entitle them to (using strict proportionality as the yardstick) – and particularly so if constituency magnitude is not too high. The d'Hondt system is therefore sometimes combined with a provision allowing parties to form electoral alliances or cartels (the French term, *apparentement,* is often used in English also), which are allocated seats in a first computational round, while individual participating parties are allocated their share of the cartel's seats in an ensuing allocation round *within* the cartel. While intended to reduce the advantages of the larger parties, *apparentement* has certain side-effects, some of which are discussed by Lijphart (1994, 134-138).

The Swedish party system of the late 1940s comprised roughly the same five parties as the other Scandinavian countries of the period: from left to right a Communist party, a Social Democratic party, a (Social-) Liberal party, an Agrarian party, and a Conservative party. The average vote support for the Swedish Social Democrats in the four elections from 1936 to 1948 was 48 per cent, while the three non-Socialist parties together won an average support of 44 per cent. Average support for the Communists during these four elections was seven per cent.

Only once, in the 1940 elections, did the Social Democrats command an absolute parliamentary majority of their own, so they depended on other parties for the formation of legislative as well as governmental majority coalitions. The Social Democracts were not interested in the Communists as coalition partners, but could nevertheless rely on them in parliament, as the Communists would not participate in replacing a Social Democratic government by any sort of bourgeois coalition. On various occasions during the 1930s, the Social Democrats and the Agrarians had been able to work closely together – even forming a coalition government on one occasion – and the relationship between the two former partners had remained generally co-operative and positive.

What Was the Problem in Sweden?
However, the Agrarians found themselves in a precarious and untenable situation which immediately affected the Social Democratic perception of how items on the political agenda should be prioritised. This development has been meticulously analysed and described by Björn von Sydow (1989) in a study of constitutional politics in Sweden eventually resulting in the introduction of the unicameral parliament (effective from 1970). An early step on this road to constitutional change was the shift in 1952, from one electoral system to another.

By the political logic of the time the Agrarians were the obvious government coalition partner for the Social Democrats. The latter were most eager to retain this government coalition which would command safe majorities in both houses and which had already proved that it could work. However, the combination of the electoral system described above and the pattern of support for the parties across constituencies practically *forced* the Agrarians to conduct electoral politics in cartels with the two other non-socialist parties, i.e., the Conservatives and the Liberals, if they were not to lose too many seats (being on average smaller than the Conservatives and the Liberals).

In October 1951, however, a coalition government of Social Democrats and Agrarians was formed, despite these unsolved electoral politics problems which had also been an issue during unsuccessful coalition negotiations between the two parties immediately after the September 1948 elections. With parliamentary elections due in September 1952, there was a prospect of seeing the junior partner of the government coalition fighting parliamentary elections in electoral cartels with the two main opposition parties.

A parliamentary committee had been looking into the issue since 1950, so part of the preparatory work was already done when it became evident to the Social Democrats that a solution to the problem of the Agrarians was urgently needed.

The task was to establish an electoral system which (1) was still basically proportional (and preferably, at least seen from the Agrarians' position, more so for middle-sized parties than the d'Hondt system), so that they would obtain their fair share of seats without having to join the non-socialist electoral cartel, and (2) at the same time were able to ensure a permanent underrepresentation of the smallest parties (i.e., those with less than ten per cent of the vote). This was very much a concern for the Social Democrats because the Communists had become stronger after World War II (not only in Sweden, of course).

The other parties also found it in their immediate interests to avoid making entry into parliament too easy for new parties (which might be splinter parties from themselves), yet they were also fully aware of the fact that it probably would be in their own best parliamentary interest to avoid situations in which the Social Democrats would have too many problems on their left flank, or become too dependent on parliamentary support from the left.

What Was, Then, the Solution?
Obviously, the solution would have to include provisions in the Electoral Act aiming at effectively securing – across the 28 multimember constituencies – a reasonable degree of proportionality (i.e., decrease the inherent advantages of the major party, the Social Democrats). This was the only way in which electoral cartels could be eliminated. The d'Hondt electoral system would therefore have to go, but the Sainte-Laguë divisor method had been (re-)invented – conveniently enough – by an Agrarian MP (Mr. Sten Wahlund) during the Autumn of 1949 (von Sydow 1989, 67). This also explains why the method, which uses as its string of divisors the odd numbers, $1, 3, 5, 7, \ldots, 2n-1, \ldots$, continues to be called (in Swedish) »the method of odd numbers«. In most other connections, however, it is named after its first inventor.

The idea of introducing compensatory seats to ensure an adequate level of proportionality had also been discussed by the Social Democrats who were seriously concerned about their »big party« bonus. However, the Social Democrats became increasingly aware of the seriousness with which the Agrarians perceived the situation, and they realized that the issue would inevitably be raised again during future rounds of government coalition negotiations. Therefore, they continued to discuss and investigate possible solutions to the problem.

Given the Agrarians' view of the problem, the Social Democrats would have to make a choice between some kind of two-tier system with compensatory seats (which they already had rejected) and a system which would permanently ensure the middle-sized parties of so much proportionality across the 28 constituencies so as to obviate incentives to form electoral coalitions.

The first option was not acceptable, but the Social Democrats had also understood that the middle-sized parties would most certainly be willing to accept an electoral threshold in each of the constituencies, in order to inhibit small or new parties from entering parliament. The first Social Democratic proposal to that effect was to exclude all parties with less than 60 per cent of the vote/seat ratio in each constituency. Among themselves the Social Democrats were not in complete agreement regarding the electoral system issue as such (von Sydow 1989, 54ff). However, Prime Minister Tage Erlander had understood that electoral system changes were a non-negotiable condition for any future resumption of government coalition negotiations between his party and the Agrarians.

On this basis, a parliamentary commission of inquiry on electoral matters had been established in 1950. Various electoral systems were analysed by the secretariat and the results made available to all interested parties through the commission's reports. A variety of quota and divisor methods were considered and different thresholds included in calculations based on the five parliamentary elections 1932-48. All the systems considered would entail Social Democratic overrepresentation, mainly at the expense of the Communists. However, the analyses also demonstrated that the three non-socialist parties did best under the two Sainte-Laguë methods: (1) in the method's ordinary form and (2) with 1.5 as the first divisor (this proposal, equivalent to reducing the vote figures by one-third, was seen as better than the exclusion of parties with less support than 60 per cent of the votes/seats ratio) as well as under a simple Hare quota system (with a threshold).

After the resumption of the government coalition negotiations in late 1951, the Agrarians, were apparently able to convince the Social Democratic leadership – especially Mr Erlander – that »the method of odd figures« was the only one acceptable to them since the systems preferred by the Social Democrats were too unfavourable for the Agrarians. However, they were willing to accept – as part of an overall compromise on government formation – some kind of threshold, even though they would clearly prefer the reduction of all party vote figures by one fourth, equivalent to having a first divisor of 1.3333 – or maybe only 1.3 (von Sydow 1989, 66-69).

As already mentioned, the secretariat of the commission of inquiry had analysed historical election results using a first divisor of 1.5, but this only maintained the same level of Social Democratic overrepresentation as in the current system (d'Hondt in multimember constituencies, allowing for *apparentement*, and with no compensatory seats).

The compromise of mid-March 1952 was not difficult to strike. If a first divisor of 1.5 was too favourable to the Social Democrats and 1.3 not favourable enough, then 1.4 would probably do, especially as 1.4 would be sufficiently unfavourable towards the formation of cartels, which, as demonstrated by other calculations, was the main point for the Agrarians (von Sydow 1989, 61ff).

The new electoral system was soon enacted, and it stood its first test in the September 1952 lower house elections. There was a closer correspondence than previously between vote and seat shares for the four major parties (see the table below), but no particular improvement for the Communists (who still suffered from the biggest discrepancy – both in absolute and relative terms – between vote share and seat share).

Stabilisation of the party system of the early 1950s, which Stein Rokkan argued was the main objective of the electoral system change, was thus quickly achieved and was maintained through the 1950s and 1960s (Rokkan 1970, 161).

Conclusion
It is most interesting to note the dexterity with which the two negotiating partners were able to strike a compromise which fitted the interests of both in a situation so unique as the one outlined above. It also explains that the divisor of 1.4 did not come about by divine inspiration but was a simple compromise between two suggestions none of which would have suited the complexities of the situation.

To search for theoretical explanations for the choice of 1.4 is thus a wasted effort. However, straightforward rational-actor-inspired party behaviour theory can help explain why the Swedish Agrarians were able to negotiate a solution to their problems and have it enacted with the assistance of their coalition partner. The Social Democrats could not allow themselves to relax until the Agrarians were (sufficiently) satisfied.

It is also interesting to note how soon the political actors concentrated on the issue of the first divisor which was considered equivalent to having a threshold in each multimember constituency. They did not seem to realise that the *threshold of representation,* which gives the lowest level at which a party might, under the most favourable conditions, gain representation in a constituency, is lower even for the modified Sainte-Laguë electoral system than for the d'Hondt system which was now abandoned (Laakso 1979, 161-163; Elklit 1981, 16-19; for further discussion see also Rokkan 1970; Lijphart 1994; Elklit 1999).

It is not enough to compare first divisors, as the distance between divisors must also be considered. For *all* combinations of number of parties and number of seats, the threshold of representation is lower for the modified Sainte-Laguë than for the d'Hondt system (Laakso 1970, 163; *Elections to the Folketing September 22, 1953*, 9). Hence, electoral system reformers are well advised to combine analyses based on historical election results with formal analyses, inasmuch as analyses based on historical results might overlook theoretically interesting combinations.

It appears that the Swedish actors were not fully aware of the difference between the threshold of exclusion (where representation is secured if a party's vote share surpasses the threshold) and the threshold of representation (where representation is only possible if a party's vote share is above the threshold) (Lijphart & Gibberd 1977; Elklit 1981, 15-20). They argued – sometimes implicitly – on the basis of the former, while in concrete situations representation might have been decided by the latter. It is probably not worthwhile to redo the calculations of the secretariat, even though it would be interesting to find out why the actors failed to realise that the new system was actually not only more favourable to medium-sized parties, but potentially also to small parties (including the Communists) than that which was scrapped to please the Agrarians – and not *less* so as so many apparently believed!

What Happened in Denmark?

Denmark was the first to follow Sweden in opting for the Sainte-Laguë system with 1.4 as the first divisor, even though one sometimes gets the impression that it was Norway (Rokkan 1970, 160). The decision to change this element in the Danish constitutional set-up was taken as part of the constitutional amendment process begun in 1946, and which ended only in 1953 (Eigaard 1993; Elklit forthcoming). An important element in the constitutional amendment process was the abolition of the Upper House, which was more easily accepted when it was decided to increase membership in the surviving, directly and more broadly elected Lower House, *Folketinget*. This decision also gave some openings for those Upper House members desiring to continue in parliament.

The Danish electoral system of 1920 differed from the two other Scandinavian proportional representation systems of the period by being a genuine two-tier system. Since 1948, 105 seats had been allocated by d'Hondt in 23 multimember constituencies (as in Sweden and Norway), but with the all-decisive difference that these 105 seats were supplemented by an additional 44 compensatory seats (Elklit 1993). The compensatory seats were allocated to parties after calculating the difference between the number of seats each party was entitled to on the basis of its entire national vote (simple Hare quotas and largest remainders) and the number of direct seats already obtained in the multimember constituencies, the latter clearly being the non-decisive tier. Apart from one specific problem (referred to below) this system had performed well since 1920, partly because of the combination of a most proportional system (Hare + largest remainders) and a low electoral threshold which together produced a much lower level of disproportionality than in Sweden and Norway.

Disproportionality index figures are provided in Table 1 below. While the figures derive from different sources and cover partly different periods, they are fully comparable, as they are all calculated according to Michael Gallagher's broadly accepted suggestion for a more powerful index than those used previously (Gallagher 1992). The upper part of the table contains Arend Lijphart's figures, using also his categorisation of electoral systems (1994, 160-162). The lower part, however, gives figures for Denmark and Norway which are more useful for analytical purposes, as they more precisely reflect the actual election systems in those countries.

Obviously, the level of disproportionality was much lower in Denmark in the period prior to the electoral system changes than in the two other countries, no matter how one constructs the periodisation of the electoral systems. Therefore, discontent with seat allocation biases because of the electoral system cannot have been a substantial explanatory factor in Denmark, regardless of the situation in Sweden and Norway. The lower part of the table provides index values for Denmark 1950-53 (April), as these two elections constitute an electoral system of their own. The previous electoral system (April 1920-1947, i.e., 12 elections) had a value as low as 1.5 which only underscores the point made above (Elklit forthcoming, Table 5).

Table 1: Level of disproportionality in Scandinavian countries in selected periods before and after the changes in 1952-53 (using Gallagher's index).

Denmark		Norway		Sweden	
DEN1	DEN2	NOR1	NOR2	SWE1	SWE2
1945-53	1953-60	1945-49	1953-85	1948	1952-68
1.81	2.01	8.53	4.38	3.51	2.36
Elklit (forthcoming) Table 5		Aardal (forthcoming) Table A5			
1950-53	1953-60	1921-49	1953-85		
0.6	2.0	5.4	4.4		

Another observation is that the electoral law changes in 1952-53 led to an increase in disproportionality in Denmark (for reasons to be discussed below), while disproportionality decreased in Sweden and Norway, as would be expected.

The level of proportionality in Denmark was more satisfactory, by all standards, than in Sweden and Norway. However, the picture would have been even more satisfactory had the Agrarian Liberals, in most elections from 1920 to 1947, not succeeded in gaining more direct seats than they were entitled to on the basis of their overall share of the national vote. This phenomenon can be explained by an uneven support and vote pattern across multimember constituencies, as the Agrarian Liberal party was particularly strong in rural Jutland. This uneven pattern meant, to mention just one example, that the Social Democrats and the Agrarian Liberals – the two major parties – in 1939 were able to gain 84 per cent of all 58 direct seats in Jutland, despite having won only a combined 63 per cent of the vote in the region. The difference between seat share and vote share reflected the bonus given by the d'Hondt system to major parties, especially when the constituency magnitude is not too high; in Jutland during this period it averaged only 5.3.

As a consequence, the Agrarian Liberals in most elections before 1950 were unable to win compensatory seats, as there were no accidental losses to be compensated for! However, the growth of the Agrarian Liberal Party during this period made it difficult for the party's activists in *urban* Denmark to accept – almost as a fact of life – that they would never be able to gain parliamentary representation (via compensatory seats) because of their party's overrepresentation in rural Jutland.

The organisational response to these frustrations was a tactical split in the party by which its metropolitan branch presented its own ticket in the 1947 elections. The »ordinary« party managed to win 46 direct seats, eight more than its vote share entitled it to. Yet the formally separate »Liberals of the Capital« were nevertheless able to take three compensatory seats because the formal separation of the two »parties« made it impossible to offset the two sets of seat allocations against each other. The »Liberals of the Capital« gained access to the pool of compensatory seats by far surpassing one of the two modest electoral thresholds of the time, namely, that requiring that a party's number of votes in one of the country's three main regions be higher than the national vote/seat ratio.

The other political parties became very upset over this conscious misuse of the electoral law, which meant that they all got one, two, or three seats less than they would otherwise have been entitled to. Thus, 1948 saw the enactment of changes to the electoral act which would make similar party behaviour impossible in future elections. The main elements in this punitive expedition were (1) that a party with too many direct seats (compared to its vote share) would not be able to retain them, and (2) that the balance between direct and compensatory seats was changed so that relatively more compensatory seats were available for correcting future biases in seat allocation. The previous distribution was 117 direct and 31 compensatory seats, but in 1948 this was changed to 105 and 44, respectively, a net increase of one seat. The proportion of compensatory seats increased from 21 to 30 per cent.

A side-effect of the 1948 reforms in electoral system legislation was a lower degree of disproportionality than ever before (or after, for that matter). The Gallagher index value for the 1950 elections – the first after the change – reached an all-time low of 0.4 (as compared to 4.2 in 1947), and all parties, including the Communists, obtained their fair share of the seats. Electoral cartels have never been allowed in Danish parliamentary elections. They are also unnecessary, as parties cannot gain from joining cartels when the electoral system effectively ensures a close correspondence between vote and seat shares.

A related issue is whether or not there is also a formal electoral threshold. As mentioned above, Denmark had an electoral threshold since 1920, but it was rather low. Parties obtained access to the pool of compensatory seats either by winning a direct seat in a multimember constituency or by gaining as many votes in one of the country's three main regions – the metropolitan area, the islands, and Jutland – as the *national* votes/seats ratio, or to put it differently, as the average price in votes for one seat. With 148 seats, this was less than 0.68 per cent of the national vote, with the additional – but crucial – requirement that the votes should have been won in only one of the three regions. In 1947, another small party – with 1.2 per cent of the national vote – did not surpass the barrier, as its votes were scattered across all three regions. Thus, the electoral threshold was not very difficult to surpass, but it was not useless either (Elklit 1993, 44-6).

The outcome of the 1950 elections was relatively unproblematic, as the »Liberals of the Capital« did not present a separate ticket again and as the Agrarian Liberals' support did not make it necessary to take back any of their direct seats (they even got a few compensatory seats). There were also a sufficient number of compensatory seats to cater to the needs of the other parties.

What Was the Problem in Denmark?
A major political problem after 1950 was the completion of the constitutional amendment process begun in 1946, but which suffered from the Constitution Amendment Commission's lack of progress. The government formed after the 1950 election was a non-socialist minority coalition government consisting of Agrarian Liberals and Conservatives. It was seen as prudent to give these two parties a central political role if the amendment process were ever to be completed successfully.

The Commission's work was conducted in various sub-committees, where »Sub-committee 1« dealt with the new cameral structure, membership size, principles of parliamentarism, and the electoral system. The minutes of the meetings are kept in the National Archives, and they apparently give a clear and reliable picture of the sub-committee's deliberations. What they do not give, however, is an equally clear picture of the motives of the involved political actors, most of whom were relatively highly placed representatives of their parliamentary parties, often with an outspoken interest in electoral and institutional matters.

A basic hypothesis concerning the 1952 electoral system decision-making process in Denmark is that the actors were officially investigating the possibilities for suggesting a new electoral system to be used under the amended constitution. However, because that brief was not too complicated, given the experiences of the two-tier electoral system since 1920, they were primarily trying to find some general solution to resolve the unendurable and awkward situation in the electoral field which had been the order of the day since the 1947-48 punitive expedition against the Agrarian Liberals.

The requirements for amending the Constitution included a popular referendum in which at least 45 per cent of the entire electorate should vote in favour. The failed amendment attempt of 1939 (the 45 per cent level of support not having been reached, due partly to the position of the Agrarian Liberals) was still part of the living memory of leading politicians. The Agrarian Liberals were still seen as capable of blocking the amendment process, and every step which could be instrumental in fully integrating them into the process should therefore be supported by those parties interested in having the amendment process brought to a happy conclusion, i.e., the Social Democrats and the Social Liberals. The same kind of reasoning lay behind the political acceptance of the coalition government of Agrarian Liberals – who had the premiership – and the Conservatives.

The 1948 amendments to the Electoral Act therefore had to be dropped. Most observers would see this as an important concession to the Agrarian Liberals, who had persistently claimed that the electoral law changes were both unwarranted and unfair. The concessions might eventually be more symbolic than real, which was probably not important – and symbolic politics is in any case not a new invention. However, the participants of the 1947-48 punitive expedition could not just revert to the situation *ex ante,* as that would mean risking a future repetition of the same politically unbearable situation as before, i.e., the Agrarian Liberals winning more seats than their vote share entitled them to.

The Solution?
The cleverly designed solution was very difficult for the system engineers to discuss openly, since that might ruin the main purpose, i.e., improving the general climate among the constitution amendment negotiators. This also means that the reconstruction and interpretation of the solution in the Danish case is difficult to substantiate with reference to, e.g., specific statements or documentation from involved decision-makers. Nevertheless, it is a reconstruction which better than any alternative explains the entire course of events as well as the changes in electoral legislation.

The solution, simple and politically elegant, took full advantage of the Danish electoral system being a two-tier system:

1. The system for allocation of seats at the lower, non-decisive level was altered so as to more precisely reflect the vote shares of all parties. The solution eventually chosen was to copy the system already implemented in Sweden, i.e., dropping the d'Hondt system and introducing the modified Sainte-Laguë system, even though it had yet to be tested in an election. The increased number of direct seats available – due to the general increase in membership of the Folketing and the decrease in the number of compensatory seats to 23 per cent - was instrumental in ensuring this.
2. With a much closer correspondence between the lower tier seat distribu-

tion and the national vote distribution, it was less risky to reverse the changes of 1947-48:

- The Agrarian Liberals could be allowed the pleasure of having the decisions concerning non-finality of direct seats and relatively more compensatory seats recalled. The distributional effects of this change back to the situation *ex ante* would be non-existent and would, therefore, only be a small price to pay for easing the general political climate.

- The overall seat allocation system at the decisive, national tier (Hare + largest remainders) was preserved, so that changes would not bias future distribution of party strength in parliament.

- It was also decided to considerably raise the electoral threshold, as the new main requirement – 60,000 votes – was the equivalent of 2.5-2.8 per cent of the national vote, somewhat more than the »Liberals of the Capital« had been able to win in 1947. It would be possible to enter parliament with fewer votes, but only if they were scattered in such a way that a party had surpassed the *regional* votes/ direct seats ratio in *all* three main regions. It would also still be possible to gain access to the pool of compensatory seats by winning just one direct seat; with the decrease in the actual threshold of representation, this was a remarkable move in the opposite direction which – together with the increased number of direct seats – ensured the established small parties with regional strongholds (the Social Libeals, the Communists, the German Minority Party) that they would not lose out because of the new threshold *per se*.

- The parties knew well that electoral thresholds which should be instrumental in discouraging new parties from running and disabling such parties from gaining representation had to be implemented at the decisive tier. A first divisor of 1.4 at the non-decisive level would in any case have no impact. The electoral threshold increase, i.e., the two new requirements, can been seen as yet another positive Social Democratic gesture *vis-à-vis* the Agrarian Liberals in line with the concessions already mentioned. These two parties, together with the Conservatives who supported that the electoral threshold be increased, were also those who had suffered most from splinter parties in the past (and the Agrarian Liberals were actually having problems with a new splinter group, called »The Independents«). Hence, it is hardly surprising that it was these three parties who were interested in making it less attractive to test one's electoral chances with a new party.

- It was also decided to recalculate the pre-election allocation of direct seats to multimember constituencies and compensatory seats to main regions at regular intervals so as to redress imbalances created by demographic development over time. Obviously, this new provision would also contribute towards continuous adaptation to changes in the political landscape.

The deliberations in Sub-committee 1 relevant to this analysis took place between late February and late May/early June 1952, when a compromise was formally presented to the parliamentary parties for approval. It is striking to see how closely developments in Sweden, referred to above, were followed. The Swedish model was considered attractive by the energetic Social Democratic sub-commission chairman, Mr Holger Eriksen, who argued against having compensatory seats (as in Sweden and Norway) and that it was necessary to see how the introduction of a Sainte-Laguë formula with 1.5 would affect the Folketing's composition (the Swedish proposal had been 1.5, but Eriksen also referred to similar considerations in the Norwegian Labour Party). The West German electoral system was also occasionally alluded to, which was only natural as there were – and still are – a number of parallels between the two two-tier systems (Elklit & Roberts 1996). Even the possibility of introducing *Überhangmandate* was mentioned on one occasion (24 April 1952), and there is no doubt that the Agrarian Liberals felt attracted to a model which combined their traditional preference for first-past-the-post elections in single-member constituencies with compensatory seats.

The balance-to-be of 135 direct seats and 40 compensatory seats was found relatively early, as calculations produced by the secretariat of the sub-commission demonstrated that this split would guarantee – as far as possible – that the Agrarian Liberals would not gain surplus directs seats; the Conservatives nevertheless continued to argue that it would be better to have more than 175 seats in total.

The use of 1.4 as a first divisor first surfaced in some seat allocation calculations by the secretariat dated 19 May, but it was never debated, at least not in any way reflected in the minutes or, later, in the Hansard. The reason given for supplementing previous calculations based on 1.5 as the first divisor and various ways of allocating compensatory seats with these new calculations was »that 1.5 apparently has too strong an effect« – but the nature of this effect was never precisely explained. The obvious explanation is that it must have been too hard on the small parties, especially as the constituency magnitude was not increased. There is no reason to doubt that the introduction of 1.4 was a simple reflection of the Swedish compromise in March. The sub-commission also used the month of May to discuss other electoral system issues, especially the Social Democratic proposal to increase the electoral threshold to five per cent. This proposal was soon reduced to four per cent and – somewhat later – to the more complex formulation mentioned above.

The entire political electoral system compromise in the sub-commission was approved by the parliamentary parties in early June and then passed to a technical drafting election law commission which presented its draft bill in February 1953 (see *Betænkning afgivet af Valglovskommissionen af 7. juni 1952*). The law was passed after the obligatory three readings in each of the two houses in late March 1953, and it is particularly interesting to note how several of the spokesmen of the parliamentary parties, as well as the Conservative Minister of the Interior, were keen to stress how the new system would enable smaller parties to win more direct seats than what was possible under the previous system (*Folketingstidende 1952-53*, cols. 2064, 2072, 2436, 2451f; see also the *Betænkning* referred to above, pp. 3-4, and *Elections to the Folketing September 22, 1953*, pp. 8-9), something clearly seen as a positive achievement. The new electoral system in Denmark was applied for the first time on 22 September 1953, in the first elections under the amended constitution.

Conclusion

The 1952 decision to introduce the modified Sainte-Laguë seat allocation system in Denmark differed from the decisions in Sweden and Norway in being implemented on the lower, non-decisive tier in an ordinary two-tier system, which differed fundamentally from the electoral systems in the two other countries. The changes would have no effect on the distribution of seats in parliament, contrary to what was expected to be the case in Sweden, and later in Norway.

The reconstruction presented above regards the political compromise negotiated in Sub-commission 1 as an elegant solution to the main problem of getting the Agrarian Liberals to accept electoral system changes which on the one hand would deprive them of any hope of again gaining surplus direct seats to keep, but on the other hand would give them the political satisfaction of having the punitive measures of 1948 recalled. In this way, the June 1952 electoral system compromise became instrumental in discouraging the Agrarian Liberals from sabotaging the popular referendum needed before the constitution could be amended.

The compromise probably contributed to the Agrarian Liberals' attitude towards the rather inconsequential proposal – at least if compared to the electoral system used in the two elections of 1950 and early 1953 – that it be accompanied by a suggestion to increase the electoral threshold considerably. The three major parties, with similar interests in this respect, were able to eventually increase the threshold, even though the final form differed from the initial proposal.

It is worth mentioning that the reconstruction presented here is primarily supported by circumstantial evidence, as the very character of the political exercise made it difficult for the politicians – particularly the leading Social Democrats and Social Liberals – to be very outspoken. This was apparently also the case in the meetings of the parliamentary parties, whose minutes are not very informative about these political and computational complexities.

It is also worth noting that Laakso's advice (1979, 168) – that political decision-makers considering electoral reform should realise that the manipulation of the first divisor is a very powerful weapon indeed – was already well understood by Scandinavian parliamentarians in the early 1950s and that in Denmark this understanding was used to facilitate the introduction of changes which could serve a political purpose without having unintended political and distributional consequences. What is still often misunderstood, however, is the *combined* effect of the Sainte-Laguë formula in its pure form and the modification of the first divisor.

... And, Finally, Norway

In many ways, the systemic situation in Norway in the early 1950s paralleled that of Sweden: an electoral system of proportional representation using the d'Hondt allocation formula in multimember districts, but with no compensatory seats. The party system had the same basic format as in Sweden: a strong Labour Party with 40-46 per cent of the vote in the 1930s and 1940s, a strong Communist vote in 1945, and four non-socialist parties (not three as in Sweden because the Norwegian Christian People's Party was tapping the religious, fundamentalist cleavage dimension).

Some of the differences, however, were important. The 29 multimember constituencies (average magnitude 5.2) were smaller than their Swedish counterparts and, more importantly, divided into rural and urban constituencies. This reflected the traditional Norwegian concern for the interests of the countryside, inherited from the political development in the 19th century.

The ratio remained 2:1 in favour of the rural constituencies, despite population changes which meant that more than 50 per cent of the entire population by the late 1940s lived in urban areas (Aardal, forthcoming, Table A3).

Apparentement was also a controversial issue, having been introduced by a legislative coalition of the non-socialist parties in 1930, and removed by the Labour majority government in 1949, just prior to the general elections of that year. The use of cartels had served its purpose by reducing the Labour overrepresentation in the elections between 1930 and 1945, without completely doing away with it, partly because of the average size of constituencies, which – as already mentioned – were considerably smaller than in Sweden.

What Was the Problem in Norway?
The basic electoral system design problem in Norway differed from Sweden for two reasons: (1) the Labour government had a (manufactured) majority of its own, commanding 85 of the *Storting's* 150 seats (57 per cent) for a vote share of 46 per cent (which therefore meant that the government did not need a coalition partner), (2) the removal, in 1949, of the provisions for *apparentement* rendered it superfluous for the non-socialist parties to even consider the formation of cartels. In some of the multimember constituencies, they managed to field joint non-socialist lists, which, however, was never any party's preferred option.

The 1:2 imbalance between urban and rural constituencies (called »the peasants' clause«) was the factor which eventually triggered an electoral system change. The parties with a strong urban support (Labour and the Conservatives, but obviously also the Communists) found it increasingly unacceptable that the urban reservoir of seats was limited in this particular manner when the urban population (and the number of urban voters) now outnumbered the rural population (and the number of rural voters).

Over the years Norway had had several electoral reform commissions mandated to examine the constituency structure problem and the allocation system (and other issues as well, such as the cartel issue). Yet another commission had been instituted in 1948, and the removal of the provision for *apparentement* in 1949 – while the commission was still contemplating – was seen as a political provocation by the non-socialist opposition parties (Greve 1964).

Labour wanted to maintain its strong position in parliament, and apparently did not view it as a major problem that its parliamentary majority was manufactured, as long as it provided for a stable (Labour) government. It is not easy to understand why Labour engaged itself in these negotiations, as the party's situation was quite comfortable. However, the key is probably that the combined effect of an electoral system change which was not too drastic and the simultaneous removal of »the peasants' clause« was perceived as not endangering existing Labour over-representation while simultaneously removing a long-time political irritant (Eide 1998, 51ff). Evidently, Labour would have to compromise in order to eliminate the constitutionally protected under-representation of the urban constituencies. The party would have to renounce – at least partly – its advantages caused by (1) the relatively small magnitude of the multimember constituencies, (2) the recently enacted elimination of *apparentement*, and (3) the application of the d'Hondt seat allocation formula, three factors which together resulted in the party's 11 per cent overrepresentation in parliament, despite the urban-rural seat imbalance.

The reports from the 1948 Electoral Reform Commission came in 1949 and 1950, but the issue was not taken up by the parliamentary constitutional committee until 1952. In order to achieve a higher level of proportionality among the parties, the majority in the Electoral Reform Commission had recommended combining (1) the (Hare) largest remainder formula, (2) compensatory seats to be allocated either on a regional or a national basis, and (3) a three per cent formal electoral threshold. The (Labour) majority in the *Storting* constitutional committee, however, did not appreciate these suggestions which, expectedly, would do away with the party's manufactured parliamentary majority.

Labour's committee members wanted the urban-rural split to be reconsidered, and they suggested as multimember constituencies the 18 administrative counties (plus Oslo and Bergen, the two major cities), disregarding the balance between urban and rural voters. However, because of Norway's geography, it was never considered to allocate seats to these constituencies proportionally, based, for example, on the number of residents or the number of voters. The concession which Labour was willing to make to the other parties for these changes was to replace the d'Hondt allocation formula with a modified Sainte-Laguë formula, but with 1.5 as the first divisor (*Storting Recommendation No. 299*, 1952, 655-656). This was, of course, the allocation system debated in Sweden in early 1952 and preferred by the Swedish Social Democrats, who were eager to have some threshold in each multimember constituency because of the perceived Communist danger. It should also be recalled that 1.5 was eventually changed to 1.4 as part of the compromise between the Swedish Social Democrats and the Agrarians.

Developments in Sweden were apparently followed closely by interested politicians and commentators, and the 1.4 compromise in March was immediately publicised in Norway. It also appears that a prominent Labour representative had tested the ground sometime during the summer of 1952 to see if the Conservatives and/or the Liberals were interested in negotiating a compromise along the lines of the Swedish model (a reference to these contacts was given by the Labour leader, Mr Gerhardsen, in Parliament on 24 November 1952, *Stortingstidende*, 1952, 2870). However, none of the two opposition parties were prepared to engage in such negotiations.

That is probably why, in November, the Labour majority fraction in the constitutional committee made a clear reference (p. 655) to the new Swedish electoral system. By then this system was known by all who were seriously interested in electoral systems and constitutional affairs, especially as the system had stood its test in the Swedish September elections. Hence, it is almost pathetic to see how the Labour fraction only referred to what they here call »a simple and natural solution«, i.e., to increase the first divisor by 0.5, when they discussed the need to increase the first divisor of the ordinary Sainte-Laguë system (*Storting Recommendation No. 299*, 1952, 655-656). Could the reason be that they wanted to have something to exchange if attractive offers were presented to them during the debate in parliament?

What Was, Then, the Solution?
As expected, a parliamentary deadlock developed when the debate reached its climax in late November 1952 (Wilberg 1958, 10) as the non-socialist opposition parties considered Labour's concessions too few and too small (despite Labour's above-mentioned attempts to open the negotiations over the summer). And it should be remembered that Labour was not strong enough to change the constitution without the support of others.

However, many Conservatives were also highly motivated to discard the urban-rural 1:2 clause. The party's vote share – and seat share – was declining compared to the situation before the war, even though the party did not do too badly in urban constituencies. It was unable to gain at least some compensation for its losses in rural constituencies. The main reason was the skewed party support patterns in urban constituencies, where Labour and the Communists together took the lion's share of the relatively limited number of seats.

It was thus also very much in the interest of the Conservatives to have the peasants' clause abolished, even though the rural wing of the party doubted the wisdom of that suggestion (Aardal, forthcoming). At the end of the day, i.e., during the sole parliamentary debate of the recommendations from the committee, on 24-26 November, the issue was opened again: on the first day of the debate, Mr Smitt Ingebretsen, the Conservative spokesman, suggested that three unsettled issues – the most important being the change from 1.5 to 1.4 – were considered carefully before any decisions would be taken by parliament (*Stortingstidende* 1952, 2865-2866). Mr Gerhardsen, chairman of the Labour parliamentary party, responded carefully, though in a positive vein. On the next day, Mr John Lyng, the Conservative leader, reiterated the very same points (*Stortingstidende* 1952, 2942). Renewed deliberations in the parliamentary parties (Labour and the Conservatives being the most interesting, as the decisions in both these parties appear to have been taken with rather narrow majorities) led to a situation in which Conservative support for removing the constitutionally established 1:2 relationship between urban and rural seats was exchanged for Labour support for decreasing the first divisor from 1.5 to 1.4 in the future application of the Sainte-Laguë electoral system. The agreement was soon enacted, so as to be in place before the upcoming 1953 *Storting* elections.

The new system had a higher constituency magnitude than the previous system (7.8 as compared to 5.2). Combined with the other electoral system changes as well as changes in party support, this resulted in a much more proportional electoral outcome in 1953 than in 1949, including a reduction in Labour's over-representation by more than 50 per cent.

Conclusion

The 1952/53 electoral system change in Norway is slightly more difficult to explain than was the case for Sweden and Denmark.

Labour wanted to retain its parliamentary majority and was not at all concerned about the low level of proportionality, but it also wanted to remove the 1:2 peasants' clause inherited from the 19th century. The suggestion was to change the constituency structure and replace the d'Hondt allocation system with the more proportional modified Sainte-Laguë system, even in (on average) larger constituencies. The suggested first divisor was 1.5, allegedly intended as a barrier against the representation of new and minor parties, such as the communists. The general idea was apparently that these suggestions would ensure a stable (Labour) government also in the future. Obviously, the inspiration came from the Swedish Social Democrats.

The Conservative leadership, and the party's urban wing, was also strongly against rural over-representation in parliament, and when they were promised a parliamentary fig leaf – i.e., a decrease in the suggested first divisor from 1.5 to 1.4 – they were willing to deliver the votes needed to amend the constitution, thereby eliminating the urban-rural seat imbalance. The consequences for the Conservatives themselves are difficult to establish because of the pattern of party support over 20 constituencies; they probably believed that it would be possible to win at least one seat in constituencies with below-average Conservative vote support.

In Denmark, parliamentarians knew that it was a misperception to see the modified Sainte-Laguë system as more effective than the d'Hondt system (under identical conditions) in barring small parties from representation when they debated and legislated the matter in 1952-53. This was apparently also understood in Norway, where two comparisons were presented more or less simultaneously during the deliberations: (1) d'Hondt versus ordinary Sainte-Laguë and (2) ordinary Sainte-Laguë versus Sainte-Laguë with an increased first divisor (*e.g., Stortingstidende* 1952, 2869).

It is not difficult to see from such comparisons which electoral system is the more proportional; but as the shift eventually was from d'Hondt to modified (1.4) Sainte-Laguë, it is not surprising that misperceptions – especially about the prospects of small parties winning a seat in multimember constituencies – might have developed (and even survived) in spite of a clear understanding among involved politicians and bureaucrats in 1952 and 1953, and academics analysing the issue later (Laakso 1979, 167).

The concession Labour gave to the Conservatives in exchange for their legislative support might on first sight appear small, at least compared to Labour's gains. However, it was probably considered high and somewhat risky – especially as Labour was so well off under the previous system, in spite of the urban under-representation. However, Labour continued to be over-represented in the *Storting*, even though the manufactured parliamentary majority in 1953 decreased from 57 to 51 per cent.

Nevertheless, the new system provided for a more proportional representation pattern, so Labour did in fact accept a decrease in its future seat share which for a political party is a high price to pay. Hence, the concession was perhaps not so small as it appears. Labour's actual over-representation in 1953 was reduced from 11.0 to 4.6 percentage points (Aardal, forthcoming, 14). It might have been considered more important that it also reduced the need for *apparentement* among the non-socialist opposition parties – or even the risk that they might merge into one large bourgeois party. Hence, whether intended or not, the formula contributed to the stabilisation of the national party system as it had developed in the early 1950s, precisely as in Sweden (Rokkan 1970, 161).

Different Problems, Similar Solutions?

Sweden
The point of departure was that it became untenable for the Agrarians (and

also, but probably less so, for the Social Democrats) that they had to fight elections in non-socialist cartels at the same time as they were members of a Social Democratic-Agrarian coalition government.

The main problem was to find an electoral system which would provide for a somewhat higher degree of proportionality for the medium-sized parties so that they would not be tempted to form electoral cartels, but without introducing compensatory seats which would do away with the big party-bonus to which the Social Democrats felt virtually entitled.

The solution, after some discussion and preparatory work, was to replace the current electoral system (d'Hondt in multimember constituencies, allowing for *apparentement*) with Sainte-Laguë in the same constituencies, but modified so that the first divisor was 1.4, instead of 1.0. The figure 1.4 was a simple compromise between 1.5 and 1.3, and the new electoral system performed as intended, making electoral cartels something of the past.

Denmark

The point of departure was the need for a constitutional amendment, which was conditioned on a popular referendum in which a least 45 per cent of the entire electorate voted in favour. This made it necessary to get all major political parties to support the constitution amendment and also to recommend their supporters to vote in favour of the amendment. One element in the constitution amendment discussion was that the Upper House should be abolished, while the number of seats in the Lower House should be increased.

The main problem was that the Agrarian Liberals had been »punished« by the other parties when a new electoral law was enacted in response to what was generally seen as the Agrarian Liberals' unacceptable exploitation, in 1947, of specific provisions in the previous law. The Agrarian Liberals therefore not only succeeded in obtaining more than their fair share of the seats, but also won additional compensatory seats in the metropolitan area. The changes to the electoral law – which had left the Agrarian Liberals rather annoyed – had to be redressed in a manner acceptable to *all* major parties because their support would be needed in the coming referendum campaign.

The solution was to retain the overall electoral system (two-tiers, with Hare + largest remainders used in the upper tier), while the seat allocation system at the lower, non-decisive level was changed in such a way that it was a foregone conclusion that a party could not again win more seats than it was entitled to. The other parties could therefore allow the Agrarian Liberals the political triumph of having the 1947-48 changes recalled, something which improved the political climate considerably, and which again made it easier to agree on other amendment issues also. This explains why the modified Sainte-Laguë system was implemented only on the lower, non-decisive tier, while the decisive seat allocation system was not changed (apart from increasing the electoral threshold which, obviously, was a significant factor). The main point is that this took away any element of risk involved in recalling the 1948 electoral law changes. This symbolic gesture was instrumental in securing the support of the Agrarian Liberals for the constitution amendment process, which was the main issue for the Social Democrats and the Social Liberals.

Norway

The point of departure was the peasants' clause, i.e., the old 1:2 urban-rural seat imbalance in parliament, which reflected power-relations in a society very different from Norway of the early 1950s. Nevertheless, the Labour Party had been continuously over-represented, due to the combined effect of the d'Hondt allocation formula, relatively small constituencies (on average), and the pattern of party support across multimember constituencies.

The main problem was that the climate for negotiating these constitutional issues was not particularly constructive, as relations between parties were not at their best. The main reason was that Labour was not particularly keen to consider electoral systems which would do away with the party's over-representation – and also because Labour had used its parliamentary majority to abolish the provisions for *apparentement*. This was important if the non-socialist parties were to be allowed the possibility of obtaining something approaching proportional representation. It was considered a particularly dirty trick that this change was enacted while a parliamentary committee was discussing possible solutions to the electoral system problems at hand. Yet Labour realised that they had to open negotiations about the electoral systems as this was the only way of obtaining support for the removal of the peasants' clause, something which they saw as being in their own best interests if they were to stay in power.

The solution for Labour was to give last minute support for lowering the first divisor of the suggested seat allocation system in exchange for support for removal of the peasants' clause.

Is a General Conclusion Possible?

The aim of this chapter has been to explain a particularly important form of institutional change in parliamentary democracies: fundamental changes to the electoral system through which seats in parliament are allocated to political parties. What makes these allocation mechanisms so interesting is that the issue is not only how many seats each party wins, but that the parties' political bargaining power in parliament is determined through that allocation.

Basic rational-choice assumptions lead us to expect that constitution makers and electoral system negotiators will primarily pursue individual as well as party interests, while more lofty ideas concerning general constitutional principles might be left for presentations on Constitution Day. This expectation, and this approach in general, has proven useful in a number of previous studies (e.g., Bawn 1993; Geddes 1998; von Sydow 1989; Elklit 1988).

The three individual – though apparently quite comparable – cases lead us to the same general conclusion, though it might be argued that the similarity as far as the dependent variable is concerned makes it difficult to reach such conclusion. The first way out is to claim that we not only have problems of a different character and with a different time-perspective but also different solutions: the modified Sainte-Laguë system was used under different circumstances in all three countries, so the solutions could not be identical – at least not in their effects. Constituency magnitude differed between Sweden and Norway, and the system was not implemented on the decisive tier in Denmark. Yet even if one argues that the dependent variables were not identical, it cannot be denied that the cases were dependent on each other, as the Swedish invention was evidently copied in the two other countries.

The general conclusion is nevertheless well in line with von Sydow's conclusion concerning the rational character of party motives in the Swedish case. Von Sydow observed that many decisions were supported by legislative coalitions much smaller than one should have expected, as the norm in constitutional and similar institutional matters was – and is – to have broad consensus (von Sydow 1989: 319). The exception from this pattern is the Danish case, but the situation was also different in Denmark, as it was viewed as a necessary condition for having the constitution amended that all major parties be party to the final agreement. To put it quite simply: a narrow coalition was not a viable possibility.

The reasons for negotiating apparently identical solutions – even though they were actually less so than is often claimed – were probably two-fold: (1) the Swedish invention – despite it being the negotiated compromise solution to a specific Swedish problem – was very timely for being considered in the two other countries as well, and (2) the similarities between the electoral systems (even though in Denmark it was only considered in relation to the lower, non-decisive level) made it easy to transfer the ideas and to understand the reasoning behind. It may even have played a role of its own that the Danish and Norwegian Social Democrats apparently saw it as an advantage that the new system had been negotiated and eventually accepted by their Swedish party comrades.

It is also interesting to note – as did Stein Rokkan (1970) – that the effects over time were quite similar across countries despite whatever other differences might have occurred: the life span of the traditional Scandinavian party system was prolonged, and it also became easier to build government and legislative coalitions (particularly in Norway and Sweden) as the need for *ad hoc* electoral cartels was now almost non-existent.

Finally, it is interesting to observe that the outcome of the electoral system changes in all three countries was what one might expect on the basis of the literature now available, i.e., decreased disproportionality in Norway and Sweden and increased disproportionality in Denmark. Shugart has examined this issue for Norway and Sweden, but his data (or his calculations) on Norway must have been flawed. Hence, he ends his discussion on a somewhat inconclusive note (Shugart 1992).

If better data are used (e.g., Lijphart 1994 or Aardal forthcoming) the picture immediately becomes as one would expect, i.e., an obvious decrease in disproportionality in both Sweden and Norway (cf. Table 1 above). In Denmark, the effect of what was the main electoral system change – the increased electoral threshold – was an obvious increase in disproportionality (Elklit 1993, 49), as is also illustrated in the table. Hence, it all worked out as expected by the then central election law negotiators – and by later theorists.

References

Aardal, Bernt (forthcoming). »Electoral Systems in Norway«, to appear in Bernard Grofman & Arend Lijphart (eds.), *Party and Electoral Systems in the Nordic Countries.*
Bawn, Kathleen (1993). »The Logic of Institutional Preferences: German Electoral Law as a Social Choice Outcome«, *American Journal of Political Science*, Vol. 37, No. 4, pp. 965-989.
Betænkning afgivet af Valglovskommissionen af 7. Juni 1952 (Betænkning nr. 74), Copenhagen: Schultz Universitetsbogtrykkeri.
Eide, Tor Myrland (1998). *Her er det godt å sitte, la oss i tillegg gjøre det tryggere. Norske valgsystemreformer i perioden 1952-1988*, Master's thesis, Bergen: Institutt for Sammenliknende Politikk, University of Bergen.
Eigaard, Søren (1993). *Idealer og Politik. Historien om Grundloven af 1953,* Odense: Odense Universitetsforlag.

Elklit, Jørgen (1981). *Det tyske mindretals parlamentariske repræsentation*, Aabenraa: Det tyske Generalsekretariat.

Elklit, Jørgen (1988). »'Den laveste partiegoismes allerbrutaleste fjæs?' Eller: Noget om valglovene i 1915 og 1920«, pp. 61-96, in Hans Chr. Johansen, Mogens N. Pedersen & Jørgen Thomsen (eds.), *Om Danmarks historie 1900-1920. Festskrift til Tage Kaarsted*, Odense: Odense University Press.

Elklit, Jørgen (1993). »Simpler than its Reputation: The Electoral System in Denmark since 1920«, *Electoral Studies*, Vol. 12, No. 1, pp. 41-57.

Elklit, Jørgen (1999). *Danske valgsystemer: Fordelingsmetoder, spærreregler, analyseredskaber*, 4th ed., Aarhus: Department of Political Science, University of Aarhus.

Elklit, Jørgen (forthcoming). »The Politics of Electoral System Development and Change: The Danish Case«, to appear in Bernard Grofman & Arend Lijphart (eds.), *Party and Electoral Systems in the Nordic Countries.*

Elklit, Jørgen & Nigel S. Roberts (1996). »A category of its own? Four PR two-tier compensatory member electoral systems in 1994«, *European Journal of Political Research*, Vol. 30, pp. 217-240.

Folketingsvalget den 22. september 1953 (Elections to the Folketing September 22, 1953) (1954), Copenhagen: The Statistical Department.

Folketingstidende (the Hansard of the post-1953 Danish Parliament as well as the pre-1953 Lower House).

Gallagher, Michael (1992). »Proportionality, Disproportionality and Electoral Systems«, *Electoral Studies*, Vol. 10, No. 1, pp. 33-51.

Geddes, Barbara (1998). »Initiation of New Democratic Institutions in Eastern Europe and Latin America«, pp. 15-41, in Arend Lijphart & Carlos H. Waisman (eds.), *Institutional Design in New Democracies. Eastern Europe and Latin America*, Boulder, Colo.: Westview Press.

Greve, Tim (1964). *Tidsrommet 1908-1964,* Volume III, in Alf Kaartvedt et al., *Det Norske Storting gjennom 150 år*, Oslo: Gyldendal Norsk Forlag.

Laakso, Markku (1979). »The Maximum Distortion and the Problem of the First Divisor in Different P.R. Systems«, *Scandinavian Political Studies*, Vol. 2 (new series), No. 2, pp. 161-169.

Lijphart, Arend (1994). *Electoral Systems and Party Systems. A Study of Twenty-seven Democracies, 1945-1990*, Oxford: Oxford University Press.

Lijphart, Arend & Robert W. Gibberd (1977). »Thresholds and Payoffs in List Systems of Proportional Representation«, *European Journal of Political Research*, Vol. 5, No. 3, pp. 219-244.

Rokkan, Stein (1970). »Electoral Systems«, pp. 147-168, in *Citizens. Elections. Parties. Approaches to the Comparative Study of the Processes of Development*, Oslo: Universitetsforlaget. A revised version of this article with the same title is in David L. Sills (ed.), *International Encyclopedia of the Social Sciences*, Vol. 5, pp. 6-21, New York: Macmillan and The Free Press, 1968.

Shugart, Matthew Soberg (1992). »Electoral reform in systems of proportional representation«, *European Journal of Political Research*, Vol. 21, No. 3, pp. 207-224.

Stortingsinnstillinger (Storting Recommendations), i.e., the official reports from *Storting* committees.

Stortingstidende 1952 (the Hansard of the Norwegian Parliament)

Särlvik, Bo (1983). »Scandinavia«, pp. 122-148, in Vernon Bogdanor and David Butler (eds.), *Democracy and Elections: Electoral Systems and Their Political Consequences*, Cambridge: Cambridge University Press.

von Sydow, Björn (1989). *Vägen till enkammarriksdagen. Demokratisk författningspolitik i Sverige 1944-1968*, Stockholm: Tidens förlag.

Wilberg, Ingeborg (1958). »Endringer i Grunnloven«, pp. 1-28, in Ingeborg Wilberg & Gunder Egge (1958). *En oversikt over de vigtigste endringer i statsforfatningsretten siden 1948*. Reprint of Jussens Venner, Serie N, Nos. 5 and 7, and Serie O, No. 2, Oslo: Universitetsforlaget.

---

* This paper has benefited from advice and assistance from Bernt Aardal, Tor Myrland Eide, Tove Elklit, Anne Birte Pade, Bjørn Rønning, Palle Svensson, and Ingeborg Wilberg. I am, however, solely responsible for any remaining errors and misunderstandings.

On Bias and Disclosure:
A Personal Pathways Perspective in Legislative Research

Heinz Eulau

Abstract

Unlike physical and natural scientists, social scientists are reluctant to connect their inquiries and discoveries to their personal careers and private experiences in other than their scholarly roles. This is likely to introduce much bias into their scientific work, and by not accounting for this bias they make it impossible to discount it for what it is in order to optimize objectivity. To remedy this fallacy, this chapter proposes a »personal pathways approach« to knowledge as part of social-scientific methodology and illustrates it by way of three research projects on legislative institutions and behavior in which the author has been involved.

Iowa City, Iowa, in the heart of the American heartland called Middle West, is the last place where one might want to look for a major research center – perhaps the only one of its kind – dedicated to the comparative study of legislative behavior, processes and institutions. Yet it was here where, some thirty years ago, serious comparative legislative studies across space and time were the topic of a conference, organized by the University of Iowa's Legislative Research Center and, in due time, nurtured by one of the world's best learned journals in the field of political science, the Legislative Studies Quarterly.[1]

It was my good fortune, in 1969, to be invited to the conference on »Comparative Legislative Behavior Research,« held at Iowa, May 26-30, 1969. Our local friends had succeeded in bringing together an extraordinarily gifted group of scholars from abroad, some of them already known in this country, others en route to recognition in their own countries and soon in the United States.[2] *Most gratifying for me personally was catching up with Austria's Peter Gerlich who five years earlier had been a member of a seminar I had given at Vienna's new Institute for Advanced Studies, and also with Denmark's Mogens N. Pedersen who had spent an academic year at Stanford University, my home turf. More important, both Mogens and Peter were doing research in which I had a hand, so to speak – in Peter's case directly, in Mogens' case indirectly. But before pursuing these »connections,« I want to provide some background for why I am writing this paper in what I like to call a »personal pathways perspective« (PPP).*

Personal Pathways in Science

The celebration of a distinguished scholar's achievements in the study of legislative behavior, institutions and processes strikes me as an altogether not inappropriate occasion to raise some questions about the private aspects of the undertaking in which Mogens N. Pedersen and so many other scholars have been involved for several decades. By »private aspects« I mean those circumstances in the scholar's career that do not often come to public attention, yet have an enormous influence on his or her work and, indirectly, on the work of others. I am not unmindful here of the wise observation of an old – now departed – acquaintance of mine, the American sociologist Everett Hughes. »Subjectively,« Hughes once wrote, »a career is the moving perspective in which the person sees his life as a whole and interprets the meaning of his various attributes, actions, and the things which happen to him. This perspective is not absolutely fixed either as to point of view, direction, or destination« (Hughes 1958, 63). Even had I come to this insight on my own, I would not have been stirred by it as much as I was if I had not met Everett Hughes in 1964 when both of us were teaching at the recently founded Institute for Advanced Studies in Vienna, Austria. Though our personal interaction was of short duration, it was intense; and its effect on how I saw myself as a social scientist has been with me for a long time. I gradually came to the conclusion that my *persona privata* was methodologically as important for how I approached the study of politics in general and of legislatures in particular as was my *persona publica* in the scientifically relevant community of scholars to which every scholar *nolens-volens* belongs. In fact, I recently gave rather formal expression to this approach as the »personal pathways perspective« on knowledge-making and, perhaps more critical, knowledge-knowing (Eulau 1996).

Curious to find out how my colleagues in the social sciences are viewing themselves as »objects, « I looked for statements – in autobiographies, autobiographical essays and other possibly serviceable sources – that linked their personal, not directly »scientific,« backgrounds and/or personal experiences with their public roles as social scientists. I found less than a handful of relevant works.[3] This struck me as rather odd, because I know of an abundance of autobiographies and other personal testimonies written by physical and natural scientists who divulge and reflect on the often subjective and even whimsical origins and nature of their scientific activities or discoveries. How come, I wondered, that social scientists, presumably sensitive to matters of human and social affairs, seem to be so reluctant to make similar self-orientational disclosures? Why this apparent »conspiracy of silence?« I have no firm answer, but I have the hunch that it has much to do with the very »personal insecurities« that a social science conceived and practiced in a mistaken image of the »hard« sciences is likely to engender among its practitioners. Instead of conceding the well-known infirmities of the social and behavioral sciences, the social scientist's personal pathways are glossed over as irrelevant to his or her »scientific« work precisely because they might reveal some bias which, a false objectivity demands, is to be disavowed. And this makes for a latent »philosophy« of science that, instead of seeing the investigator's personal pathways as an essential component of the research process, is »in denial« and seeks external validation *pro vita sua* in embracing one »paradigm« after another. How different, for instance, the orientation one finds in Michael Polanyi's *Personal Knowledge* (1958, 322-23):

> As I acknowledge, in reflecting on the process of discovery, the gap between the evidence and the conclusions which I draw from them, and account for my bridging this gap in terms of my personal responsibility, so also will I acknowledge that in childhood I have formed my most fundamental beliefs by exercising my native intelligence within the social milieu of a particular place and time. I shall submit to this fact as defining the conditions with which I am called upon to exercise my responsibility.

As I noted after reading Polanyi's book, »here is a 'real' scientist of unchallenged distinction who made no bones about the connection between the private and the public in scientific inquiry.... I had been well aware of the importance of imagination or free association in scientific thought; but that scientific thought also has roots in personal experiences – in addition, of course, to its social groundings in a community of scholars – is a notion that evolved only gradually« (Eulau 1996, 25).

Treating oneself as a »case» of what one wants to write about without, however, making oneself the center of the case, is not an entirely unembarrassing venture. It may appear like a dog's effort to chase its own tail. To avoid such circularity, the personal pathways perspective as a methodological adjunct in scientific inquiry requires a high degree of self-consciousness and self-understanding. It demands of the »self» to transcend itself (»its self«) so that the resultant report will be sufficiently authentic to be accepted as credible in the community of concerned scholars. Put differently, the pathways perspective seeks to *account* for the scientist's subjectivities in a way that allows the reader to *discount* these subjectivities in an assessment of the scientific product which may be affected by them. Rather than disguise what may create bias in the research process, PPP seeks to *disclose* it. If all this sounds rather abstract, I hope to give it concrete meaning by making myself a »case« in question (without probably giving a satisfactory answer).

All of this forced itself on my attention only *after* I had escaped the life of an active, perhaps hyperactive, research scholar and had come to enjoy enough leisure to reflect on what I had been doing in all those decades of a frolicsome research life which, in many respects, leaves little time for disclosure by way of PPP. As I now look back at how I came to what one might call an »automethodological« exercise – a forbidding neologism really no more esoteric or absurd than the established and familiar term »autobiographical,« I find that it was largely in reaction to much mischief being made of Thomas Kuhn's concept of »scientific revolution.« Lest I be accused of indulging in twenty-twenty hindsight, I shall draw on what I wrote as I slowly came to the non-Kuhnian notion of PPP as an important factor in the research process. PPP is of course not in competition with the Kuhnian idea of all scientific knowledge being »social knowledge« created by the community of scholars. It supplements and enriches it. I shall do this with reference to my own adventures in legislative studies.[4]

A Non-Kuhnian View of Legislative Studies

One of the interesting things about the study of parliamentary institutions and legislatures in the past half century – my generation's half century – is that it never really succumbed to whatever fashions swept through other sub-fields of political science. Although there was subsequently much talk of a »behavioral revolution« that presumably began after World War II and represented a turning point in the development of political science, there was more continuity than discontinuity in research on legislatures from the late nineteenth century on. Throughout the century legislative studies have ranged from the statistical treatment of parliamentary roll-call votes through more or less detailed institutional descriptions to intensive, analytic studies of single cases of legislation. And there has been amazingly little philosophical or methodological controversy in this field. There were temporary enthusiasms, of course, but in general legislative studies evolved as some new notions were added to old ones. The idea of there having been – in the sense of Kuhn's scientific revolution – a »behavioral revolution« circa 1950 is largely a latter-day fabrication to justify a »post-behavioral revolution.« But this »new (post-) revolution« was nowhere to be seen in research on legislatures. Nevertheless, so great was the pressure to assume the »revolutionary mantle« that I felt a need to speculate – but only speculate – about why it was that the metaphor of a post-behavioral *revolution* was so palatable to at least some political scientists. I attributed it to the contemporary popularity of Kuhn's (1962) conception of scientific development:

> Whatever validity this conception might have in regard to fundamental transformations in the natural and physical sciences (where it is far from being noncontroversial), it is inappropriate for explaining and understanding the development of the social sciences. Yet, in an era in which the word »revolution« was fashionable, it was of no concern that Kuhn's theory of scientific revolution did not really fit the scientific circumstances of a field like political science. It was sufficient that the theory supplied a vocabulary that was congenial and that could serve to rationalize and legitimize the misgivings of those who had never been comfortable with the scientific orientation introduced into the discipline in the wake of the behavioralists' ascendancy, or of those who did not like the discipline's pragmatic commitment to the established political order. In a scientific perspective, the irony that the »new revolution,« had it come off, would be counter-revolutionary and even reactionary was lost on the self-styled post-behavioralists (Eulau 1981, viii).

I am reasonably sure that I never heard anybody talk about a disciplinary revolution during the 1950s. David Truman, in his famous 1955 essay, had spoken of the impact *on* political science of the revolution *in* the behavioral sciences and not of a behavioral revolution *in* political science. This is a rather specious point to make in this particular connection – specious because the use of the word »revolution« at that time, in the quietist era of the 1950s, could not be linked either to the real world of American politics as it later emerged in the 1960s or to Kuhn's history-driven view of the philosophy of science. All this was in the future and could not have been known (or, I suppose, predicted).

When Kuhn's book was published, in 1962, I was not particularly enthusiastic about its relevance for the social sciences. My reading of the history of political science in particular had led me to reject the notion that changes in the discipline's topics, theories and methods, however drastic they might appear to the contemporary eye, were ever revolutionary in the sense in which one could legitimately speak of the Copernican Revolution in astronomy or the Newtonian Revolution in physics. In a 1950s historical review of the discipline's literature I put it this way:

> The history of political science as an independent field of inquiry can be written as a history of successive emancipations from earlier limitations and false starts. Yet, these successive emancipations have been additive rather than cumulative: *the old survives with the new, and the old acquires new defenders as the new relies on old apostles.* It is impossible to say, therefore, that anything has been disproved as long as conventional tests of proof – the requisites of scientific status in any field of knowledge – are not commonly accepted by political scientists, or, in fact, are rejected by some as altogether irrelevant in political inquiry (Eulau 1959, 94).

I had met Tom Kuhn in 1958-59 during his residence at the Center for Advanced Studies in the Behavioral Sciences in the hills above Stanford University. He gave a seminar about his ideas. I was more impressed by his notion of »communities« of scholars doing »normal« science than by any talk about »scientific revolution.« Here's what Kuhn himself wrote about his interaction with the social scientists at the Center:

> ... spending the year in a community composed predominantly of social scientists confronted me with unanticipated problems about the differences between such communities and those of the natural scientists among whom I had been trained. Particularly, I was struck by the number and extent of the *overt* disagreements between social scientists about the nature of legitimate scientific problems and methods. Both history and acquaintance made me doubt that practitioners of the natural sciences possess firmer or more permanent answers to such questions than their colleagues in social science. Yet, somehow, the practice of astronomy, physics, chemistry, or biology normally fails to evoke the controversies over fundamentals that today often seem endemic among, say, psychologists or sociologists. Attempting to discover the source of that difference led me to recognize the role in scientific research of what I have since called »paradigms.« These I take to be universally recognized scientific achievements that *for a*

time provide model problems and solutions to a community of practitioners. Once that piece of my puzzle fell into place, a draft of this essay emerged rapidly (Kuhn 1962, ix-x; italics added).

Kuhn clearly misunderstood and overestimated the significance of what he called »controversies« in the social sciences. These are usually rather endemic intra-family disputes over sundry temporary fashions which peter out without being resolved in one way or another. They are not the kind of controversies which lead to revolutionary transformations of paradigmatic significance as articulated by Kuhn. It strikes me as ironic that the »new revolutionaries« in political science used – or should I say misused? – Kuhn's work which, as he so vividly tells us, was influenced by his (quite mistaken) understanding of social science as it appeared to be practiced and not by some preconception about one paradigm being replaced by another in a cycle of scientific revolutions. As I noted in an essay published in the same year as Kuhn's book, when David Truman spoke of a revolution in the behavioral sciences, he »did not envisage the kind of *fundamental* paradigmatic change« that Kuhn had in mind when using the word »revolution« in connection with the physical sciences. On the contrary, I averred, »it was the contention of Truman's essay that the new tendencies [i.e., political behavior study] were a continuation of traditional political science« (Eulau 1962, 29).

A Bicephalous Doctoral Dissertation

Until the middle 1960s, when the academic community throughout the world was shaken by what was euphemistically called »student unrest« (there being no better word for what was going on), I had seen myself as a social or political »scientist« in the image of the physical or natural scientist as this role was generally and mistakenly interpreted – a cold-blooded, objective seeker of the truth wherever it might be found and whatever consequences it might have. I still cannot really account for the fact that as a graduate student working for the doctorate in political science (1937-1941) I came to adopt this vision of the political scientist as »scientist.« Although I was *privately* devoted to »history« and »literature« in their eminently humanistic and non-scientific aspects, the *public* person I pretended to be in at least one part of my doctoral dissertation was that of the methodologically sophisticated political *scientist*. As a student »majoring« in political science as it was taught before World War II, I was critical of the discipline's prevailing legalistic-deductive and historical-positivistic approaches and their methodological naiveté. Relying on just two contemporary expositions of what a *science of politics* might look like (Dimock 1937; Elliott 1931), I argued that »it is impossible to investigate concrete constitutional formations [like parliamentary government] without the aid of a pre-existing hypothetical concept of the object of inquiry.« I then propounded that »because political concepts, in order to achieve a certain degree of validity, must be fairly accurate reflections of real political processes, political theory finds itself in a sea of abstractions whenever it fails to refer constantly to empirical situations.« However, I added, this kind of concept must not be understood »as a copy of the real world, but merely a useful working basis for studying the empirical situation« (Eulau 1941, 85-86). *Und so weiter.* What was funny about this stance was that in the German *Gymnasium* I had attended before coming to the United States, the sciences proper, physics, chemistry and biology, were my least favorite subjects, while I did reasonably well in literature, history and geography – precisely the topics which, at least on the face of things, led me to the study of politics. I am not much given to psychologically eccentric and fungible interpretations of anybody's state of mind, but I can also not exclude the possibility that this »scientific« stance was in fact an attempt to prove (to myself, as I didn't tell anybody else about it) that I could »do science« as well as the next fellow. In psychologese it is called »reaction formation.«

Yet, the dissertation's pretentious title, *A Historical and Analytical Inquiry into the Theory of Parliamentarism,* revealed an unacknowledged ambivalence, at least not acknowledged at the time. The simplest and, in fact, most parsimonious explanation for my doing a »historical« as well as what I thought of as a »scientific« study was that the dissertation would not have been accepted without its historical component. This kind of opportunistic strategy is of course quite common in an environment like the university where »discipleship« is often the price paid for mentorship. But, again, this sort of explanation is too simple. The fact was (and still is) that I *do* like »historical« interpretations, if not explanations, of social phenomena. I think that exploring and writing about the origin and development of parliamentary theory in France, Germany and England from circa 1800 to 1870 had a profound influence on my later work in legislative research.[5]

All this does not explain, of course, why more than a century later European parliamentary theory as rooted in history ignited my scholarly interest on the West Coast of the United States. The story is quite straightforward. By the time I came to think about a dissertation, I had been in the United States barely four years. I was still much involved, at least intellectually and certainly emotionally, in the overthrow of the Weimar Republic whose parliament, with its unfortunate name, *Reichstag,* had been a parliamentary monstrosity. And, more immediately, there was the attempt of the young Spanish Republic to survive in a civil war that really symbolized the death of parliamentarism in that country. All other things equal, the primary weakness of both the Weimar Republic and Republican Spain had been that from the beginning their legislative institutions had been the playgrounds of a struggle for power among parties some of which, on the extreme Left and extreme Right, rejected the principal tenet of parliamentarism – the responsibility of the ministers to parliament and implicitly the institutionally-sanctioned circulation of the political elites. Though I was sitting in a library far away from the scene of action, my ears were ringing with slogans about the »crisis« of parliamentarism. These events were potent real-world stimuli for scholarly research on a topic which, in later jargon, would be labeled »relevant.« I cannot assert that these retrospective musings reflect the truly catalytic effect of my long-term interest in legislative institutions, but I can also not disprove this explanation. I cannot guarantee that my contemporary political biases did not affect the doctoral research, but I am reasonably certain that a bias in favor of the legislature as democracy's central institution was something that I recognized only many years later, though early enough to be discounted for what it is.

Ecological as Personal Knowledge

A scholar's bibliography is, unfortunately, not something like the portfolio of clues a white-collar thief leaves behind to be detected only upon the most careful discovery and scrutiny. Its items are there for all to see, even if their groundings in one or another personal pathway remain obscure if not revealed by the author.[6] As an example let me take a minor item in my own bibliography entitled »The Ecological Basis of Party Systems,« published in the late fifties (Eulau 1957). Whatever noble things I wrote about why I considered there to be a »problem« in how urban and rural environments impacted the fortunes of political parties and the competitiveness of the two-party system, how did it come about that this topic interested me?[7] There were a number of circumstances potentially biasing this research, but they were nowhere mentioned in the published report. The most direct incentive was an invitation by the Social Science Research Council to compete for a research grant in the broad field of comparative political studies focused on the American states. But this does not really explain why I chose the topic of the impact of urban-rural differentiation on the outcome of legislative elections rather than some other topic. I was living then (in the

1950s) in a small village (population 3,000) in rural Ohio, after having previously spent over six years in the metropolitan cities of Washington, D.C. and New York City. The transfer from these urban centers to Ohio's agricultural hinterland could have been something of a traumatic shock, enough to sensitize me to tensions I noted in the state's party politics, but it was not. Where, then, did this sensitivity come from? I must pick up a pathway that leads back to my childhood. I was born and, until I left Germany in 1934, lived in an industrial town, Offenbach-am-Main, (population then about 60,000). But I was frequently shuttled and, when old enough, often went on my own from this urban environment to a small rural town in Upper Hessia, Buedingen, where my parental grandmother still lived as did many other relatives. The Eulau family had been in agriculture or business related to agriculture (as cattle and grain merchants) from about 1800 on, until the fourth generation took off to the big cities nearby. But there never was a sharp break between the rural and urban members of the clan, and I grew up as a »rurbanite,« feeling equally at home in the two environments. And I learned very early that I could behave or had to behave quite differently in the (dangerous) urban and (untroubled) rural contexts. Hence the transfer from the urban East Coast to the rural Midwest was less disturbing than might have been expected, and I brought to my observation of Ohio state legislative elections in the years I lived there (1947-1957) a disinterested perspective which I think was not unrelated to the relevant pathway I have reconstructed. The article itself gives no inkling of this »understanding.«[8]

An Ultimate Root

I must now make clear why the 1969 conference at Iowa and, especially, my encounters there with Peter Gerlich and Mogens N. Pedersen were particularly enjoyable to me personally, but not simply for the obvious reason I mentioned in the opening paragraph of this chapter. Nor is it due to the fact that Mogens delivered a splendid chapter later published under the title »Lawyers in Politics: The Danish Folketing and United States Legislatures« (Pedersen 1972), or that Peter Gerlich presented a paper on »Orientations to Decision-Making in the Vienna City Council« (Gerlich 1972). Of course, both papers were of personal interest to me. Mogens' paper took off from and, by way of comparison of the American and Danish cases, extended some research on lawyer-legislators I had published some years earlier (Eulau & Sprague 1964). Peter's paper, in turn, was an application of role analysis as originally formulated in a research project on four American states in which I had participated (Wahlke et al 1962). It was also influenced by an American project on city councils which I had begun at just about the time the Vienna study was in its planning stage (see Eulau & Prewitt 1973).

All this is true enough, but the reason for my screening out Pedersen's and Gerlich's papers is not strictly »scientific.« I mention them because in making a »great leap forward« from circa 1940 (when I wrote my doctoral thesis) to circa 1970, I want to suggest that PPP on scientific discovery does not implicate either some sort of logical or chrono-logical process. Rather, PPP is triggered whenever it is relevant, whatever the order of things in historical time. Past, present and future merge into a continuum without beginning and without end. Mentally, infinite regression just as infinite progression is possible. Unlike in the story teller's story which must have a beginning and an end, in PPP where one begins or ends varies depending on what one *discovers* to be germane.

Now, back in 1969, Mogens may have thought that I came to the study of lawyers in politics and the theory of »professional convergence« featured there because lawyers constitute what John Dewey, the philosopher, would have called a »problematic situation« in the real world. As scholars and other cognoscenti know, lawyers are highly overrepresented in the world's legislative bodies where they play an eminent role by virtue of their legal expertise. They are worthy of social-scientific investigation because one suspects that »legal minds« are poor instruments of *vox populi*. There was certainly nothing in the text of *Lawyers in Politics* to suggest that it was interlarded with »personal knowledge« in Polanyi's sense. And Peter may have thought that centering the 1964-65 Vienna seminar in an empirical study of the city's *Gemeinderat* (which simultaneously functions as a *Landtag*) was ordained (scientifically, not divinely) by my having recently completed a comparative study of state legislatures in the United States, and by being currently involved in the massive study of over 90 city councils. Of course, these »models« were there and undoubtedly propelled the Pedersen and Gerlich explorations and extensions, thereby making significant contributions to the comparative study of legislatures. In this respect, then, they were evidence of Kuhn's view of how scientists normally proceed as members of a community of scholars. But what Mogens and Peter did not know, and what only I »knew« at the time, though without the benefit of PPP, was that all of these studies – involving lawyers, legislators and lawyer-legislators – were deeply anchored in several of my own pathways (including, of course, my formal education and concerns as a citizen).

When I first thought of the lawyers-in-politics project and interested John Sprague to join me, the fact of my father having been not only a lawyer but also, at least for a time, a politician, was only a vague glimmer in my memory.

Even assuming that some latent comprehension was going on, as the research was a collaborative affair, any mention of personal knowledge stemming from paternal influence would have been quite unseemly. As a result, neither introduction nor footnotes nor methodological appendix gives the slightest inkling of the nexus between the senior investigator's potential personal knowledge and the object of the investigation. I cannot say whether at some lower level of consciousness this nexus may have motivated me and driven or enlightened the investigation. Whatever objections to the theory of »professional convergence« were or could be raised in critiques of the published research, nobody could even remotely charge me with personal bias in suggesting that lawyers often do things that politicians do, and vice versa. It would have been interesting to know what reception the research might have been if its being rooted in a personal pathway had been disclosed in accordance with PPP as part of its methodological baggage. Alas, this we will never know.

I can also not tell how my many collaborators on the San Francisco Bay City Council Project or Peter Gerlich (and his Austrian collaborator, Helmut Kramer)[9] would have reacted if I had told them that in picking city councils as research sites I was perhaps something less than the totally disinterested observer as fantasized in scientific lore. As I have found out only recently from surviving documents, my father was not just an ordinary attorney but also a town councillor in Offenbach-am-Main (where I was born) and evidently a hyperactive politico, belonging to the city council's educational committee, law and finance committee, a development commission, a sociopolitical commission as well as the presidency of the *Stadtbad* (the public, city-owned swimming pool).[10] Now, I'm not about to propose that my interest in city councils was genetically driven as my father was a member of his city's local council at the very time when I was biologically conceived and magically delivered as a prospective student of legislative institutions. Yet, even though I (or my younger brother) cannot recall any conversation with my father about it, I cannot get away (today, as I write) from the idea that many years later my »knowing« about his legislative career may have made for a dormant research agenda which had something to do with my manifest research interests. Again, I can only speculate about the relevance of these disclosures for the scientific work I was involved in. I have a very strong hunch, however, that my *professing* to be a legislative scholar might have been quite different if I had not been *called* by one of my particular pathways to be what I became. As I look back, I can only concede that I have always valued, in the normative sense, the legislative-electoral over the executive and judicial branches of government. What better explanation is there for this bias than to seek it in a pathway? Though how it may have biased my work on lawyers and legislators, and the work of those who leaned on and extended it, is for others to say.

Notes

1. The emergence of the Iowa-based CLRC was due to the happy circumstance that the University's Department of Political Science had become the home of a small cadre of legislative scholars whose research interests spanned several levels of organizational complexity – national, state and local – and, even more importantly, diverse geographical arenas. This made *comparison* across levels and arenas emblematic of both the Center's and, later, the *LSQ's* mission. The most notable members of this group were John C. Wahlke, with whom I had labored for many years in the first genuinely comparative study of four American state legislatures; Gerhard Loewenberg, originally the author of a splendid study of a single legislature, the German Bundestag, but later a geographically wide-ranging author and devote impresario of the *LSQ*; Samuel C. Patterson whose appetite for understanding legislative things small and large has been insatiable and who, with Malcolm E. Jewell – the *LSQ's* first editor and continuing faithful associate – has been the author of a for many years leading textbook that was broadly comparative and creatively analytic; Joel D. Barkan, primarily an Africanist, and Chong Lim Kim, primarily an East Asia specialist, both interested in studying legislative developments in their areas of special competence but in a comparative perspective; and G.R. Boynton who brought methodological sophistication to the enterprise.
2. A National Science Foundation grant made it possible to bring in a number of scholars from abroad. Among the better known were Norway's Henry Valen, Finland's Pertti Pesonon, the Netherlands' Hans Daalder and France's Mattei Dogan. For a compilation of the conference papers, see Patterson & Wahlke, eds., 1972.
3. I am limiting myself to American works exclusively. See Simon 1991; or Bendix 1986.
4. In my book, *Micro-Macro Dilemmas in Political Science* (1996), I elaborated PPP at some length and applied it to the methodological problems of aggregation and disaggregation, wholes and parts, and so on.
5. Fortunately, no journal would publish my »scientific« exposition of parliamentarism. A summary of the historical part was almost immediately accepted and published (Eulau 1942).
6. However, I have seen some scholarly bibliographies that, for one reason or another, omit items. This happens when an item is deemed sufficiently embarrassing by an author to be jettisoned. I have myself engaged in this sort of honorable self-censorship. The rationale simply is, »Who cares?«
7. The »noble thing« I'm referring to here was expressed as follows: »A viable democratic political system, as any social system, has to meet certain internal-structural requisites that can be shown to be functional for achieving the goals of the system.« And so on. It is obvious that I was conceptualizing the »noble thing«

in terms of the then fashionable structural-functional mode of analysis – today a victim of a much-trodden contemporary pathway I shared with many others.
8. Although I use the word »understanding« here, let me emphasize that I am not using it in the sense in which Wilhelm Dilthey or Max Weber used it when they spoke of »verstehende Wissenschaft« as a mode of social analysis in conflict with the deductive-empirical method.
9. Kramer was also a member of the seminar at the Vienna Institute. See Gerlich & Kramer 1969, 7-8.
10. Archiv der Stadt Offenbach, Signatur 314, referenced in Werner 1988 (vol. 2, 225).

References

Bendix, Reinhard (1986). *From Berlin to Berkeley,* New Brunswick, N.J.: Transaction Publishers.
Dimock, Marshall E. (1937). »Scientific Method and the Future of Political Science,« in *Essays in Political Science in Honor of Westel Woodbury Willoughby,* Baltimore: Johns Hopkins University Press.
Elliott, William Y. (1931). »The Possibility of a Science of Politics: With Special Attention to the Methods Suggested by William B. Munro and George G. Catlin,« in Stuart Rice (ed.), *Methods in Social Science, A Case Book,* Chicago: University of Chicago Press.
Eulau, Heinz (1941). *A Historical and Analytical Inquiry into the Theory of Parliamentarism.* Ph.D. Dissertation, Berkeley, Ca.: University of California.
Eulau, Heinz (1942). »Early Theories of Parliamentarism,« *Canadian Journal of Economics and Political Science* 8, pp. 33-55.
Eulau, Heinz (1957). »The Ecological Basis of Party Systems: The Case of Ohio,« *Midwest Journal of Political Science* 1, pp.125-35.
Eulau, Heinz (1959). »Political Science,« in B.F. Hoselitz (ed.), *A Reader's Guide to the Social Sciences,* Glencoe, Ill.: Free Press.
Eulau, Heinz (1962). »Segments of Political Science Must Susceptible to Behavioristic Treatment,« in J.C. Charlesworth (ed.), *The Limits of Behavioralism in Political Science,* Philadelphia: American Academy of Political and Social Science.
Eulau, Heinz (1981). »Foreword: On Revolutions That Never Were,« in S.L. Long (ed.), *The Handbook of Political Behavior,* New York: Plenum.
Eulau, Heinz (1996). *Micro-Macro Dilemmas in Political Science: Personal Pathways Through Complexity,* Norman: University of Oklahoma Press.
Eulau, Heinz & Kenneth Prewitt (1973). *Labyrinths of Democracy: Adaptations, Linkages, Representation, and Policies in Urban Politics,* Indianapolis: Bobbs-Merrill.
Eulau, Heinz & John D. Sprague (1964). *Lawyers in Politics: A Study in Professional Convergence,* Indianapolis: Bobbs-Merrill.
Gerlich, Peter (1972). »Orientations to Decision-Making in the Vienna City Council,« in Samuel C. Pattterson & John C. Wahlke (eds.), *Comparative Legislative Behavior: Frontiers of Research,* New York: John Wiley & Sons.

Gerlich, Peter & Helmut Kramer (1969). *Abgeordnete in der Parteiendemokratie,* Wien: Verlag für Geschichte und Politik.

Hughes, Everett C. (1958). *Men and Their Work,* Glencoe, Ill.: Free Press.

Kuhn, Thomas S. (1962). *The Structure of Scientific Revolutions,* Chicago: University of Chicago Press.

Patterson, Samuel C. & John C. Wahlke, eds. (1972). *Comparative Legislative Behavior: Frontiers of Research,* New York: John Wiley & Sons.

Pedersen, Mogens N. (1972). »Lawyers in Politics: The Danish Folketing and United States Legislatures,« in Samuel C. Patterson & John C. Wahlke (eds.), *Comparative Legislative Behavior: Frontiers of Research,* New York: John Wiley & Sons.

Polanyi, Michael (1958). *Personal Knowledge,* Chicago: University of Chicago Press.

Simon, Herbert A. (1991). *Models of My Life,* New York: Basic Books.

Truman, David B. (1955). »The Impact on Political Science of the Revolution in the Behavioral Sciences,« in *Research Frontiers in Politics and Government,* Washington, D.C.: Brookings Institution.

Wahlke, John C., Heinz Eulau, William Buchanan & LeRoy. C. Ferguson (1962). *The Legislative System: Explorations in Legislative Behavior,* New York: John Wiley & Sons.

Werner, Klaus (1990). »Offenbacher Juden in Politik und öffentlichen Leben der Weimarer Republik,« in *Zur Geschichte der Juden in Offenbach am Main.* Band 2: *Von den Anfängen bis zum Ende der Weimarer Republik,* Offenbach am Main: Magistrat der Stadt.

European Union Regional Policy – Not So Inclusive?[1]

Mike Goldsmith

Abstract

This chapter examines social inclusion within the European Union, both in the context of EU decision making and more specifically in that of regional policy. It begins with an examination of three models of decision making within the EU. It first considers the EU as a state centred organisation, in which nation states are predominant, as with de Gaulle's Europe de Patries. It then considers the EU as a contested hierarchy, more akin to Delors' Europe of the Regions. Finally, it looks at the EU as an example of multi-level governance or a Europe with the Regions.

The chapter then continues with a review of the different meanings that can be given to the phrase social inclusion, reflecting three lines of policy debate within the Union. What follows is a review of EU regional policy, its operation and the pressures for change that it has faced recently. The chapter concludes that much of regional policy has been concerned with economic development rather than explicitly with social inclusion, despite the objective of regional policy being one which seeks to narrow the gap between richest and poorest parts of the EU. It goes further in suggesting that the pressures for change on regional policy means that it is less likely to reduce social exclusion in future, and that the main opportunities for dealing with problems of exclusion will continue to lie in regulation policies rather than in any likely extensions of welfare or of citizen rights within the EU.

Introduction

This brief essay considers issues of social inclusion within the context of European Union decision making and especially in the context of European regional policy. Whilst such a policy has been interpreted as a means by which integration within the EU could be improved, this paper will argue that it has been less successful in terms of reducing social exclusion within the EU, and that such exclusion is likely to be widened rather than reduced when the EU finally expands towards central and eastern Europe in the next Millennium. But such expansion is not the only feature of the EU which supports such an argument. Studies (Cheshire 1990; Cheshire *et al.* 1992; Cheshire 1995) show that there has been relatively little change in the hierarchy of EU regions and cities over the last twenty to thirty years, despite the EU emphasis on policies and programmes designed to redress the balance between the richest and poorest regions.

Furthermore, other studies (see inter alia Harding *et al.* 1994; Urban Studies 1998a; 1998b) also reveal increasing social polarisation occurring in most major urban centres across Europe. Cities are becoming increasingly divisive, with a widening gap between the rich and the poor. All of this suggests that the processes of social exclusion are likely to increase before they decrease.

Decision Making in the European Union

Since its inception, decision making in the European Union has been characterised in a variety of ways, changing as the Union and its institutions have developed. Remembering that the Union is a treaty based organisation – as distinct to a federal or confederal system such as the United States – it is first and foremost a *state centred* organisation, in which the member states are at the centre of the decision making process. Hence decisions on policies and programmes, on levels of finance etc, come to be ratified at the periodic meetings of the Council of Ministers, at which heads of state have frequently negotiated different terms to those originally proposed by the Commission, or negotiated opt out arrangements (the UK over the Social Charter, for example), or achieved specific deals (the famous occasion on which Margaret Thatcher secured the British budget rebate, for example), or exercised a veto on proposals. Whilst such actions have become more difficult with the introduction of Qualified Majority Voting on a number of EU areas, it is still the case that nation states and their governments play a major role in the EU decision making process.

As such under this model European integration can be perceived as an international regime, designed by sovereign states, who seek to regulate the development of economic and political interdependence through a process of international collaboration. Change comes about incrementally, with more significant changes brought about through a succession of new Treaties, such as those agreed at Maastricht in 1992 and Amsterdam in 1997. For those who argue that the EU conforms to such a model, control remains vested in dominant units (nation states), and changes depend on voluntary cooperation and bargaining between powerful member states (Hoffman 1982). As writers such as Hooghe (1996a, 177) suggest, decision making in this model is essentially elitist, closed, opaque and not readily accountable – and we have a Gaullist »Europe de Patries« rather than some other form of arrangement.

The second model, more prevalent in the 1990s[2], is essentially the supranational model, closest to the one propounded by the advocates of a federal Europe. In essence it found its strongest advocate in Jacques Delors, who thought of the EU as having a strong supranational core (i.e., the Commission)[3] working with weakened nation states and a strengthened, but fragmented, regional periphery. This model is Delors' Europe of the Regions writ large. Effectively such a model would give rise to a contested hierarchy, since the regions compete with each other and with the nation states over territorial representation. The Commission – as the supranational body – during the nineties tended to be on the side of the sub-national level, which it has sought to mobilise on a functional basis around a series of specific European-wide policy issues (Tommel 1998) – see for example the development of widespread functional and territorial networks which have both been established and encouraged to grow by the various Commission directorates – especially on regional, environmental, innovation/technology and information society issues.[4] In turn these networks target such institutions as the Commission and the European Parliament in seeking support for new initiatives as well as funding from existing EU programmes, leading to a kind of by-passing of the nation state, even though the latter remain the most important actors in the game. Decision making in this model is likely to be much more pluralistic and competitive, somewhat more open and accessible, but no more accountable than the elitist style described earlier.

More recent thinking[5] is to see the European Union as a system of multi-level governance, not so much as a Europe *of* the Regions as a Europe *with* the Regions. But it is not only the Commission, Parliament and regions who are involved, but national and local levels as well. The result is a system of decision making in which there are multiple access points, multiple opportunities to exercise influence and pressure and multiple places at which decisions are made. The result is extensive sub-national mobilisation, including non-governmental organisations (NGOs), as various actors/levels seek to play grantsmanship style games, and in which there is no predominant territorial principle. The result is a pattern of uneven development and distribution of resources and a system in which decision making is what Hooghe (1996a, 179) calls »pluralist with an elitist bias« in that only actors with valuable resources can effectively participate. Nation states are no longer able to act as gatekeepers, able to close off the European agenda and political arena. On the other hand, multi-level governance does not imply a level playing field for all participants – some actors are more skilful, have more resources, or understand and play the game better than others.

Social Inclusion

At this point we must turn to a consideration of issues relating to social inclusion and social exclusion. To begin with what does social inclusion mean? To quote Padraig Flynn, lately Commissioner Responsible for Employment, Industrial Relations and Social Affairs (DG V):

> social inclusion means that every person in society has the possibility to participate in that society[6]...

However much of a motherhood statement that may sound, this »possibility of participation« has been associated within the EU with three lines of policy debate.[7] The first of these centres around what it means to be a citizen of Europe – or rather of the EU. In this debate »participation« is achieved by individuals exercising their »citizen rights«, including social rights, and other matters such as mobility and equality. Despite the Schengen agreement on mobility and the abolition of passport controls at borders, citizenship in this context has largely been determined in terms of membership of nation states, in the sense that those born in member states acquire both national and European (EU) citizenship, whilst others (guest workers/immigrants) are excluded.

The second line of policy debate is based on what I will call welfarism/welfarist issues. The essence here is how far the basic pattern of welfare associated with the Northern European welfare states can and should be extended throughout Europe (Groes *et al.* 1994). Developed very much as part of the social democratic consensus in the post war 2 years, countries like Sweden, Denmark, the Netherlands, Germany and Britain developed extensive education, housing, transport, social security and health care systems. Whilst the ability of these countries to maintain current and improved levels of provision is very much an issue for the present debate (Taylor-Gooby 1996), the general pattern of provision in these countries has been more universalistic, and with a greater stress of matters of equity and equality than is true for some Southern European countries, as Ferrara (1996) and Cousins (1998) have demonstrated. Ferrara (1996, 17) suggests that a number of common features exist in the welfare systems of countries such as Italy, Spain, Portugal and Greece and these set them apart from Northern Europe. First, income maintenance is based on a highly fragmented but corporatist system, »displaying a marked internal polarisation; peaks of generosity (e.g., pensions) accompanied by macroscopic gaps of protection« (Ferrara 1996, 17). Second, whilst health care is generally provided on a universal basis, there are variations in the extent to which health care is universally available in the different countries. Portugal for example retains a form of compulsory health care insurance which allows better off workers privileged access and conditions of care (Ferrara 1996, 23), whilst Greece is still further from a universal system - access to care is still largely mediated through occupational insurance schemes (Ferrara 1996, 24). Third, there remains a greater reliance on private and voluntary sector provision than would be the case in most of the Northern European countries, Britain possibly excepted – for example through the provisions made by Catholic institutions. Last, but by no means least, the persistence of clientelistic forms of politics and patronage in countries like Italy, Portugal, Spain and Greece simply means that access to welfare may be determined by factors other than need. For example, the influence of parties as »mass distributors of welfare« in Italy has been well documented (see inter alia Ferrara 1996, 25-27).

In part one explanation for the difference between the two sets of countries lies in the fact that ideas about social democratic welfare systems came late to Southern Europe, especially to the newer democracies which emerged in the late seventies and early eighties. But, as Northern Europeans know full well, universal welfare does not come cheap. The ability of states to provide extensive and improving welfare benefits depends on both an increasing GDP (as in the case of Norway for example), a willingness amongst tax payers to bear the costs in the form of high levels of taxation as well as a general political consensus, at least amongst voters, that such benefits are both desirable and necessary. Contrast this with experience in Sweden where the 1990s saw several major changes in the way in which welfare was provided as the country adopted policies more in tune with those associated with Thatcher and Reagan.

Within the European Union, however, there has really been little debate about extending the Northern model fully through the Union (Taylor-Gooby, 1996). Again this is largely because welfare has been seen as an issue for which national states are responsible or claim responsibility. In part this may also be because different conceptions of ideas about social inclusion/exclusion exist through the Union. For example, as Cousins (1998, 129-130) demonstrates the British have shown a persistent concern for the elimination of individual poverty whilst the French talk more of social exclusion as a »deficiency of solidarity« or a »break in the social fabric« (Cousins, op.cit. 129). Whilst this nation state focus might change in future, especially as changing demographics and the consequences of economic globalization make themselves felt, in the past and currently the notion of a European welfare system has not been high on the EU agenda.

This gives rise to a third policy debate about how EU institutions might deal with problems of social inclusion and in practice the method by which the Commission has extended its influence over matters of social inclusion, namely through a process of social regulation. Under a process of social regulation, inclusion is extended through regulatory measures which are designed to change behaviour – of individuals, organisations, businesses etc. – or are used to improve the conditions of the most disadvantaged. One example of such a regulation is the European Working Week Directive which limits the number of hours people are supposed to work in any seven days.

It would be true to say that up until the beginning of the 1990s and beyond, in so far as there has been an European social policy, it is this latter approach which has generally been associated with it.[8] Notwithstanding the introduction of the Social Charter and the changes produced by the Amsterdam Treaty, it seems to me that this social regulation approach is likely to remain the main thrust of European social policy in the future.

In other words the EU has not really penetrated the social policy agenda. This result is, as Cram (1993) notes, both surprising on one extreme – the Rome Treaty's Title 3 is devoted to social policy, and equally surprising at another extreme that there is any social policy at all. In addition to the reason already given – that the state centred model of the EU would see social policy very much as the responsibility of nation states, thus limiting EU intrusion into this area – it is possible to suggest why the EU, via the Commission, has become involved and in the way it has.

Given that within the EU network of institutions the power to initiate proposals and also to regulate largely lies with the Commission, it is hardly surprising, given what we know about organisations and bureaucracies, that the Commission has sought to extend its sphere of influence as the EU has developed. In particular, under the strong leadership of President Delors, the Commission sought successfully to push the EU project forward on a number of fronts, with the creation of the Single European Market being a major success.

But expansion of activity through the more backdoor and less visible method of regulation has also increased the Commission's influence. As Cram (1993;1997) and Majone (1996) both point out, such expansion is all the more likely to occur if the cost of regulation can be off-loaded on agencies and actors other than national governments, for example on to industry, local governments or the voluntary sector in some way. Thus, for example, it tends to be sub-national agencies who bear the brunt of enforcement costs for consumer protection enforcement and industry who bear the costs of implementing some aspects of the Social Charter or of the Working Week Directive. One familiar mechanism, well analysed by Cram (1993; 1997), by which social regulation has been achieved is the health and safety regulations and directives which fall most heavily on industry, but do help improve the conditions of those in work. Such regulations and directives can have even more force if they are backed up by European Court of Justice decisions when cases eventually come to that level, but it also has to be said that failure to implement such regulations properly occurs more frequently than one might wish. Furthermore, the capacity of the Commission to police these matters is extremely limited, so allowing firms and individuals to avoid compliance – indeed at the heart of the resignation of the Commissioners in March 1999 was the inability or unwillingness of Commissioners to police their own affairs properly.

By the late eighties and early nineties, as the extent of social exclusion within the EU became more apparent, it rose higher up the Commission agenda. It was asked to become more heavily involved, especially at Amsterdam where employment creation was given highest priority. But despite this change, the approach to problems of social inclusion/exclusion within the EU have, I would maintain, been limited and largely designed to support the macro economic strategy of developing and introducing the Single Market. Where initiatives have been taken, other than those of a regulatory nature, they have been largely of the pilot variety (Quartiers en Crises for example), or concerned with »state of the (national) art« studies, or concerned with network building (e.g., building up pan EU networks of NGOs), agenda raising (the creation of the Social Policy Forum) or designed to lead to »exchange of experience.«[9] This is not to say that in particular regions or cities such developments do not achieve some beneficial results. On the contrary they frequently do – the problem has been to turn the successes into policy and practice on a wider scale. For example a recent call for a bid from DGV centred on activities »improving knowledge of current experience in tackling social exclusion«; exchanging experience on promoting social inclusion; promoting networking amongst NGOs on best practice and on "civil dialogue" on tackling exclusion (EU 1998). The overall result is that the Commission and the EU remain heavily reliant on strategies of social regulation to improve social inclusiveness rather than on programmes designed to bring about redistribution. One policy area where this has not been the case, however, has been regional policy, and it is to this I wish to turn.

EU Regional Policy and Social Inclusion

EU regional policy has probably attracted more research attention than any other in the general field of EU studies in recent years (see inter alia Jeffrey 1996; Jones & Keating 1995; Rhodes 1995; Hooghe 1996b; Goldsmith & Klausen 1997; Balme 1996). But most of this work concentrates on economic development aspects of policy rather than on social inclusion. For our purposes here, I do not wish to do anything more than draw on some elements of this work.

Broadly defined, EU regional policy is also a mechanism for aiding social inclusion. It is also a policy for redistribution, in that it has largely been designed to help narrow the gap between the poorest and richest regions within the European Union. Using what are known as the structural funds (ERDF and ESF) regional policy is at best a »compensation for acknowledged losers from the market integration process.« (Hooghe 1996b, 5), though it has never had the same status as the policy concerned to promote the single market itself. Whilst some successes might be claimed, for example in Ireland (Laffan 1996; Coyle 1997) and Catalonia in Spain (Morate & Munoz 1996), overall the structural funds have not significantly narrowed the gap between the declining (socially excluded) periphery and the richer core (Cheshire 1990; 1991; 1995). At its best regional policy has slowed the processes of social exclusion. It has certainly helped develop institutional partnerships and build networks linked to the European Union and its institutions (see inter alia Hooghe 1996b; Jeffrey 1996).

What is interesting for our purposes here is the way in which the focus of regional policy has changed; how the area has been colonised by a wide range of actors, and how these actors vary in their ability to exploit the different possibilities offered. A further interesting dimension to explore is the way in which the Commission and its various directorates have operated, and finally to consider how the level of activity under regional policy is at least partially threatened, except for Objective 1 regions, and is certainly likely to change after the Millennium as the EU expands to the East.

The initial use of the structural funds was very much infrastructure and input orientated. The period under what was known as Delors 1, covering the period between 1988 and 1994, saw both Objective 1 and Objective 2 regions investing EU structural funds in a large number of infrastructure projects – buildings designed to attract inward investment; regeneration of disused coal and steel plants or vacated docklands, and improved transportation routes – better roads, trains etc. Between 1994-99, over which time what was known as Delors 2 has been in operation, the use of the funds has become much more output orientated, with an emphasis on new firm creation; help to small and medium enterprises (SMEs) and on the number of jobs created. Certainly as the Commission, and especially DGXVI responsible for regional policy, has improved its monitoring capacity and has increased awareness about other possibilities for improving regional competitiveness, the policy emphasis has shifted much more towards a process and output orientation. And following Amsterdam, the emphasis has become more people (or at least jobs, innovation and training) orientated, a trend which one would expect to continue after 2000.

Over this period the size of the funds has increased up to 27.4 billion ECU in 1999 from 7 billion in 1987, or a rise from 19% of the EU budget to 35%, making the structural fund the second largest item of expenditure under the EU budget. In addition, the proportion of population covered by the EU structural funds has reached around 50%, with the consequence that funds were less concentrated on the most heavily deprived areas than they had been before, notwithstanding the fact that Objective 1 regions were significant beneficiaries under the policy. In part this change was because, as with all EU policiy areas, each member state has to draw some benefits from the operation of the structural funds. Thus before reunification, Germany received very little from the structural funds, though since 1999 some of the former East German regions have been major beneficiaries.[10]

These structural funds are made up by two types – the regional develoment funds (ERDF) and the social fund (ESF). If ERDF has largely been infrastructure orientated, then one might have expected ESF to have been focused on direct measures to combat social exclusion. In practice, it has been used much more indirectly, focusing on post 16 education and training, and on cross-national mobility, especially of students. A minor part of the fund has also underpinned postgraduate training for unemployed graduates. The use of the fund to deal directly with social exclusion has been much more limited, largely concerned with pilot projects and exchange of experience. Certainly it has not been used to develop an explicit *urban social* policy even if cities have often been the major beneficiary. Nor has the use of ESF moved away from its largely training focus – again there has only been limited NGO activity and involvement, notwithstanding the emphasis given in the programme to *regional* partnerships as the basis on which it operates.[11]

Whilst most studies often report some of the major successful players in the EU structural funds game, what others show is that these regional and local actors respond to EU initiatives in a variety of ways (Goldsmith & Klausen 1997). Whilst eligibility for funds is the main determinant of who becomes involved, money is not the only determinant. Some regions and cities are simply *counter reactive* – basically uninterested in or even opposed to the European project. Politicians and bureacrats in these areas are often suspicious or sceptical about the Union or are isolated from Brussels. This group in practice contains quite large numbers of sub-national governments.

Others operate in a largely *passive* fashion – and comprise the largest category uncovered by Goldsmith and Klausen (1997, 239). They learn about the work of the EU by accident rather than design, having little more than a postbox with which to deal with European affairs. There is little political or bureaucratic commitment to or involvement with European matters over and above that required by law. At best such regions and cities can most accurately be described as making »an incremental adjustment to Europe.« (Goldsmith & Klausen 1997, 240). Politicians and paid officials in such areas are likely to think they are too small to be involved with Europe, or that they had better wait and see what happens. At best such passive authorities are adjusting gradually and reluctantly to change in Europe.

The third group identifed by Goldsmith and Klausen is what they would call *reactive* municipalities and regions. As such they demonstrate a positive interest in European matters, but they are followers rather than leaders. Slowly taking or joining initiatives, collaborating with other local governents and regions, or joining some existing European network. Importantly, they learn from others, and their politicians and bureaucrats are both aware of »the need to internationalise and to orientate themselves towards Europe, even if they are unsure of how to do it.« (Goldsmith & Klausen 1997, 240). But as such they remain unsure about the European game in which they have become involved and are not yet accomplished at the bidding operation which lies at the heart of European grantsmanship.

The last category are what Balme and Le Gales (1997, 146) call »bright stars«, the *proactive* cities and regions at the heart and soul of the European regional policy arena. It is this group which frequently attracts attention, and includes such regions as Nord Pas-de-Calais; South Wales, Catelonia, Nord Rhine Westfalen, Sachsen Anhalt, or cities such as Barcelona, Birmingham, Lyon and Montpellier amongst others. They have strong political leadership, and the »necessary bureaucratic and political infrastructure for them not only to win in the grantsmanship stakes, but also to have a view of how those stakes could be changed to their advantage.« (Goldsmith & Klausen 1997, 241). They are likely to belong to such well-established European networks and lobbying groups as RETI and Eurocities, or to the Association of European Regions, with their leaders playing a key role in the Committee of the Regions – the formal consultative body established by the Commission following the Maastricht treaty with its emphasis on subsidiarity. These politicians and their attendant paid officials are at home on the European stage, working well with the European Parliament and more frequently with Commissioners and Directorate staff. In ever increasing numbers they have established or share a Brussels office, which »acts as a listening post in the corridors of Brussels, as an information channel to feed comments and data to the Commission, and likely to include someone who can perform as a lobbyist over the table in the Brussels eateries.« (Goldsmith & Klausen 1997, 242). Thus for example all the German Länder have such offices, as do the two Brussels regions (from which they effectively conduct their foreign policies), and Scotland and Wales. Cities like Birmingham, Manchester, Montpellier, Barcelona and Seville also have similar offices.

It is these regions and cities who lead the process of European integration from below, who give meaning to the term subsidiarity, and who effectively make the European Union the system of multi-level governance – a Europe with the Regions – it has become. But the diversity of participants, together with different eligibility for assistance and varying skills at playing the game, add to the process of exclusion within Europe, rather than reducing it.

Partly because of this, and notwithstanding the EU 1997 report on social and economic cohesion, regional policy and funding are under pressure. Post Delors nation states have pushed to re-establish their place at the centre of European decision making. By basically rejecting deepening the Union in favour of widening it by a process of expansion to central and eastern Europe at Amsterdam and at the same time setting limits to the EU budget, member states have ensured that regional policy must change. 1999 will see the final setting of funds post 2000. Fewer regions and cities will benefit. Whilst Objective 1 regions will continue to receive substantial aid, there will be fewer Objective 2 regions, and aid will be more clearly targeted within them.

Hooghe (1998, 462-467) sees regional policy as being under four different pressures. First, there is pressure from proponents of neo-liberalist economics. She believes that regional policy is a form of regulated capitalism, and as such has been the bedrock against change of neo-liberalist orientation. In this sense cohesion policy, of which regional policy is the mainstay, distorts market competition. Thus, for those who believe that the market should rule regional policy is something that should be changed or avoided if at all possible. However, given the current political disposition of both the European Parliament and most EU national governments (in that the majority are under the control of social democratic countries), moves towards a more market orientated European economy seem unlikely, notwithstanding the clear differences between leaders such as Blair on the one hand and Jospin and Schröder on the other. A bigger threat to regional policy is expansion to the east of Europe, bringing in countries who are as poor if not poorer than current peripheral members. New members will expect significant help in integrating their economies into the EU system. Within a fixed budget, which current member states have indicated they wish to maintain, such expenditure can only be met by cutting back existing programmes, as current debates over the British rebate and the Common Agricultural Policy indicate. Regional policy cannot expect to escape. Only in so far as such changes further the Single European Market can they be regarded as neo-liberal.

The second pressure which Hooghe suggests is threatening regional policy is national assertiveness. At one level this is a reflection of the re-assertion of the state centred model in the post Delors era, whilst on the other the balance between beneficiaries and contributors has changed over the years. The southern states, for whom regional policy was largely designed and who have been the major beneficiaries, seem, in Hooghe's terms (1998, 463) »in a weaker position to demand side-payments than in 1988 or 1993«.

The third pressure comes because national governments are under some budgetary pressure themselves, especially from increasing welfare costs associated with rising or persistent unemployment, as well as from rapidly rising health care costs and the need to support and care for aging populations. If national governments face budgetary pressures, they will certainly seek to limit the size of EU expenditure...with consequences for regional programmes and expenditure.

National governments are also likely to exert pressure because operational principles such as subsidiarity and partnership have allowed other actors, especially sub-national governments a more legitimate role within the European decision making system. At the same time this development has undermined the traditional role of national governments within that system, namely that of gatekeepers able to control access to decisions and funds.

The last pressure suggested by Hooghe is that of policy dysfunctionality. Two arguments are employed here. First, that regional policy, far from reducing inequalities, has in fact increased them, both within and between regions. If this is indeed so then it is not a very efficient way of solving the problem of regional disparity, especially as it acts in rather an indiscriminatory way. Furthermore, as with other aspects of some EU policies, benefits from regional policy are expected to trickle down. Such an approach is slow and does not necessarily benefit all – in other words the policy may again increase rather than decrease social exclusion.

The second argument concerns the mode of operation for the policy, namely the partnership principle. Critics point out that it is laborious to administer, taking time to establish – and even when established partnerships may well be symbolic rather than real. They are also vulnerable to clientelism and possible corruption, which as events have shown is difficult to track and monitor. Furthermore, add the critics, the relationship between growth and partnership may well be spurious – in that the fastest growing regions have generally received little or no EU aid.

As a result these pressures pose choices for EU decisions makers, with different outcomes being dependent on the nature of the decision making process. Following Hooghe (1998), the results in each area might be as follows. In terms of the budget the choice is between consolidation or cuts. The likely outcome is that there will be budget cuts for regional programmes. The extent of the cuts again depends on the decision making process – likely to be larger if the state centrist approach applies, whilst a multi-level governance approach would help minimise cuts. Decisions on this are expected in 1999. The policy has been subject to heavy lobbying from those most likely to lose from changes, and signs are they have met with some limited success, even if it will not stop some regions from losing out quite heavily from the changes.

The second area of change is in the procedures or rules for allocating the funds. Currently structural funds reach some 50% of the EU population, with the consequence that the redistributive effect is weakened. It is clear that more targeting of funds is likely, even if the so-called »lagging behind« regions which have Objective 1 status will still do quite well. It is the former Objective 2 regions who will lose most heavily, since the status will only be given to those regions who face serious problems of economic and social conversion, though provision has initially been made to help wean such regions off their dependence on such funds – in effect a win for the multi-level governance approach. In addition regional policy is likely to have a new third objective or priority, designed to adapt and modernise national and EU policies for employment, education and training.

The final area subject to change concerns the rules which govern spending of monies. The introduction of partnership was a major EU institutional innovation arising from regional policy, bringing many more actors into the decision making process. It was expected to achieve a number of goals following the agreement on subsidiarity at Maastricht. For example the identification of common problems and the pooling of resources to deal with them was one objective, whilst allowing partners in effect to govern themselves was another (Heinelt 1996), strengthening sub-national actors and enhancing democracy a third. Critics, especially those in Northern Europe, would argue that partnership has fallen short on all these and, in so far as they want to change, they would prefer to see much more divided rather than shared responsibilities for expenditure, with each partner being accountable for what it does best. Against this, the strongest advocates for partnership tend to be those sub-national actors at loggerheads with their national authorities – as many British local governments were under the Conservative regimes of the eighties and early nineties (Hooghe 1998, 471; Marks *et al.* 1996).

In practice what is likely to be proposed is a simplified partnership model. Two reforms have been suggested in 1998. First, that partnerships be extended to bring in »social and economic partners on the ground« – that is to make partnerships more meaningful than they have been in many cases. Second, and in direct contrast, it is expected that there should be a clearer division of responsibilities between the different partners than exists at present.

An Inclusive Europe? The Consequences of Change

What are the likely consequences of changes such as those proposed for regional policy for the social inclusiveness of an expanded European Union? One has to admit that one does not feel particularly optimistic that the gap between the richest and poorest regions will be significantly narrowed – indeed it seems more likely to widen. One major change, however, has not been discussed so far – namely the placing of employment at the top of the EU agenda and at the centre of its strategies by the Council of Ministers in 1997. Four core themes can be identified at the centre of these strategies – employability, entrepreneurship, adaptability, and equal opportunities. The first three of these clearly fit a neo-liberal agenda, whilst equal opportunity (aimed at women) might be said to help the social inclusion agenda.[12] Thus moves in the direction currently proposed seem to be closer to a neo-liberal agenda than to that of regulated capitalism, with the consequence that social inclusion continues to be of a lower order of importance.

What is also clear is that the welfarist approach is still not high on the agenda, despite signs that issues such as health care are moving up on the agenda of the Commission and DGV in particular. Critics would argue that DGV has not been a particularly influential actor in the Commission and EU policy debates, with its Commissioner regarded as more affable than able, and that other directorates, such as DG13 with its information society agenda, and DG16, with some of its urban policy initiatives, have been more active in the attempts to deal with social exclusion directly. Notwithstanding the efforts of DGV to put a best face on the social policy debate, it has really met with little success beyond »widening and deepening the policy debate« (agenda building); »building networks with NGOs« (support building), and limited policy initiatives, such as its Action Plan for the free movement of workers and its Anti-Racialism Year. To make matters worse, as of June 1998, it would appear that even those NGO's who had received approval for specially targeted DGV projects have still to receive funding following an adverse European Court of Justice decision on the legality of these programmes!

By contrast, the new ESF programme continues to have neo-liberal themes at the centre of its four priorities – namely sustainable economic development; competitiveness and innovation, and employment (job creation) and human resources. Only equality of opportunity reflects any aspect of the social inclusion agenda. Job creation and training are likely to be the key measures and actions included – regulation of equality of opportunity in the job market, designed to increase female labour market participation, comes a poor third.

Not a lot of this agenda represents significant change. Social inclusion is still expected to »trickle down« from economic inclusion, which itself »trickles down« from economic development and improved competitiveness. Notwithstanding the possibility (remote?) that there may be room for some improvement if programmes are both better specified and targeted, or if the level of regulation increases and widens out further, the worst excesses of social exclusion will remain untreated at a general level. As a result wider issues of citizenship and social rights, increasing urgent problems of welfare follwing patterns of demographic change, and other issues of social inclusion (poverty, housing, racial discrimination, migrant rights) seem likely to continue receiving symbolic rather than real attention.

Notes

1. The author first met Mogens Pedersen in the 1980s as part of his ECPR activities. I came to know him better during the time spent together on the ECPR Executive Committee in the 1990s and during periodic visits and study leave spent at Odense University. This essay is in part a tribute to MNP's efforts in promoting European integration and social inclusion over the years – in some respects more successful than those of the EU itself.
2. See for example the writings of Haas (1968) and Sbraggia (1992).
3. This piece was written just before and during the wholesale resignation of the European Commission on March 16, 1999. The outcome of this débâcle seems that a strong Commission, led by a dominant European leader of the status of Delors, is unlikely to emerge again in the foreseeable future. Both the member states and the European Parliament are likely to use the opportunity presented by the downfall of the current set of Commissioners to improve their own position within the EU's institutional arrangements.
4. On these developments see inter alia Goldsmith and Klausen (1997).
5. See for example Marks, Schmitter et al. (1996): Hooghe (1996a; 1998).
6. Padraig Flynn, June 1998: Social Forum Chatline Report. WWW.
7. A fourth line concerns the debates initiated by Commissioner Bannerman in relation to the information society. Here it would seem that some of the weakness associated with the EU democratic deficit would be overcome by the use of appropriate information technologies.
8. A fourth approach, based on extending consumer ability to participate in the market place, so helping economic development as well as extending inclusion, also formed part of Delors strategy for the introduction of the Single Market. I am grateful to Robert Moores, University of Liverpool, for drawing thispoint to my attention. See also Hooghe L. (1996b): *Cohesion Policy and European Integration*, Oxford: Clarendon Press, pp. 5-6.
9. For a discussion of the role of NGOs in EU matters see inter alia Greenwood and Aspinall (1997); Marks and McAdam (1996).
10. Whilst undertaking work for another piece of research, the author was also told by an Objective 2 region in a relatively prosperous part of the EU that the regional authority would have difficulty spending its current allocation of funds and would not be able to spend the increased allocation it was expecting the following year! The allocations in question went some way to making up that country's share of the structural funds.
11. Though some individual NGOs are very capable of participating in such regional activities, if the experience of the author in some British partnership meetings is any guide, they are likely to be quite daunting occasions, often dominated by government and Commission officials speaking a technocratese unknown to the lay person,or else most of the decisions may well have been taken in smoke filled corridors and rooms from which the (largely female) lay NGO representatives might well have been excluded by their (predominantly male) local and regional government »part-ners«.

12. And if one accepts the arguments used by Delors for increasing employment as a means of raising both the numbers of consumers and the level of consumer activity, then, trickle down fashion, there might be a higher level of social inclusion – more people working and spending more, thus generating more jobs etc. However, this author is not convinced by this line of argument.

References

Internet Chat, European Social Policy Forum, June 1998.
Balme, R. (ed.) (1996). *Les Politiques du Neo-Regionalisme*, Paris: Economica.
Balme, R. & Le Gales (1997). »Stars and Black Holes: French Regions and Cities in the European Galaxy«, pp. 146-171, in M. Goldsmith & K.K. Klausen (eds.), *European Integration and Local Government*, Cheltenham: Edward Elgar.
Cheshire, P. (1990). »Explaining the Performance of the European community's Major European Regions«, *Urban Studies*, Vol. 22, pp. 311-333.
Cheshire, P., R.P. Camagni, J.-P. De Gaudenar & Roura J. Cuadrado (1992). »1957 to 1992: Moving Towards a Europe of Regions and Regional Policy«, pp. 268-300, in L. Rodwin & H. Sazanami (eds.), *Industrial Change and Regional Economic Transformation: The Experience of Western Europe*, London: Harper Collins.
Cheshire, P. (1995). »A New Phase of Urban Development in Europe«, *Urban Studies*, Vol. 32, pp. 1045-1063.
Cousins, C. (1998). »Social Exclusion in Europe«, *Policy and Politics*, Vol. 26, No. 2, pp. 127-145.
Coyle, C. (1997). »European Integration – A Lifeline for Irish Local Authorities?«, pp. 75-94, in M. Goldsmith & K.K. Klausen (eds), *European Integration and Local Government*, Cheltenham: Edward Elgar.
Cram, L. (1993). »Calling the Tune without Paying the Piper? Social policy regulation: the role of the Commission in European Community Social Policy«, *Policy and Politics*, Vol. 21, No. 2, pp. 135-146.
Cram, L. (1997). *Policy-making in the EU*, London: Routledge.
EU (1998). *ESF 2000: A guide to the new Structural Fund Regulations*, Brussels: EU.
Ferrara, M. (1996). »The 'Southern Model' of Welfare in Social Europe«, *Journal of European Social Policy*, Vol. 6, No. 1, pp.17-37.
Goldsmith, M. & K.K. Klausen (eds.) (1997). *European Integration and Local Government*, Cheltenham: Edward Elgar.
Greenwood, J. & M. Aspinwall (eds.) (1998). *Collective Action in the European Union*, London: Routledge.
Groes, N., M. Møller & E. Boll Hansen (1994). »To Have and Have Not«, pp. 57-66, in E. Boll Hansen (ed.), *Challenges to Local government in European Welfare Development*, Copenhagen: AKF.
Haas, E.B. (1968). *The Uniting of Europe*, Stanford: Stanford University Press.
Harding, A., J. Dawson, R. Evans & M. Parkinson (eds.) (1994). *European Cities Towards 2000*, Manchester: Manchester University Press.

Heinelt, H. (1996). »Multi-level governance in the European Union and the Structural Funds« pp. 9 - 25, in H. Heinelt & R. Smith (eds.), *Policy Networks and European Structural Funds*, Aldershot: Avebury.

Hoffman, S. (1982). »Reflections on the Nation State in Western Europe Today«, *Journal of Common Market Studies*, Vol. 20, pp. 21-37.

Hooghe, L. (1996a). »Subnational Mobilisation in the European Union«, *West European Politics*, Vol. 19, No. 2, pp.175-198.

Hooghe, L. (ed.) (1996b). *Cohesion Policy and European Integration*, Oxford: Clarendon Press.

Hooghe, L. (1998). »EU Cohesion Policy and Competing Models of European Capitalism«, *Journal of Common Market Studies*, Vol. 36, No. 4, pp. 457-77.

Jeffrey, C. (ed.) (1996). *The Regional Dimension of the European Union*, London: Frank Cass.

Jones, B. & M. Keating (eds.) (1995). *The European Union and the Regions*, Oxford: Oxford University Press.

Laffan, B. (1996). »Ireland: A Region without Regions: the Odd Man Out?«, pp. 320-341, in Hooghe (ed.) *Cohesion Policy and European Integration*, Oxford: Clarendon Press.

Majone, G. (ed.) (1996). *Regulating Europe*, London: Routledge.

Marks, G. & D. McAdam (1996). »Social Movements and the Changing Structure of Political Opportunity in the European Union«, *West European Politics*, Vol. 19, No. 2, pp. 249-278.

Marks, G., J. Salk, L. Ray & F. Nielsen (1996). »Competencies, Cracks and Conflict: Regional Mobilization in the European Union«, *Comparative Political Studies*, Vol. 29, No. 2, pp. 164-92.

Marks, G., F.W. Scharpf, P.C. Schmitter, & W. Streeck (1996). *Governance in the European Union*, London: Sage.

Morate, F. & X. Munoz (1996). »Vying for European Funds: Territorial Restructuring in Spain« pp. 195-218, in L. Hooghe (ed.), *Cohesion Policy and European Integration*, Oxford: Clarendon Press.

Rhodes, M. (ed.) (1995). *The Regions and the New Europe*, Manchester: Manchester University Press.

Sbraggia, A.M. (ed.) (1992). *Europolitics*, Washington: Brookings.

Taylor-Gooby, P. (1996). »Eurosclerosis in European Welfare States: regime theory and the dynamics of change«, *Policy and Politics*, Vol. 24, No. 2, pp. 109-124.

Tommel, I. (1998). »Transformation of Governance: The European Commission's strategy for creating a 'Europe of the Regions'«, *Regional and Federal Studies*, Vol. 8, No. 2, pp. 52-80.

Urban Studies (1998a). Special Issue on International Migration and Ethnic Segregation in Urban Areas, Vol. 35, No. 3.

Urban Studies (1998b). Special Issue on Ethnic Segregation in Cities, Vol. 35, No. 10.

Opinion Structures in Political Parties - The Law of Increasing Polarization?

Roger Buch Jensen

Abstract

In 1973 John D. May put forward the theory and empirical evidence behind the famous law of curvilinear disparity, which claims that opinion structures within political parties position voters as moderates; activists or sub-leaders as extremists; and politicians as trapped in the middle of the two groups, which exercise different but very important powers over the politicians: electoral success and nomination respectively. The analysis of three different attitudes: ideological self-placement, general fiscal attitudes and specific fiscal attitudes, provides no support for the law of curvilinear disparity. On the contrary there is a tendency towards increasing polarization. Differences of opinion among people who vote for different parties are much less than political disagreements between the local party chairmen of different parties or between politicians from different parties.

A classical element in the public as well as scientific debate about political parties is the question of parity or disparity in opinions between a party and the party's voters or members. The normative position underlying most of these debates is a claim saying that there ought to be a high degree of parity if democracy flourishes within the party or in society at large. But the most common empirical claim or observation is that there is a degree of disparity in opinions between the top and the bottom of parties no matter whether the bottom is defined as the rank-and-file members or as the voters.

One of the first to report this observation was Ostrogorski, who in the late 19th century wrote that »it is an almost general fact that the (local caucus) is more Radical than the mass of the party, more so even than the MP who has to submit to its demands.« (Ostrogorski, 1902/1964: 170).

Similar conclusions are found in Michels' study of the German Social Democratic party in the early 20th century. Party democracy is portrayed as a top-down system where the survival of the party and the interests of party leaders and the party bureaucracy becomes more important than the initial political goals of the party and its members, as well as party democracy. As an example Michels points to Engels foreword to Marx's »Die Klassenkämpfe in Frankreich 1848-49«, whose reformist political tone was later explained by Engels as the result of threats from anti-socialist legislation in Germany. In Michels' interpretation organizational survival became more important than the political ideals and goals set by the members (Michels, 1911/1962: 336).

Today the »old classics« in studies of opinion structures are often neglected because of a »modern classic«, John D. May's study from the early 1970s (May, 1973). May puts forward the theory of the so-called »special law of curvilinear disparity«, where the opinions of party leaders (politicians) are closer to the moderate opinions of voters rather than those of the sub-leaders -the party activists -who are more radical or pure in their opinions -which creates the curvilinear opinion structures as illustrated by Party 1 and Party 2 in Figure 1.

Figure 1. Illustration of May's special law of curvilinear disparity - example: idological self-placement on a left-right scale where 1 is very left-wing and 10 is very right-wing.

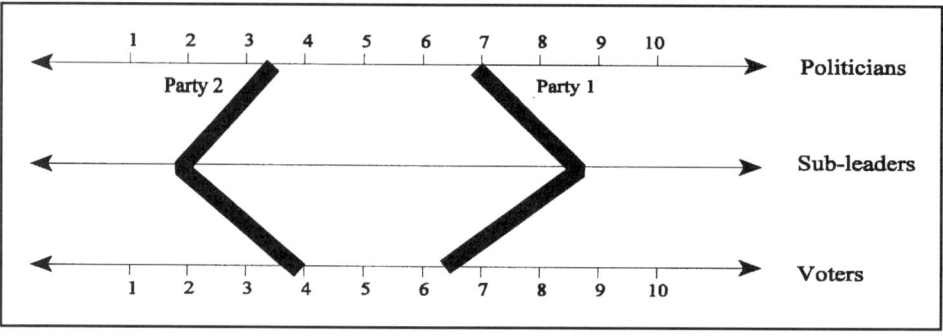

This opinions structure is in May's words »...the normal configuration of major or semi-major parties operating where overt, organized, electoral competition for governmental office is institutionalized.« (May, 1973: 139). This chapter will first examine whether these curvilinear opinion-structures can be found in Danish local politics and, secondly, discuss why this is not the case!

Opinion-structures in Danish local politics

In the early 1990s Danish local politics was studied intensively in the research project »Leadership in Local Politics« (Mouritzen, 1993). Three of the many data-sets generated by the project will be used to test the special law of curvilinear disparity. First, a postal survey with a sample of every fifth local politician in the 72 municipalities, which were selected so that they were representative of all the 275 Danish municipalities. 1,238 questionnaires were mailed and 912 (74 per cent) were returned. Second, a postal survey with the party chairmen of all local party organisations in the 72 selected municipalities. In all, 926 local organizations were included in the survey and 610 (66 percent) returned the questionnaire. Third, a survey involving 1,002 voters, carried out by the Gallup Institute in the form of personal interviews. These three surveys contained many questions about beliefs, values and attitudes to different aspects of democracy and local politics. The analysis below focuses on three aspects:

- Ideological self-placement on a right-left scale
- General fiscal attitudes
- Specific fiscal attitudes

Ideological self-placement on a right-left scale

In political science ideological self-placement serves as a rough gauge of individuals' political identity and almost all respondents were willing to answer the question about self-placement. May's special law of curvilinear disparity finds very little support in this respect, only the Social Democratic Party showed the expected pattern, with the local party chairmen as extremists. Conservative Party and Progress Party voters turned out to have the most extreme attitudes, while it is the politicians in the Liberal Party who are most extreme. The clearest tendency is that there are no tendencies! In some parties all three strata have a high degree of parity, while in other parties disparities are considerable; in some parties politicians are extremists, in others the party chairmen are most extreme, while others have voters as the most extreme stratum. It is impossible to talk of any kind of law of the structures of opinion, and this fact calls for a re-evaluation of the data with the focus not on each party, but instead on the party system as such.

  A second look at figure 2 shows a tendency to increasing polarization the higher the strata evaluated. Politicians had a range of 4.9 scale-points – from the politicians in the Socialist People's Party (2.7) to the Progress Party (7.6). The local party chairmen had a range of 4.3 scale-points – from party chairmen in the Socialist People's Party (2.8) to the Conservative Party (7.1), while the voters only had a range of 3.6 scale-points – from the Socialist People's Party voters (4.3) to the Progress Party (7.9). Whether this tendency towards increasing polarization is valid or not can only be concluded by reviewing other ways of gauging political attitudes.

Figure 2. Ideological self-placement of politicians, sub-leaders and voters in Danish parties, on a left-right scale where 1 is very left-wing and 10 is very right-wing.'

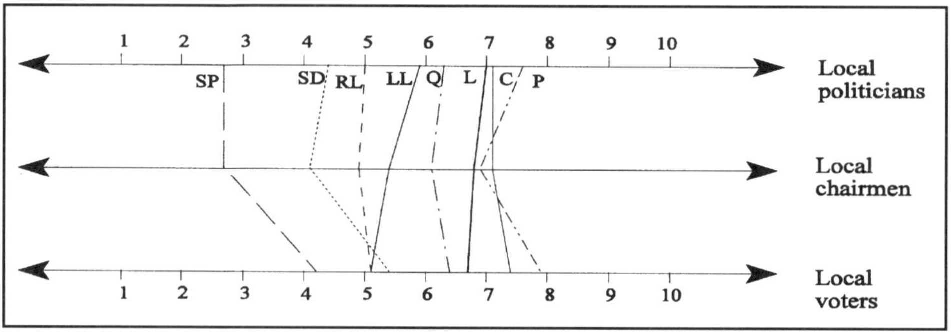

* C ' The Conservative Party, L ' The Liberal Party, LL ' Local Lists, P ' The Progress Party, Q ' The Christian People's Party, RL ' The Radical Liberals, SD ' The Social Democratic Party, SP ' The Socialist People's Party.

General fiscal attitudes

The attitudes to the level of taxation and public expenditure in Danish local politics have been examined both at a general level and in various more specific fields of public service such as schools, roads etc. The general question on the extent of the Danish welfare state was phrased as a question – »If you could decide what ought to happen with the local taxation and the way the municipality spends the money, would you prefer« – 1) less tax and less service; 2) same tax and same service, and 3) higher tax and more service. The answers were coded respectively -1, 0 and 1. An average was calculated for each party and each stratum, and this varied from -1 (if all respondents in a stratum want less tax and service) to 1 (if all respondents in a stratum want higher tax and more service). The results for each stratum and party are given in Figure 3.

Again, the Social Democratic Party shows the curvilinear pattern, but is this time joined by the Conservative Party. The variation between the parties, however, was extensive, both with regard to the level of parity and to the patterns found. So once again, the conclusion is that there is almost no support to the law of curvilinear disparity in Danish local politics.

This time the shift of focus from each party to the party system shows a variation of 1.41 scale-points among politicians, 1.37 scale-points among local party chairmen and 0.56 among local voters. Polarization clearly increases with the higher strata, but there is no significant difference between the local politicians and the local party chairmen. A more detailed analysis of the opinion structures of spending can be based on the attitudes to spending on numerous different kinds of public service.

Figure 3. Attitudes to tax and services. -1 ' all support less service and less tax, and 1 ' all support more service and more tax'

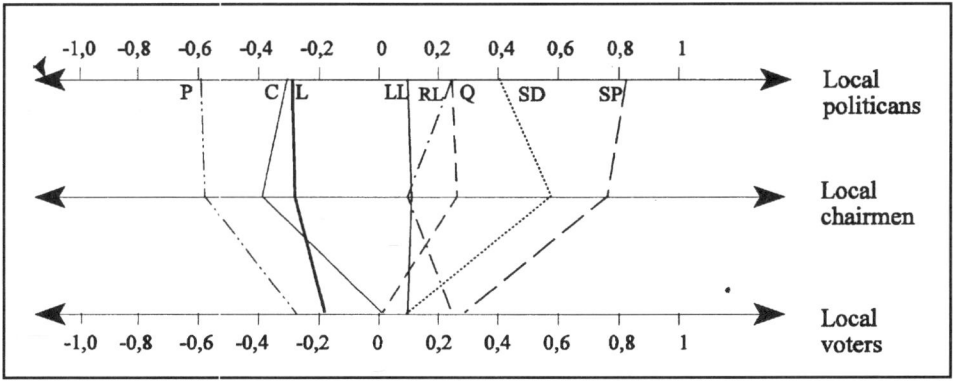

* C ' The Conservative Party, L ' The Liberal Party, LL ' Local Lists, P ' The Progress Party, Q ' The Christian People's Party, RL ' The Radical Liberals, SD ' The Social Democratic Party, SP ' The Socialist People's Party.

Specific fiscal attitudes

The last test of the law of curvilinear disparity is on specific attitudes to municipal spending on thirteen different areas of municipal service. The voters were asked whether their municipality was spending too little, sufficient, or too much money on:

- schools
- care for elderly people
- sports facilities
- roads and streets
- day-care and kindergartens
- social welfare
- libraries
- the environment

Opinion Structures in Political Parties   141

- road safety
- employment initiatives
- public transport
- culture
- administration

The answers were coded respectively 1, 0 and -1. The average was calculated for each stratum and each party.

The overall result was that voters had a positive attitude to more spending on almost every kind of service. Only on social welfare, and particularly on administration, were averages negative and indicated a desire for less spending. The positive averages on the other services indicated a willingness to spend more money. This contrasts to the general fiscal attitude of most voters who want the same tax and service (71 per cent) or less tax and service (14 per cent) -although this is not shown clearly by Figure 3, and could be interpreted as a sign of fiscal illusion -a phenomenon also widespread among politicians and local party chairmen (Buch Jensen, 2000).

The results of the analysis of the different public services were never exactly the same, but spending on traffic safety is shown as an example of the results (cf. Figure 4). Within many of the public services local party chairmen were moderate in their willingness to spend more money, while politicians and especially voters were more positive towards extra spending. With regard to the law of curvilinear disparity the findings are unclear. For some parties and some services the law finds support: the party chairmen are more extreme, the voters are the least extreme, and the politicians lie in between the two extremes. But for other parties or other services willingness to spend more increases with higher strata or decreases with higher strata or simply has no pattern at all. Once again, the very clear conclusion is that the law of curvilinear disparity finds no solid empirical support in the study of Danish local politics.

With the shift of the analysis to the party system as a whole, it once again becomes clear that voters are much less polarized than local politicians and local party chairmen. This holds true for nine of the thirteen types of services. Of the remaining four services three (sports facilities, roads and streets and employment initiatives) show the same polarization of the different strata, while the last service (schools) shows voters as the most polarized stratum. Much more variation is seen in the relationship between politicians and party chairmen, sometimes politicians are most polarized, sometimes local party chairmen are the most polarized stratum.

Figure 4. Attitudes to spending more on road safety. -1 ' all support less service and lower tax, and 1 ' all support more service and more tax'

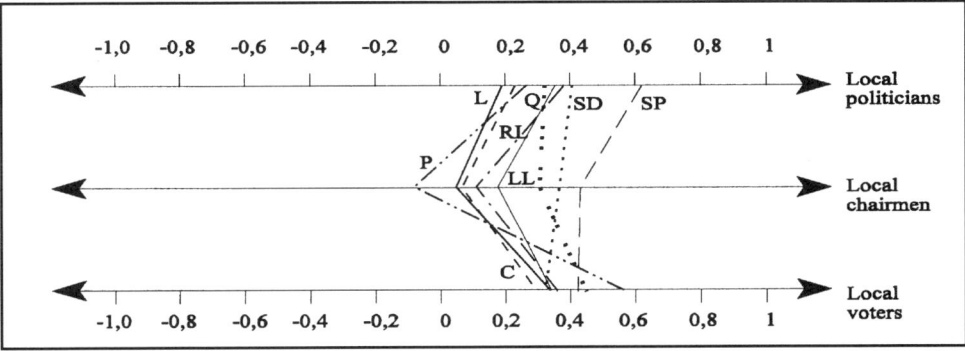

* C ' The Conservative Party, L ' The Liberal Party, LL ' Local Lists, P ' The Progress Party, Q ' The Christian People's Party, RL ' The Radical Liberals, SD ' The Social Democratic Party, SP ' The Socialist People's Party.

The analysis above provides two clear conclusions.

1) The law of curvilinear disparity found no support in this study of Danish local politics. Regardless of whether the focus was on ideological self-placement, general or specific fiscal attitudes, the curvi linear pattern was rarely seen and was never in evidence for all or most parties, not even for the »major or semi-major« parties mentioned by May in the quotation above. The major parties in Danish local politics are the Social Democratic Party and the Liberal Party, and there was only support for the Social Democratic Party on ideological self-placement and general fiscal attitudes, not on specific fiscal attitudes and never for the Liberal Party!

2) A shift in focus from the individual parties to the party system as a whole revealed support for – if not a law – at least a tendency towards an increase in polarization, when the level shifts from voters to sub-leaders or to politicians, and sometimes also with the shift from the level of sub-leaders to that of politicians.

The two conclusions raise two new questions: a) Why was there no support for the curvilinear disparity? and b) Why was there no tendency towards increasing polarization?

Opinion Structures in Political Parties   *143*

Why was there no support for the curvilinear disparity and why was there no tendency towards increasing polarization?

One simple answer to the questions is that May's law was developed with the focus on national party organizations and this is the explanation for the lack of empirical support in Danish local politics. However, this is not a very good answer as there is no reason to believe that the characteristics, dynamics and logic of internal control, bias in recruitment patterns and political socialization in parties and elected assemblies, etc., used by May, should only have an impact on national politics. The fundamental powerful position of activists as well as voters are no less important in local politics than in national politics, due to their different prerogatives and resources: on the one hand, nomination and campaign support and on the other, electoral support and success. Another characteristic feature of Danish local politics is that voters' personal knowledge about each candidate is crucial to the electoral outcome. This should give politicians more incentives and freedom to move closer to voters, but this is clearly not what is actually happening.

Another answer is a methodological answer pointing to local party chairmen as poor representatives of the sub-leaders – they can in fact be claimed to be leaders, or to have very close connections with politicians. Local party chairmen often have a position as brokers or negotiators between activists and politicians and can be much more easily socialized to accept the attitudes, values and beliefs of politicians than the other, »purer« activists. It is not possible to test this explanation with the available data, but it clearly has a weakness: even with the influence of politicians the local party chairmen need the support of activists to be re-elected, and we could therefore expect to find them on the opposite side to politicians relative to voters – creating a weak curvilinear pattern – which, as mentioned, is often not found at all.

It is difficult to give a good explanation for the lack of support for the law of curvilinear disparity, but how can the tendency towards increasing polarization be explained? A probable answer is that the tendency is the result of invalid measures, because politicians and party chairmen reflect much more about their own political attitudes than do voters and that they are in a political world where the manifestation of disagreement is important. The lack of clear patterns within each party can be seen as the result of the very different party systems in Danish municipalities (Elklit, 1997). In different municipalities different degrees of ideological conflict give different manifestations within the same party, while the general tendency towards polarization can be explained by the general need for ideological or attitudinal manifestation. This interpretation moves the explanation away from the May's world of power and self-interest into a much more complex world of discursive processes, which are almost impossible to test with the quantitative methods used here. The analyses needed should examine the link between attitudes and real-world political decisions, and the expectation would be not to find clear links between outspoken attitudes and actual political decisions on the individual level. This expectation is supported by analysis on municipal level, where Mouritzen (1991) show that there is no correlation between which party who has the power in a municipality and the municipal policy. Socioeconomic and sociodemografic variabels turns out to be more important. However it is not possible to compare decisions in municipalities, which vary in size, demographics and history, with the available data set in this study.

To move from May's world of power and self-interest to a world of meaning and discourse would seem to render the question of opinion structures trivial for local and party democracy, but this is not the case – it will only move the debate into the complicated and interesting debate of »standing for« as opposed to »acting for« within the theories of representation (Pitkin, 1979)

In support of the interpretation, which cuts the link between the attitudes analysed here and the real political decisions, is the fact that Danish local politics is dominated by a consensus culture. Asked whether a politician should a) fight for his views even though it could lead to defeat or b) should always be willing to make a compromise, 88 per cent of the politicians in the survey chose the latter statement (Anderson, Berg & Mouritzen, 1996: 41). Most decisions in local councils and their committees are made either unanimously or with very broad support – as is the case in Danish national politics. All in all the consensus model (Goldsmith, 1992) not only of Denmark but the whole of Scandinavia could be the crucial factor in explaining the analysis reported here, but this would only be a provisional explanation – because what are the causes that create a consensual political climate? The discussion will stop here, without giving the final answers to why increasing polarization, and not curvilinear disparity is found in Danish local politics, but with strong indications of a fundamental weakness in May's theory, namely the neglect of the interparty discursive processes and political games between the competing parties which might be the real explanation for the many disparities in opinions structure in political parties. Much more empirical research is needed and it would probably be more fruitful to search for a tendency towards increasing polarization, rather than to search for patterns of curvilinear disparity -at least this seems to be the case in

Denmark, but probably also in many other countries – in particular when local politics is studied, but probably also in studies of national politics!

Conclusion

In 1973, May formulated the law of curvilinear disparity, which claims that opinion structures within political parties places voters as moderates; activists or sub-leaders as extremists; and politicians trapped in the middle of the two groups, which exercise different but very important powers over the politicians: electoral success and nomination respectively. The analysis of three different attitudes: ideological self-placement, general fiscal attitudes and specific fiscal attitudes, provides no support for the law of curvilinear disparity. On the contrary support is found for a tendency towards increasing polarization. Differences of opinion among people who vote for different parties means much less than political disagreement between the local party chairmen of different parties and between politicians from different parties. This conlusion is a conclusion not on the analytical level of indiviual parties, but on the contrary on the level of the party system, which on the one hand make predictions on individual parties less precise compared to May's law, but on the other hand is much closer to the empirical facts in Danish local politics.

References

Anderson, Lene, Rikke Berg og Poul Erik Mouritzen (1996). *Undersøgelse af kommunalbestyrelsesmedlemmer*, Local Government Studies from Department of Political Science and Public Management, University of Southern Denmark - Odense University, No. 12/ 1996.
Buch Jensen, Roger (2000). *Lokale partiorganisationer*, Ph.D.-thesis, Department of Political Science and Public Management, University of Southern Denmark - Odense University.
Elklit, Jørgen (1997). "Kommunernes partisystemer", in Jørgen Elklit & Roger Buch Jensen (eds.) *Kommunalvalg*, Odense: Odense University Press.
Goldsmith, Michael (1992). "The Structure of Local Government" in Poul Erik Mouritzen (ed.). *Managing Cities in Austerity*, London: Sage.
May, John D. (1973). "Opinion Structure of Political Parties: The Special Law of Curvilinear, Disparity", *Political Studies*, vol. 21, No. 2, pp. 135-51.
Michels, Robert (1911/1962). *Zur Soziologie des Parteiwesens in der modernen Demokratie*, Leipzig.
Mouritzen, Poul Erik (1991). *Den politiske cyklus*, Aarhus: Politica.

Mouritzen, Poul Erik (1993). *Forskningsprogrammet om Det kommunale Lederskab*, Local Government Studies from the Department of Political Science and Public Management, University of Southern Denmark - Odense University, No. 1/1993.

Ostrogorski, Mosei (1902/1964). *Democracy and The Organization of Political Parties*, 2. Vols., Chicago: Quadrangle Books.

Pitkin, Hanna Fenichel (1967). *The Concept of Representation*, Berkely, Los Angeles & London: University of California Press.

Saturation Without Parity: The Stagnating Number of Female Councillors in Denmark

Ulrik Kjær

Abstract

This article argues that a continuing increase in the proportion of female local councillors in Denmark should not be taken for granted. A stagnation in the percentage of women in Danish local governments will be demonstrated, and this will lead to a discussion of the saturation hypothesis. A state of saturation can emerge before mathematical parity has been reached. The role of the electorate, the local party organizations and the eligible women themselves will be assessed with regard to the saturation hypothesis, drawing on election result data as well as survey data.

Introduction: The Saturation Hypothesis

Since the local elections in 1909, when women used their newly won eligibility (gained the year before) to obtain 1.3 per cent of the seats in the local governments (Dahlerup 1978, 146), the proportion of female councillors in Denmark has been growing steadily. The increase acquired momentum during the 1970s and 1980s, but as figure 1 demonstrates, the trend has been altered in the 1990s, and the percentage of local offices held by women has stagnated. In the 1993 elections, the percentage of female candidates decreased for the first time since 1950, and in the 1997 elections this decline was supplemented by a decrease in the percentage of women among elected councillors (a decrease not seen since 1937).

Figure 1. Percentage of women among candidates and elected councillors in Danish local elections, 1970-1997.

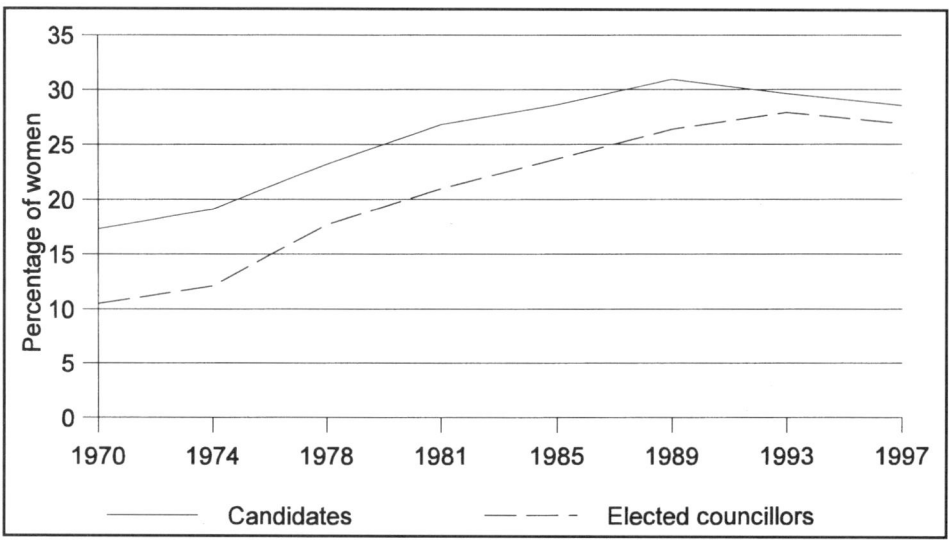

Source: The Danish Statistical Bureau, various publications.

When Sue Thomas a few years ago wrote about women legislators at the gubernatorial level in the U.S., she prophecized: »If the past is any guide, the proportions of women in legislatures will increase steadily but incrementally« (Thomas 1994, 153).

Predicting the future is difficult, and it seems that one cannot be content by simply making extrapolations from the past. The case of Danish local governments has demonstrated that the past has not turned out to be a reliable guide to the future. The same signs have been observed in other Scandinavian countries (Pikkala 1997), a trend to be discussed further below.

It could be claimed that no one who observes women's inclusion in the formal political life sees women occupying one hundred per cent of the seats in the polity in question. It seems more likely if we operate on the implicit assumption that the discussion is relevant only when the group in question is a minority. Hence, the progress, or at the least the focus on it, will come to a »natural« end when some kind of parity is reached. In strictly mathematical terms, this parity will reflect a fifty-fifty composition, but for practical purpose, a share of say 45 or 40 per cent can be sufficient for some to accept that a state of parity has been obtained.

In the Danish councils, the steady increase in womens's share of the seats has stopped (at least momentarily) below a percentage of 30, and probably even the most unpretentious advocates of female representativeness will not assess this as gender parity. A threshold of parity will not be introduced here. Actually, the entire normative question as to how many women ought to be in a given polity should not be adressed in this article. However, it can be mentioned that recent research on Danish local government, which has dealt with the question of female representativeness, demonstrates that the normative arguments for a given percentage of female councillors are not as straightforward as sometimes claimed (Kjær, forthcoming).

An interesting question, of course, is whether it can be justified to pay this amount of attention to a minor decrease in the percentage of women in Danish local governments. The answer is, »yes«, because Denmark and the other Scandinavian countries are often referred to when discussing women's inclusion in legislative bodies in representative democracies (e. g., Darcy *et al.* 1994, 50). There is widespread knowledge of the fact that in comparison with other western democracies these countries have a high percentage of women in their legislatures both at national and local levels. Presently, there are few commentators within the Scandinavian context who do not operate with a continual closing of the gender gap as an implicit premise. The purpose of this article is to draw attention to the somewhat unexpected downturn in the proportion of women in Danish councils, and to assess if the demonstrated decrease should be seen as an omen or just as an anomaly.

How should the stagnation in the number of female councillors be explained? At first glance, it seems difficult to point to changes in the institutional arrangements regarding local politics or more broadly defined societal trends that could be thought responsible for the development.[1] This is not to say that no such potential explanations exist, but if they do, they have not yet been proposed. Instead, the combination of a polity with a comparatively high proportion of women and a stagnation whose occurence lacks an immediate explanation might lead us to change the focus from the »90s« to the »30s«. The explanation has not to do with the calendar having reached the 1990s, but to the fact that the percentage of female councillors has reached the 30's.

On an intuitive basis, we could hypothesize that part of the stagnation in the number of female councillors can be explained by the occurence of a state of saturation. Momentum is not lost because of some incident but because the potential for raising the proportion of women at the councils has already been fully capitalized. The hypothesis does not have parity as its necessary condition, as saturation can emerge such that the proportion of women in the legislative body is other than 50 per cent.

The theoretical point of departure for this claim could be that in the mind of the voters and the party nominators, the dimension of gender recedes into the background when some progress has been made. This is not to say that a certain level of women in the legislatures generates hostility towards female councillors and candidates but, rather, that it might lead to a lack of any affirmative action regarding the characteristic of gender.

After introducing this hypothesis of saturation, it should be applied to some aspects of the present Danish situation in the following discussion. Unfortunately, data which allows relevant comparisons across time are not available. The broad historical approach to the question of why the women's share of the seats in local governments increased during the 1970s and 1980s but stagnated during the 1990s, cannot be pursued, when the goal is to present empirical evidence. Instead, we must be satisfied with a strategy that makes use of the fact that the stagnation coincides with a series of intensive studies of Danish municipalities carried out as part of the research programme Leadership in Local Governments. Mogens N. Pedersen has been a leading figure in this programme, especially in the project on recruitment of local politicians conducted as part of the programme. The data collected as part of this study allows us to assess if the present situation is characterized by a lack of *potential* for further increase in the proportion of female councillors. The aim of this article is not to discuss why the proportion increased substantially in the 1970s and 1980s. Rather, it seeks to show that one of the reasons why this did not continue in the 1990s was that no potential existed for such an increase.

The discussion of the saturation hypothesis will focus on three selected aspects of the recruitment process. The process can be described by a demand-supply model, which assumes that recruitment to political office is a result of the interaction of a supply- and a demand-side. While »on the *demand-side* the model assumes selectors choose candidates depending upon their perceptions of the applicants, abilities, qualifications, and experience« (Norris & Lovenduski 1995, 14), the »supply-side explanations suggest that the outcome reflects the supply of applicants wishing to pursue a political career« and that »constraints on resources (such as time, money and experience) and motivational factors (such as drive, ambition and interest) determine who aspires« (Norris & Lovenduski 1995, 15). On the demand side, two actors can be identified: the voters and the nominating organizations, i.e., the political parties and independent local lists. Initially, the voters' gender attitudes at the electoral stage will be assessed. This will be followed by a discussion of the influence of the political parties at the nominating stage on the gender composition of the electoral tickets. Recognizing the importance of including the supply side, the final part of the article addresses the question of potential differences between the two sexes at the supply side of the model.

Demand-side Explanations: The Voters

Studying figure 1, it can be seen that the proportion of female candidates is constantly slightly above the proportion of elected female councillors. This could lead to the conclusion that the electorate (here denoting the aggregate of the voters who cast their vote) is to some degree hostile to the female candidates. This need not necessarily be the case, however. At the elections in 1985, it became possible for the parties to nominate their candidates on open tickets, which means that it is the number of preferential votes cast for each of the candidates which determines who will actually get elected. Since the introduction of open tickets, where 48 per cent of the lists used this possibility, the share has been constantly increasing, reaching 72 per cent at the 1997 elections. The remaining lists run on semi-closed tickets, and during the elections prior to 1985 this meant all the lists. At that time there was no alternative. On semi-closed tickets, not only the preferential votes but also the preceding prioritizing of the candidates by the parties are considered when the gained seats are assigned.[2] Because of this spill-over effect from the nominating stage into the electorial stage, the election result has to be cleansed of this »heritage« from the nomination process before the effect of the electorate on the gender composition can be assessed.

In previous research on this question, no attempt has been made to eliminate this spill-over effect (Bentzon 1981, 35). The conclusions reached about the situation in the 1970s should therefore be treated with some caution. It is argued that some partiality for female candidates existed in the electorate, but that a combination of the parties giving female candidates low priority and the electoral system's consideration of this prioritizing led to a net decrease in women's share during the electoral stage (Bentzon 1981, 35). On the basis of the data presented, it is not possible to produce a final assessment of the validity of this conclusion. Instead, we turn to the detailed information on the 1993 elections, which allows us to isolate the effects of voters' preferential voting and of the parties' priorities. This has been done by simulating an election result where the priorities made by the parties are neglected (all lists are treated as open); this result has then been compared to the actual election result (Kjær 1997). The findings of this analysis are shown in table 1.

Table 1. Difference in the percentage of women among candidates and elected councillors in Danish local elections in 1993, and the effect of the electorate's voting behaviour and the political parties's prioritizing, respectively.

	Semi-closed lists	Open lists	Total
Percentage of lists	31	69	100
Percentage of women among candidates	33.7	27.6	29.6
Percentage of women among elected councillors	31.7	26.2	27.8
Difference in percentpoints from candidates to elected councillors	÷2.0	÷1.4	÷1.8
- effect of the electorate's voting behavior[a]	+1.3	÷1.4	÷0.8
- effect of the parties's priorities and the election system's consideration of these[b]	÷3.3		÷1.0

a Calculated as the percentage of women, which would have been obtained if no consideration had been paid to the parties' priorities (all lists are treated as open lists in a simulation) minus the percentage of women on the lists of candidates. A positive value expresses that the electorate would have raised the percentage of women councillors compared to the percentage of women candidates if they had had the possibility and vice versa.

b Calculated as the percentage of women elected minus the percentage which would have been obtained if no consideration had been paid to the parties' priorities (all lists are treated as open lists in a simulation). A negative value express that the proportion of female councillors due to the political parties prioritizings and the electoral systems consideration of these was lowered in the election phase compared to a situation where the voters' preferential votes alone determined who was to fill the posts.

Source: Election reports from all 275 Danish municipalities.
N=2,168 (number of lists).

Table 1 demonstrates that when the minority of lists which ran on semi-closed tickets is studied, the traditional hypothesized pattern is found. The proportion of women decreased through the electoral stage because the parties' priorities, due to the electoral system, dominates the otherwise women-partial electorate. The effects are minor, however. And more important, if we examine the majority of lists which ran on open tickets, we find that the electorate is not favourable to women. On the contrary, for these lists, where voters through their preferential voting are in full control of the selection among the candidates, they use this possibility to lower the proportion of women.

This somewhat paradoxical finding does not alter the main conclusion of the analysis, namely, that the electorate are not generally favourable to women, when they go to the polls. We do not know for sure whether the gender of the candidates influences the specific voter's voting behavior at all, or whether the gender question influences some voters more than others. However, this is not relevant for the testing of the saturation hypothesis, just as it is not necessary to know if the electorate used to be favourable to the women in the 1970s. The point to be made on the basis of the data presented is that when the group of candidates is turned into the group of councillors no potential for raising the proportion of women (by letting gender dominate all other characteristics of the candidates) exists in the Danish electorate at large in the 1990s.[3]

Demand-side Explanations: The Political Parties

Considering the subordinate role played by the political party, through their prioritizing of the candidates, in regard to the electoral stage, table 1 also demonstrates that there exists no potential for raising the proportion of women among the political parties. On the contrary, in terms of ordering the candidates on the semi-closed tickets, women are generally ranked lower than men. In order to fully assess the influence of the political parties, the focus should change to the nomination stage, where they play a leading role. And it should be recalled that it is during the nomination process that the proportion of women drops dramatically, from approximately 50 per cent of the voters (and potential candidates) to approximately 30 per cent of the actual candidates.

The relationship between the female proportion of candidates and the elected councillors is not straightforward, but it seems likely that an increase in the proportion of female councillors will be facilitated by a corresponding increase in the group of candidates.[4] Hence, it seems relevant to examine, if there exists a potential in the political parties for raising the proportion of female candidates.

Adapting the saturation hypothesis, it will be claimed that the stagnating proportion of female candidates is a result of a tendency among the nominating organizations to approximate a certain level of female candidates. Lists which usually score low on female candidates will continue to raise the proportion, while lists which have already reached a relatively high level will experience a stagnation or decrease. Alternative hypotheses could be that stagnation is to be found to the same extent on all lists, independent of their initial level, or that the lists will tend to become more polarized, such that the lists with few women get even fewer and lists with more women become more »feminized«.

If the lists are pooled according to the national label under which they run, as is usually done, it is the polarization rather than saturation hypothesis which seems to best describe the situation at the 1997 elections. Ranking the twelve national parties according to the percentage of female candidates on the tickets who used their labels leads to an order pretty much consistent with the parties' usual location on a right-left political spectrum.[5] The more leftist the party, the higher proportion of female candidates. And while most parties at the 1997 elections experienced a decrease in the proportion of female candidates compared to the elections of 1993, the two parties on the left (The Socialist People's Party and The Unitary List) had the most significant increases.

In order to test the saturation hypothesis, however, pooling has to be carried out according to the lists' initial level of female councillors. This is done in figure 2, which shows the extent to which lists with different levels of women candidates in the 1993 elections experienced an increase or decrease in this proportion at the subsequent 1997 elections. The measure used is a PDI, calculated as the percentage of lists in the group which experienced an increase, minus the percentage of lists which experienced a decrease.

Figure 2. Change in the proportion of female candidates on the tickets from 1993 to 1997 according to initial level. PDI.[a]

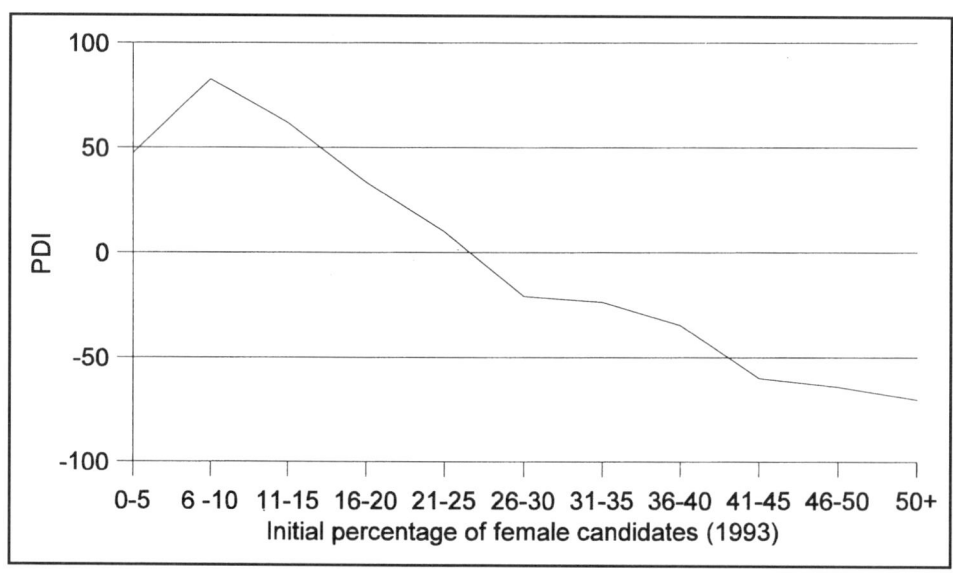

[a] PDI calculated as percentage of lists, who experienced an increase minus those who experienced a decrease in the percentage of women among the candidates.

Source: The Danish Statistical Bureau, various publications. N = 1,403 (number of lists).

With a negative slope of the line, figure 2 lends support to the saturation hypothesis as formulated above (the two alternative hypotheses would have led to horizontal and increasing lines, respectively). It is difficult to assess the level of adaptation (whether the slope is high or low), but the analysis demonstrates an aspect of saturation not captured when the lists are aggregated according to party label.

A more straightforward interpretation can be made of the intersection with the X-axis. At this level of initial proportion of female candidates, the number of lists, which experience an increase equals the number which experience a decrease. At lower levels, the majority of the lists are in progress, while at higher levels there is a decline in the proportion of female candidates at the majority of the lists. If the analysis is re-run with no groupings of the independent variable, an estimated line of linear regression intercepts the X-axis at 31 per cent of female candidates at the 1993 elections. This intersection differs among the party labels, however. Running the analysis for the lists under each of the six major party labels separately, it can be demonstrated that a tendency for saturation exists among all these parties, but the level at which the balance tips varies from 20 per cent (The Progress Party) to 42 per cent (The Socialist People's Party).[6]

However, this finding does not lead to any conclusions regarding the behaviour of the lists as nominating organizations. The more substantial part of the saturation hypothesis relates to the idea of the lists as being satisfied with a certain level of gender representativeness and therefore not putting any efforts into raising the proportion of female candidates any further. Data from the election reports used so far can also be influenced by supply-side factors; hence, in order to assess the »women-friendly« potential among the lists, we need to focus more specifically on these nominating organizations.

The decision to nominate specific candidates is determined by several factors. One of these could be to present a somewhat socio-demographically representative ticket, such that the candidates reflect the electorate at large along certain socio-demographic dimensions. In a survey conducted among leaders of local party organizations during the 1993 elections, the leaders were asked to rank six different characteristics of potential candidates considered in the nominating process. The result is shown in table 2.

Table 2. Local party leaders' indications of whether the distribution of certain characteristics among the candidates was a preference taken into consideration in the nomination process during the 1993 election. In sum and by party label. Percentage of leaders indicating that the characteristic was very important or important.[a] (Ranking)

	Total	Party label[b]						
		F	A	B	C	V	Z	Other
The list should include persons with broad recognition in the community	82 (1)	54 (4)	67 (5)	97 (1)	92 (1)	90 (3)	84 (3)	85 (1)
Young persons should also be included	81 (2)	67 (2)	88 (3)	89 (2)	82 (4)	80 (4)	90 (1)	77 (2)
Candidates from all parts of the municipality should be included	78 (3)	61 (3)	91 (1)	79 (3)	90 (2)	92 (2)	85 (2)	65 (4)
There should be candidates with different occupations	75 (4)	46 (5)	68 (4)	76 (4)	86 (3)	93 (1)	79 (4)	74 (3)
The list should include about the same number of men and women	67 (5)	76 (1)	88 (2)	75 (5)	65 (5)	52 (5)	42 (6)	65 (5)
The list should include persons with leadership occupations	39 (6)	6 (6)	20 (6)	38 (6)	57 (6)	52 (6)	63 (5)	39 (6)
N =	412	59	29	51	35	63	22	153

a The third option was to answer »Less important/not important«.
b The parties are: The Socialist People's Party (F), The Social Democratic Party (A), The Social Liberal Party (B), The Conservative Party (C), The Agrarian Liberal Party (V), The Progress Party (Z) and smaller parties and local lists without a national label (Other).
Source: Survey among leaders of local party organizations 1993 (Elklit et al. 1995).

Table 2 demonstrates a preference for equal gender composition among the candidates, a factor taken into consideration by no less than two out of three organizations. However, this finding should be compared to the even greater preferences for most of the other items. In comparison with other considerations, the attempt to reach an equal proportion of candidates of the two sexes is not ranked very highly (Buch Jensen & Kjær 1997, 101).[7] Table 2 also shows substantial differences among the political parties, and once again these tend to agree with the left-right wing position of the parties on the political spectrum. The more leftist parties tend to be more eager to pursue numerical equality between the two sexes.

The party leaders were also asked if they thought that their intentions to present a gender-balanced ticket were fulfilled. More than half the leaders who thought that including about as many women as men on their ticket was important assessed that they had been successful in their efforts. On first sight, this seems inconsistent with the fact that on these tickets, the average proportion of women was less than 30 per cent, and only a little more than one out of ten could present a ticket on which half or more were women. On the other hand, if the saturation hypothesis is to explain the present stagnation, it will have as an assumption that the nominating organizations reach a point of saturation which is lower than 50 per cent. To which extent this is true is examined in figure 3, where the assessment of whether the wish for a gender balanced ticket has been fulfilled is combined with the achieved proportion of female candidates.

Figure 3. Percentage of lists who thought that their gender-balancing wishes were fulfilled in the 1993 elections, according to different proportions of female candidates obtained. [a, b]

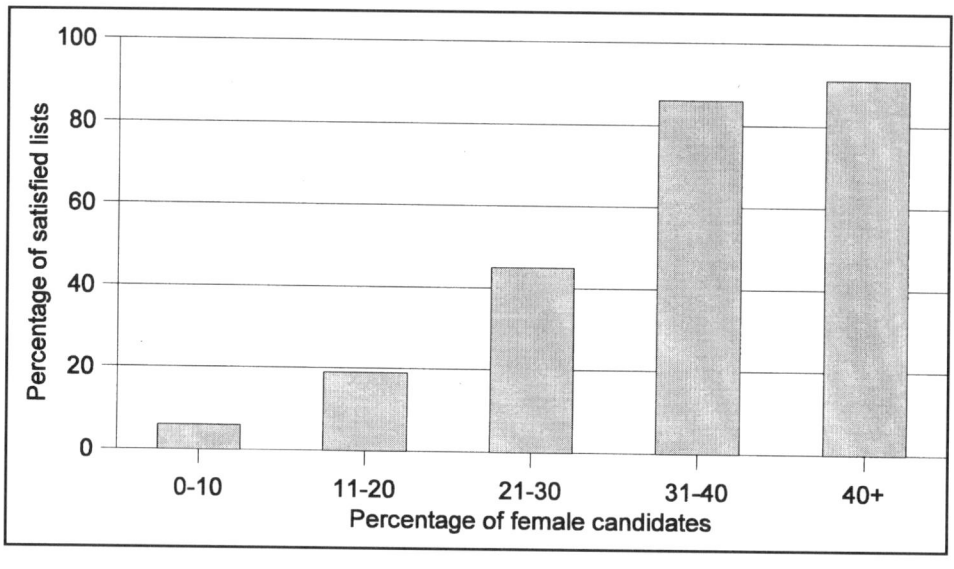

a Lists, who answered that their vishes were highly fulfilled or more or less fulfilled. The Third category was labelled not fulfilled.
b Only lists, who at a subsequent question indicated, that they gave priority to a gender-balanced list is included (N = 256).

Source: The Danish Statistical Bureau, various publications. N = 1,403 (number of lists).

Figure 3 demonstrates that the level at which the desire for numerical gender equality is fulfilled is not fixed, and that it is certainly not fixed at 50 per cent. It is not obvious, for example, that a proportion of between 31 and 40 per cent female candidates meets an objective of presenting a ticket with »about the same number of women and men«. Yet this is the assessment among almost 9 out of 10 of the lists in the survey which had this share of women on their tickets. By conducting a more detailed analysis, it is found that the critical point, the percentage of female candidates where half the lists having this proportion are satisfied, is 31 per cent.[8] Again, it is possible to find saturation without parity in regard to female representativeness among one of the important actors in the recruitment process.

One third of the party organizations expressed no intentions to present a gender balanced ticket (on these tickets the proportion was 23 per cent), and most of the two-thirds, who had the ambition did not need 50 or even 40 per cent female candidates as a necessity to meet this objective. It can be asked whether the intentions of the nominating organizations with regard to female socio-demographic representativeness have any influence at all on the gender composition of the tickets. In any case, it can be concluded that no significant potential for raising the proportion of female candidates exists among the majority of the nominating organizations.

Supply-side Explanations

The analysis has so far shown that the actors on the demand-side are characterized more by apathy than hostility or partiality in regard to the number of women in local politics. In order to fully assess the gender-question, it is therefore necessary to include the supply-side. Why do the women not come forward when the seats in the local councils are to be distributed? The group of potential candidates is rather difficult to sample (Darcy et al. 1994, 43), and therefore we have to rely on indirect measures. In the 1993 elections, almost a thousand candidates were asked why there were fewer women than men in local office, and these people will be used as informants in this section. The candidates were asked to assess eight explanations often discussed in the popular debate. The results are shown in table 3.

Table 3. Views of the candidates of the 1993-election on why fewer women than men were running. PDI (Percentage who answered »fully agree« and »partly agree«, minus the percentage who answered »partly disagree« or »fully disagree«).[a]

	Women	Men	Total
a. Women often give priority to family considerations	86	64	70
b. Men are less modest at the nomination stage	56	47	49
c. Women are less interested in politics than men	÷18	14	5
d. Women lack self-confidence	14	÷23	÷12
e. The political parties do not sufficiently support women	÷20	÷45	÷39
f. Women are not getting as many preferential votes as men	÷38	÷57	÷51
g. Women lack experience and education	÷42	÷50	÷48
h. Women are not as qualified for politics as are men	÷94	÷79	÷83
N =	275	660	935

[a] The fifth option was to answer »neither agree or disagree«.
Source: Survey among candidates 1993 (Kjær & Pedersen 1996).

Explanations relating to the uneven qualifications among the sexes (items g and h) is rejected by virtually everyone. Explanations relating to hostility among selectors (items e and f) are assigned very low importance, which is in harmony with the findings presented above.[9] Instead, the women are thought to lack the ability to promote themselves in the game of political nomination (items b and d), have less interest in politics (item c) and especially to stay out of politics because of family concerns (item a). It should be noted that these findings are not a result of the male majority in the pool of candidates. Table 3 shows only minor discrepancies between the responses of the candidates of the two sexes.

Where does this leads us in terms of the stagnating proportion? In light of table 3, it seems reasonable to assess the process of political socialization and the general status of equality among the sexes as critical for the recruitment of women to local political office. Lack of comparable data prevent us from making a dynamic analysis that could answer questions such as »Are women (and girls) socialized into seeing themselves as potential politicians to a higher extent than earlier?« and »Are women's comparably greater perceived obligations towards home and hearth vanishing?«.

Instead, following the strategy of this article consistently, the potential for change should be assessed. Unfortunately, the static data are not sufficient for risking a conclusion. Instead, two different interpretations of table 3 should be offered. On the one hand, it can be claimed that there exists some potential for an increase in the proportion of women. By changing the relations between the two sexes in society as such, it will be possible to raise the proportion of women. If one assesses the current trend as working for equality among the sexes, this interpretation would be appropriate and a potential could be assumed. On the other hand, if the data are seen as demonstrating that after years of focussing on these issues substantial differences between the attitudes to running for political office of the two sexes still exist (or have returned), and if no revolutionary changes in these attitudes are discerned in the horizon, the potential for an increase in female representativeness must be assessed as weak at least in a short run perspective.

Conclusion

Discussions of gender representativeness in political assemblies such as the Danish councils are often characterized by an implicit belief in an equalization tendency. The proportion of women is slowly but steadily increasing, and a continuation of this progress until a state of parity has been reached has normally been taken for granted (Darcy *et al.* 1994, 49). As the Danish case illustrates, however, the momentum can be lost. Saturation can occur before parity. The optimism held by some advocates of an equal gender distribution in political polities is built mainly upon a lag hypothesis, which states that time will solve the »problem« (Raaum 1995, 30). Two of the main theoretical foundations for this hypothesis, which lies in opposition to the saturation hypothesis introduced in this article, should be included in the discussion.

First, a time-lag could be explained by incumbency effects. It is often assumed that holding initial office can be advantageous at the electoral stage. If this is the case, the flow of persons through the councils can be very slow, being a disadvantage for traditionally socio-demographically under-representative groups such as women (Pedersen 1994, 231). It will take some time for changes in gender attitudes to crystallize, so that the impact in terms of a higher proportion of seats will be delayed. In the 1993 elections, the ratio of success varied significantly between incumbents and candidates not already elected (0.80 and 0.13 respectively) indicating the presence of some kind of incumbency-effect.[10] However, when the flow of candidates is to be assessed, it is also important to include voluntary derecruitment (Pedersen 1997, 71). Twenty-three per cent of the councillors in office did not run again, and combining the voluntary and the involuntary derecruitment, it can be calculated that no less than 38 per cent of the councillors have been replaced. At the same time, the proportion of women among the newly elected councillors was 31 per cent, and even though this is higher than the average 28 per cent, it is still socio-demographically underrepresentative to the electorate. In order to demonstrate a significant incumbency-caused lag, derecruitment should be very minor, and the proportion of women among non-incumbents close to 50 per cent or higher. This has not been shown to be the case. An incumbency-caused lag could also exist if women had a higher ratio of voluntary derecruitment and, therefore, less chance to exploit the incumbency-effect. According to the empirical evidence, however, there is no significant difference between the ratio of women and men (0.24 vs. 0.23, respectively). Finally, it could be hypothesized that the incumbency-effect is different among politicians of the two sexes, but again the data do not confirm this: female incumbents have about the same ratio of success in elections as do males (0.79 vs 0.80, respectively).

Another theoretical point of departure for a lag-hypothesis could be the question of gender equality and the socialization into gender-specific roles, as touched upon briefly in the previous section on the supply-side of the recruitment equation. According to a socialization-caused lag-hypothesis it could be claimed that even though gender equality is predominant in the public debate, it has not as yet crystallized into equal gender distribution in the polities. It will take time before we will see the impact of the fact that early stages of the recruitment process will be experienced in a gender equal environment. As mentioned above, however, we do not know for sure, if such a state of total equality between the sexes has been reached in Denmark. This question lies beyond the bounds of this article, but it should be emphasized that the status of equality in the society as such can affect the proportion of female councillors we observe in the future. As has been demonstrated, no further intentions of affirmative action with regard to women exists among the electorate or the political parties. The voters and parties are not hostile to women. It is simply that other characteristics of the candidates tend to dominate the selections.

The saturation-hypothesis may not be the only explanation for the stagnating number of female councillors in Denmark. However, it probably constitutes some of it.[11] Nevertheless, generalizations in time and space should be made with caution. Comparisons with other Scandinavian countries, which also score high on proportions of female councillors, show the picture to be only somewhat supportive, and definitely not clear-cut. In Iceland, which has lagged behind the other Scandinavian countries in terms of female councillors, the percentage is still growing, reaching a 28 per cent high in the elections of 1998. Finland also experience a continual increase in the proportion of women in local governments but at a decreasing rate (current level of 31 per cent). In Norway, the percentage of female councillors dropped from 31 to 29 per cent in the 1991 elections, increasing again to 33 per cent in the latest elections in 1995. And in Sweden, a stagnation was observed in 1991, where the level remained at some 34 per cent. The proportion then jumped to 41 per cent in the 1994 elections and reached a Scandinavian record of 42 per cent in 1998.[12] More comparative research is needed in order to assess whether the saturation hypothesis will find universal support. It is tempting to conclude with a prediction as to the proportion of women in the Danish local councils after the next elections in the autumn of 2001. On the other hand, drawing on the experience of the chapter, I will abstain from such an attempt.

Notes

1. The next section states that in 1985 it became optional whether to run as a traditional semi-closed list or as an open list. Table 1 demonstrates that the proportion of women is higher on semi-closed than on open lists. This could lead to the immediate conclusion that the introduction and widespread use of open lists, can explain some of the decrease in the proportion of women. However, this is not the case. The picture can be explained by the fact that The Socialist People's Party at the same time favours semi-closed lists and has a high percentage of female candidates and councillors. There is no relationship between the type of list used and the proportion of women when a control for political party is added.
2. All votes cast on the list, and not on a person, are given to the highest ranked candidate, who has not received enough preferential votes to secure a seat.

3. This conclusion could be seriously weakened, of course, if there are simply not enough women on the tickets to choose from. However, this is not the case. In the elections of 1997, 4,961 women ran for the 4,685 seats. The female candidates were not equally distributed among the municipalities. In 136 of the 275 municipalities, the number of female candidates was lower than the number of seats at the council. In the case of an extreme women-friendly electorate, this would have led to 4,129 (88 per cent) female councillors. If the electorate would have remained loyal to the party, they actually voted for, and then afterwards through preferential voting tried to have as many women elected as possible, a total of 3,188 (68 per cent) women would have gained seats in the 1997 elections. Even under the assumption that the electorate would have stopped their women-friendly attitude, when a level of 50 per cent women was reached in a municipality, a total of 2,135 (46 per cent) women would have been elected.

4. This claim is not based solely on the experience of the elections included in figure 1. A multiple regression analysis with the lists as level of analysis and with the proportion of female councillors as the dependent variable supports the claim. The standardized beta-coefficients for the included independent variables are as follows: $.36^{***}$ (proportion of female candidates), $.13^{***}$ (urbanization – percentage of the inhabitants of the municipality, who live in a town with more than 10,000 inhabitants), $.08^{*}$ (number of seats obtained by the list), $.05^{N.S}$ (proportion of women in the workforce), $-.03^{N.S.}$ (number of seats in the council), and the party labels (reference group: The Socialdemocratic Party, the minor parties not reported) $-.01^{N.S.}$ (The Social Liberal Party), $-.04^{N.S.}$ (The Conservatives), $-.02^{N.S.}$ (The Socialist People's Party), $-.03^{N.S.}$ (The Agrarian Liberal Party), $-.08^{**}$ (The Progress Party), $.05^{N.S.}$ (The Unitary List). Levels of significance: ***: $p<.001$, **: $p<.01$, *: $p<.05$ and $^{N.S.}$: not significant at a .05-level. N=1365, R^2=.19.

5. The percentage of female candidates for each of the labels at the elections in 1997 were as follows: 41.3 (The Unitary List), 39.2 (The Socialist People's Party), 32.1 (The Social Liberal Party), 30.1 (Schleswig Party), 30.0 (The Socialdemocratic Party), 28.9 (The Christian People's Party), 28.7 (Danish People's Party), 28.0 (Lists without a national label), 28.1 (The Center Democrats), 26.6 (The Conservatives), 25.0 (Democratic Renewal), 24.6 (The Agrarian Liberal Party) and 21.3 (The Progress Party).

6. The point of saturation for the remaining four parties are: 37 per cent (The Social Liberal Party), 32 per cent (The Social Democratic Party), 28 per cent (The Agrarian Liberal Party) and 25 per cent (The Conservatives). Again, this ranking is consistent with the parties' positions on a left-right continuum.

7. The fact that the only item included not relating to socio-demographic representativeness comes out with the highest ranking might indicate that socio-demographic representativeness tends not to play a major role in the nominating process.

8. The number of respondents is not sufficiently high to make comparisons among the parties, but a rough analysis indicates no major differences. The eagerness to obtain gender balanced tickets can differ between the parties, but the level at which saturation occurs seems to be universal.

9. This could serve as a validation of answers given by these informants, just as the fact that almost identical answers are found in the survey among party leaders (n=412) and in a survey of councillors retiring from office in 1993 (n=192).

10. These and the following ratios are calculated with the 1993 election reports from all 275 Danish municipalities as source. For further details, see Kjær (forthcoming).
11. An alternative hypothesis is that with the demonstrated differences in the proportion of women between the political parties, a positive election result among the parties with relatively few women and vice versa could negatively influence the total number of female councillors. This hypothesis is falsified by the data from the 1997 elections. The two parties on the left-wing (with a high proportion of women) gained extra seats in the election, while the The Conservatives, The Agrarian Liberal Party and The Progress Party, all on the right wing (and with a low initial proportion), lost seats.
12. Sources for these figures are the national statistical bureaus: Iceland (Hagstofa Íslands), Norway (Statistisk sentralbyrå), Sweden (Statistiska Centralbyraaen), and for Finland the source is Pikkala (1997).

References

Bentzon, Karl-Henrik (1981). *Kommunalpolitikerne*, Copenhagen: Samfundsvidenskabeligt Forlag.

Buch Jensen, Roger & Ulrik Kjær (1997). »Rekrutteringsprocessen: Udvælgelse og selvudvælgelse«, pp. 88-105, in Jørgen Elklit & Roger Buch Jensen (eds.), *Kommunalvalg*, Odense: Odense University Press.

Dahlerup, Drude (1978). »Women's Entry into Politics: The Experience of the Danish Local and General Elections 1908-20«, *Scandinavian Political Studies*, Vol. 13, No. 2, pp.139-62.

Darcy, R., Susan Welch & Janet Clark (1994). *Women, Elections & Representation*, 2. ed., Lincoln: University of Nebraska Press.

Elklit, Jørgen, Roger Buch Jensen & Ulrik Kjær (1995). »Svarfordelinger fra undersøgelse af lokale valgkampe«, *Kommunalpolitiske Studier*, No. 6, Odense: Det samfundsvidenskabelige Fakultet, Odense Universitet.

Kjær, Ulrik & Mogens N. Pedersen (1996). »Svarfordelinger fra undersøgelse af kandidater ved kommunalvalget den 16. november 1993«, *Kommunalpolitiske Studier*, No. 9, Odense: Det samfundsvidenskabelige Fakultet, Odense Universitet.

Kjær, Ulrik (1997). »Konsekvenser af den personlige stemmeafgivning«, pp. 295-308, in Jørgen Elklit & Roger Buch Jensen (eds.), *Kommunalvalg*, Odense: Odense University Press.

Kjær, Ulrik (forthcoming). *Kommunalbestyrelsernes sammensætning - rekruttering og repræsentation i dansk kommunalpolitik*, Ph.D.-dissertation, Odense: Faculty of Social Sciences, University of Southern Denmark.

Norris, Pippa & Lauri Lovenduski (1995). *Political Recruitment: Gender, Race and Class in the British Parliament*, Cambridge: Cambridge University Press.

Pedersen, Mogens N. (1994): »Incumbency Success and Defeat in Times of Electoral Turbulences: Patterns of Legislative Recruitment in Denmark 1945-1990«, pp. 218-50, in Albert Somit, Rudolf Wildenmann, Bernhard Boll & Andrea Römmele (eds.), *The Victorious Incumbent: A Threat to Democracy?*, Aldershot: Dartmouth.

Pedersen, Mogens N. (1997): »De, der selv siger stop«, pp. 62-73, in Jørgen Elklit & Roger Buch Jensen (eds.), *Kommunalvalg*, Odense: Odense University Press.

Pikkala, Sari (1997): »Kvinnor i kommunfullmäktige«, pp. 347-362, in Voitto Helander & Siv Sandberg (eds.), Festskrift till Krister Ståhlberg, Åbo: Åbo Akademis Förlag.

Raaum, Nina (1995). »The Political Representation of Women: A Bird's Eye View«, pp. 25-55, in Lauri Karvonen & Per Selle (eds.), *Women in Nordic Politics: Closing the Gap*. Aldershot: Darthmouth.

Thomas, Sue (1994). *How Women Legislate*, New York: Oxford University Press.

Bringing the Politics Back in
The Public Accountability of Regulators

Michael Laver

Abstract

Even the most free of »free« markets requires heavy government intervention to create and maintain property rights and to regulate »arm's length« transactions in these. Proponents of markets advocate that such regulation be carried out, not by the core bureaucracy, but by »independent« public agencies, such as courts, central banks, and other state agencies with terms of reference that free them from direct »political« intervention. The big problem is that, in a democracy, the core public bureaucracy is at least formally accountable to the population it serves, thereby conferring legitimacy on the public policy process. Quasi-independent government agencies, precisely by virtue of being »freed« from direct political intervention, typically have no direct public accountability for their actions. The public legitimacy of such actions, especially when these are unpopular, ceases to be self-evident. This chapter argues that the next generation of thought about public policy-making must bring politics back into the equation.

Rumours of the End of Politics Greatly Exaggerated

This chapter argues that it is high time for public policy specialists to begin thinking about the look and feel of post-libertarian policy implementation and analysis. To deconstruct my argument a little before it has even been put together, readers do need to know that I was born in Britain in 1949, and reared in the golden era of the British welfare state, in an age of innocence and hope when Margaret Thatcher was known only as a grocer's daughter from Grantham.

The free market had disgraced itself with the Great Depression and the world had been rescued by an economic model based upon the premise that politics makes a difference because governments can spend their way out of recessions and smooth out the business cycle – a model that had been tried, had been tested, and had been shown to work. World War 2 had created so much physical damage and social disruption that central planning on a grand scale was clearly the only way to get things back on the rails. Huge sections of key infrastructures had been destroyed in the fighting. Vast numbers of returning soldiers had needed jobs and homes fit for heroes. The middle classes had learned to live without servants. A new social order had well and truly arrived.

In Britain, war hero Winston Churchill had been thrown out on his ear as soon as the war ended, and a Labour government installed with a landslide majority, a government committed to taking over the commanding heights of the British economy and systematically constructing a comprehensive welfare state. Post-war reconstruction generated an economic boom and, even when right wing governments took over from the social democrats, they did not dismantle one tiny bit of the welfare state. Instead they told people, as in Harold Macmillan's famous slogan for British voters, »you've never had it so good«.

It all seems so very different now. Believing in government intervention has come to be like smoking, or drinking and driving, or clear-cutting the rain forest. People still do it but when they do they're treated, at least in public, as either morons or psychopaths. As far as social scientists are concerned, this means that our job is now typically defined as searching for ever neater new ways to take things away from the Fat Controller at the centre of things and give them back to consumers, people who know what they want and by golly have a right to get it. The fundamentally libertarian ideological message in all of this is that the best thing governments can do is to keep their noses out of other people's business. This, in turn, has stunted public debate about what, apart from keeping their noses out of things, governments might usefully be doing. Well, I was brought up to believe that government is about *taking care* of the people's business, not keeping its nose out of this, and what I want to do here is launch a counter-attack.

Before doing this, I want you to believe me when I tell you that I am not a Luddite. My friends will tell you that my main failing is to be far too fascinated by what is strange, new and curious, and far too little concerned to keep the best of what we have already. If they were foolish enough to indulge in a little freelance deconstruction of their own, they might tell you that Laver has just got bored with the current, by now tired and tawdry, libertarian orthodoxy; that he's on the look-out for new thrills. They might even be right, but what is important right now is that I'm not going to take you back to the good old days of hoping that handing the job over to big government was the cure for all our ills. What I want to do is to look forwards rather than backwards, beyond present-day fundamentalist belief in the magic of the market to what I sincerely do feel is the essential inevitability of the political. I have to warn the faint at heart, however, that this does involve fresh thinking about the continuing and utterly central role in our lives for government intervention of some form or another.

Robinson Crusoe and the Collective Action Problem

A lot of what I will have to say here has to do with how we solve what is perhaps the most fundamental problem of all human social interaction. This is the collective action problem, which arises because nearly every one of us desires things that we consume as individuals, but which can only be produced as a result of the co-ordinated action of groups of people, functioning as a society.

Even in Daniel Defoe's *Robinson Crusoe* – a book that should be required reading for anyone interested in public policy – the eponymous hero of charming but eccentric self-sufficiency survived only by making regular visits to a shipwreck that conveniently provided him with a range of invaluable artefacts that were the result of complex social production processes. It is quite clear that in anything that looks even vaguely like the modern world, moreover, that the collective action problem provides the context within which we must pursue the gratification of almost every desire that we might have.

The easiest way to think about this problem is to work with a real-world example. The example I have chosen concerns what is for sophisticated modern human beings such as thee and me the relatively primitive desire that the food and drink we consume should be safe, and not contain things that will either kill us or cause us great pain. You can get a feel for this atavistic desire for safe food and drink when you watch the reactions of any tourist who has eaten a T-bone steak in London over the past twenty years or so when you mention, doing your public duty of course, that the current medical orthodoxy is that eating beef on the bone in Britain is a way to catch CJD, a disease that takes up to 20 years to incubate, but which ends up killing people after first turning their brains into sponges. The people you helpfully tell this to may swagger around whistling loudly and pretending not to care, but look behind their eyes and you'll see that this news really scares them. The threat of catching an incurable brain disease, quite simply, does not make any sensible person feel better off.

Those of us who are not in a position to take to the wilds, grow our own food from seeds that we gather from nature and dig our own deep artesian wells, must rely upon others for the safety of the food and drink that we put into our mouths every day. We do this in the certain knowledge that the individual producers of the products we all eat and drink face continual incentives to cut corners, to shave costs and to increase their private profits. If they are not sensitive to these pressures then, quite simply, they are not the successful entrepreneurs whose behaviour patterns are so central, at least in theory, to the effective operation of any market.

Most mere mortals who spend any time at all in a slaughterhouse, or indeed any other food processing plant that is working to its normal routine, typically find the experience quite shocking. Pieces of food find their way back from dirty floors onto the production line and thence into packages that end up on supermarket shelves and ultimately in our mouths. Mould and slime get scraped off the ingredients of all sorts of soon-to-be tasty and inviting dishes. Things that nobody in this room would eat in a million years if they were put naked on their plate in a restaurant get minced and mashed and sauced and tossed into processed foods. Rats, mice and and other wild-life rule the roost in the store-rooms. I could go on and on and on but I think you get the picture.

The bottom line is that almost anyone I can think of – except perhaps the very most perverse and cranky of survivalists – agrees that we derive great benefits from a public health and hygiene regime that sets minimum standards for the quality of what we eat and drink, and which results in the enforcement of these standards. It is, furthermore, very hard indeed to construct an argument that the setting and enforcement of such standards should be left entirely to the swashbuckling entrepreneurs of a free market in food. Their incentive and the ability to increase private profits by cutting corners are just too great. Most sensible people would agree, I think, that we need »outside« regulatory agencies to set and enforce health and hygiene standards for what we eat and drink. Attempts to find a way around the need for such agencies look more like preposterous ideological contortions than serious policy analysis. In some very important situations, in short, there is a fundamental need for state regulation of »private« markets.

This need for state regulation does not just derive from the particularly emotive matter of the safety of what we eat and drink. Every »private« market fundamentally requires the intervention of external agencies to define, regulate and enforce the property rights that are actually traded on the market. The difference between property and possession, after all, is why someone can be thrown into jail (by the iron fist of the state, naturally) for having »your« TV set in their living room. The difference between freedom and a prison cell often has to do with the public definition and regulation of private property rights.

The march of technology continually creates new potential property rights that need to be defined, regulated and defended by external agencies, whether these concern airport landing slots, broadcasting frequencies for mobile phone networks, satellite orbits or, no doubt in the future, launch windows for flights to the Moon or to Mars. As we saw very clearly when the former Warsaw Pact states set out to change modes of production in the post-Soviet era, »free« markets only really get going as a result of robust government action to define and defend a particular set of property rights.

The real questions, therefore, concern who creates, regulates and enforces these property rights and associated obligations, which are fundamentally political and not at all self-evident? And to whom are the regulators of the market in these rights responsible?

The move away from big government, originally associated in Europe with conservative libertarianism, but now supported quite widely around the world and across the political spectrum, typically involves advocating an »arm's length« approach to regulation by government. The essential conception of the policy process embedded in this approach is that the political system defines a set of property rights and a set of obligations associated with these. It then establishes and maintains a legal regime within which a »free« market in these rights can operate in an orderly way.

Proponents of »free« markets typically argue that, despite the fact that the property rights upon which they rely depend crucially upon government action, markets can nonetheless be made free by ensuring that the key public sector roles are performed, not by the core bureaucracy, but by »independent« public agencies such as courts, central banks, and other state agencies. These agencies are set goals that are admittedly the product of a very political public policy process, but they are given the job of achieving these goals under terms of reference that protect them from direct »political« intervention. The theory is thus that the policy making process is fundamentally political, while the policy implementation process is fundamentally legal-administrative. The magic of the market, it is claimed, can only operate if policy, once made, is implemented in a »neutral« technocratic manner with as little political input as possible.

»Arm's length« rule implementation may be performed directly by the judicial system, which in most western democracies is at least in theory clearly protected under the constitution from political interference. This is rare, however, not least because the regulation of a sophisticated set of property rights in the modern world typically involves a vast volume of technical knowledge and specialised analytical skills, as well as continuous monitoring and action. All this is hardly a job for a court of law, which tends to deal with cleaning up messes after they have happened, and to become familiar with the technicalities of these matters only on a »need to know« basis.

It is thus far more usual for front-line regulation in a specialised policy area, if not handled directly by government but instead in an arm's length manner, to be dealt with, not by the courts, but by an »independent« regulatory authority. While ostensibly legal-administrative in character, this typically operates in a rather ill-defined limbo to be found between the political, administrative and judicial systems.

The ideal of those who advocate rolling back the state is thus to push regulatory agencies firmly into the legal-administrative arena, in theory free from »political« interference. This ideal involves defining regulatory agencies as being, in essence, technocratic and hands-on branches of the judicial system. Ultimately, of course, the classical doctrine of the separation of powers means that the judicial system is not accountable to the political system, and this conception of a regulatory authority thus involves paying a high price in terms of the public accountability of regulators. Low-level stupidity and ineptitude can be handled within the internal career structure of the regulatory agency itself as presently happens, at least to some extent, within the judiciary. However, if this model is pursued, there is little by way of ultimate recourse against stupidity and ineptitude at the top, which must just be accepted as the price to be paid for the independence of the regulatory system.

Even for those who are prepared to pay this price, however, a much bigger problem is that it is simply not realistic to expect the explicitly »political« arena of a policy-*making* system that is dealing with any complex policy area to be able to define a set of property rights and associated obligations in a sufficiently exhaustive and internally consistent manner to enable purely mechanical policy *implementation*. General principles can be set out and books full of very detailed rules can be written. As any lawyer will tell you, however, it is just not possible in advance to cover every potential future eventuality. Not only that, but particular real-world cases will inevitably arise that highlight inconsistencies in any given set of general regulations. Thus regulators cannot always be neutral rule-implementation machines – it is just not possible to write rules in sufficient detail to cover every possibility and avoid every possible inconsistency. In short, and whether we like it or not, regulators must inevitably exercise discretion.

The exercise of discretion by a regulatory agency is vital to my argument because, when regulators do exercise discretion, they involve themselves in the political process of policy making rather than the legal-administrative process of policy implementation. One of the fundamental principles of a democracy, of course, is that those involved in making political decisions are accountable to the public.

We have now got to the nub of the argument. Given that »independent« regulators inevitably must exercise substantive discretion in the policy area under their jurisdiction, how can they be held accountable to the public for their discretionary actions, while at the same time remaining independent? Indeed, are the twin desires for the independence and the accountability of our regulators not fundamentally in contradiction?

The traditional political model of regulation by the core government bureaucracy, so much in disfavour during the current vogue for independent regulatory authorities, solves this problem in a simple but effective manner by tilting the scales firmly in the direction of accountability. The core - bureaucracy is divided into government departments with a well-defined hierarchical structure. Each government department is the ultimate responsibility of a political appointee who is at all times politically accountable for actions taken by his or her department. In European-style parliamentary democracies, there is a government minister responsible to a cabinet and Prime Minister, who are in turn responsible to a parliament elected by the people. In US-style presidential systems, the political heads of government departments are responsible to a directly elected president, while the committees of an elected legislature also play an important role.

In either system, the buck for controversial decisions is passed up the hierarchy and ultimately, if a political issue is at stake, the buck stops in the political arena. Someone who is accountable to the public is left holding it. In a democracy, this provides ultimate public accountability for administrative decisions with significant and substantive policy content.

A key implication of the more recent model of an independent regulatory agency is that such agencies have powers, granted with the intention of giving them independence from political interference, that make them look rather like latter-day absolute dictatorships. When controversial discretionary decisions are made by regulators operating in such an environment, it is by no means necessary that the buck stops with someone who is accountable to the public. Indeed, on this model of the public regulator, public accountability looks more like unwarranted political pressure, and is something to be guarded against rather than sought after. The scales are thus tilted firmly in the direction of independence and against accountability, for reasons that are often not clearly articulated.

There is, it seems to me, a deep and serious contradiction within the very notion of an »independent« regulatory authority acting at all times in the public interest but steadfastly insulated from political pressure. The only hope for such a system to work is to find an unending supply of Platonic Guardians to staff senior positions in regulatory agencies. If this were possible, then we could assume regulatory agencies to be benevolent dictatorships run by an enlightened caste of administrators, quite unlike ordinary people but with the sole aim, nonetheless, of furthering the interests of ordinary people.

Even in this unlikely event, the best intentioned of philosopher-kings will make mistakes from time to time. One very unfortunate consequence of the insulation of regulation from politics is that, if some public policy atrocity is committed within an »independent« regulatory agency, then mainstream politicians who would have found themselves being held accountable had the civil service been doing the job can now wash their hands of the matter. They can argue, quite rightly in their own terms, that they cannot be held responsible for the behaviour of an agency that of its very essence is beyond their control. If the matter goes to court then, provided the regulator is not acting *ultra vires* and does indeed have the right to exercise the discretion at issue, then there may also be little public accountability for whatever blunder has been committed.

All of this will mean that the victim of a policy atrocity performed by an independent regulator legally exercising his or her discretion will be in a position very much like the powerless and bewildered victim of Franz Kafka's *Castle*. (This seminal critique of unaccountable big government is another must for all interested in the policy process in general and policy implementation in particular). The bottom line will be that there will be no place at all in the system where the buck can be seen to stop in the hands of someone who can be made responsible to the public for holding it.

In a nutshell, there is a real danger that the independent regulatory authority so beloved of those who hate big government is far more likely to resemble the Kafka-esque caricature of big government than the core public service that it replaces. Core public servants, at least, have bosses who are ultimately accountable to the public, and who will kick ass down the line to avoid having to pay the price for the mistakes of their subordinates.

What this highlights is that a much stronger case must be made by those who want to tilt the scales in favour of the independence of public regulators, and against their accountability. This case will need to be argued in terms of the incentive structure that can be put in place to ensure that regulators with feet of clay, who are not Platonic guardians, will not come to behave as unresponsive and increasingly out-of-touch-tyrants.

All of this matters for many reasons but the one I wish to focus on for the remainder of this chapter has to do with the legitimacy of the political system. Legitimacy is admittedly a rather vague notion that is somewhat unfashionable these days, but it seems to me to be crucial if we want to understand the political role of regulators in the policy process. Legitimacy ultimately means that those who live in a society cede the right to govern themselves to some political regime. It involves individuals accepting, and abiding by, all decisions »legitimately« made by the regime according to agreed principles and procedures, even when they disagree with the substantive outcomes of particular decisions.

Obviously, when you accept a decision with which you agree, this tells us nothing about how you view the decision making regime involved. It is when you accept a decision with which you disagree substantively, because you accept the right of the regime to make the decision and the procedures by which the decision was made, that we see you accepting the legitimacy of the regime in question. You accept the outcome of decisions with which you disagree because you recognise that, if everybody were to challenge the basis of every collective decision that was made within the society in which you choose to live, then life would be chaotic and intolerable. People on the losing side of every collective decision would disobey it, and would have to be tracked down and punished at massive cost. Many, many collectively valuable policies would not be worth implementing in the face of such costs. Collectively, therefore, members of a society gain by tacitly accepting the legitimacy of the public policy process that governs most aspects of their daily lives, reserving unto themselves the right to challenge, or to exile themselves from, the incumbent regime on matters that go to the core of their very existence.

In this sense, the notion of legitimacy is closely bound up with the collective action problem. A political regime that prevails because of its legitimacy can be seen to lie somewhere between the traditional Hobbesian ruler who is the bogey of those who hate big government – a ruler who forces people to cooperate »for their own good« under the threat of state sanctions – and an anarchistic regime under which a principle of reciprocity allows people to solve collective action problems for themselves on the basis of conditional cooperation.

A regime that prevails because of its legitimacy is one which makes governmental decisions that for the most part do not have to be enforced by costly sanctions, because its subjects accept that, taken as a whole over the long term, the substance of these decisions will be good for them. While subjects face an incentive not to obey particular decisions with which they disagree, to do so would be to defect from a tacit »anarchistic« agreement that those who choose to live under this regime will abide by its decisions, even when they disagree with some of these, provided the decisions are legitimately taken. This leads to the well established constitutional principle that decisions should be taken according to principles that all accept as correct when viewed from behind a »veil of ignorance« about their substantive implications in particular cases.

Once people can be seen to defect from legitimate decisions, then this begins to unravel the social contract which underpins the operation of a legitimate political regime. In any large society, the fear of the resulting social chaos would almost certainly not in itself be enough to prevent individual free riding, of course. We will undoubtedly need to rely upon some form of individual reputational effect whereby those seen to defect from legitimate decisions will be treated as being generally less trustworthy than others, and will therefore find it harder to do profitable business in general. This is a large and complex problem, but a key conclusion for my purposes, one that I take to be relatively uncontroversial, is that the legitimacy of a public policy process is very valuable, compared to the alternatives, for most of those who are subject to it.

Now, honest fool that I am, I have to warn you that we have come to the point in my argument that does require a leap of faith. (In my defence I should point out that every argument that really gets you somewhere new involves at least one leap of faith). My leap here concerns the link between legitimacy and accountability – specifically the relationship between the legitimacy of a public policy process and the public accountability of key decision makers within this.

Logically, I suspect, there is no strict link between the two concepts. In other words, if we could indeed find a caste of Platonic Guardians who we all agreed were benign philosophers to run our public policy process for us (and of course the self-image of many key public servants in the real world is not a million miles away from that of a benign and enlightened guardian of the public interest), then we might accept the legitimacy of this process, even if those making key decisions were utterly unaccountable to us for what they decided to do. But most of the problems of politics, of course, would disappear if such a caste existed – we would just lie back, surrender ourselves to our guardians and live happily ever after.

In the absence of such paragons I suspect, and this is an empirical generalisation rather than a logical deduction, that mere mortals feel decision-makers are taking decisions that are legitimate only if they can be held accountable for these in some way. In other words I am claiming that the public accountability of decision makers is a key principle that people will demand of a decision making process before they accept it as legitimate.

This implies that undermining the accountability of decision makers undermines the legitimacy of the regime within which they operate.

As they say in the west of Ireland having at last fixed a troublesome tractor engine, »NOW she's suckin' diesel«. Everything is now in place for me to drive home my main argument about why we have to bring the politics back into the public policy process.

We have seen that the current vogue for shifting the role of regulator away from the core state bureaucracy towards »independent« public agencies that are ostensibly free from political interference, of its very essence, must also involve tilting the scales against the political accountability of decision makers. This also tends to undermine the legitimacy of the regulatory process, as unpopular outcomes are taken to result more from the arbitrary exercise of power, even when this is exercised strictly within the terms of reference of the decision maker, than from hard choices made in the public interest. Clear lines of public accountability for decision makers provide practical demonstrations that they make their choices as agents of the public. Given this, citizens accord these decisions legitimacy and do not force the state to hunt down and punish every citizen who disagrees with a particular public policy decision.

The basis of legitimacy in social reciprocity means that there is much less of a social obligation on any individual to abide by a public decision that is not legitimate. Narrow cost-benefit decisions on policing and enforcement are then all that are needed in the face of an illegitimate decision, since in such cases no public opprobrium falls upon those who can get away with breaking the law.

In this way a loss of legitimacy by a decision making regime, provoked by a loss of accountability on the part of its decision makers, can have huge social costs. Reducing the accountability of decision makers can cause major collective action problems, problems that are completely ignored by those who favour spinning off the core regulatory role to independent public agencies.

What is the solution to this problem? It has of course taken me so long to state the problem that I conveniently have little time left for the much more difficult business of solving it. In any event this solution will not easily be found, and is something I take to be one of the core projects of those who are concerned with the nature of the public policy process in a post-libertarian era. It will be a big job and for the most part I leave it to others.

»Bringing the state back in« has become a fashionable enough slogan in reaction to some of the excesses of 1980s' Thatcherism, but it risks being interpreted as no more than the plea for a return to the golden age of the welfare state, a call to step backwards rather than forwards. »Bringing the politics back in« or »bringing the people back in« to the process of public administration, however, presents us with the challenge of looking for new solutions rather than rediscovering old ones.

Regulation by a core bureaucracy under direct political control is not the only way to ensure the accountability of decision-makers engaged in the implementation of key public policies. Building a fire-wall between the making of public policy and its implementation is not in itself a bad thing. It is perhaps the most powerful argument of the post-welfare state public policy analysts, and has never been challenged in this paper. What has been objected to has been undermining the legitimacy of the public policy process by severely curtailing the accountability of those whose job is to implement policy.

It is easy to say, of course, that we must preserve the idea of a fire-wall between a political process of policy making and a legal-administrative process of implementation, but must nonetheless give much more thought to how to make the implementation process accountable. It's easy to say but hard to do because, given conflicting tastes among members of the public, any real form of public accountability is essentially political. Keeping that fire-wall means dealing with two quite independent political processes and, of course, reconciling potential conflicts between the two.

My hunch is that this is going to involve a completely new type of politics, the like of which we haven't yet seen in operation anywhere. We are all very familiar with the various forms of politics associated with making public policy decisions. We are much less familiar with the politics of holding the implementation process accountable when this is not done via the political system that makes the decisions in the first place.

We are most of us, furthermore, accustomed to the notion that legal-administrative decision makers can do the job that they do precisely because they are not subject to direct political pressure. Most Europeans, for example, shrink in horror at the image, so common in US movies and television, of judges and district attorneys running for office and trimming their legal decisions with an eye to the next election. While a system of accountability for those who implement public policy decisions need not be quite so nakedly populist as this, there is no doubt that the flip side of accountability is susceptibility to public pressure and a dilution of what is of course in reality no more than a myth of legal-administrative impartiality.

Finding a new and innovative way to trade off the accountability and the impartiality of those who implement public policy should thus be one of the main tasks that all of us who are interested in public policy set ourselves as we prepare for the post-libertarian era.

When Should a Minority Government Resign?

Leif Lewin

Abstract

In a parliamentary system, internal disunity and lack of parliamentary confidence can lead to the fall of governments. The effect of the electoral outcome on minority governments is harder to foresee, however. At what level should a government already below the magic 50-percent level resign? The decisive factor is the kind of supporting majority a minority government can reckon with during negotiations. Votes count but bargaining decides. The doctrine of parliamentarism must be reformulated, but in such a manner, though, that it does not conflict with the principle that citizens must be able to hold their representatives accountable.

Classical democratic theory prescribes majority rule: the party or coalition of parties controlling a majority ought to form the government. When this majority is lost, the government should resign (Bagehot [1867] 1928). But what about a situation in which already at the start the government controlled fewer than 50 percent of the seats in Parliament? At what point should a minority government resign? When it has 40 percent, 30 percent? At some other critical point?

Size, however, is not the only requisite of classical parliamentarism. In a majoritarian democracy, the government must command a legislative basis which is not only large enough to control Parliament but also unified enough to pursue consistent policies (Lewin 1998b). Furthermore, the government should enjoy Parliament's confidence. With majority governments this is seldom a problem; party discipline means that such governments can reckon with majority support in Parliament. A minority government, on the other hand – which is common in Continental Europe – maintains its position by bargaining over policies with its various supporters. It may thus enjoy parliamentary confidence in the one case and lose it in the next (Laver & Schofield 1990).

Against this background, I have suggested dividing the factors behind government resignation into three categories: those reflecting *the electoral outcome*, those arising from *disunity*, and those brought about by a vote of *no confidence*. The data for the empirical illustrations accompanying the following discussion are furnished by the 23 resignations of government which have taken place in Swedish parliamentary history (Lewin 1996, 136). I agree with Damgaard (1994) that, in this kind of analysis, the problem is not so much how we define the »termination« of a government as what we mean by »a government.« I have followed Strom (1990) in using the following definition in my studies: a new government is one formed in either of the two following events: 1) a new prime minister is appointed (except in cases where the previous prime minister died or resigned as party leader, and was replaced by a new party leader); and 2) a change takes place in the party composition of the government.

The Desire to Resign

According to mainstream Downsian political science - modelled as it is on majoritarian democracy - »office« rather than »policy« is the strongest motive behind politicians' behaviour. The attractions of power decline, however, when a government does not have a majority. The leader of a government that has difficulty implementing its program on account of its minority position, will be strongly disposed to resign. In only exceptional cases – as in Sweden in 1998 – will a prime minister cling to power after having suffered a serious electoral setback. A minority government founded on negotiation and compromise is constantly on the verge of betraying its program; the concessions involved can prove so painful that resignation comes as a liberation in the end. Loyalty to ideology, rather than holding on to power, is what wins praise. Party leaders who resign from government for ideological reasons often meet with plaudits and appreciation (e.g., the Swedish Moderate Party leader in 1981 and the Swedish Center Party leader in 1994).

Where minority parliamentarism is concerned, then, it is more appropriate to say that parties formulate policies in order to win elections than to say that they win elections in order to formulate policies (Downs 1957, 28). If such difficulties arise that central electoral promises cannot be kept, the prime minister usually prefers to tender his resignation. Not *everything* is negotiable for a minority government. Selling out the party program just to keep power is considered a sign of political decadence. Swedish parliamentary tradition was summarized aphoristically in the words spoken by a Swedish prime minister upon resigning in 1926: »It is better that this government fall than that the power of government be allowed to fall« (Swedish Parliamentary Proceedings AK 1926, 44, 29).

This attitude existed in Sweden already in pre-parliamentary times. The political interest of the Swedish people was awakened during the political struggle over the introduction of tariffs, leading to the emergence of the democratic idea that ministerial power should depend on the judgement of the voters and not on the confidence of the king. In the eye of the storm was a prime minister who was very much of two minds. He repeatedly asked the king to be relieved of his duties, invoking the electoral advances achieved by the opposing party (Petré 1945, 249-252).

After the Left had achieved a majority and the principle of parliamentary responsibility had been accepted, the triumphant Social Democrats were swept by a wave of great expectations. Notwithstanding this, the leader of the first socialist party in the world to gain power by peaceful means was most unwilling to shoulder the burdens of government. He justified his caution with the plea that the government would not be able to implement its program in the manner expected by the voters (Gerdner 1946, 198-199).

For fully 23 years - between 1946 and 1969 - another Social Democratic prime minister governed the country. With superior tactical skill, he split his non-socialist opponents and implemented his program of building a »Strong Society« with a large public sector. Privately, however, this highly successful prime minister longed to escape the policy of negotiation to which he was forced by his minority position. He wished to resign. For a long time, in fact, he regarded his leadership as but a provisional solution in the shadow of the colorful politicians of an earlier generation. He wished »quietly to vanish.« He gave serious consideration to repeated offers to be appointed Chancellor of the Swedish Universities. And even at the time of his greatest political victories, he inquired into whether or not he might be allowed to resign; time and time again, he was persuaded to stay (Ruin 1986, 64-71).

At what point, then, does a minority government *wish* to resign? An empirically founded answer would be: more often than one might think.

Electoral Outcome

In the Swedish material, electoral outcome is the most common motivation for governments to resign. As can be seen from Table 1, 12 of 23 resigna-

Table 1. Resignations of Swedish governments 1917-94.

	Electoral Outcome	Disunity	No Confidence	Other
Edén 1917-20 MAJ		x		
Branting I 1920 MIN	x			
De Geer/von Sydow 1920-21 MIN	x			
Branting II 1921-23 MIN			x	
Trygger 1923-24 MIN	x			
Branting III/Sandler 1924-26 MIN			x	
Ekman I 1926-28 MIN	x			
Lindman 1928-30 MIN			x	
Ekman II/Hamrin 1930-32 MIN	x			
Hansson I 1932-36 MIN			x	
Pehrsson i Bramstorp 1936 MIN	x			
Hansson II 1936-39 MAJ				x
Hansson III 1939-45 MAJ		x		
Hansson IV/Erlander I 1945-51 MIN	x			
Erlander II 1951-57 MAJ		x		
Erlander III/Palme I 1957-76 MIN	x			
Fälldin I 1976-78 MAJ		x		
Ullsten 1978-79 MIN	x			
Fälldin II 1979-81 MAJ		x		
Fälldin III 1981-82 MIN	x			
PalmeII/Carlsson, 1982-91 MIN	x		x	
Bildt 1991-94 MIN	x			

tions can be explained in this manner. One noteworthy fact is that only minority governments have resigned for this reason in Sweden (on the resignation of Swedish majority governments, see below).[1]

Yet when, as we asked earlier, should a government resign if it has only enjoyed minority support even prior to an election just held? Table 2 charts some of the issues that a prime minister must consider when confronting this question. The point of departure for the analysis is that under conditions of minority parliamentarism, the head of government cannot restrict his attentions to the share of votes garnered by his own party. He must also determine whether or not he can reckon with a supporting majority. A simple two-by-two table may serve to illustrate this:

Table 2. When should the government resign? Table of the prime minister's deliberation.

	No supporting majority	Supporting majority
More votes	1	2
Fewer votes	3	4

If the government receives more votes than in the previous election, it may seem peculiar for it to consider resigning. In the case of a minority government, however, there may be reason for it to do so if the government lacks a supporting majority (this situation is represented by square 1). Electoral success may furnish the fortitude needed to initiate negotiations aimed at broadening the parliamentary basis of the government (Erlander II in 1951 was such a case).

It may seem still less incumbent on a government to resign if it has increased its share of the vote even while being able to rely on a supporting majority (this situation is represented by square 2). Sometimes, however, the strength of electoral winds is considered to be more important than who holds a majority. A party in opposition may have advanced more strongly still, strengthening its claim on governmental responsibility (this was the case with Trygger in 1924, who resigned to make way for the Social Democrats).

A minority government which has received fewer votes, and which lacks a supporting majority besides, naturally finds it difficult to retain power (square 3). Palme in 1976 and Carlsson in 1991 were instances hereof.

Finally, we have the case of a government which has received fewer votes but which retains a supporting majority. The outcome here is particularly uncertain. Three Swedish cases may be recalled here: 1932, 1979 and 1998. In all three, one could imagine an outcome contrary to what actually occurred. In 1932, a Liberal prime minister resigned after his party had lost votes in the election - even though there was still a non-socialist majority in Parliament. Once again, electoral winds combined with fixity of purpose on the part of the Social Democratic minority secured governmental power for the latter. Contrary to what is sometimes claimed, therefore, the assumption of power in 1932 by the Swedish Social Democrats – an event which lay the foundation for a half-century at the helm of government – was far from an obvious and historically given victory. The result could perfectly well have been different.

In 1979, the relative strength was the same but the outcome was the reverse. This time, the Social Democrats did not ask for the chance to form a government. During the entire election campaign, moreover, the Liberal Party leader (whose party ended up losing votes), had been playing with the idea of retaining the prime ministership precisely in a situation of this kind. He was attracted by the idea of acting as a pivot between the Social Democratic and non-socialist groupings in Parliament. The Social Democrats were about as strong in 1979 as in 1932 (with 44 percent and 45 percent of the seats, respectively). Moreover, the divisions between the non-socialist parties were roughly as great: the right-wing leaders had been been strongly skeptical of cooperating in 1932, and sharp tensions in connection with nuclear power divided the bourgeois parties in 1979. In the end, the Liberal prime minister resigned, making way not for the Social Democrats (who had gained in the election) but, rather, for a bourgeois coalition.

The election of 1998, finally, resulted in the most severe setback ever suffered by the Social Democrats. Nevertheless, the Social Democratic prime minister continued serenely at the head of a minority government. During the election campaign he had not indicated, whether in the event of a continued minority position he would seek to cooperate with parties to his left or to his right. Following the election, however, he entered into negotiations with the Left Party (formerly the Communists) and with the Greens. The leftist bloc which took shape had lost 11 seats in Parliament to the parties of the right. The Left's parliamentary strength was still sufficient, however, to provide the prime minister with a supporting majority. It was this support that proved decisive. The prime minister's refusal to resign, notwithstanding the record losses sustained by his party, impelled the leader of the Moderates to request a parliamentary vote of »no confidence«. However, this motion garnered only the support of a minority (consisting of the parliamentary deputies of the Moderate Party).

In sum, there is no established parliamentary practice, covering the case of a minority government which has sustained an electoral defeat even while retaining a supporting majority. Inter-party negotiations may produce a result whereby even a party which lost out heavily in elections can remain at the helm of government.

Disunity

Resignations due to disunity generally reflect a situation in which a government has been formed along *one* conflict dimension but subsequently dissolves along another. A striking feature of the Swedish data is that all of the resignations tendered by majority governments have arisen for this reason.

An analysis of how conflict dimensions have succeeded one another in Sweden yields a thumbnail sketch of the country's political history. The program of the first government in Table 1 was to establish parliamentary democracy and institute universal suffrage. When this program had been accomplished, the economic dimension assumed primacy: now that »formal democracy« had been introduced, the Social Democrats deemed the time ripe for »socialism.« As a result, the Liberals and the Social Democrats went their separate ways, reflecting their differences regarding tax levels and the role of the state in the business sector.

The economic dimension has since dominated political conflict in Sweden, as in other European countries. In our data, it accounts for four of the five resignations listed in the disunity column. This conflict dimension re-emerged after World War II, when left parties had great expectations of a »Harvest Time« during the post-war period. The result was the dissolution of the Grand Coalition which had governed the country during the war. In the course of the prosperous 1950s, the Left position on this scale acquired a more advanced formulation: in the struggle over supplementary pensions, the Social Democrats proposed that the state bear responsibility not only for the citizens' basic welfare, but also for the individual's right to retain a high standard of living during retirement. The non-socialist partner in the ruling coalition rejected this, however, as a new kind of »socialism.« In 1981, finally, the economic dimension again proved decisive when the middle parties, governing together with the Moderates, surprised their partners by concluding an agreement on taxes with the opposition Social Democrats.

In 1978, a new dimension caused a government to resign. This non-socialist government, the first in 44 years, had been formed two years earlier along the economic dimension. In the preceding election campaign, moreover, the Social Democrats had again been criticized for »socialism« - indeed, for »East European Socialism.«[2] Having constituted the government, however, the bourgeois parties split over nuclear power, and the government resigned over this issue (Lewin 1998a, 238-273).

No Confidence

As in the cases found in the »electoral outcome« column, only minority governments have resigned upon suffering a vote of »no confidence.« Here too, the Swedish data present us with five cases.

Placing the government's very existence at risk by calling for a »vote of confidence« is the ultimate means by which a prime minister can force dissidents within his party or coalition to acquiesce in his policies. In this way, the leader of the Swedish Conservatives silenced critics within his party who opposed universal suffrage for men. Similarly, a Social Democratic prime minister, in 1959, forced the Communists to support a proposal for a sales tax. And in this way the Moderate Party leader faced down an attempt by a right-wing party in 1994 to block the government's economic policy (Lewin 1996, 154).

The first two resignations in this category (in 1923 and 1926) had to do with unemployment, a Social Democratic government in both cases seeking to conduct a more »humane« policy than the bourgeois majority would allow. The third resignation had to do with tariffs: in this case, a Conservative government named the terms for its continuation in office, and resigned when these were not met. The resignation of 1936 was unique. The Social Democratic government had lost a vote on defense expenditures. Yet it remained in place a little while longer, in order to be able - in the face of an approaching election - to choose a tactically more favorable question on which to fall than over a proposal to cut defense spending (in a situation where many believed that a large-scale war was soon to break out). The government then proposed an unrealistically large increase in pensions. Sure enough, this proposal was voted down, and the Social Democrats were able to enter the election campaign with their flags held high. The resignation of 1990, finally, reflected disagreements over economic policy: the Social Democratic government had proposed a »freeze program,« freezing prices, rents, municipal taxes and – remarkable for a Labour government – a wage freeze and a temporary ban on strikes. These latter two measures were more than the Left Party Communists could accept. The Communists then joined with the non-socialist parties in voting »no« when the prime minister called a vote of confidence.

The striking thing about the resignations in the »no-confidence« column is that the prime ministers in question knew *beforehand* that they would lose. Thus, the setbacks did not lie in a failure to tame the opposition, as suggested in the introductory example. In cases of this kind, the prime minister deliberately chooses to lose. He does not do this for instrumental reasons, as he knows that he can no longer influence policy. Rather, the reason is ideological: he wishes to demonstrate his convictions and hopes in the long run to win favor with the electorate. Acordingly, it is a party's core issue that presents the best occasion for such a demonstration: unemployment for the Social Democrats, tariffs for the old Conservatives.

The initiative for a vote of »no confidence« can also come from Parliament. No such attempt has been successful in Sweden and we thus find no such instance in Table 1. However, some attempts have been made in this direction. In 1980, the Social Democrats asked Parliament to declare that the non-socialist government had mismanaged the economy. However, the government had a majority, party discipline held, and the declaration was voted down. Some years later, the relations of strength in Parliament were altered. The bourgeois parties asked Parliament for an expression of lack of confidence in the minister for foreign affairs, in view of the minister's statements regarding submarine intrusions into Swedish territorial waters. The result was the same as in the preceding case: the parliamentary strength of the different parties determined the outcome, and the proposal was voted down. Finally, as mentioned earlier, the Moderate Party requested of Parliament in 1998 that it express a lack of confidence in the prime minister, in view of the latter's refusal to resign in the face of the worst electoral setback ever suffered by his party. This proposal did not garner the support of a majority, either.

The behavior of the opposition cannot be characterized as instrumental in these cases. Proposals that Parliament withdraw its confidence serve in such instances as an ideological signal - a dramatization of the criticism routinely hurled at the government by the opposition.

This does not mean the instrument is ineffective. Parliament's prerogative to withdraw its confidence »is intended as the ultimate guarantee of parliamentarism,« the Swedish constitutional fathers write. »It would seem reasonable to assume that it will be used only in exceptional cases« (Holmberg & Stjernquist 1980, 210). The power of this prerogative is thus latent. The possibility of a withdrawal of parliamentary confidence hangs like a threatening cloud over the political landscape. It is clear that this has affected the outcome in two cases: in 1981, when the Moderates forced the government to resign on account of disunity over taxes; and in 1988, when the minister of justice resigned »voluntarily« (it was regarded as a foregone conclusion that Parliament would have otherwise withdrawn its confidence from her) (Lewin 1996, 162).

How much, then, does political trust matter for a minority government? A great deal. Since the government has a majority against it, Parliament can at any time rally behind a vote of no confidence. Should this happen, the government must resign. In order to avoid such an outcome, minority governments must maneuver carefully. If the difficulties prove insurmountable even so, the government can choose to resign before losing a vote of confidence. If the lack of confidence concerns just a particular minister, this minister can decide individually to resign.

Bargaining Decides

Minority governments were scarcely foreseen in classical parliamentary doctrine, and they were certainly not regarded as desirable. »According to the basic rules of the parliamentary system, every minority cabinet is an unwanted crisis symptom,« writes the German political scientist Klaus von Beyme in his authoritative thousand-page tome on modern parliamentarism. »A long period of minority parliamentarism threatens to lead to political sclerosis« (von Beyme 1970, 570-571).

An alternative to this dismissive attitude, as we have seen, is to extend the doctrine to embrace minority governments too. In such a context, it is customary to speak of »negative parliamentarism.« In contrast to classical parliamentarism, minority parliamentarism is not characterized by an active manifestation of will, i.e., an express approval on the part of Parliament. Rather one should say that parliamentarism is a system of government in which the cabinet is »tolerated« by a parliamentary majority (Brusewitz 1929).

At what point does this tolerance cease? When should minority governments resign? As noted in this article, electoral outcomes are rarely decisive on their own. Minority parliamentarism is one long negotiation process, in which political trust and tolerance are built up. One could perhaps say - to travesty the famous formulation of a Norwegian political scientist - that »votes count but bargaining decides« (Rokkan 1966, 105-106).[3] How such negotiations are carried out is of decisive importance for the vitality of the system. If negotiations nullify the ability of voters to hold their representatives accountable, if citizens cannot in practice vote the government of the day out of office, if the faces in the government are always the same (even if appearing in varying constellations) - if all this obtains, the danger is plain that public suspicion of politicians will only increase further. The signs are not lacking that negotiation and consensus formation in modern minority parliamentarism have brought democracy to a new and problematic stage (Lewin 1998b). A reformulation of the doctrine of parliamentarism to include minority government must therefore be paired with a pertinent analysis of how citizen influence over government can be safeguarded in a system characterized by politics of negotiation.

Notes

1. Prime Minister Carlsson, who resigned in 1990 after a vote of »no confidence«, reassumed the prime ministership after a mere eleven days. He resigned more permanently after an electoral defeat the following year.
2. The proposal for employee investment funds had called forth this criticism.
3. It was Stein Rokkan who declared that »Votes count but resources decide.« The reference here was not to political resources but to economic ones – of the sort possessed by labor, business and the farm interests.

References

Bagehot, Walter [1867] (1928). *The English Constitution*, London: Oxford University Press.

von Beyme, Klaus (1970). *Die Parlamentarische Regierungs- systeme in Europa*, München: Piper.

Brusewitz, Axel (1929).»Vad menas med parlamentarismen?« *Statsvetenskaplig Tidskrift.*

Damgaard, Erik (1994).»Termination of Danish Government Coalitions: Theoretical and Empirical Aspects,« *Scandinavian Political Studies*, vol. 17, pp. 193-212.

Downs, Anthony (1957). *An Economic Theory of Democracy*, New York: Harper & Row.

Gerdner, Gunnar (1946). *Det svenska regeringsproblemet 1917-1920. Från majoritetskoalition till minoritets- parlamentarism*, Uppsala: Almqvist & Wiksell.

Holmberg, Erik & Nils Stjernquist (1980). *Grundlagar med tillhörande författningar*, Stockholm: Norstedts.

Laver, Michael & Norman Schofield (1990). *Multiparty Government: The Politics of Coalitions in Europe*, Oxford: Oxford University Press.

Lewin, Leif (1988). *Ideology and Strategy: A Century of Swedish Politics*, Cambridge: Cambridge University Press.

Lewin, Leif (1996). *Votera eller förhandla? Om den svenska parlamentarismen*, Stockholm: Norstedts Juridik.

Lewin, Leif (1998a).»*Bråka inte!« Om vår tids demokratisyn*, Stockholm: SNS.

Lewin, Leif (1998b).»Majoritarian and Consensus Democracy: The Swedish Experiment,« *Scandinavian Political Studies*, vol. 21, pp. 195-206.

Petré, Torsten (1945). *Ministären Themptander*, Uppsala: Almqvist & Wiksell.

Rokkan, Stein (1966).»Numerical Democracy and Corporate Pluralism,« in *Political Oppositions in Western Democracies*, ed. by Robert Dahl, New Haven: Yale University Press.

Ruin, Olof (1986). *I välfärdsstatens tjänst. Tage Erlander 1946-1969*, Stockholm: Tiden.

Strom, Kaare (1990). *Minority Government and Majority Rule*, Cambridge: Cambridge University Press.

Swedish Parliamentary Proceedings (1926).

Types of Democracy and Generosity with Foreign Aid: An Indirect Test of the Democratic Peace Proposition

Arend Lijphart and Peter J. Bowman

Abstract

Because full-fledged democracy is mainly a post-1945 phenomenon and because the Cold War offers an alternative explanation for the peaceful relations among democracies, it is difficult to test the democratic peace proposition directly; most tests have therefore been indirect ones. This chapter offers another indirect test, based on the cultural and structural differences between consensus and majoritarian types of democracy – comparable to the differences between democracy and non-democracy – and based on differences with regard to one kind of peaceful foreign policy – the supply of economic development assistance. The hypothesized relationship between consensus democracy and generosity with foreign aid is strongly confirmed.

The democratic peace proposition states that democracies are more peaceful, especially in their relations with each other, than non-democratic systems. This proposition is not new; in fact, it can be traced back as far as Immanuel Kant's famous treatise *Perpetual Peace*, first published in 1795. Woodrow Wilson's aim to »make the world safe for democracy« also included the idea that a more democratic world would necessarily be a safer and more peaceful world. In the 1970s and 1980s, political scientists like Melvin Small and J. David Singer (1976) and Rudolph J. Rummel (1983) started the latest phase of scholarly attention to the democratic peace proposition, and the interest in it as well as the debate about its merits have blossomed in the 1990s.[1]

The proposition is a very strong one, especially in its dyadic form – which states that democracies do not fight *each other* – and especially for the post-

World War II era. Significantly, the major exceptions to the democratic peace proposition that critics frequently mention – the War of 1812 between the United States and Great Britain, the American Civil War (1861-65), the Spanish-American War (1898), the Boer War (1899-1902), the First World War (if Germany can be regarded as democratic on account of its elected parliament), and democratic Finland's participation in the Second World War – are all pre-1945 examples (Ray 1997, 54).[2] The proposition is also important because of its extremely significant policy implications: in a world in which all states are ruled democratically, »perpetual peace« would be guaranteed.

The democratic peace proposition can take three forms: dyadic, monadic, and systemic. It is the most robust and least controversial in its dyadic form, mentioned above, which postulates that democratic states tend to be peaceful toward each other, but are not necessarily peaceful toward non-democracies. One explanation that is cited for this divergent behavior of democracies is based on internal differences between democratic and autocratic polities. Margaret G. Hermann and Charles W. Kegley (1996) argue that democracies have markedly better bargaining capabilities and superior institutional resources than autocratic states, and that it is these strengths that make them less likely to be the target of attack by other states, rather than the fact that they have democratic and liberal forms of government. Conversely, democracies themselves are often self-righteous and belligerent toward authoritarian states whose governments they regard as repugnant. In addition, Arvid Raknerud and Havard Hegre (1997) find that democracies will often join other democracies in wars against non-democratic states.

Nevertheless, several scholars – especially Kenneth Benoit (1996) and Rudolph J. Rummel (1997, 63-83) – have argued in favor of the monadic proposition: that democracies are generally more peaceful even in their relations with non-democracies. A drawback of Benoit's analysis is that his time frame pertains only to conflicts in the 1960s and 1970s and that it can therefore only make a limited contribution to determining the full scope of democratic-autocratic relations. Writings that have a broader time frame but are still limited to the Cold War era are challenged by Henry S. Farber and Joanne Gowa (1997) as well as by Paul D. Senese (1997). Their analyses look at wars in the pre-Cold War years and find that not only are there weaknesses to monadic explanations, but there are also flaws in the dyadic postulate. Farber and Gowa (1997) emphasize that wars were more likely to be fought between democratic states in the pre-1945 era before the Cold War could have a strategically unifying effect on democracies. Hence, they argue, the democratic peace was brought on by structural balance-of-power conditions, not by genuine differences in internal political dynamics.

We shall give this »realist« perspective more attention later on in this chapter.

A new perspective – the third variant of the democratic peace proposition – was added by Nils-Petter Gleditsch and Havard Hegre (1997) to the theoretical debate: the systemic level. Their argument is that as more states become democratic, the international system as a whole becomes more peaceful. While Gleditsch and Hegre found that war actually increased with the advent of new democracies in the pre-Cold War era, the systemic proposition becomes more persuasive in the period of the Cold War. Here again, the Cold War is introduced as a key variable.

Testing the Democratic Peace Proposition

In all three forms, the proposition has been difficult to test, first, because *before 1945* there were almost no full-fledged democracies and, second, because *after 1945* the democratic peace can also be explained in »realist« terms. Let us look at each of these problems in greater detail.

First, »democracy« is a controversial concept, but there is general agreement on Robert A. Dahl's (1971, 3) eight criteria for democracy: not just universal suffrage is required, but also such institutional guarantees as free and fair elections, freedom of expression, freedom to form and join organizations, and alternative sources of information. What is often neglected, however, is that while universal suffrage is not a sufficient condition for democracy, it *is* a necessary condition. The first country to meet this condition was New Zealand when it instituted truly universal suffrage, that is, the right to vote for both men and women and also for the Maori minority, in 1893.[3] This means that, before 1893, there were no full-fledged democracies at all.[4] Several countries – such as Germany, the Netherlands, and Sweden – adopted universal suffrage, including full and equal suffrage for women, after the First World War. However, in the United Kingdom women did not get the right to vote on the same basis as men until 1928, and Belgian, French, and Italian women had to wait until the end of the Second World War to become voters.

Moreover, it is difficult to accept as »democracies« those countries with large colonial possessions whose inhabitants completely lacked the right to vote; for instance, even after 1928, the vast majority of the people ruled by the British government had no say in its selection. These limitations on universal suffrage were lifted after the Second World War as a result of the rapid dissolution of the colonial empires and the near-universal adoption of full women's suffrage – the one notable exception being that Swiss women had to wait until 1971.⁵ It is often said that democracy is a twentieth-century phenomenon, but it would be more accurate to call it a post-1945 phenomenon. The democratic peace proposition can therefore only be properly tested in the post-1945 era.

The second problem is that the democratic post-1945 era coincides almost exactly with the era of the Cold War and that »realists« insist that the Cold War can account for the peace among the post-1945 democratic polities as well as or even better than the fact that these polities were democratic. In the words of Farber and Gowa (1997, 393-94), »the advent of the Cold War induced strong common interests among democratic states [and these] common interests rather than common polities explain the post-1945 democratic peace.« Because the Cold War pitted most of the world's democracies against the major non-democracies, the relative impacts of democracy and Cold War are almost impossible to disentangle.⁶

Indirect Tests

In response to the above analytical problems, most scholarly analyses have either explicitly or implicitly – usually the latter – resorted to various forms of indirect tests. One example is James Lee Ray's (1997, 56-57) answer to the Farber-Gowa explanation. He argues that if the complete absence of wars between democracies in the Cold War era can be explained in realist terms, one would also expect the absence of wars between states in the Communist camp and the absence of wars between any of the states, including non-democracies, on the »free world« side of the struggle. As he points out, however, there were several wars of both kinds: armed conflicts within the Communist camp (the Soviet attacks on Hungary, Czechoslovakia, and Afghanistan, Soviet border clashes with China, and Vietnam's invasion of Cambodia) and wars involving at least one undemocratic state in the non-Communist camp (the El Salvador-Honduras war in 1969, the Greek-Turkish clash over Cyprus in 1974, and the 1982 British-Argentinian war over the Falkland Islands). Hence, he concludes, the democratic peace proposition is much more persuasive than the realist proposition.

The other indirect tests all derive further propositions from the proposition that democracies do not or rarely engage in war with each other; if the derivative propositions are validated – which is the case in the majority of studies – they lend support to the original democratic peace proposition. Four such indirect tests can be distinguished. The first explores the link between democracy and actions that fall short of full-scale war but that are clearly not pacific in nature: military interventions (Hermann and Kegley

1996), militarized disputes (Oneal & Russett 1997), and the tendency to escalate conflict (Senese 1997). The second category of indirect tests includes the many studies that focus on the period before 1945, when there were very few democracies, and the period before 1893, when there were no democracies at all; an example is the pioneering Small-Singer (1976) study which covers the period from 1815 to 1965. Here, the independent variable is not democracy but the degree of non-democracy.

The third indirect test focuses on democratizing states and hypothesizes that these states tend to become more peaceful as they democratize. This hypothesis has been partly disconfirmed in one study, which shows that states in transition to democracy are less pacific than stable polities of both the democratic and autocratic type (Mansfield & Snyder 1995), but confirmed in another (Ward & Gleditsch 1998). The fourth and final test is based on the argument that, if the democratic peace proposition is correct, we can also expect democracies to be peaceful internally and not to conduct civil wars. For instance, one skeptic (Layne 1994, 41) uses the American Civil War as a key disconfirming case – not very convincing evidence, of course, since neither side was fully democratic and one side even practiced slavery. On the basis of broad comparative evidence, Rudolph J. Rummel (1997, 85) concludes that democracy »sharply reduces the severity of domestic collective violence, genocide, and mass murder by governments,« and Ted Robert Gurr (1993, 290-92) shows that democracies have an especially good record of peacefully resolving ethnic conflicts.

Another Indirect Test: Democracy and Foreign Aid

We offer still another indirect test. Our argument begins with the cultural and structural explanations of the democratic peace, which are the two most common and most plausible theoretical rationales for the phenomenon. The cultural explanation is that democracies, as noted earlier, externalize their domestic norms of settling conflicts by discussion, negotiation, and compromise instead of by force. The structural explanation is that democratic checks and balances, along with transparency and accountability, give policy-makers a political and electoral motivation to avoid the material costs of war (Chan 1997, 77; Solingen 1996, 811-82). Moreover, the cultural and structural forces for peace reinforce each other. The culture of compromise strengthens compromise-inducing institutions, and compromise-oriented structures can shape accommodating political attitudes.

Our second step is to point out that democracies differ with regard to how compromise-oriented their political cultures and structures are. The distinction here is between majoritarian and consensus democracies (Lijphart 1984; 1999). Consensus democracies are more compromise-oriented than majoritarian democracies and, according to the rationale presented above, can therefore also be expected to be more peace-oriented. In other words, we assume that there is a continuum in these respects from non-democracy to majoritarian democracy to consensus democracy instead of a simple contrast between democracy and autocracy.

Our third step is to specify a dependent variable that differs from wars or other military confrontations – since these are extremely rare among democracies – but that still captures degrees of difference in the peacefulness of foreign policies. Our choice here is the supply of foreign aid – economic development assistance, not military aid – which is arguably the most peaceful and most generous of foreign policies that nations can engage in. Our hypothesis is that consensus democracy is positively correlated with levels of foreign aid giving. If this hypothesis is correct, it indirectly strengthens the democratic peace proposition.

We focus on those countries that indisputably meet the criteria of full and consolidated democracy. The precise definition is: political systems with populations over a quarter of a million that, as of 1996, can be regarded as fully democratic according to Dahl's criteria and that had been continuously democratic since 1977 or earlier.[7] Thirty-six countries fit this definition, and 21 of these gave economic development assistance in the 1980s and 1990s: 16 West European countries plus the United States, Canada, Japan, Australia, and New Zealand. These 21 democracies are listed in Table 1, in descending order according to their degree of consensus democracy.[8]

Given the importance of the Cold War in the debate about the democratic peace, we chose two four-year periods for our examination of levels of foreign aid: 1982-85, clearly well before the end of the Cold War – when, in fact, very few people expected that the Cold War would end so soon! – and 1992-95 when the Cold War had clearly ended. We use multi-year averages in order to even out annual fluctuations in foreign aid (although, in practice, very few large fluctuations occurred). The figures presented in the second and third columns of Table 1 are the average annual economic development assistance as a percentage of the gross national product of each country. In the 1982-85 period, foreign aid ranged from a high of 1.04 percent of gross national product (Norway) to a low of 0.04 percent (Portugal); from 1992 to 1995, the highest percentage was 1.01 percent (Denmark and Norway) and the lowest 0.14 percent (the United States). For the 1992-95 period, the fourth column also presents foreign aid as a percent of defense expenditures, as calculated by the United Nations Development Programme. The

Table 1. Degrees of Consensus Democracy (1971-96), Economic Development Assistance as a Percent of GNP (1982-85 and 1992-95), and Economic Development Assistance (1992-95) by 21 Democracies.

	Degree of consensus democracy (1971-96)	Aid as % of GNP (1982-85)	Aid as % of GNP (1992-95)	Aid as % of defense spending (1992-95)
Switzerland	1.87	0.29	0.37	24
Finland	1.66	0.34	0.42	22
Denmark	1.45	0.79	1.01	52
Belgium	1.42	0.57	0.36	21
Netherlands	1.16	0.98	0.81	37
Italy	1.16	0.24	0.27	13
Sweden	1.04	0.88	0.94	36
Norway	0.92	1.04	1.01	34
Japan	0.85	0.31	0.28	30
Portugal	0.36	0.04	0.32	12
Luxembourg	0.29	0.08	0.34	39
Austria	0.26	0.32	0.31	35
Germany	0.23	0.47	0.34	18
Ireland	0.12	0.23	0.22	18
United States	-0.52	0.24	0.14	4
Spain	-0.59	0.09	0.26	17
Australia	-0.67	0.50	0.36	15
France	-0.93	0.59	0.60	19
Canada	-1.07	0.46	0.43	23
New Zealand	-1.12	0.26	0.24	17
United Kingdom	-1.39	0.34	0.30	9

Source: Based on data in Lijphart 1999, Appendix A; United Nations Development Programme 1994, 197; United Nations Development Programme 1995, 204, 206; United Nations Development Programme 1996, 199, 201; United Nations Development Programme 1997, 214-15.

highest foreign aid as a percent of defense expenditure was Denmark's 51 percent, and the lowest that of the United States, 4 percent.

The first column of Table 1 shows the degree of consensus democracy of the 21 countries, based on five institutional characteristics in the 1971-96 period: the degree of executive power-sharing, the relative power of the executive and the legislature, the party system, the electoral system, and the interest groups system. Majoritarian characteristics are one-party majority cabinets, executive dominance over the legislature, a two-party system, a disproportional electoral system, and a pluralist, competitive, free-for-all interest group system. Consensus characteristics are broad coalition cabinets, a balance of power between executive and legislature, a multiparty system, relatively proportional election outcomes, and a corporatist interest group system with frequent tripartite consultations and agreements between the government, employers, and labor unions. These five variables were measured on different scales and therefore had to be standardized before they could be averaged (and standardized again). Each unit on the standardized average score represents one standard deviation. The range is from 1.87 for highly consensual Switzerland to -1.39 for the highly majoritarian United Kingdom.[9]

It is worth highlighting that two of the five characteristics that distinguish consensus from majoritarian democracy can be extended to non-democratic forms of government – which strengthens the theoretical rationale for our assumption that there is a continuum running from consensus to majoritarian to non-democracy. First, consensus democracies tend to have relatively weak executives and relatively strong legislatures; majoritarian democracies have executives that predominate over their legislatures; and non-democracies tend to have extremely strong executive power and extremely weak legislatures or no legislatures at all. Second, the multiparty systems of consensus democracy contrast with the two-party systems of majoritarian democracy and further with the typical one-party or no-party systems of autocratic regimes.

Consensus Democracies are Indeed More Generous

Table 2 presents the bivariate relationships between degree of consensus democracy and the three foreign aid variables. The estimated regression coefficient is the increase or decrease in the dependent variables (foreign aid as a percent of GNP and as a percent of defense expenditures) for each unit increase in the independent variable – in our case, each increase by one standard deviation of consensus democracy. Because the table reports bivariate regression results, the standardized regression coefficient in the second column equals the correlation coefficient. The statistical significance of the correlations depends on the absolute t-value, shown in the third column, and the number of cases (the 21 countries in our analysis). Whether or not the correlations are significant is indicated by asterisks; three levels of significance are reported, including the least demanding 10 percent level.

The range in degrees of consensus democracy is 3.26 standard deviations. Most democracies are not in extreme positions, however, and it would be more accurate to say that the »typical« consensus democracy and the »typical« majoritarian democracy are roughly two standard deviations apart. This means, for instance, that, based on the value of 5.94 percent in the first column, the economic development assistance (expressed as a percent of defense expenditure) provided by the typical consensus democracy was almost 12 percentage points higher than the aid given by the typical majoritarian democracy.

Table 2. Bivariate Regression Analyses of the Effect of Consensus Democracy on Economic Development Assistance (as a Percent of GNP and as a Percent of Defense Expenditures) Provided by 21 Democracies, 1982-85 and 1992-95.

	Estimated regression coefficient	Standardized regression coefficient	Absolute t-value
Aid as % of GNP (1982-85)	0.09*	0.30	1.38
Aid as % of GNP (1992-95)	0.10**	0.39	1.86
Aid as % of defense spending (1992-95)	5.94***	0.51	2.58

* Statistically significant at the 10 percent level(one-tailed test).
** Statistically significantat the 5 percent level (one-tailed test).
*** Statistically significant at the 1 percent level (one-tailed test).
Source: Based on the data in Table 1.

In the bivariate regression analysis, consensus democracy is significantly correlated with all three foreign aid variables, albeit at different levels; the strongest correlation, at the 1 percent level, is with aid as a percentage of defense spending. Figures 1 and 2 present the scattergrams for the relationships between the degree of consensus democracy and foreign aid as a percent of GNP and as a percent of defense spending, both in the most recent period. The scattergrams for the relationship between consensus democracy and aid as a percent of GNP in 1982-85 and in 1992-95 are very similar and, in order to save space, we are not showing the scattergram for the earlier period. The close similarity between the patterns in the two peri-

Figure 1. The Relationship Between Consensus Democracy and Economic Development Assistance (as Percent of GNP), 1992-95.

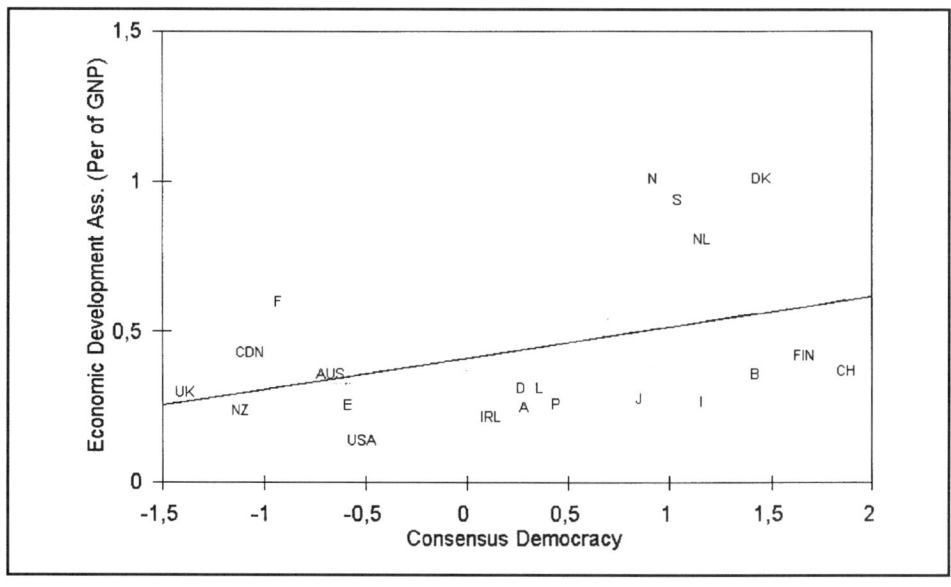

Types of Democracy and Generosity with Foreign Aid

ods is theoretically very significant, of course: it shows that the end of the Cold War had relatively little influence on the relative levels of foreign aid given by our 21 countries.

Figure 1 shows that the Netherlands and three of the Nordic countries – Denmark, Norway, and Sweden – are the countries that are mainly responsible for the high average level of foreign aid that the consensus democracies dispense. This generosity is neither a general Nordic characteristic nor a general Benelux quality: Finland and Belgium are also consensus democracies and Luxembourg partly so, and these three countries do not supply unusually high levels of aid. On the majoritarian (left) side of the scattergram, five Anglo-Saxon countries and Spain are located in close proximity to each other, all with foreign aid levels below 0.5 percent of GNP. France is the exceptional case of a majoritarian country with considerably greater generosity (0.60 percent of GNP) – in fact, the fifth highest level among the 21 democracies. There is clearly also a contrast between the more generous Continental European countries, including France, on the one hand, and the less generous countries with a British political heritage, including Ireland, on the other. The average aid levels for the 14 Continental European countries is 0.53 percent – almost double the average of 0.28 percent for the six Anglo-Saxon countries (which is also Japan's percentage).

Figure 2. The Relationship Between Consensus Democracy and Economic Development Assistance (as Percent of Defense Spending), 1992-95.

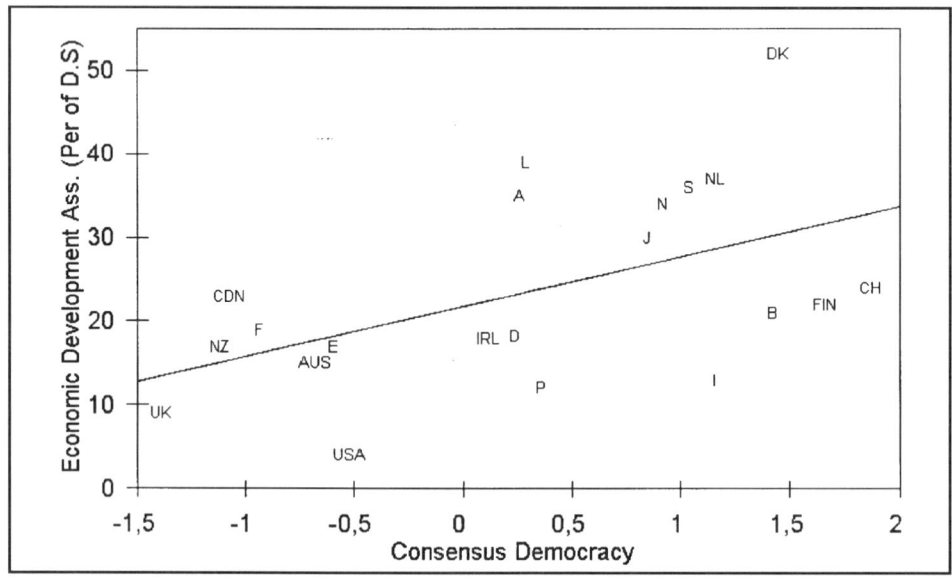

Figure 2 relates the degree of consensus democracy to foreign aid as a percent of defense spending, and the scattergram resembles that of

Figure 1 in most respects. The same three Nordic countries and the Netherlands are again in high positions, but they are now joined above the regression line by consensual Japan and moderately consensual Austria and Luxembourg. On the majoritarian side, France is no longer an outlier, and the United States – already the least generous democracy in Figure 1 – is now in an even more pronounced low position.

These findings clearly support our hypothesis concerning the relationship between type of democracy and economic development assistance. Before we declare this hypothesis confirmed, however, two important controls need to be introduced. First, since wealthier countries can better afford to give foreign aid than less well-to-do countries, the level of development should be controlled for. We used the United Nations Development Programme's (1997, 46-48) broadly based »human development index« as our measure of development.[10] The bivariate correlations between level of development and foreign aid all have positive signs, indicating that the richer countries indeed give more foreign aid than the less rich ones. However, only one of the correlations, between development level and foreign aid in 1982-85, is strong enough to be statistically significant (at the 5 percent level).

Second, since large countries tend to assume greater military responsibilities and hence tend to have larger defense expenditures, which can be expected to limit their ability and willingness to provide foreign aid, population size (logged) should be used as a control variable.[11] Here again, the bivariate correlations all have the expected sign – in this case, a negative sign: population size and foreign aid are indeed inversely related to each other. The correlation between population and aid as a percent of defense spending is very strong and highly significant (at the 1 percent level), but the other two negative correlations are not statistically significant.

When these three variables are simultaneously entered into the multiple regression equations, they all turn out to have a strong impact on levels of foreign aid: with just one exception (the influence of population size on aid in 1982-85), all of the correlations are now statistically significant. For the purposes of this study, it is especially important to note that, with population size and development level controlled for, the correlations between consensus democracy and the three measures of foreign aid remain significant – now all at the same 5 percent level. With the controls in place, the typical consensus democracy gave about 0.20 percentage points more of its GNP in foreign aid than the typical majoritarian democracy in both periods – the relationship was only fractionally stronger in the Cold War years – and its aid as a percent of defense spending was about 9.5 percentage points higher.

Conclusion

On the basis of the evidence presented above, we can conclude that type of democracy and foreign aid are closely related. We have assumed a continuum from consensus democracy to majoritarian democracy to non-democracy. This assumption is highly plausible and, if it is correct, it means that the difference in peaceful orientations that we found between consensus and majoritarian democracies can be extrapolated to non-democratic forms of government. Hence our analysis offers indirect support to the democratic peace proposition – somewhat more indirect support than that offered by the other indirect tests described earlier, but nevertheless very strong and persuasive support.

Notes

1. For excellent reviews of the literature, see Chan (1997), Maoz (1997), and Ray (1997).
2. As we shall argue below, most of the participants in these wars cannot be regarded as truly democratic.
3. However, women did not have the right to be candidates for public office in New Zealand until 1919.
4. In Samuel P. Huntington's (1991, 13-16) well-known identification of three waves of democratization, he sees the first wave starting much earlier: in 1828. However, he uses a much too lenient definition of universal suffrage: the right to vote for at least 50 percent of adult males. This means that he accepts as democratic a system in which 75 percent of all adult citizens do not have the right to vote.
5. Moreover, Australian Aborigines (about 2 percent of the population) could not vote in federal elections until 1962, and universal suffrage in the United States was not fully established until the passage of the Voting Rights Act in 1965.
6. One example of an attempt to disentangle the variables is Erik Gartzke's (1998). He contends that similar preferences among nations (measured by means of roll-call votes in the United Nations General Assembly from 1950 to 1985) takes precedence over the degree of democracy in these nations: it is their similar preferences rather than their shared democracy that makes democratic states unwilling to go to war with each other.
7. Our reliance on Dahl's criteria differs from the reliance by most democratic peace researchers on the Polity II and Polity III data sets (see Jagger and Gurr 1995). However, our set of democracies largely coincide with the countries that receive the top ratings on the Polity II and III measures.
8. The other 15 democracies are the Bahamas, Barbados, Botswana, Colombia, Costa Rica, Greece, Iceland, India, Israel, Jamaica, Malta, Mauritius, Papua New Guinea, Trinidad and Tobago, and Venezuela.

9. These five characteristics jointly constitute the executives-parties dimension of the contrast between consensus and majoritarian democracy. There is a second dimension to this contrast – the federal-unitary dimension – also based on five characteristics, such as federal and decentralized vs. unitary and centralized government and strong bicameralism vs. unicameralism (see Lijphart 1999). In this chapter, we focus exclusively on the executives-parties dimension.
10. The index is based on three main variables: income, life expectancy, and educational attainment.
11. Robert A. Dahl and Edward R. Tufte (1973, 122-23) found a strong link between population size and defense spending.

References

Benoit, Kenneth (1996). »Democracies Really Are More Pacific (in General): Reexamining Regime Type and War Involvement«, *Journal of Conflict Resolution*, Vol. 40, No. 4, pp. 636-657.

Chan, Steve (1997). »In Search of the Democratic Peace: Problems and Promise«, *Mershon International Studies Review*, Vol. 41, No. 1, pp. 59-91.

Dahl, Robert A. (1971). *Polyarchy: Participation and Opposition*, New Haven: Yale University Press.

Dahl, Robert A. & Edward R. Tufte (1973). *Size and Democracy*, New Haven: Yale University Press.

Farber, Henry S. & Joanne Gowa (1997). »Common Interests or Common Polities? Reinterpreting the Democratic Peace«, *Journal of Politics*, Vol. 59, No. 2, pp. 393-417.

Gartzke, Erik (1998). »Kant We All Just Get Along? Opportunity, Willingness and the Origins of the Democratic Peace«, *American Journal of Political Science*, Vol. 42, No. 1, pp. 1-27.

Gleditsch, Nils-Petter and Havard Hegre (1997). »Peace and Democracy: Three Levels of Analysis«, *Journal of Conflict Resolution*, Vol. 41, No. 2, pp. 283-310.

Gurr, Ted Robert (1993). *Minorities at Risk: A Global View of Ethnopolitical Conflicts*, Washington, DC: United States Institute of Peace Press.

Hermann, Margaret G. & Charles W. Kegley (1996). »Ballots, a Barrier Against the Use of Bullets and Bombs: Democratization and Military Intervention«, *Journal of Conflict Resolution*, Vol. 40, No. 3, pp. 436-460.

Huntington, Samuel P. (1991). *The Third Wave: Democratization in the Late Twentieth Century*, Norman, Oklahoma: University of Oklahoma Press.

Jaggers, Keith & Ted Robert Gurr (1995). »Tracking Democracy's Third Wave with the Polity III Data«, *Journal of Peace Research*, Vol. 32, No. 4, pp. 469-482.

Layne, Christopher (1994). »Kant or Cant: The Myth of Democratic Peace«, *International Security*, Vol. 19, No. 2, pp. 5-49.

Lijphart, Arend (1984). *Democracies: Patterns of Majoritarian and Consensus Government in Twenty-One Countries*, New Haven: Yale University Press.

Lijphart, Arend (1999). *Patterns of Democracy: Government Forms and Performance in Thirty-Six Countries*, New Haven: Yale University Press.

Mansfield, Edward D. & Jack Snyder (1995). »Democratization and the Danger of War«, *International Security*, Vol. 20, No. 1, pp. 5-38.

Maoz, Zeev (1997). *Regional Security in the Middle East, Past, Present and Future*, London: Frank Cass.

Oneal, John R. & Bruce Russett (1997). »The Classical Liberals Were Right: Democracy, Interdependence, and Conflict, 1950-1985«, *International Studies Quarterly*, Vol. 41, No. 2, pp. 267-294.

Raknerud, Arvid & Havard Hegre (1997). »The Hazards of War: Reassessing Evidence of the Democratic Peace«, *Journal of Peace Research*, Vol. 34, No. 4, pp. 385-404.

Ray, James Lee (1997). »The Democratic Path to Peace«, *Journal of Democracy*, Vol. 8, No. 2, pp. 49-64.

Rummel, Rudolph J. (1983). »Libertarianism and International Violence«, *Journal of Conflict Resolution*, Vol. 27, No. 1, pp. 27-71.

Rummel, Rudolph J. (1997). *Power Kills: Democracy as a Method of Nonviolence*, New Brunswick, New Jersey: Transaction Publishers.

Senese, Paul D. (1997). »Between Dispute and War: The Effect of Joint Democracy on Interstate Conflict Escalation«, *Journal of Politics*, Vol. 59, No. 1, pp. 1-27.

Small, Melvin & David Singer (1976). »The War-Proneness of Democratic Regimes, 1816-1965«, *Jerusalem Journal of International Relations*, Vol. 1, No. 4, pp. 50-69.

Solingen, Etel (1996). »Democracy, Economic Reform, and Regional Cooperation«, *Journal of Theoretical Politics*, Vol. 8, No. 1, pp. 79-115.

United Nations Development Programme (1994). *Human Development Report 1994*, New York: Oxford University Press.

United Nations Development Programme (1995). *Human Development Report 1995*, New York: Oxford University Press.

United Nations Development Programme (1996). *Human Development Report 1996*, New York: Oxford University Press.

United Nations Development Programme (1997). *Human Development Report 1997*, New York: Oxford University Press.

Ward, Michael D. & Kristian S. Gleditsch (1998). »Democratizing for Peace«, *American Political Science Review*, Vol. 92, No. 1, pp. 51-61.

New Political Parties in Established Party Systems: How Successful Are They?

Peter Mair

Abstract

Despite the ever-increasing attention devoted to analyses of party system transformation in recent years, there has been remarkably little systematic analysis concerning the emergence and success of new political parties as such. With old parties supposedly being challenged and subject to decay, we might reasonably expect an increasing role for new parties. Accordingly, this chapter explores two simple hypotheses: (a) that major growth has occurred in the number of new parties contesting elections; and (b) these new parties together account for an increasing share of electoral preferences. The analysis suggests that while new political parties have indeed proliferated over the past few decades, and while together they now sometimes account for a substantial share of electoral preferences, the aggregate evidence of genuine novelty in the long-established European party systems remains surprisingly limited. New parties sometimes flourish briefly, but then die away. Others persist, and sometimes even manage to gain a stable foothold within their respective party systems. But the most successful of these tend to be new in name only, while even those who flourish in the shorter-term are those who can point to some linkage to the past.

Introduction

The end of the 1990s affords a suitable opportunity to assess the real weight of electoral support now gained by new political parties. Since at least the late 1970s, a substantial and varied discussion has taken place concerning changes in West European party systems. Indeed, the discussion has gone on so long that it has become part of the so-called classic literature. Moreover, by this stage the notion that politics has changed – even dramatically – has become part of the conventional wisdom. How such change can and should be discerned, however, remains a matter of debate. On the one hand, there are those who suggest that change might best be seen in the aggregate, as it were, in that it is likely to be manifested in the emergence and success of new political parties, in the decay and failure of old political alignments, and in evidence of increasing flux and volatility from election to election. On the other hand, there are those who suggest that change might often be absorbed, and that despite the shifting orientations of voters, and the transformation which has ensued within the broader socio-structural environment, traditional alignments can prove sufficiently adaptive so as to accommodate new demands and ride out the potential storms. In one case, older parties attempt to resist new challenges and, failing that, help to accelerate the changes which then become visible in the aggregate. In the other case, the parties both anticipate and accommodate; hence, while change may not be readily visible in the aggregate, it nevertheless permeates the system as a whole. Paradoxically, it would appear that it is the attempt to persist which more likely leads to change, whereas an ability to adapt is more likely to facilitate survival.

Questions such as these have now been debated back and forth among European political scientists for more than two decades, with Mogens N. Pedersen having played a prominent, if not formative role within this debate. Indeed, if the watershed studies of Lipset and Rokkan (1967), and Rose and Urwin (1970), can be seen as marking the high point of the »persistence in the aggregate« position, Pedersen's (1979) article marks the point of departure for the literature which sought to emphasise change. I use the term point of departure advisedly here, since although Pedersen was careful to note the sheer variability of the European experiences, with some polities registering quite substantial electoral shifts and others appearing to settle down into even more stable patterns, this frequently-cited article has nonetheless been seen as marking one of the first publications to herald the importance of the coming flux. Partly through the impact of his work, which also coincided with other empirical studies based on survey data, as well as with some theoretical expectations, it soon became clear that a consensus had emerged stating that party systems were indeed changing, that the hold of older, traditional parties was weakening, and that new challengers were emerging to upset old apple carts. As noted, Pedersen himself was more cautious than most in concluding this, and in fact the evidence of pervasive aggregate change, certainly up through the end of the 1980s, was not wholly convincing (Bartolini & Mair 1990; Mair 1993). Moreover, work on some of the new challengers, in particular, that is on the small parties who intended to challenge the hold of their bigger rivals, showed that much of the supposed alternative politics was not really that impressive after all (e.g., Müller-Rommel & Pridham 1991).

Perhaps more surprising, however, is that while this debate prompted an increase in research devoted to the role and performance of small parties in established party systems, and while more and more attention also began to be paid Green parties in particular, it has provoked remarkably little systematic analysis concerning the emergence and success of *new* political parties as such. More to the point, with old parties supposedly being challenged and subject to decay, we might reasonably expect that the resulting vacuum would be filled by new parties, and that such new parties would therefore merit serious attention. Indeed, given a situation in which party systems were believed to be subject to substantial aggregate flux, and in which traditional alignments were subject to a substantial threat, then we might reasonably hypothesise: (a) an increase in the number of new parties in contention (an expansion of »the offer«, to use Bartolini's (1999) term); and (b) these new parties would account for an increasing share of electoral preferences (a growth in the »demand« (Bartolini 1999)).

Up to now, however, neither of these hypotheses has been systematically tested. To my knowledge, the closest anybody has come to such test in a somewhat preliminary but nonetheless valuable early inventory of new party success carried out by Matthew Shaddick, then an undergraduate student at the University of Manchester (Shaddick 1990). Beyond that, evidence has come only indirectly, through the attention paid to changing levels of electoral fractionalization in European party systems. Yet as Pedersen (1980) has pointed out, this particular indicator tells us little about changes over time, and hence is of little value in analyzing the emergence and success of new parties. In this chapter, I will therefore attempt an initial test of both hypotheses regarding new parties. In so doing, I also hope to tap into yet another issue raised by Pedersen, which is the analysis of party lifespans (Pedersen 1982; 1991).

The data for this analysis consist of the aggregate data on electoral outcomes as drawn from the valuable handbooks of Mackie and Rose (1991; 1997), with updates drawn from the regular *Political Data Yearbook*, published as part of the *European Journal of Political Research*. The analysis presented in this chapter covers all elections in long-established European democracies from 1960 through to the end of 1998. Although these electoral sources are reasonably authoritative, they have some limitations as far as the present analysis is concerned. In particular, the Mackie-Rose data inevitably fail to include a number of the very small new parties, some of which poll just handfuls of votes, and almost all of which end up being grouped into a general »others« category. In this sense, the data as so drawn will tend to underestimate the number of new actors that actually emerge into the political light. On the other hand, these data are sufficiently reliable so that no significant political actor is likely to have been missed, and certainly none with any reasonable hope of winning representation in parliament.

My definition of a *new* party is both simple and generous: new parties are those which first began to contest elections no earlier than 1960. Hence, any party that began to contest elections in the 1950s or earlier is for these purposes an »old« party. It should also be emphasised that the definition of new parties adopted here takes no account of the origins of the party in question – although this will be examined later in the paper – in that a new party is regarded as such even if it involves simply the merger (in the 1960s or later) of two or more pre-existing »old« parties. The criterion is ageist.

The Electoral Performance of New Parties: An Overview

The first of the two hypotheses listed above is easily tested and confirmed. As can be seen in Table 1, of 292 parties recorded as having contested election in the period 1960-1998, 60 per cent (N = 176) are new parties. In other words, across this period, only somewhat more than one-third of the parties began contesting elections prior to 1960. Of course, it must be borne in mind that we are dealing here with almost four decades of electoral competition, and that the number of elections contested under conditions of mass democracy in this period far exceeds that prior to 1960. Nonetheless, the figures speak for themselves: the offer is substantial, and the number of new parties significantly exceeds that of old parties. The most extreme example is the exceptionally fragmented Italian case, where new parties account for some 75 per cent of all parties contesting elections in this period. Belgium and the Netherlands, both highly fragmented, also include substantial numbers of new parties. At the other extreme are the United Kingdom and Sweden, where relatively few new parties have emerged, and where the systems themselves are relatively unfragmented. At first sight, therefore, we might consider these latter cases to be relatively strong party systems, at least in the sense that they appear to discourage the formation of new alternatives.

Not all these new parties are successful, of course, and many then disappear almost immediately after their first electoral outing. They need to be winnowed out. I have used two very minimal criteria for this process, the

Table 1. Number of New Parties* in Established Party Systems, 1960-1998.

Country	No. of parties contesting elections	No. of new parties* contesting elections	No. of new parties polling at least 1 per cent	No. of new parties polling at least 1 per cent *and* contesting at least two elections	No. of new parties (from previous column) no longer contesting elections by 1998
Austria	11	7	6	5	2
Belgium	27	17	9	9	4
Denmark	19	10	10	9	4
Finland	18	9	9	6	2
France**	21	12	12	10	4
Germany	21	12	8	5	1
Iceland	16	11	10	5	4
Ireland	15	8	6	4	0
Italy***	44	33	20	12	6
Luxembourg	15	11	10	6	4
Malta	7	4	3	3	2
Netherlands	25	15	10	9	3
Norway	13	7	5	5	2
Sweden	8	3	3	3	1
Switzerland	20	11	8	8	2
United Kingdom	13	6	2	1	1
All Countries	292	176	131	100	42

Notes:
* Here as elsewhere in this paper, »new parties« are defined simply as parties that first begin to contest elections no earlier than 1960.
** The French data exclude groupings reported in Mackie and Rose under such catch-all headings as »other right«, »other left«, »regionalist parties«, etc.
*** The Italian data from 1994 and 1996 refer to the votes in the PR constituencies only.
Sources:
For this and all other tables: Mackie & Rose (1991, 1997), *Political Data Yearbook*, various years (published as part of the *European Journal of Political Research*).

results of which are also summarised in Table 1. First, I have counted those parties polling at least 1 per cent of the vote at least once – an exceptionally minimal threshold – but one which nevertheless serves to reduce the number of new parties from 176 to 131. In other words, of the total number of new parties that began contesting elections from the 1960s onwards, some 45 (25.6%) fail to achieve even this minimal success. The offer clearly exceeds the demand. The second criterion is that the party in question should exhibit some minimal degree of longevity – that is, it should have contested at least two elections. Note, however, that this second criterion may underestimate the appeal of some very recently formed new parties, particularly in the very volatile Italian case, in that those that emerged to contest only the most recent election are also hereby excluded. Nonetheless, although this is also a very low threshold of qualification, it serves to winnow out a further 31 of the cases, leaving just 100 new parties (56.8% of the total) which meet the criteria of polling 1 per cent at least once and also contesting at least two elections to date.

Given that we are dealing with 16 countries across a forty-year period, a total of 100 parties does not seem remarkably large. Again, Italy leads the field, but this time with just 12 new parties surviving the winnowing out process. Notwithstanding the potential long-term future which may be enjoyed by some of the parties which first emerged to contest Italy's 1996 election, and which are excluded from this last category, it has clearly proven easier to form a new party in Italy than to achieve even a minimal degree of success. France follows Italy, having shed just two parties in the winnowing out process. In the French case, therefore, new parties do relatively well. New parties also enjoy relatively good chances of success in Belgium and the Netherlands, and particularly in Denmark, where only one of the ten new parties recorded in 1960-98 has failed to meet the two minimal criteria (the Danish People's Party which, at the time of writing, had contested only the 1998 election, albeit with substantial success). Malta, Sweden and the UK fall at the opposite end of the spectrum. In both Malta and Sweden, only three parties have managed to meet both criteria. In the UK, only the short-lived Social Democratic Party has managed this. These latter systems are clearly resistant to new formations.

As shown in Table 2, the second hypothesis is also easily confirmed. These figures report the mean total vote for *all* new parties by decade, that is, they also include the results for those parties which contested only one election and/or which failed to poll at least 1 per cent (N = 176). As can be expected, this total vote has tended to increase steadily across the period in question, averaging just 4.5 per cent across all the long-established democracies in the 1960s, increasing to 9.1 per cent in the 1970s, 14.4 per cent in the 1980s, and finally to 21.8 per cent to the end of 1998. By the 1990s, new parties accounted for more than two-thirds of the total Italian vote, and for close to half the total vote in the Netherlands and France. Given that the Italian party system had been remade almost in its entirety by the mid-1990s, and that the 1992 election marked more or less the last serious electoral outing for the old established parties, this is clearly an exceptional case. In fact, since the 1992 elections, new parties have begun to account for close to 100 per cent of the Italian vote. Even without Italy, however, the total new party vote averaged 18.8 per cent across the remaining long-established democracies, still well above the figure recorded during the 1980s. Thus, new parties are more commonly found in contemporary elections, and they enjoy substantially increasing support within their respective party systems. Also notable is the steady increase in the number of new parties emerging over time. As indicated in Table 2, 30 of the 176 parties involved here began to contest elections in the 1960s, 48 began in the 1970s and 50 in the 1980s. The 1990s – i.e., through to the end of 1998 – have seen 48 new parties emerge. As many as one in three of this last figure can be accounted for by the extraordinary Italian experience, however, and excluding Italy from the data as a whole results in decade by decade figures for party starts of 28, 41, 42 and 32, respectively.

The secular growth of new party support is far from universal, however.

Table 2. Mean Share of the Total Vote Given to New Parties, by Country and by Decade.

	1960s %	1970s %	1980s %	1990s %
Austria	1.7	0.1	4.1	11.1
Belgium	2.8	11.4	12.9	22.4
Denmark	8.7	26.9	30.7	24.9
Finland	1.6	8.2	13.7	22.7
France	16.3	29.1	27.1	41.7
Germany	4.3	0.5	7.5	13.9
Iceland	2.4	4.7	19.3	11.9
Ireland	0.3	1.4	7.9	10.0
Italy	9.5	3.3	7.1	66.8
Luxembourg	3.1	12.0	11.5	20.0
Malta	13.1	0	0.1	1.5
Netherlands	2.3	26.6	44.5	45.9
Norway	3.9	13.6	15.1	19.7
Sweden	1.1	1.6	4.5	14.5
Switzerland	0.4	5.3	12.2	18.1
United Kingdom	0	0.8	11.6	2.3
All (National Mean)	4.5	9.1	14.4	21.8
Total no. of new parties first beginning to contest elections, by decade	30	48	50	48

Finland, Norway and Sweden, as well as Ireland, Belgium, the Netherlands and Switzerland, all mirror the cross-national pattern, in that all exhibit a more or less steady growth in new party support across the four decades. In Denmark, Iceland and the UK, by contrast, new party support in the 1990s falls below the levels recorded in the 1980s. The remaining countries also fail to record a secular trend. Support for new parties in Austria, Germany, Italy and Malta initially faltered in the 1970s – indeed in Malta the initial surge for new parties in the 1960s disappeared completely in the 1970s, and since then Malta has proved the least hospitable system for new challenges. In France and Luxembourg support faltered in the 1980s. However, despite the absence of a pervasive secular trend, it is clear that new parties in general are doing better now than at any other time in post-1950s elections. It is only in Denmark, Iceland, Malta and the UK that the peak in new party support occurs prior to the 1990s. Moreover, only in Malta and the UK did support for new parties fail to reach double figures by the 1990s.

These are cumulative figures, of course, in that they reflect the total vote (averaged by decade) gathered by all new parties in each of the elections in the countries concerned. As more of these parties enter the fray, and particularly when they consolidate themselves, they will account for an increasing share of the total vote. It is also likely that not all these new parties will prove equally successful, however, nor will all of them endure, and in this sense the figures for total new party support may overestimate the actual gains recorded by individual parties in the various systems. In fact, support levels for individual parties vary enormously, and on average, paint a far less rosy picture than that derived from the cumulative vote reported in Table 2. A first impression of this contrast can be seen in Table 3, which reports the

Table 3. Mean Vote per New Party per Election (ranked by country).

Country	Mean Vote per new Party per Election (in per cent)	Total number of Electoral Outings by new New Parties
United Kingdom	10.65	2
Netherlands	7.16	47
France	5.76	45
Italy	5.53	35
Iceland	5.19	14
Denmark	5.07	71
Luxembourg	4.70	12
Norway	4.41	28
Malta	4.21	7
Sweden	3.53	19
Finland	3.47	29
Austria	3.31	13
Ireland	2.93	20
Germany	2.76	23
Belgium	2.54	50
Switzerland	2.30	32
ALL	4.42	447

mean vote per contest (per election) for each of the new parties. It should be noted that not all new parties have been included in these calculations, but only those that meet the minimum requirements of having contested more than one election *and* having on one occasion polled at least 1 per cent of the vote (see Table 1). By winnowing out the weakest and most short-lived (or most recent) of the new parties, these figures will therefore tend to exaggerate average success levels. Even allowing for this exaggerated effect, however, the average results for these new parties do not seem overly impressive. It is only in the UK, for example, that the average new party has polled double figures in individual elections. And since the British data involve just one party, the Social Democratic Party, who contested just two elections, these figures are scarcely representative. Leaving aside the British case, we can see that the Dutch figure is clearly the most impressive. New parties in the Netherlands have thus far presented themselves to the voters on 47 occasions (across the eleven Dutch elections that were held between 1960 and 1998), and have each polled an average of more than 7 per cent of the vote. France, Italy and Denmark also appear quite impressive, with as many as 45, 35 and 71 appearances of new parties, respectively, and yet with each of these new parties polling an average of more than 5 per cent of the vote. However, the fact that an average support of 5 per cent pulls a country towards the top of this set of national rankings is sufficient indication of the fact that many new parties remain on the peripheries of mass politics. In other words, even when it survives, the average new party carries little weight. In Ireland, Germany, Belgium and Switzerland, for example, where new parties appear frequently, their average vote per contest is less than 3 per cent. Across all the established democracies, and across 447 electoral engagements, the average new party has polled less than 4.5 per cent per contest.

Moreover, and especially in light of Pedersen's (1982) discussion of party lifespans, it is also worth emphasising that not all of these new parties manage to survive. Taking as an indicator of its demise a party's absence at elections subsequent to its having an actual vote recorded in the Mackie-Rose data, a total of 42 of the 100 new parties which have contested more than one election and which have polled at least 1 per cent of the vote have since ceased to exist – or, at least, have since ceased to contest elections as separate entities (see Table 1). In other words, more than 40 per cent of these minimally successful new parties have since disappeared.

Births, Marriages and Divorces:
The Origin and Success of New Parties

New parties emerge in three general ways. First, some new parties emerge as the result of a merger between two or more pre-existing parties. The most obvious – and, indeed, most successful – example of this process is the Christian Democratic Appeal (CDA) in the Netherlands, formed as the result of a merger between two long-established Protestant Parties, the Anti-Revolutionary Party and the Christian Historical Union, together with one long-established Catholic Party, the Catholic People's Party. Second, there are those new parties which emerge as the result of a split in an existing party. In some cases, the old party continues alongside the new splinter party, and in other cases the split results in the emergence of two or more new parties. Deciding which of these two modes is the case in an analysis such as this will inevitably involve some arbitrary judgements. In the present analysis, for example, I regard the two parties which emerged from out of the Italian Communist Party (PCI), the Democratic Party of the Left (PDS) and Communist Refoundation (RC) as being new parties, whereas I regard the Social Democratic split from the British Labour Party as creating one new splinter party which then ran alongside the established Labour Party. Conversely, I do not regard the splits which gave rise to separate linguistic versions of the Belgian Christian, Socialist and Liberal Parties as having created any new parties, since the two wings of each of these parties had already maintained separate electoral constituencies for some time prior to the formalized division. Third, there are those new parties which are genuinely new, in the sense that they cannot be adequately regarded as having derived from either a merger among, or a split from, pre-existing parties. Inevitably, of course, many of these »new« new parties will have drawn elements of both their leadership and active support from existing parties, but they can nonetheless be regarded as genuinely novel – or at least as novel as possible within the relatively closed confines of established party systems. Examples of such »new« new parties include many of the Green parties, as well as the Irish Progressive Democrats and the Dutch Democrats 66.

Assumptions about the success of new parties, as well as some of the more far-reaching implications which have been associated with the challenge of the new politics, tend to be based most closely on this last category of new parties; that is, on those new parties which appear to reflect a relatively novel alignment. Once we are dealing with mergers between already established parties, or even with those parties which have split from already established parties, it seems less plausible to speak in terms of realignment or challenge. Old wine in new bottles is in this sense less dramatic than new wine in whatever sort of container modern tastes might find appealing.

Table 4. New Parties, Classified by Origin.

Type of origin:	Number (%)	Number Surviving to Most Recent Election (% of Category)
»New« new party (birth)	118 (67.0)	56 (47.5)
Merger between pre-existing parties (marriage)	19 (10.8)	10 (52.6)
Split from pre-existing party (divorce)	39 (22.2)	13 (33.3)
ALL	176 (100.0)	79 (44.9)

Moreover, as can be seen from Table 4, these »new« new parties also clearly predominate in terms of supply. Of the 176 new parties which first emerged since 1960, more than two-thirds are genuinely new, with just over 10 per cent emerging as the result of mergers between existing parties, and with little more than one-fifth emerging as a result of splits from older parties. These figures are largely comparable to the distribution within the category of the 100 parties which meet the minimum criteria for success identified above (contesting at least more than one election and winning at least 1 per cent of the vote on at least one occasion), where the balance is 62, 10 and 28 per cent, respectively. On the other hand, these newly-born parties tend to be a little less enduring. Table 4 indicates that whereas more than half the newly »married« parties have survived through to the most recent election, slightly fewer than half the genuinely new parties can claim this degree of longevity. These differences are relatively slight, however, and both categories appear to survive much better than those newly »divorced« parties, of which only one in three has managed to survive (see also Mair 1990).

Nevertheless, it is important to emphasize that the divorced parties outperform the newly-born parties in terms of their average electoral support. Among the 100 parties which meet the minimal success requirements, those emerging from a split with an existing party have polled an average of just over 4 per cent across their electoral lifespan, as against just 3.5 per cent for those parties which appear genuinely new. Not surprisingly, however, merged parties outperform the other two categories, polling an average of almost 9 per cent. Most striking of all, however, is how poorly all these new party categories perform. In no case does the average vote by category reach double figures, even when the one-off or very poorly performing parties are excluded, that is, even with the N of 100. In fact, of these 100 individual parties, only seven can claim an average vote running into double figures, while only one in five can claim to have reached double figures in at least one election.

Table 5. The Most Successful New Parties, by Rank-Order (N = 100).

A: NEW PARTIES WITH A MEAN VOTE OF MORE THAN 10.0% (N = 7)				
Country	Party Name	Period (n elections contested)	Mean Vote	Origin
NL:	Christian Democratic Appeal	1977-98 (7)	28.8	alliance
IT:	Forza Italia	1994-96 (2)	20.8	new
IT:	Democratic Party of the Left	1992-96 (3)	19.2	split
FR:	Union for French Democracy	1978-97 (6)	18.3	alliance
FR:	Democratic Centre	1967-68 (2)	12.3	alliance
UK:	Social Democratic Party	1983-87 (2)	10.7	split
FI:	Left Wing Alliance	1991-95 (2)	10.7	alliance

B: NEW PARTIES WITH A PEAK VOTE OF MORE THAN 10.0% (N = 20)				
Country	Party Name	Period (n elections contested)	Peak Vote	Origin
NL:	Christian Democratic Appeal	1977-98 (7)	35.3	alliance
FR:	Union for French Democracy	1978-97 (6)	22.0	alliance
IT:	Democratic Party of the Left	1992-96 (3)	21.1	split
IT:	Forza Italia	1994-96 (2)	21.0	new
DK:	Progress Party	1973-98 (11)	15.9	new
NL:	Democrats 66	1967-98 (10)	15.5	new
NO:	Progress Party	1973-97 (7)	15.3	new
FR:	National Front	1978-97 (6)	15.2	new
DK:	Socialist Peoples Party	1960-98 (16)	14.6	new
FR:	Democratic Centre	1967-68 (2)	14.1	alliance
IR:	Progressive Democrats	1987-97 (4)	11.8	new
SWE:	Christian Democratic Union	1964-98 (11)	11.8	new
UK:	Social Democratic Party	1983-87 (2)	11.6	split
NO:	Socialist Left	1961-97 (10)	11.2	new
FI:	Left Wing Alliance	1991-95 (2)	11.2	alliance
IC:	Citizens Party II	1987-91 (2)	10.9	new
FI:	Rural Party	1962-95 (10)	10.5	split
IC:	Womens Alliance	1983-95 (4)	10.2	new
LU:	Social Democratic Party	1974-79 (2)	10.1	split
IT:	Lombard League/Northern League	1987-96 (4)	10.1	new

These last figures are reported in Table 5, which ranks the individual new parties in terms of their mean vote over their electoral lifespan (Section A) as well as in terms of their peak vote (Section B). If we examine the mean vote first, then we see just seven of the 100 parties polling more than 10 per cent of the vote across all their contested elections: two Italian parties, Forza Italia (FI) and the PDS; two French parties, the UDF and the Democratic Centre (CD); a Dutch party, the CDA, which heads the list; a British party, the SDP; and a Finnish party, the Left-Wing Alliance. Of these seven parties, just one – Forza Italia – is genuinely new. Moreover, of these seven parties, two have since ceased to contest elections, the CD and the SDP, and two are part of the massive shake-up in Italian politics, in which the scope for new parties was massively enhanced by the effective remaking of the party system as a whole. This effectively leaves three new parties that can be safely said to have established a major foothold within an established party system: the CDA, the UDF, and the Left-Wing Alliance. Strikingly, all three represent alliances of pre-existing parties – indeed, they reflect alliances of very long-established parties. In these terms at least, the new party challenge hardly seems to be that at all. While certainly being new parties, they largely reflect old politics.

Figures on peak support (in Section B) offer a somewhat more nuanced perspective. In this case, there are twenty new actors who prove relevant, in that each has enjoyed a peak vote of more than 10 per cent, with the list again being clearly headed by the CDA (35.3 per cent in 1989), followed by the UDF. What is different here, however, is that 12 of the 20 are »new« new parties, including the top performer, Forza Italia, and being otherwise led by the Danish Progress Party, the Dutch D 66, the Norwegian Progress Party, and the French National Front, each of which has polled a peak vote in excess of 15 per cent. Moreover, of the four parties on the list which have failed to survive, only one – the Icelandic Citizens Party II – was a genuinely new party. In these terms at least, newly born parties appear to have had an impact, albeit perhaps short-lived.

They also, by any standards, constitute an interesting array. Three of the 12 newly-born parties on this list are of the new politics generation, albeit all of a non-Green variety and also Nordic: the Danish Socialist People's Party, the Norwegian Socialist Left, and the Icelandic Women's Alliance. Two others might also be regarded as involving concerns related to the new politics, in that both D 66 and the Irish Progressive Democrats reflect what is essentially a more recent but increasingly fashionable combination of social liberalism and economic conservatism, with both being also relatively committed to institutional reform. Almost all the others – the possible exception being the Swedish Christian party – are firmly on the right, however. They include both the Danish and Norwegian Progress Parties, as well as the French National Front and the Italian Northern League. All these parties have served to push the political spectrum in their respective countries quite sharply towards the Right. Forza Italia might also be considered as relevant for inclusion here, although this party is probably more accurately placed on the Centre Right.

We are thus witnessing the temporary surge of the first generation of New Left or New Politics parties, as well as that of the Far Right. What we do not witness, at least as yet, is evidence of a Green or genuine post-materialist surge; as yet, in other words, no Green party has managed to poll more than 10 per cent of the vote in any election in any of the established systems. This is interesting in itself, and suggests that while even newly-born parties can achieve some success, their chances of doing so will be enhanced when they can forge some connection to more long-established alignments. The new, and sometimes Extreme Right has indeed emerged as something relatively novel on the European political landscape. As Ignazi (1992) has suggested, these new parties of the Right might even be seen as a manifestation of the silent »counter-revolution«. Nonetheless, and despite their novelty, they inevitably hark back to older, long-established divisions within the European ideological mosaic (Mudde 1998), and it is this echo which may well have proven crucial to their relative success. The first generation of the new politics, protagonists from which also figure prominently on this list, was also often linked to the older concerns, in that these parties frequently emerged from attempts to renew traditional Marxism within an increasingly post-industrial setting. When new politics does manage to break through, then, it appears to do so with one hand stretched back to the past. Those who have sought a more radical break with traditional politics, on the other hand, still tend to remain on the margins.

In conclusion, while new political parties have proliferated over the past few decades, and while they may now account for a substantial share of electoral preferences, the aggregate evidence of genuine novelty in the long-established European party systems remains surprisingly limited. New parties sometimes flourish briefly, but then die away. Others persist, and sometimes even manage to gain a stable foothold within their respective party systems. The most successful of these, however, tend to be new in name only, while even those which flourish in the shorter-term are those who can point to some linkage to the past. In sum, despite the proliferation of new parties, it is the inertia of the old politics, and of the older political organizations in particular, that still remains quite palpable.

References

Bartolini, Stefano (1999). »Collusion, Competition, and Democracy«, *Journal of Theoretical Politics*, forthcoming.

Bartolini, Stefano & Peter Mair (1990). *Identity, Competition and Electoral Availability: The Stabilisation of European Electorates, 1885-1985*, Cambridge: Cambridge University Press.

Ignazi, Piero (1992). »The Silent Counter-Revolution: Hypotheses on the Emergence of

Extreme Right-Wing Parties in Europe«, *European Journal of Political Research*, Vol. 22, No.1, pp. 3-34.

Lipset, S. M. & Stein Rokkan (1967). »Cleavage Structures, Party Systems and Voter Alignments: an Introduction«, pp. 1-64, in S. M. Lipset & Stein Rokkan (eds.), *Party Systems and Voter Alignments*, New York: The Free Press.

Mackie, Thomas T. & Richard Rose (1991). *The International Almanac of Electoral History*, (3rd ed.), London: Macmillan

Mackie, Thomas T. & Richard Rose (1997). *A Decade of Election Results: Updating the International Almanac*, Glasgow: Centre for the Study of Public Policy, University of Strathclyde.

Mair, Peter (1990). »The Electoral Payoffs of Fission and Fusion«, *British Journal of Political Science*, Vol. 20, No. 1, pp. 131-42.

Mair, Peter (1993). »Myths of Electoral Change and the Survival of Traditional Parties: the 1992 Stein Rokkan Lecture«, *European Journal of Political Research*, Vol. 24, No. 2, pp. 121-133.

Mudde, Caspar (1998). *The Extreme Right Party Family: An Ideological Approach*, Ph.D. Thesis, Leiden: University of Leiden.

Müller-Rommel, Ferdinand & Geoffrey Pridham (eds.) (1991). *Small Parties in Western Europe: Comparative and National Perspectives*, London: Sage Publications.

Pedersen, Mogens N. (1979). »The Dynamics of European Party Systems: Changing Patterns of Electoral Volatility«, *European Journal of Political Research*, Vol. 7, No.1, pp. 1-26.

Pedersen, Mogens N. (1980). »On Measuring Party System Change: A Methodological Critique and a Suggestion«, *Comparative Political Studies*, Vol. 12, No. 4, pp. 387-403.

Pedersen, Mogens N. (1982). »Towards a New Typology of Party Lifespans and Minor Parties«, *Scandinavian Political Studies*, Vol. 5, No. 1, pp. 1-16.

Pedersen, Mogens N. (1991). »The Birth, Life and Death of Small Parties in Danish Politics«, pp. 95-114, in Ferdinand Müller-Rommel & Geoffrey Pridham (eds.), *Small Parties in Western Europe: Comparative and National Perspectives*, London: Sage Publications.

Rose, Richard & Derek W. Urwin (1970). »Persistence and Change in Western Party Systems Since 1945«, *Political Studies*, Vol. 18, No. 3, pp. 287-319.

Shaddick, Matthew (1990). »New Political Parties in West European Party Systems«, B.A. Thesis, Manchester: University of Manchester.

Appendix 1

New Political Parties, 1960-98:
New Parties Polling at Least one Per Cent *and*
Contesting at Least Two Elections

	Period (n elections contested)	Mean Vote	Peak Vote	Origin
AUSTRIA (No. of NEW PARTIES = 5)				
Democratic Progressive Party	1966-70 (2)	1.9	3.3	split
United Greens	1983-94 (3)	1.4	2.0	new
Green Alternative	1986-95 (4)	5.4	7.3	alliance
Liberal Forum	1994-95 (2)	5.7	5.9	split
No-Citizens Initiative	1994-95 (2)	1.0	1.1	new
BELGIUM (N = 9)				
Francophone Democratic Front	1965-91 (10)	2.8	5.1	new
Walloon Rally	1968-91 (9)	2.6	6.7	alliance
Brussels Liberal Party	1974-78 (3)	1.1	1.3	split
Ecolo	1977-95 (7)	2.5	5.1	new
Agalev	1977-95 (7)	2.9	4.9	new
Respect for Labour	1978-87 (4)	1.2	2.7	new
Flemish Blok	1978-95 (6)	3.4	7.8	new
Rossem/Banaan	1991-95 (2)	2.0	3.2	new
National Front	1991-95 (2)	1.7	2.3	new
DENMARK (N = 9)				
Socialist Peoples Party	1960-98 (16)	8.3	14.6	new
Liberal Centre	1966-68 (2)	1.9	2.5	split
Left Socialists	1968-88 (10)	2.2	3.7	split
Christian Peoples Party	1971-98 (12)	2.8	5.3	new
Centre Democrats	1973-98 (11)	4.9	8.3	split
Progress Party	1973-98 (11)	8.8	15.9	new
Common Course	1987-90 (3)	2.0	2.2	new
Greens	1987-90 (3)	1.2	1.4	new
Unity List	1990-98 (3)	2.5	3.1	alliance
FINLAND (N = 6)				
Rural Party	1962-95 (10)	5.3	10.5	split
Constitutional Peoples Party	1975-91 (5)	0.7	1.6	new
Finnish Peoples Unity Party	1975-83 (3)	0.7	1.7	split
Greens	1983-95 (4)	4.7	6.8	new
Pensioners	1987-95 (3)	0.6	1.2	new
Left Wing Alliance	1991-95 (2)	10.7	11.2	alliance
FRANCE (N = 10)*				
Republican Party	1962-73 (4)	5.9	8.4	split
Unified Socialist Party	1962-81 (6)	2.0	3.9	alliance
Democratic Centre	1967-68 (2)	12.3	14.1	alliance
Workers Struggle	1973-86 (4)	0.9	1.7	new
Left Radicals	1973-97 (7)	1.7	3.0	split
Greens	1978-97 (6)	2.1	4.1	new

National Front	1978-97 (6)	8.0	15.2	new
Union for French Democracy	1978-97 (6)	18.3	22.0	alliance
Generation Ecology	1993-97 (2)	2.7	3.7	new
New Ecologists	1993-97 (2)	1.8	2.6	new

GERMANY (N = 5)

German Peace Union	1961-65 (2)	1.6	1.9	new
National Democratic Party	1965-98 (9)	1.0	4.3	new
Greens	1980-98 (6)	5.6	8.3	new
Party of Democratic Socialism	1990-98 (3)	4.0	5.1	new
Republicans	1990-98 (3)	1.9	2.1	new

ICELAND (N = 5)

Union of Liberals & Leftists	1967-78 (4)	5.1	8.9	split
Social Democratic Federation	1983-87 (2)	3.9	7.6	split
Womens Alliance	1983-95 (4)	7.2	10.2	new
Citizens Party II	1987-91 (2)	6.1	10.9	new
Humanist Party	1987-91 (2)	1.7	1.8	new

IRELAND (N = 4)

Workers Party	1973-97 (9)	2.2	5.0	split
Greens	1982-97 (5)	1.3	2.8	new
Progressive Democrats	1987-97 (4)	6.7	11.8	new
Democratic Left	1992-97 (2)	2.7	2.8	split

ITALY (N = 12)**

Soc. Party of Proletarian Unity	1968-76 (3)	2.7	4.4	split
Proletarian Unity	1972-79 (2)	1.1	1.4	split
Radical Party	1976-87 (4)	2.4	3.5	new
Proletarian Democracy	1979-87 (3)	1.3	1.7	alliance
Pensioners Party	1983-92 (2)	1.0	1.4	new
Lombard League/Northern League	1987-96 (4)	6.9	10.1	new
Greens	1987-96 (4)	2.6	2.8	new
La Rete	1992-94 (2)	1.9	1.9	new
Democratic Party of the Left	1992-96 (3)	19.2	21.1	split
Communist Refoundation	1992-96 (3)	6.7	8.6	split
Pannella List	1992-96 (3)	2.2	3.5	split
Forza Italia	1994-96 (2)	20.8	21.0	new

LUXEMBOURG (N = 6)

Independent Movement	1964-68 (2)	3.1	5.8	new
Social Democratic Party	1974-79 (2)	8.3	10.1	split
Independent Socialists	1979-84 (2)	2.2	2.4	split
Green Alternative	1984-89 (2)	4.0	4.2	new
Pensioners	1989-94 (2)	8.1	8.3	new
Luxembourg for Luxembourgers	1989-94 (2)	2.5	2.6	new

MALTA (N= 3)

Christian Workers Party	1962-66 (2)	7.8	9.5	split
Democratic National Party II	1962-66 (2)	5.3	9.3	new
Democratic Alternative	1992-98 (3)	1.1	1.7	new

NETHERLANDS (N = 9)

Democrats 66	1967-98 (10)	7.5	15.5	new
Middle Class Party	1971-72 (2)	1.0	1.5	new
Democratic Socialists 70	1971-81 (4)	2.7	5.3	split
Radical Political Party	1971-86 (6)	2.2	4.8	split

Christian Democratic Appeal	1977-98 (7)	28.8	35.3	alliance
Reformed Political Federation	1977-98 (7)	1.3	2.0	split
Socialist Party	1986-98 (4)	1.4	3.5	new
Centre Democrats	1986-98 (4)	1.0	2.5	split
Green Left	1989-98 (3)	5.0	7.3	alliance

NORWAY (N = 5)

Socialist Left	1961-97 (10)	6.2	11.2	new
Liberal Peoples Party	1973-85 (4)	1.5	3.4	new
Progress Party	1973-97 (7)	7.1	15.3	new
Pensioners Party	1985-93 (3)	0.5	1.0	new
Red Electoral Alliance	1985-97 (4)	1.1	1.7	new

SWEDEN (N = 3)

Christian Democratic Union	1964-98 (11)	3.4	11.8	new
Ecology Party	1982-98 (6)	3.6	5.5	new
New Democracy	1991-94 (2)	4.0	6.7	new

SWITZERLAND (N = 8)

National Action	1967-95 (8)	2.4	3.3	new
Republicans	1971-79 (3)	2.5	4.0	new
Progressive Organizations	1975-91 (5)	1.3	2.2	split
Greens	1979-95 (5)	3.7	6.1	new
Alternative Greens	1983-95 (4)	1.5	2.7	new
Freedom Party	1987-95 (3)	3.9	5.1	new
Ticino League	1991-95 (2)	1.9	1.9	new
Federal Democratic Union	1991-95 (2)	1.2	1.3	new

UNITED KINGDOM (N = 1)

Social Democratic Party	1983-87 (2)	10.7	11.6	split

Notes:
* The French data exclude results reported for such catch-all categories as »other right«, »other left«, »regionalist parties«, etc.
** The Italian data from 1994-96 refer to the votes in the PR constituencies only.

Sources:
Mackie & Rose (1991, 1997), *Political Data Yearbook*, various years (published as part of the *European Journal of Political Research*).

To Hell with Athens' Agora

Jørn Henrik Petersen

Abstract

The contribution argues that complaints about journalism follow from the societal ideal regarding the media as an institution of direct democracy expected to present us with a true picture of the external world in which we are interested. The illusory nature of this ideal is enhanced by the characteristics of the edited society in which information 'providers' try to involve the media in a political struggle over opinion-shaping, agenda-setting, personal profiling, economic control and political influence. Journalism and politics both concentrate on the specific, the short-term, the individualized and the tangible, rejecting the attention attached to the general, the long-term, the collective and the abstract. The core of the problem appears to be the intolerable and unworkable myth that each of us must acquire a competent opinion about all public affairs. This fiction, partly a product of the voters' rational ignorance, creates a tension between our ideals of democracy and the realities.

> Behold! human beings living in a sort of underground den, which has a mouth open towards the light and reaching all across the den; they have been here from childhood and have their legs and necks chained so that they cannot move, and can only see before them; for the chains are arranged in such a manner as to prevent them from turning round their heads. At a distance above and behind them, the light of a fire is blazing, and between the fire and the prisoners there is a raised path; and you will see, if you look, a low wall built along the way, like the screen which marionette players have before them, over which they show the puppets.

»I see«, he said.

»And do you see«, I said, »men passing along the wall carrying vessels, which appear over the wall; also figures of men and animals, made of wood and stone and various materials; and some of the prisoners, as you would expect, are talking, and some of them are silent?«

»This is a strange image«, he said, »and they are strange prisoners.«

»Like ourselves«, I replied; »and they see only their own shadows, or the shadows of one another, which the fire throws on the opposite wall of the cave?«

»True«, he said: »how could they see anything but the shadows if they were never allowed to move their heads?«

»And of the objects which are being carried in like manner they would see only the shadows?«

»Yes«, he said.

»And if they were able to talk with one another, would they not suppose that they were naming what was actually before them?«

Plato, *The Republic*, Book Seven

Introduction

The mass media and the profession of journalists have for many years been strongly criticised. This contribution argues that the core of the problem is the intolerable and unworkable fiction that each of us must acquire a competent opinion about all public affairs. The problem of the media is confused because the critics and the apologists expect the media to make up for all that was not foreseen in the theory of democracy. This has to do with: a misinterpretation regarding the concept of news and the criteria of news; a change of society towards an edited society; the difficulties of reconciling the general and the specific, the collective and the individualized, the short- and long-term perspectives, the abstract and the tangible; and the rational ignorance of voters. These factors reflect a tension between our ideals and the reality of politics, media and their interaction. Finally, this contribution reflects whether the new public journalism may reduce the tensions.

Two Currents

For many years, a current of general hostile feelings has been diffused concerning the mass media. The critics suggest that newspapers and television covering our complex daily life are out of all proportion, tame, thin, sensation-mongering, faddish, dominated by single cases, individualising, etc. Initially it was the elitist groupings who tended to voice these criticisms. In recent years, however, the critique has not only persisted but has evolved from among ranks of the journalists themselves.

My colleague, Peter Harms Larsen (1998), recently crystallized the criticism in 12 claims dealing with the nuisance of journalism. Individually, and in sum they adopt a sharply critical perspective on the work of the journalists in Denmark today. They tell a story of a profession undergoing a crisis, of professional standards in a state of disorganization and of a societal role of journalists under erosion. All these claims can be debated. None of them are new. What is new is that the criticism is so very persistent.

Running parallel to this 'mess of journalism', is another critical current reflecting a widespread political fin-de-siècle feeling in the Occident. It is a sense of an epoch with institutions, traditions, norms, standards and rules concerning social life coming to an end.

About News and Truths

»Who is the most dishonest: the media knowing that they make a one-track propaganda out of the prime minister's statements, or the prime minister, who very likely has expressed himself in short sentences without finer nuances [an admission, JHP], but who has lived up to his promise about securing the voluntary early retirement pension [an interpretation, JHP]. A main problem is that the media want to make a drama and to create its own reality instead of informing the citizens about the real incidents in real life [an ideal, JHP]«. This was how the Danish minister of taxation, Ole Stavad, expressed his opinions in the newspaper *Jyllands-Posten* on January 3rd, 1999 following the popular 'rebellion' provoked by changes in the early retirement payment scheme adopted following parliament's approval of the state budget. I do not want to comment on Mr. Stavad's admission and the interpretation, but it is worth commenting upon the problem and the ideal. Let us start with the latter.

The news cannot mirror, nor can it reproduce 'real incidents in real life'. The news is the report of an aspect that has obtruded itself, (Lippmann, 1922, 216). The news deals with a part of the reality that has become visible with something which has happened. The news tells us that a sprout has broken through the surface of the ground. The sprout can be seen, but it does not tell when the seed was put into the soil or how it germinated. At best, the news can tell what somebody says about the seed, about the intention, about the development, about time etc.

News and truth are not the same thing. The news tells about an event, while the truth assumes that the hidden facts are brought to light, set into relation with each other, thus making a picture of reality on which men can act (Lippmann 1922, 226).

Only a small part of reality is absolutely recognizable. There exists but a very small body of exact knowledge which requires no outstanding ability or training to deal with. The rest is at the journalist's discretion. If the persons who know about the intention, the development, the time etc. fail to pass on this information (knowingly or unknowingly), the news will be coloured by the journalist's stereotypes, way of interpretation, codes and the urgency of his or her own interests. We all view and interpret the world through our subjective lenses.

Criticism of the media is due to the fact that in our societal ideals, the media have come to be regarded as an institution of direct democracy, charged on a much wider scale, and from day to day, with the function often attributed to the initiative, referendum, and recall, (Lippmann 1922, 229). The media are burdened with the unreasonable illusion that they are to spontaneously provide us the truth which democrats had hoped was inborn. Democratic theory assumes that the press is able to create a mystical force, 'Public Opinion', that will take up the slack in public institutions. By this assumption, the theory employs a misleading standard of judgment. The limited nature of news and the unbounded complexity of society are overlooked, while the human endurance, public spirit, and omnicompetency are overestimated, (Lippmann 1922, 228). »Universally it is admitted that the press is the chief means of contact with the unseen environment. And practically everywhere it is assumed that the press should do spontaneously for us what primitive democracy imagined each of us could do spontaneously for himself, that every day and twice a day it will present us with a true picture of all the outer world in which we are interested«, (Lippmann 1922, 203).

However, the media is no substitute for institutions. They are like lighthouses. The beam of the searchlight sweeps over the reality and focuses for a moment on this, a moment on that, bringing one episode and then another out of darkness into vision. The lighthouse keeper reports on what he is observing, but he does not observe everything. And he does not observe things at the same time. Therefore, he reports on incidents. Spasmodically and sporadically, the media report the news, but there is no necessary connection between the various events.

We all know that subjects and problems are not isolated asteroids. They are connected. The Danish debate about voluntary retirement pay has something to do with the discussion about home care. They are both attached to the pressure of taxation determining the spending capacity of the government. The level of taxation is a function of the taxable capacity, which is determined by the size of the labour force, the number of working hours and, thus, by the amount of work done. Such relations and comprehensive views, however, are not the media world's cup of tea. It has to do with 'food chains' of the media and with the citizens.

The media have generally promoted the idea that they could do what a naive democratic theory expects them to do. At a great moral cost to themselves, they have encouraged a democracy still bound to its original premise that for every organ of government, for every social problem, the media could provide the machinery of information which these do not normally provide by themselves, (Lippmann 1922, 228). Contradictory ideals and realities yield only great frustrations, however.

The Edited Society

The problem is due partly to the fact that the information is not available; but it is not only that. Information is often available in a form which does not aim at imparting knowledge, enlightenment or the uncovering of 'the truth'. We live in an edited society, as my colleague, Anker Brink Lund (1999), influenced from Ekecrantz and Olsson (1998), emphasized in his inaugural lecture. In the edited society it is not only the mass media which assess the reality from the perspective of the editorial news criteria. (As far back as 1922, Lippmann wrote [p. 217]: »It is safer to hire a press agent who stands between the group and the newspapers. Having hired him, the temptation to exploit his strategic position is very great«). Danish Prime minister Poul Nyrup Rasmussen, minister of taxation Ole Stavad and minister of finance Mogens Lykketoft know the full story of the early retirement pay. I do think that I know it. Maybe one day it will be told. It will be a story about the difficult relationship between media and politicians, about the rules which control their interaction and about the relationship between news and truth. This kind of story would broaden our minds and deepen our knowledge.

The News Criteria

It is difficult for most people to come to terms with the fact that from a journalistic perspective a 'good story' is often a bad story about death and accidents, trickery and humbug, violence and crime, as was discussed recently by Peter Harms Larsen (1999). Established news criteria are a key part of the journalist's knowledge and tool kit, because they are founded on a solid knowledge of readers' psychology, cross-cutting classes, gender and age groups. The criteria reflect several hundreds of centuries of knowledge and experiences by journalists and editors, as to how information should be collected, edited and transformed into news, so that it stimulates people to buy and read their newspaper, or watch their television broadcast.

Usually there are four criteria:

- the sensation: the unusual, the unexpected, the surprise;
- the conflict: the dispute between persons and interests;
- the identification: people, proximity, relevance for the readers and the viewers;
- current interest: something that has just happened and is the subject of a current debate.

It is obvious that lying beyond these subjects are the everyday occurrences, events void of conflicts, impersonal and distant phenomena, abstract discussions, and work according to rules and expectations. A good story is definitely not 'a good story' and it is definitely not part of the news.

One might fear that the criterion of significance had been excluded. And there is some truth to this. The criterion of significance seems to be used in journalism only if an important and significant subject can be elucidated, so that the story can be placed in the spotlight of the news criteria. Significance is generally not used as the sole criterion.

Consequently, in trying to influence the public, it is expedient for politicians, managers and heads of interest groups to make use of exaggeration, simplification, polarisation, intensification, concretization and personification, if they want penetration in the media. And they know it.

We all know how journalists think and what affects them. This is a necessary aspect of modern, general education. However party leaders, organisations and firms do not only know the journalistic mind-set. They exploit it. They have learned the news criteria in order to lead the media's hunt for news in a direction conditioned by their own interests. They know that feeding the journalists with photo-opportunities, sound bites, punch lines, good stories, critical reports, and surprising scientific results gives them excellent opportunities for influencing the editorial process in its production of the daily news.

We witnessed this process in the Danish documentary TV2 programme called 'The Candidates'. The programme followed the Prime Minister and the leader of the opposition through the election campaign and included situations which we – the spectators – normally do not see. One feature was necessary: to ensure the attention of the media and to set the agenda, something which the press subsequently reflects. The focus was on the media and coverage by the press.

The activities of the two politicians were characterized by efforts to control, to regiment and to arrange. The information provided to the media was centrally controlled. It was regimented and arranged with the maximum impact in mind. The objective was to ensure that the campaign would function. Spontaneity was reduced to planned spontaneity.

Journalists frequently risk being reduced to marionettes deceived by their own news criteria because all sources around them, their 'food chains', become more and more professional in controlling, regimenting and arranging events which then replace the news which journalists are supposed to cover. Journalists appear to be setting the agenda, but in fact it is often others who have pulled the strings and written the lines.

Today the focus has been turning away from the media and the journalists. More attention is being paid to the professional sources and information 'suppliers' trying to involve the media in a political struggle over opinion-shaping, agenda-setting, personal profiling, economic and political influence. We are approaching the thesis of Noam Chomsky that the efficiency of the efforts of the American Power Center regarding media influence and control of the news has grown so much that the so-called free press has been led by the nose via planned campaigns initiated by ever-growing numbers of communication consultants, marketing specialists and information departments. This is but a modern version of Walter Lippmann's observation that during wars, the armed forces indirectly involve journalism in military strategy.

Back to the Edited Society

Elected representatives, administrators and heads of interest groups also use the journalistic interpretative frameworks to bring about order and consistency in the plurality of the events. In daily life, this effort is reflected in the negotiating games and in assessments of what is viewed as journalistically significant. In a more radicalized form, we see it exemplified by the extensive use of the 'spin-doctors', i.e., specialists in the art of placing their client and his interests in a favourable light.

Those trying to 'play' the media act consciously on the established news criteria. The sensation attracts attention. The agenda is influenced if the stories are recognisable, understandable and meaningful, if the readers or the viewers are able to identify themselves with the subject being read about or seen on the TV screen.

The result is the 'serial media story' or 'the single-case' journalism. The professional journalists are placed in a complex network of blustering sources, each of them trying to attract attention. Strategically, the sources manipulate the news criteria and play on the fear of boring the audience. Obviously, the risk is that journalists are pulled around by manipulative sources.

The journalists no longer play the decisive role they once did. The rules of communication of news manifest themselves outside the mass media in the narrow sense; but it is not only the journalists who have lost their agenda-setting role. Previously they shared this role with the elected representatives and to some extent with the central administration. Now they, too, have lost their authority to define what is news. Many others know the journalistic and the parliamentary rules enabling them to exert an influence. This amplifies the endeavours of the politicians and the authorities to apply the journalistic perspective themselves. The interest groups intensify their 'public relations' efforts. Everybody wanting to influence and to cultivate his or her interests places a professional journalist as spokesperson and gatekeeper. The authoritative decisions, on the other hand, are increasingly made behind closed doors, as recently witnessed by the compromise on the Danish budget bill. By this procedure, the decision-makers avoid unpleasant surprises in the wake of improvised decisions as well as the impact of free, unimpeded debate.

This mirrors Pierre Bourdieu's (1998) 'evil circle of information'. The media is affected by cultural inbreeding: if one asks, perhaps a bit naively, how those entrusted with the task to inform us are themselves informed, it turns out that by and large they are informed by others whose task it is to inform.To know what you have to say, one needs to know what others are saying.

It is to Bourdieu's credit that he has so carefully explained how dangerous, i.e., regimenting, standardising, repressive and ultimately censoring, information about information is. It leads to a levelling or a homogenization of the hierarchies of significance.

Single-Case Journalism

Single-case journalism has other consequences as well. As emphasized by Anker Brink Lund, it gradually redefines the public's status from being citizens and electors to consumers and clients. It legitimates roles as victims and 'consequence experts' on an equal footing with other democratic roles. Individuals are free to express their difficulties and problems without first having to channel their problems and demands through the representative channels.

It is a symptom of our day, intensified by single-case-journalism. It is no coincidence that the Roskilde historian Henrik Jensen (1998) has called his recent book 'The Century of the Victim'. The strategy of emphasizing one's victimization has become a symbol of our social life in a complicated world. The role of the victim is successful – starting with the immediate attention from the surroundings, which for a moment pushes a person out of the grey mass and into the limelight. Still more people push themselves impulsively and without deeper moral reflections into the role as 'defenceless victims of brutal conditions'. The victim gains temporary attention by telling about the accidents and the injustice to which he or she has been subjected. »I am not to be blamed. Blame lies with the others. Society is at fault«.

The irresponsible victim has obtained a privileged status in society and in the media. 'To find the victim' is a typical journalistic angle. The public reacts with a strange mix of compassion, fear, suspicion, shame, contempt and envy.

From the perspective of Henrik Jensen's exciting analysis, it is worth emphasizing that it is neither the media nor the journalists, who have produced the victims. The media simply reflect and intensify the 'Zeitgeist', and single-case journalism is a parallel to single-case politics. It would be a waste of time to discuss which came first: the chicken or the egg.

Single-Case Politics

When political activity develops into day-to-day management, the single cases overshadow the wider, general perspectives. One of the basic deficiencies of public political debate is precisely the absence of the wider perspective. Neglect of the general, long-term perspective leads to the dominance of short-term politics, and this may cause quite insurmountable and unanticipated problems.

Most political decisions must solve a short-term problem: the original idea of the voluntary early retirement pay was to facilitate the entry of young people on the labour market and to reduce the youth unemployment. The result has been a still lower retirement age. With last year's political intervention in the labour market agreements, including extended holidays, the politicians coped with an acute problem; yet the long-term problem concerning the shortage of labour, the decline in the number of hours worked and in the taxable capacity was intensified, thus subjecting the welfare model to greater financial strain.

It is easy to criticize the media for not attending to the general and long-term perspectives, but solving the problem demands that the legislative branch itself takes its time and puts the problems into their proper perspective.

It is difficult to reconcile the general and the specific, the collective and the individual, the abstract and the concrete, the short- and the long-term interests. This was clearly documented by the recent agreement on the state budget bill.

The objective of the agreement was to prevent a future unpleasant situation from occurring if no interventions were made in, say, the voluntary early retirement payments, the rent subsidy scheme and the structure of the labour market. The benefits, however, are vague, abstract and hard to communicate. What do 'flexibility on the labour market', 'competitiveness', 'fixed exchange rates', 'the status on the balance of payments' and 'lower pressure of taxation in ten years' time' mean to ordinary citizens?

It is easy to understand the immediate and tangible disadvantages of these measures: voluntary retirement payments smaller than expected; reduction in the rent subsidies; more years spent in the labour force; shorter duration period for daily allowances; and accumulated pension claims to be deducted against the early retirement pay. It is easy to form an opinion on matters like these. If anything, we are opposed.

The public, therefore, reacted like an insulted child. They felt victimized by the treachery of politicians, because the objectives were abstract, vague, collective and the benefits belonged to the future. The disadvantages, on the contrary, were tangible, individual and had an effect here and now. This basic asymmetry is difficult to cope with for the political parties as well as for the media. The risk is that the media conspire with the victims against the system. However, 'the system', too, is certainly to blame.

Another problem is that the benefits are collective by nature and belong to the future, while the costs concern easily identifiable people and groups and belong to the present. It is difficult, therefore, to promote the comprehensive perspective. The worried voices of the professional victims make themselves heard more easily.

When the short-term perspective and the tangible replace the long-term point of view and the abstract in both politics and media, the illustrious ideal of the informed citizenry able to form a competent opinion on all public affairs is subject to erosion. The political negotiations have moved from the traditional, formal frameworks – law-preparing commissions for instance - to the closed professional compartments governed by private rules and inhabited by politicians, officials and interest groups. Serving as campaign magicians, they set the political agenda in a strategic interaction with the media. This is the response to single-case journalism and the assessment experts. Or is it the other way around?

However it may be, it is experts who decode and interpret the universe of knowledge motivating the political decisions. There emerges a powerful class of well-informed people separated from a general public absorbed in single cases, personal cases and scandals. The bond between the electorate and the elected is cut.

The Two Publics

The public has been divided into two publics. We have an elite public which develops a code-based and professional communication marked by political trial balloons, signals about compromise possibilities and coded party issues. It is a serious public whose members market their positions in close cooperation with the leading politicians. Together they create the strategies of greatest importance for the political desicions.

Next to this elite we have a popular public concerned with single-cases, scandals and strange events. Society is divided into two separate subcultures. This separation, together with the commercial pressure on newspapers and television, leads to new societal roles to the journalists.

We are placed in a dangerous game between media and politics, with which we have not yet come to terms. The core of the problem appears to be the intolerable and unworkable fiction that each of us must acquire a competent opinion about all public affairs. The problem of the media is confused because the critics and the apologists expect the media to make up for all that was not foreseen in the theory of democracy. Democrats regard media as a panacea for their own defects. Analysis of the nature of news and of the economic basis of journalism, however, shows that the media necessarily and inevitably reflect, and therefore, in greater or lesser extent, intensify, the defective organization of public opinion (Lippmann 1922, 19). Most criticism of journalism seems to be based on this fiction.

The Rationally Ignorant Voter

When we buy kitchen hardware, cars or homes, we usually know what we are doing. As consumers we read about the different makes of cars and their qualities. We consult friends and acquaintances in order to learn from their experiences. We collect knowledge about the cost of spare parts and the expected price of the used car. We act as informed and rational consumers.

And it all makes sense because the benefits of choosing rationally are individualized. It is the individual who saves money because the car is not a petrol guzzler. I am the one who earns money, because the spare parts are cheap. And I am the one who earns the profit when the price of the used car increases. The expenses following from a stupid choice are born by me. Therefore, in my private choices, I have a strong incentive to be well informed and rational.

My behaviour in the political system is different. Now it is no longer a matter of private choices, but about decisions with consequences for all of us. Perhaps it should mean that I paid special attention to the collective choices, but I do not. Because I am rational, I know that my decisions are insignificant. In a referendum I count for only one out of four million voters. Only a small part of the possible benefits is mine, and I share the costs of a stupid decision with several million other Danes.

Even if I did use plenty of time to get acquainted with a given public issue, my influence is minimal. Even if I act as the best informed voter, my influence is not greater than that of the most ignorant voter. So why use time and energy trying to know everything, when it is all about matters of common interest? I would rather tend my garden and enjoy my whisky. But if I think like that, I imagine that most other people will think the same. The citizens choose to be ignorant, a quite reasonable choice of action.

One of Anthony Downs' (1957) most influential contributions to the science of politics is the concept of 'rational ignorance'.[1] When two candidates compete for the votes of a large electorate, the vote of each individuals voter has a negligible probability of affecting the outcome. Realizing this, rational voters do not expend time and money gathering information about candidates. They remain 'rationally ignorant' of both the issues in the election and the opposing candidates' positions on these issues. Although Downs deserves credit for making 'rational ignorance' part of the parlance of political science, the idea is clearly present in Schumpeter's (1950, 256-64) classic discussion of democracy:

> When we move .... away from the private concerns of the family and the business office into those regions of national and international affairs that lack a direct and unmistakable link with those private concerns, individual volition, command of facts and method of inference soon cease to fulfill the requirements of the classical doctrines. What strikes me most of all and seems to me to be the core of the trouble is the fact that the sense of reality is so completely lost. Normally, the

great political questions take their place in the psychic economy of the typical citizen with those leisure-hour interests that have not attained the rank of hobbies, and with the subjects of irresponsible conversation. These things seem so far off; they are not at all like a business proposition; dangers may not materialize at all and if they should they may not prove so very serious; one feels oneself to be moving in a fictitious world.

This reduced sense of reality accounts not only for a reduced sense of responsibility, but also for the absence of effective volition. One has one's phrases, of course, and one's wishes and daydreams and grumbles; especially, one has one's likes and dislikes. But ordinarily they do not amount to what we call a will – the psychic counterpart of purposeful responsible action. In fact, for the private citizen musing over national affairs, there is no scope for such a will and no task at which it could develop. He is member of an unworkable committee, the committee of the whole nation, and this is why he expends less disciplined effort on mastering a political problem than he expends on a game of bridge....

Thus, the typical citizen drops down to a lower level of mental performance as soon as he enters the political field. He argues and analyzes in a way which he would readily recognize as infantile within the sphere of his real interests. He becomes a primitive again. His thinking becomes associative and affective. And this entails two further consequences and ominous significance.
First, even if there were no political groups trying to influence him, the typical citizen would in political matters tend to yield to extra-rational or irrational prejudice and impulse ..... Moreover, simply because he is not 'all there', he will relax his usual moral standards as well and occasionally give in to dark urges which the conditions of private life help him to repress. But as to wisdom or rationality of his inferences and conclusions, it may be just as bad if he gives in to a burst of general indignation. This will make it still more difficult for him to see things in their correct proportions or even to see more than one aspect of one thing at a time. Hence, if for once he does emerge from his usual vagueness and does display the definite will postulated by the classical doctrine of democracy, he is as likely as not to become still more unintelligent and irresponsible than he usually is. At certain junctures, this may prove fatal to his nation.

Acknowledging the rational ignorance and the impossibility of a dialogue among four million people, we have chosen to live in a representative democracy. The four million voters elect 179 members of Parliament, who make decisions on behalf of the four million. But to elect these 179 is complicated in itself.

Therefore, we have simplified the process by allowing the 179 to be members of political parties, in principle representing different views of the world.

This is the reality, but we still abide by the fiction that decisions follow from a democratic dialogue in which we all participate. Every single citizen is regarded as sovereign and omnicompetent (Lippmann 1927, 11). This creates a tension between the reality and the ideal. From this tension springs frustration. Lippmann describes the ideal as a fiction: »I do not mean an undesirable ideal. I mean an unattainable ideal, only in the sense that it is bad for a fat man to try to be a ballet dancer. An ideal should express the true possibilities of its subject. When it does not it perverts the true possibilities. The ideal of the omnicompetent, sovereign citizen is, in my opinion, such a false ideal. It is unattainable. The pursuit of it is misleading. The failure to achieve it has produced the current disenchantment,« (Lippmann 1927, 29).

The representative system means that I do not need to take a stand on well-defined issues. Intermittently, I make a choice among a number of political parties. I know about the rough contours of the parties, but I do not know in any detail which problems the parties will be dealing with in the period to come. To vote is like buying a lottery ticket. My only criteria of assessment are whether the salesman inspires confidence and whether I have dealt with him or her before. As a voter, I deposit my 'influence' with someone I have confidence in. And my next decision depends upon whether I think this person has been worthy of my deposit or not.

Some people argue that 'the salesman' represents an ideology or worldview: yes, perhaps. But we are citizens in Denmark, where only a few people are able to act on the basis of principles, much less to formulate such principles.

Rather we endeavour to procure the petty and paltry pleasures with which we glut our lives and to focus on the immediate consequences to ourselves. Politicians, citizens and the media, ideally entrusted with the task of linking the electorate and those elected, have a strong incentive to atomize the debate so that the overall perspective is lost. The 'consequence journalism' focuses mainly on the effects for individuals – frequently, the outcomes for the consequence experts, i.e., the victims – or the turnout for selected groups. The prospect of the general point of view being advanced is, however, poor.

Another problem is, that we have no common standards for our assessments. This means that it is difficult to determine whether the benefits to be derived from a contemplated initiative compensate for the costs, because we do not agree on the definition of costs and benefits. Therefore, nothing is 'true'. The truth is what the majority decides. This paves the way for the sophists to play an important role. To some extent, democracy means a dissolution of all values. If anything is valid, everything is unimportant.

For the above-mentioned good reasons, the citizens, i.e., the highly-prized public, do not have the same knowledge about the social conditions as the people who are daily preoccupied with these subjects:

> We must assume that the members of a public will not anticipate a problem much before its crisis has become obvious, nor stay with the problem long after its crisis is past. They will not know the antecedent events, will not have seen the issue as it developed, will not have thought out or willed a program, and will not be able to predict the consequences of acting on that program. We must assume as a theoretically fixed premise of popular government that normally men as members of a public will not be well informed, continuously interested, nonpartisan, creative or executive. We must assume that a public is inexpert in its curiosity, intermittent, that it discerns only gross distinctions, is slow to be aroused and quickly diverted; that, since it acts by aligning itself, it personalizes whatever it considers, and is interested only when events have been melodramatized as a conflict. The public will arrive in the middle of the third act and will leave before the last curtain, having stayed just long enough perhaps to decide who is the hero and who the villain of the piece (Lippmann 1927, 54-55).

An unattainable ideal leads only to disillusionment. This is precisely what happened subsequent to the agreement on the Danish government's law on the state budget.

When far-reaching decisions are agreed upon as part of a compromise accepted behind closed doors, many people consider it a threat to our ideas of democracy, at least as voiced on the Danish Constitution Day:

- Subjects which should be scrutinized by introducing a bill and debating in committee are discussed in a closed decision-making process.
- The parties involved in the political accord almost obtain a veto regarding changes in the settlement.
- The parties obtain an autonomous existence, acting superior to the legislature.

- The legislature is placed in a passive position. Decisions are made in a closed group of party leaders.
- There has been limited previous discussion, which has only been »caught« by a few well-informed observers.
- Circumstances important during the draft stage of the bill are neglected.

Government by the people has been suspended. It is replaced not only by the government of elected representatives, but by government of a group of party leaders. It is, however, difficult to see how you can avoid the 'closed' decision-making process. We know for sure that if parts of a 'package' leak too soon, it will be 'shut down' at once. Nothing affects the minute-by-minute politics so much as the change of moods in public opinion and in the mass media. The corollary is the need for 'closed-door' politics. The parties have different preferences. Compromise, therefore, is an absolute necessity, but if it is to be stable, the parties have to commit themselves before their supporters' booing crowds are let loose.

We, the public, ought to praise our elected politicians for having dared to act, even if we did not have the possibility to react until the compromise was formed. Maybe the understanding would increase if we – the voters – would recognize that we are (rationally) ignorant. Hence, we need politicians who dare to make decisions. And who dare stand by their decisions.

A Preliminary Summary

Now we can conclude that we face the nuisance of journalism, the nuisance of politics, the nuisance of interest groups, and the nuisance of the public. Not because journalists, politicians, leaders of interest groups and citizens are thieves or gangsters. In some way or other, the bad guy in the game is 'the rules' which determine our behaviour. There is no reason to shoot at one person or another. The problem appeals to reflection.

The Dilemma

Ideologically our thinking on democracy is based on the idea of the sovereign, omnicompetent, omniscient citizen. This idea colours the discussion about the relationship between the media, the politicians and the public. The idea is classical, so let me illustrate by a quote from C.N. David, the editor of the National Liberal daily *Fædrelandet*, which began publishing in 1834, 15 years prior to the Constitution:

> The paper will try to draw the public's attention to public matters, to awaken and to nourish the citizens' interest in the civic, and, thus, endeavour to rouse the self-importance, which for the people as well as the individuals, is the primary condition of a vital life. To describe the excellent and the good characterizing our society, to point out our deficiencies and what we wish should be changed and improved and to heighten our awareness of what we still want to accomplish. The people, therefore, must develop a comprehensive knowledge about the essence of the State, insight into the nature of the State, knowledge of the objectives and the activities of the institutions in and for the State, assurance about the condition of the State, recognizing what each member of the State owes the whole and what the whole owes to him. Void of this accumulated knowledge, insights and recognitions from which follow an intense interest in the State, the people will always be a mass of inhabitants instead of a unity of citizens (quoted from *Dansk Mediehistorie*, 1, 1996, pp. 113-115, my translation).

The quote mirrors the confidence in the responsible public and urges the newspapers to act as the bridge connecting the public and its representatives. The editor warns the citizens of the risk of the people degenerating into a mass of inhabitants, or to quote Anker Brink Lund, that the citizens degenerate into consumers and clients.

If this happens, we face the kind of problem so powerfully developed by one of David's contemporaries, the French historian Alexis de Tocqueville. In 1831-32 de Tocqueville spent 9 months in the 'brave new world'. Back home, he wrote his locus classicus about democracy in America. Chapter 56 is called: »Which Form of Despotism Must the Democratic Countries Fear«:

> The first thing that strikes the observation is an innumerable multitude of men, all equal and alike, incessantly endeavoring to procure the petty and paltry pleasures with which they glut their lives. Each of them, living apart, is a stranger to the fate of all the rest – his children and his private friends constitute to him the whole of mankind; as for the rest of his fellow-citizens, he is close to them, but he sees them not; he exists but in himself and for himself alone; and if his kindred still remain to him, he may be said at any rate to have lost his country. Above this race of men stands an immense and tutelary power, which takes upon itself to secure their gratifications, and to watch over their fate. That power is absolute, minute, regular, provident, and mild. It

would be like the authority of a parent, if, like that authority, its object was to prepare men for manhood; but it seeks, on the contrary, to keep them in perpetual childhood: it is well content that the people should rejoice, provided they think of nothing but rejoicing. For their happiness such a government willingly labors, but it chooses to be the sole agent and the only arbiter of that happiness; it provides for their security, foresees and supplies their necessities, facilitates their pleasures, manages their principal concerns, directs their industries, regulates the descent of property, and subdivides their inheritances: what remains, but to spare them all the care of thinking and all the trouble of living ?...

[The supreme power] covers the surface of society with a network of small complicated rules, minute and uniform, through which the most original minds and the most energetic characters cannot penetrate, to rise above the crowd. The will of man is not shattered, but softened, bent and guided; men are seldom forced by it to act, but they are constantly restrained from acting: such a power does not destroy, but it prevents existence; it does not tyrannize, but it compresses, enervates, extinguishes, and stupefies a people, till each nation is reduced to be nothing better than a flock of timid and industrious animals, of which the government is the shepherd...

Our contemporaries are constantly excited by two conflicting passions; they want to be led, and they wish to remain free: as they cannot destroy the one or the other of these contrary propensities, they strive to satisfy them both at once. They devise a sole, tutelary, and all-powerful form of government, but elected by the people... they console themselves for being in tutelage by the reflection that they have chosen their own guardians. Every man allows himself to be put in leading-strings because he sees that it is not a person or a class of persons but the people at large who hold the end of the chain.

By this system, the people shake off their state of dependence just long enough to select their master, and then relapse into it again... [a strange] sort of compromise between administrative despotism and the sovereignty of the people (Tocqueville, 303-304).

Like in other cases we find ourselves in a field of tension between the ideal and the reality.

Public Journalism

One enters this field of tension by reading the very stimulating book by Peter Bro, '*The Journalist as an Activist*' (1998). Bro explicates the tension by discussing the ideas of Walter Lippmann (1922; 1927; 1955) and John Dewey (1927). Lippmann coined the view that the existence of a well-informed public was an impossibility. Public leadership, therefore, had to be entrusted to a well-informed, well-educated elite able to manage society sensibly and for the benefit of everybody. The unrestricted right of the press to publish should be a counterweight to the elite. Dewey, in contrast, emphasized that the great social decisions would sooner or later fail if they did not emerge from a discussion in the public space. For Dewey, wide open discussion was as important as an effective result; but he was not blind to Lippmann's arguments: if »the Great Society is not converted into a Great Community the Public will remain in eclipse«.

In modern America, Dewey's ideals are mirrored by Robert Bellah's (1985, 1991) contributions to sociological theory, and by the literature developing the idea of 'Public Journalism'. The concept can be defined in many ways. Bro identifies public journalism with the intent to 'reconstruct the public'. Bro's interpretation, while it has my sympathies, is not without problems. To the extent to which principles are concerned, public journalism seems to be opposed to the (necessary) representative system. It represents a dream of Athens' Agora. Nevertheless, it is easily transformed into something else.

On March 19, 1999 Conservative politician Per Stig Møller published a comment in the newspaper *Berlingske Tidende*. Møller told about a message put on the agenda of the Danish Parliament on February 11: »Danmarks Radio, DR2 'Indefra' will hold a demonstration on Parliament Square on February 11, 1999 at 12:00 p.m. until February 12, 1999 to 3:00 p.m. in order to make visible the problems of the homeless people«.

The editors of 'Indefra' did not, however, cover a demonstration arranged by the homeless. It was the editors themselves who arranged the demonstration. On his way to the parliamentary session, Møller was presented with an invitation to the demonstration and was asked about his attitude to this while the camera was directed right against him.

This example represents a strange disconnection of actual reality to be replaced by a media-created reality.

I do not argue here that this is an example of 'Public Journalism'. However, it is a variety. In Chapter four of his book, Peter Bro describes different examples from the United States. I shall give one example only (p. 71):

> In the first project the Wichita *Eagle* invited ordinary citizens to de-

cide what the issues of the gubernatorial-election should be about. This was done by providing a public space for the politicians' actions and the journalists' information activities. In a second project, however, the newspaper and the media-partners went further and allowed the citizens to figuratively step into this public space and become political participants on an equal footing with the politicians. The media provided this symbolic space in the newspaper, on television and radio, through town meetings, by arranging focus-group discussions, workshops, etc. The arrangements took place in the traditional media and elsewhere. The media opened up a public space in which a political discussion could take place and problems could be solved. The overriding objective was to reconstruct the public. (My translation).

The *Eagle* and its journalists *created* a public space and *allowed* the citizens to step inside. The newspaper and the media-partners *opened up* and *turned themselves* into a public sphere. The public was *reconstructed*. The important question is whether these activities have freed 'the crowd' from tutelage. Have the masses not simply gotten themselves a new self-appointed shepherd? Does the whole exercise not reflect the journalists' attempt to recapture their previous defining role? Is it not simply an effort to maintain the myth that the mass media and the journalists are a democratic institution on equal terms with other democratic institutions?

Notes

1. From the perspective of this contribution, influenced as it is by the writings of Walter Lippmann, it is of interest that Downs writes: »Few of our conclusions are new; in fact, some have been specifically stated by Walter Lippmann in his brilliant trilogy on the relation between public opinion and democratic government. However, our attempt to trace what rational men will do, both as citizens and in government, is novel as far as we know. It tends to prove logically contentions that Lippmann and others have reached by observing politics empirically« (Downs 1957, 14).

References

Bellah, Robert N., et al. (1985). *Habits of the Heart*, Berkeley: University of California Press.
Bellah, Robert N., et al. (1991). *The Good Society*, New York: Vintage Books.
Bourdieu, Pierre (1998). *Om tv – og journalistikkens magt*, København: Tiderne Skifter.

Bro, Peter (1998). *Journalisten som aktivist – om presse, politik og demokratisk dialog,* Copenhagen: Fremad.

Bruhn Jensen, Klaus (ed.) (1996). *Dansk mediehistorie vol. 1-3,* København: Samleren.

Dewey, John (1927). *The Public and Its Problems,* Denver: Allan Swallow.

Downs, Anthony (1957). *An Economic Theory of Democracy,* New York: Harper and Row.

Ekecrantz, Jan & Tom Olsson (1998). *Det redigerade Samhället,* Stockholm: Carlssons Bokförlag.

Jensen, Henrik (1998). *Ofrets århundrede,* København: Samleren.

Larsen, Peter Harms (1998). »Journalistikkens uvæsen«, *Politiken November 19th, 1998.*

Larsen, Peter Harms (1999). »Dansen om nyhedskriterierne«, *Jyllands-Posten February 3rd, 1999.*

Lippmann, Walter (1922). *Public Opinion,* New York: The Free Press.

Lippmann, Walter (1993) [1927]. *The Phantom Public,* New York: MacMillan, Reprinted by Transaction Publishers, New Brunswick and London.

Lippmann, Walter (1955). *The Public Philosophy,* London: Hamish Hamilton.

Lund, Anker Brink (1999). »Det redigerede samfund«, *Fyens Stiftstidende, February 6th, 1999.*

Schumpeter, Joseph A. (1950). *Capitalism, Socialism, and Democracy,* New York: Harper and Row.

Tocqueville, Alexis de (1956) [1835/1840]. *Democracy in America,* (ed. by Richard D. Heffner), New York: A Mentor Book from New American Library.

The Danes and Direct Democracy

Palle Svensson

Abstract

Referendums have a central place in certain theories of democracy, and a renewed interest in a more frequent application of referendums has developed in Denmark, as in other countries. Even though the Danish political system is one of representative democracy, referendums are quite common. Thus, Denmark is a good case for studying public beliefs in forms of direct democracy. This chapter focuses on recent voter studies in order to show, how the demand for more direct democracy operates as a defensive weapon chosen by those with few resources and who distrust politicians, rather than an offensive instrument for a further democratisation of the political system.

Introduction

During the 1990s Denmark has had three referendums about European integration. The first was about the Maastricht Treaty in 1992, the second on the Maastricht Treaty and the Edinburgh Agreement in 1993, and the third on the Amsterdam Treaty in 1998. Previous, referendums had been held in 1972 on Danish membership in the European Community and on the Single European Act in 1986. Apart from these referendums, a large number of demands and proposals have been advanced in the public debate about holding further referendums – both from the Government and from the Opposition. Finally, all parties supporting the so-called »National Compromise« – an agreement between seven of the eight parties in Parliament to form the Danish basis for negotiations leading to the Edinburgh Agreement – have announced that all future changes in Denmark's relationship to the European Union must be submitted to national referendum for final acceptance or rejection (Petersen 1999).

Parallel to the more frequent application of referendums the 1990s have seen the emergence of public debate regarding the proper balance between representative and direct democracy. This debate was initiated by one of the leaders of the centrist Social Liberal Party, Niels Helveg Petersen, who in 1991 suggested more referendums in order to stimulate public interest in politics and increase the active participation of Danish citizens (Petersen 1992). The debate, however, has to some extent been taken over by individuals and parties with a more critical view on representative democracy, such as the right-wing Progress Party and the Danish People's Party, both of whom advocate a more direct form of democracy.

So far, neither a constitutional change nor any legal provisions have been carried through or even put on the political agenda, but the increased interest in referendums and direct democracy makes relevant the need to analyse how Danish citizens look upon various aspects of direct versus representative democracy and active participation versus elite rule and party competition. An understanding of these attitudes is a prerequisite for further progress towards understanding constitutional reforms.

In this chapter, Danish referendums as an element of direct democracy are discussed by raising a number of vital questions. Will more frequent application of referendums develop the political system and contribute to further democratisation? Or have referendums been taken over by political elites as an instrument to manipulate the voters? How are referendums perceived by the voters themselves? What does the increased use and further discussion of referendums mean for the perception of this institution? In short, who supports and who rejects this element of direct democracy?

The position of referendums in democratic theory will be briefly outlined and their role in the Danish political system delineated. Democratic values and the perception of referendums among Danish voters are then analysed in terms of developments over recent years and as regards their distribution among social and political groups. Finally, the results of the empirical analysis are discussed with a view to the situation of the 1990s and possible future of referendums in Denmark.

Democratic Theory

The ideal democratic process – based on the principles of popular sovereignty of the people and political equality, i.e., all citizens having equal and adequate opportunities to influence decisions affecting their life conditions (Dahl 1989, 108-115, 119-131) – has never been fully implemented anywhere. All adult citizens are presumed to have the necessary qualifications to participate on equal terms in political life, but resources are not sufficiently distributed in any polyarchy to ensure equal influence to all citizens. Consequently, some people have better opportunities for freedom, personal development and actual interests than do others (Dahl 1989, 88–96). However, to what extent should citizens become more involved in politics and how could such increased involvement be achieved?

The issue about improving citizen participation and possibilities of influence has often been articulated in terms of a balance between representative and direct democracy. As a general principle, a distinction can be made between two opposing notions called liberal and radical theory (Holden 1974, 68-71).

Liberal democratic theory claims that representative democracy is a value in itself because representatives are able to bring political issues up for free debate. In accordance with this conception, representative democracy is more than a mere technical aid because the elected representatives represent an elite which better and more truly than the people itself expresses the demands prevalent among the citizens (Ross 1953, 180).

As voters generally have limited possibilities to participate in politics in a rational and independent way, Joseph A. Schumpeter suggested reversing the sequence of the two defining elements in what he called »the classical doctrine«: (1) the decision of issues and (2) the election of leaders. Whereas the classical view – according to Schumpeter – had perceived the decision of issues as primary and the election of leaders as secondary, Schumpeter argued that it is both more realistic and more in line with the intentions of democracy to regard the election of leaders as the primary function of the voters and the popular decision of issues as the secondary. The voters' primary function is to produce a government. In this way Schumpeter arrived at this revised definition of democracy: »The democratic method is that institutional arrangement for arriving at political decisions in which individuals acquire the power to decide by means of a competitive struggle for the people's vote« (Schumpeter 1942, 269).

Among the advantages of this democratic revision, Schumpeter emphasised that this definition of democracy recognises the need for leadership. This need had been neglected in the classic view, which quite unrealistically had given the initiative to the common voters. Furthermore, this definition focuses on the competition between elites for the people's vote. Even if this competition may not be completely perfect, it is regulated by the electoral method – a free competition for a free vote – which excludes other methods used by competing elites to acquire power (e.g., military coup or court intrigues).

Contrary to the liberal view, radical democratic theory claims that representative democracy is only a practical measure. It is necessary since it is impossible to let *all* citizens participate directly in *all* discussions concerning common matters *all* of the time. Radical democrats do not reject the notion that political decisions in a modern, complex society have to be taken by a smaller group of individuals. They neither attack the representative system as such nor do they claim that some kind of elite can be completely avoided. In fact, insofar as competition between two or more groups of elites results in establishing a correspondence between elite decisions and the interests of the population, radicals would say that a *necessary* condition for democracy is fulfilled.

The radicals do not accept, however, that elite competition and policy correspondence is a *sufficient* condition for a full democracy – or that it could be taken as its defining characteristic: hence, »democracy in the traditional sense involves a great deal more than the correspondence of individual wills and collective decisions; it involves, for example, political equality, active consent about the form of government and the rules of the game, widespread discussion and participation, political and otherwise, through all kinds of activities and channels« (Duncan & Lukes 1963, cited from Kariel 1970, 202).

Thus, these conflicting theories of democracy offer quite different perceptions of the value of citizen participation. It follows that the view on forms of participation in general and on referendums also differ.

In liberal democratic theory, referendums are alien to a representative democracy. Referendums should not be used in such a system and if they are it should be only as a rare exception, observing very restrictive conditions (Ross 1953).

In radical democratic theory, there is no difference in principle between direct and indirect democracy, and in order to neutralise tendencies towards expert dominance and to engage the citizens politically, it would be feasible to introduce elements of direct democracy such as institutions like the initiative and referendum (Barber 1984, 281–89).

In a democracy, citizens must choose between various political possibilities. If they do not do so themselves, economic and intellectual elites will do it for them. Human beings live in communities and must necessarily cooperate and make joint decisions. It is therefore important to make this cooperation as rational as possible, but it is also important to do it in a way that reflects the views and interests of the citizens in terms of their active consent.

Accordingly, radical democratic theory sees elements of direct democracy such as initiative and referendum as increasing public participation and responsibility because these institutions constitute a perpetual instrument for political education. Furthermore, they give the political debate the reality and the discipline required in order to be efficient. The citizens' possibility to submit a proposal to direct voting (initiative) and their possibility to take a position on the decisions of elected representatives (referendum) unite debate and action. These possibilities express the national will and transform public opinion into political decisions. Thus, for radical democrats, the application of referendums should be limited only for practical reasons.

To sum up, the question whether an increased application of referendums can develop the political system and contribute to further democratisation depends on the applied democratic theory. If a liberal theory is taken as point of departure, referendums have to be rejected as a means to further democratisation (for a recent example of this position in the Danish debate, see Højlund 1993). If, on the other hand, the radical theory is taken as point of departure, more referendums may contribute to further democratisation. This presupposes, however, that political leaders and citizens are motivated to use this possibility, and that referendums are not used for other purposes.

In the next sections, the role of referendums in the Danish political system is indicated and prospects for further democratisation discussed by surveying basic democratic attitudes and attitudes toward referendums among Danish citizens.

Direct Democracy in Denmark

The Danish political system is not a realisation of any specific democratic theory. Rather, it should be seen as a result of a prolonged process, in which various ideas and group interests have confronted each other under changing social and political conditions. Basically, this process has led to a continued democratisation of the political regime even though there have been serious defeats and setbacks for the democratic forces. Thus, applying the terminology of Robert A. Dahl, the political system in Denmark is a polyarchy (Svensson 1993).

The principle of popular sovereignty has been achieved to an increasing extent. However, it is also important to emphasise that this achievement has taken place within a representative form of government. Danish citizens have to a larger extent obtained possibilities for an equal influence on the composition of the Danish Parliament – the Folketing – and on the composition of the Government, and thus *indirectly* on policy-making. The combination of the two main principles of Danish democracy – popular sovereignty and representative government – is expressed primarily in the principle of universal suffrage defining »the people« as all adult citizens; in proportional representation ensuring equal representation in the Folketing of all political opinions; and in the parliamentary principle making the Government responsible to the majority of the Folketing.

The democratisation process has also allowed Danish citizens the possibility to exert more *direct* influence on policy-making by means of referendums. Yet such elements of direct democracy have come rather late and have been met by severe opposition from spokesmen of representative democracy.

Today the Danish polyarchy allows for six possibilities for holding referendums whereas there are no constitutional possibilities for popular initiative. Five of the possibilities of referendums are explicitly mentioned in the Constitution and are all legally decisive: (1) an obligatory referendum on constitutional amendments; (2) an optional law referendum; (3) an obligatory law referendum on the voting age; (4) an obligatory law referendum on delegation of constitutional powers to international authorities; and (5) a voluntary and decisive referendum on laws about treaties.[1] In addition to these constitutional provisions, it is possible by law to hold voluntary referendums. Traditionally, it has been claimed that such referendums would have only advisory status, as they could not restrict the authorities which are competent according to the constitution (Sørensen 1969, 178f). However, this view has recently been challenged, the argument being that the legal distinction between advisory and decisive referendums is rather formalistic inasmuch as all referendums are in fact politically decisive, and as the Constitution makes no mention of any prohibition against voluntary and binding referendums, they may be adopted (Zahle 1996, 126ff).

A closer analysis of the adoption of referendums in the Danish constitutional system makes it clear that the principle of popular sovereignty has penetrated the constitutional framework in forms of direct democracy only to a limited extent. The majority of the people have the possibility to exert direct political decision-making with regard to constitutional amendments. Even this possibility is made difficult because it is demanded that a favourable majority must comprise at least 40 per cent of the electorate. Facultative law referendums leave the voters without any possibility to demand that a passed bill be submitted to a referendum. If a minority in the Folketing puts forward such a demand, the constitutional provisions clearly favour representative democracy on behalf of direct democracy, as a majority, comprising at least 30 per cent of the electorate, is required to reject the passed bill. What is left of direct democracy is in reality only a right to veto, a right to stop bills passed by the Folketing.

Even if some possibilities of direct democracy have been introduced in Denmark, there is still room for a much larger application of referendums. The question is whether and to what extent further elements of direct democracy are desired not only by parts of the political elite but also by Danish citizens. The following analysis of attitudes of Danish citizens examines the general view on political equality, followed by beliefs about a more frequent application of referendums.

Democratic Values in Denmark

Results from numerous studies on political participation have shown that some citizens are more active than others. The most active persons are characterised by their personal resources, e.g. education, work position or economic situation (see Milbrath & Goel 1977; Damgaard 1980; Togeby 1989). Higher participation is also related to higher political interest, knowledge and self-confidence. Low political activity is not only associated with few resources, but also with little motivation and the belief that it is of no use to fight for one's ideas and interests. A Norwegian study has labelled this relationship »political poverty« (Martinussen 1973).

In the development of democracy, a central issue has been whether inequality in participation and inequality in political influence are an inevitable condition for all societies and all forms of human co-operation, or whether democracy and political equality are perceived as a possibility. Is it realistic, by spreading resources and deliberate efforts for instance, to motivate passive groups and to obtain a higher degree of equality in political participation and influence? One precondition for activating the citizens could be whether various, particularly passive groups consider it possible to overcome inequalities. The more people believe in democratic equality, the larger the possibilities that existing inequalities are not simply accepted but challenged and perhaps even circumscribed.

To identify Danish citizens' view of democracy's possibilities, the following question has been used in Danish surveys: »It will always be necessary that a few competent individuals decide everything«. In the 1990s this item was included in the national surveys after the Danish referendums of June 1992 and May 1993 (see Siune & Svensson 1993; Siune, Svensson & Tonsgaard 1994), and in a survey conducted after the referendum on the Amsterdam Treaty in May 1998. The results are shown in table 1.

Table 1. The Possibility of Democracy,[1] 1992, 1993 and 1998. Per cent.

	1992 (N=712)	1993 (N=934)	1998 (N=939)
All	59	54	58
Men	60	53	58
Women	59	55	58
18-29 years	62	61	57
30-49 years	69	56	63
50 years -	51	46	53
Basic School	47	43	48
Grammar School/O-levels	63	52	54
High School/A-levels	75	74	74
Unskilled workers	58	44	49
Skilled workers	48	53	57
White collar	69	60	67
Self-employed	56	54	58
Very much interested in politics	65	61	66
Somewhat interested in politics	63	58	61
Only a little interested in politics	52	44	51
Not at all interested in politics	47	17	50
Socialist People's Party	77	72	69
Social Democrats	68	49	59
Centre parties[2]	67	51	66
Conservatives	46	53	57
Liberals	52	52	55
Progress Party[3]	61	49	39

Notes:

1) The figures show the percentages disagreeing on the item: »It will always be necessary that a few competent individuals decide everything.«

2) The centre parties comprise the Social Liberals, the Centre Democrats and the Christian People's Party.

3) In 1998 both the Progress Party and the Danish People's Party.

Table 1 shows that most Danes have a strong belief in democracy. The majority (59 per cent in 1992, 54 per cent in 1993 and 56 per cent in 1998) dissociate themselves from the allegation that political inequality is inevitable. The belief in more democratic equality is significantly higher among the well-educated, among those with an interest in politics, and among supporters for parties on the left-wing compared with supporters of right-wing and centrist parties. No gender difference is apparent on this issue. Age differences are not very large and form no clear pattern beyond the tendency for older people to be more sceptical than the young and the middle-aged regarding the possibility to eliminate political equality. It can be shown that this is not only a result of lower education among the elderly. The main difference between social classes is that white collar people have a higher belief in democracy than do other classes. On closer analysis, however, it is revealed that this is, to a large extent, due to higher education among white collar individuals.

In general, the belief in larger democratic equality is strongest among the young and the middle-aged, well-educated, politically interested, left-wing oriented groups – the same groups among whom we find post-materialistic values (compare Inglehart 1990). Belief in inequality is weakest among voters with few individual resources and low interest in politics.

From these findings and from the value given to referendums in the radical democratic theory, it could be expected that a large number of Danes, and particularly those who are well-educated and politically interested, favour increased use of referendums.

Referendums

Research regarding the view of Danish citizens on referendums has been carried out for some years, with various opinion poll institutes having collected data on this issue. Practice varies regarding the extent and registration of the »don't knows,« and there may also be some differences in weighting procedures. Nevertheless, it is now possible to describe trends in attitudes toward referendums over a period of almost 20 years.

These trends are shown in figure 1. The curve describes developments from the late 1970s to the late 1990s in terms of the proportion of people agreeing to the item: »Many more political issues should be decided by being sent to a referendum.«[2]

The figure indicates an overall stability in the attitude of the Danish population towards direct democracy. From the late 1970s, about half the respondents committing themselves (46 per cent) supported the idea of more referendums. After a rise during the 1980s a decline in the 1990s is noticed in support for more issues to be decided by referendum. From a high of 56 per cent in 1991, it dropped to 43 per cent in 1993, reaching a low point of 38 per cent after the referendum on the Amsterdam Treaty in May 1998.

A possible interpretation of these trends may be that support for more referendums is generally increasing among Danes but that it drops in the period after the holding of a referendum. Thus, the two rapid referendums on the European Union in 1992 and 1993 eroded popular support for more direct democracy, and a similar effect occurred after the Amsterdam Treaty in May 1998. This indicates that a number of Danish citizens were disap-

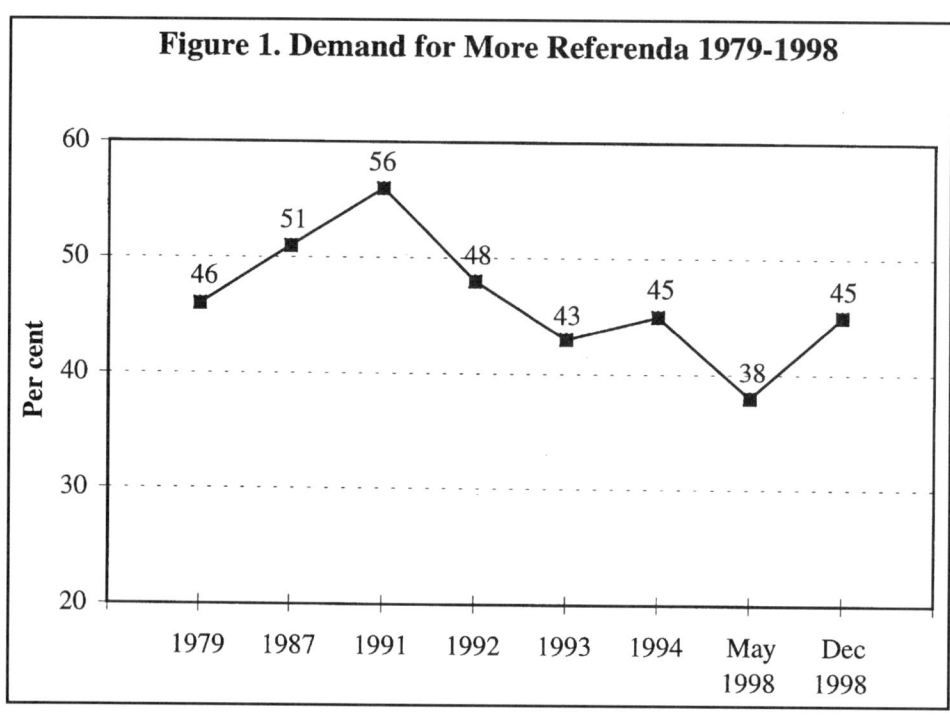

pointed by the actual use of referendums. Whether this disappointment is caused by dissatisfaction with unequal terms for opponents in the campaign up to the referendum, by rejection of the ways in which the political elite is seen to use the referendum to manipulate voters, or by other factors – exclusive use of referendum in relation to the EU issue in the 1990s, for example – is impossible to say without further analysis. However, it seems evident that after some time support rises again. Thus, the overall picture is one of a rather stable division of Danish citizens into two, almost equally large groups of supporters for more direct democracy and supporters for maintenance of the existing representative democracy. The question is, »Who belongs to the two groups?«

Table 2 shows in more detail which Danes appreciate the idea of having more referendums. Throughout the entire period, women have been more positive than men. As a general rule, young people have been more positive than older people, but the pattern has not been quite stable. In 1992, the difference in age was hardly significant, while in 1993 and 1998 the young were clearly the most enthusiastic. The data do not allow for a closer analysis of differences between generations. Consequently, we are unable to see whether those who were young in the 1970s are more positive than later generations. Nevertheless, nothing indicates that this should be the case.

Throughout the entire period, the higher educated have been more sceptical towards a frequent application of referendums than those with a lower education. The educational differences have not been very profound and are somewhat blurred in 1998, but they contribute to revealing a more general structure in public beliefs on referendums. This structure indicates that those

Table 2. Demand for More Referendums,[1] 1992, 1993 and 1998. Per cent.

	1992 (N=712)	1993 (N=931)	1998 (N=950)
All	48	43	38
Men	46	43	34
Women	50	44	40
18-29 years	49	56	55
30-49 years	45	39	34
50 years -	49	39	33
Basic School	52	44	37
Grammar School/O-levels	50	46	41
High School/A-levels	38	38	35
Unskilled workers	56	53	50
Skilled workers	56	46	38
White collar	39	36	31
Self-employed	43	38	22
Very much interested in politics	47	42	34
Somewhat interested in politics	44	42	33
Only a little interested in politics	50	46	43
Not at all interested in politics	72	54	47
Socialist People's Party	55	47	42
Social Democrats	51	44	37
Centre parties[2]	40	30	31
Conservatives	33	35	29
Liberals	35	34	35
Progress Party[3]	72	57	56

Notes:

1) The figures show the percentages agreeing on the item: »Many more political issues should be decided by referendums.

2) The centre parties comprise the Social Liberals, the Centre Democrats and the Christian People's Party.

3) In 1998 both the Progress Party and the Danish People's Party.

strong on individual resources do not prefer referendums as a way to increase citizen participation and influence. On the contrary, referendums are mostly preferred by those with few individual resources. This observation is confirmed by the fact that the blue collar workers, especially the unskilled, have most consistently favoured the idea of more referendums, while white collar workers and the self-employed have been more reserved. In addition, the less politically interested have been most favourable to the idea of more referendums, which again confirms that mainly those with few resources want to introduce a more direct democracy.

During the entire period, the desire to increase the number of referendums is strongest on the political wings, among the voters for the Socialist Peoples' Party and the Progress Party, respectively. Voters supporting the centre parties – i.e., parties around the government and centre of political power – are more reserved. This reservation is particularly outspoken for the voters of the Conservative People's Party and the Liberal Party.

The results shown in table 2 do not fit very well with the results shown in table 1, nor by the expectations raised by these results. If we assume that those wanting to develop democracy as part of post-materialistic values should welcome more referendums as a means to such a development, it follows that not only the young but particularly the well-educated and politically interested should be more positive towards referendums than indicated in table 2. According to expectations voters for the Socialist Peoples' Party favour more referendums. Somewhat surprisingly, however, the same applies to voters for the Progress Party and the Danish Peoples Party. These parties are mainly anti-establishment, supporting a rolling back of the state, favouring market forces and authoritarian, traditional national values as expressed in hostility towards immigrants.

In short, the assumption on which the expectations were drawn from table 1 may not hold. A belief in democracy and the possibility to ensure political equality may not be related to a demand for more referendums as strongly or unambiguously as assumed on the basis of radical democratic theory. Table 3 explores how and to what extent the attitude towards the possibility of democracy and the demand for more referendums are related among Danes in the 1990s.

Table 3 shows no association between a belief in political equality and support for more referendums. Only in 1992 is any sort of positive relationship found, but it is a very weak one. Whereas 46 per cent of those finding political inequality inevitable agreed that more issues should be decided by referendum, 48 per cent of those believing in political equality did the same. In both 1993 and 1998, the relationship was the opposite of the one expected. More citizens with an authoritarian perception of political life (49 per cent in 1993, 42 per cent in 1998) wanted more referendums than those with a democratic perception (39 per cent in 1993, 36 per cent in 1998). Obviously, hope and commitment to democratise the political system are not the main explanations behind the demand for a more direct democracy and more referendums.

In view of the fact that individuals with few resources, such as unskilled

Table 3. Possibility of Democracy and Demand for More Referendums, 1992, 1993 and 1998. Per cent.

	The Possibility of Democracy			
	Agree that a few will always decide	Neither nor	Disagree that a few will always decide	All
1992: Agree that more issues should be decided by referendums	46	50	48	47
Neither nor	3	4	5	5
Disagree that more issues should be decided by referendums	51	46	47	48
All	100	100	100	100
N	259	26	416	703
1993: Agree that more issues should be decided by referendums	49	49	39	44
Neither nor	3	11	3	3
Disagree that more issues should be decided by referendums	48	40	58	53
All	100	100	100	100
N	389	34	507	925
1998: Agree that moreissues should be decided by referendums	42	31	36	38
Neither nor	5	14	5	6
Disagree that more issues should be decided by referendums	53	55	59	56
All	100	100	100	100
N	334	62	537	933

workers and people with low political motivation, are more in favour of referendums than individuals with many resources, it is conceivable that more direct democracy has greater support from those marginalised from the present political system, those who have little political influence or perception of own political influence, and those who do not trust the politicians running the representative institutions, than by those who want a further democratisation of the political system.

In order to test this hypothesis, table 4 examines the relationship between trust in politicians, where the demand for more referendums is correlated with the responses to the question: »In general, how high is your trust in Danish politicians? Would you say that you have very high trust, rather high trust, rather low trust or very low trust in Danish politicians?«

Clearly, the relationship between demand for referendums and trust in politicians is much stronger than the relationship with the possibility of democracy. Moreover, the relationship is as expected. With declining trust in politicians, the demand for referendums grows stronger. Thus, the demand for referendums in Denmark in the 1990s seems to be more of a defensive protection against the present political system and its representatives than an offensive weapon in the struggle for further democratisation. Enthusiasm for more referendums seems to be directly related to the distance to the power centre: The longer the distance to the power centre, the higher the enthusiasm for more referendums. The close relationship between lack of trust in politicians and the demand for more direct democracy is shown even more clearly in figure 2, where trust in politicians is measured on a ten-point

Table 4. Trust in Politicians and Demand for More Referendums, 1992, 1993 and 1998. Per cent.

	Trust in Politicians				
	Very high	Rather high	Rather low	Very low	All
1992: Agree that more issues should be decided by referendums	27	37	60	75	48
Neither nor	5	3	7	6	4
Disagree that more issues should be decided by referendums	68	60	33	19	48
All	100	100	100	100	100
N	37	368	224	65	694
1993: Agree that more issues should be decided by referendums	27	31	46	60	43
Neither nor	3	2	4	3	3
Disagree that more issues should be decided by referenda	70	67	50	37	54
All	100	100	100	100	100
N	30	333	319	223	905
1998: Agree that more issues should be decided by referendums	19	30	42	53	38
Neither nor	5	6	8	2	6
Disagree that more issues should be decided by referendums	77	64	50	45	57
All	100	100	100	100	100
N	43	401	327	144	915

scale in 1993. More referendums and more direct democracy are apparently the alternatives which those with few resources choose when they distrust politicians and feel powerless towards them.

However, table 4 also indicates that the relationship between demand for more referendums and lack of trust in politicians – though high during the entire decade – has, nevertheless, become weaker. This is demonstrated by the decline in demand for more referendums among those with lowest trust in politicians, from 75 per cent in 1992 to 60 per cent in 1993 to 53 percent in 1998. Yet it is even more apparent if the correlation coefficients are compared: Pearson's r: drops from .30 in 1992 to .23 in 1993 and .19 in 1998. Referendums as a defensive weapon seem to be somewhat undermined during the 1990s, a conclusion strengthened by a closer look at some of the figures in table 2. Decline in support for more referendums from 1992 to 1993 is particularly pronounced among voters for the Progress Party

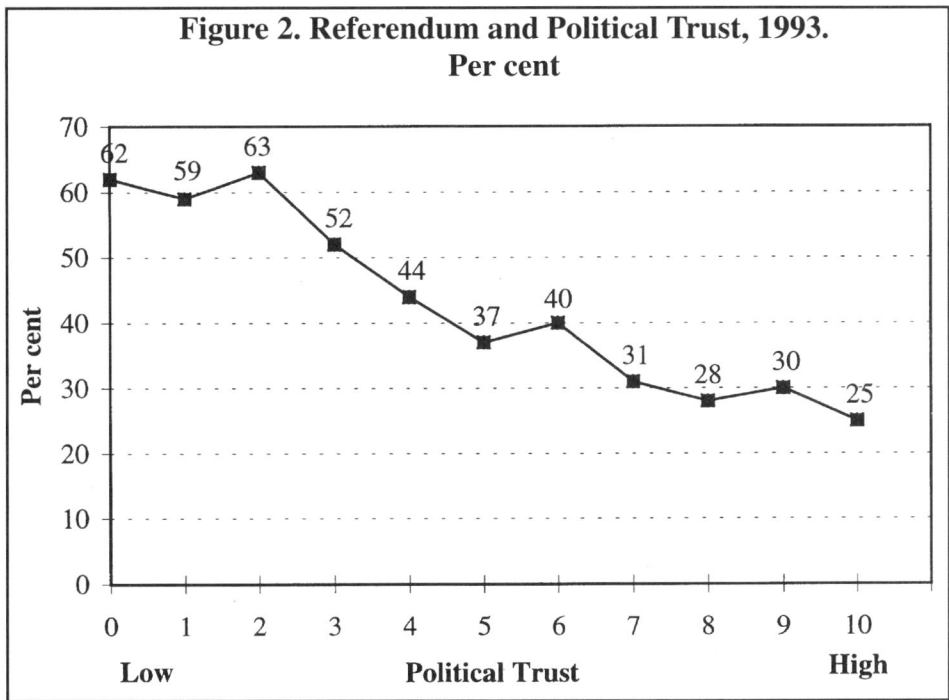

and those with the lowest interest in politics, i.e., among those most alienated from the representative political system.

Weak, powerless and disillusioned voters hoping for more referendums in order to renew the political system seem to have lost faith in referendums as a defensive device in the beginning of the 1990s. With some misgivings, one might speculate which alternatives this group of voters would turn to in order to defend themselves against the establishment. From the radical democrats' point of view, little hope is to be drawn from these results. The only bright aspect is that young people still favour the idea of referendums, but generally the desire to increase citizen influence on their own destiny is becoming less associated with elements of direct democracy.

Conclusions

During the 1990s, the discussion about democracy has been renewed in leading circles in Denmark. The idea to supplement existing, representative democracy with elements of direct democracy, primarily by holding more referendums, has been introduced by both political theorists and practitioners. There have been three referendums concerning Denmark's relation to the European Community. The EC issue was put on the agenda and copiously discussed in the mass media. Finally, there are prospects of additional referendums in the coming years.

Overall, the Danish population is evenly divided in their views on referendums and direct democracy. The number of people who welcome and reject the idea of deciding more issues by referendums has remained largely constant. During the 1990s, a gradual increase in the demand for more referendums has temporarily ceased. This trend may have been caused by the experiences of the referendums stimulating some citizens to change their minds about referendums generally – especially those people who distrust politicians. Following the rejection of the Maastricht-Treaty in June 1992, it was claimed that many voters felt manipulated when they had to vote again in May 1993. The result of that referendum may explain the drop in support for more referendums. Supporters of the Progress Party have especially deserted the idea.

The drop from 1992 to 1993 among Progress Party voters corresponds with a proportional drop among those not interested in politics and those distrusting the politicians. This pattern indicates that groups previously supporting referendums become less enthusiastic because they feel that the established system has taken over the referendum institution and is using it to manipulate the voters.

According to democratic theory, the trend in referendum patterns in Denmark during the 1990s represents a paradox. The preference toward more referendums, especially among the weak and powerless groups who had supported the idea, has changed. This coincides with elite discussions to introduce more direct democracy, putting the EC on the agenda, holding three referendums, and outlining the prospects of future referendums.

In summary, the perception of referendums among Danish citizens apparently rests on a structural and a procedural basis. Structurally, voters with few individual resources, weak interest in politics and low trust in politicians tend to give more support to the application of referendums than do voters with more individual resources, stronger interest and higher trust. Those with many resources do not prefer referendums to achieve higher equality, expressing the (liberal democratic) fear about leaving decisions with people who do not have enough knowledge about the issues and a scepticism towards ordinary people's ability and will to competently acquaint themselves with the details. More referendums primarily appear to be the alternative chosen by those with fewer resources when they distrust the politicians and feel powerless towards them.

The desire for more referendums in Denmark is not mainly an offensive weapon for democracy's continued development. Rather, it expresses the defensive reaction of the powerless and the alienated towards the political elite and towards what they view as elitist groups growing up in a post-industrial society. The groups with the strongest belief in political equality do not want to use referendums as a means for continued democratisation of the political decision-making process, whereas the groups most sceptical towards representative democracy and the elected politicians and favouring referendums are also sceptical of the possibility of political equality.

The procedural element has to be studied closely in the future in order to develop a better understanding of the underlying mechanisms. The Danish case demonstrates that more frequent application of referendums may not increase their popularity in the short run, not even among those usually supporting them. It may depend strongly on who calls them, on what issues are being decided, and under which circumstances the referendum is being held.

Notes

1. The last mentioned possibility has often been forgotten. It has been used only once, in 1993, and has been seen as a special combination of constitutional possibilities in order to hold a referendum even though the required 5/6 majority for delegation of constitutional powers to the EU had been obtained. I have myself been guilty of making this mistake (see Svensson 1996, 34 and the note to table 3.1, 39).
2. The 1979 figures are from the project on the political decision-making process in Denmark (Damgaard *et al.* 1980). The Social Research Institute was responsible for collecting the data. The 1987 data were collected by AIM (Elklit & Tonsgaard 1989, 439). The 1991 figures are from a Sonar opinion poll published in the newspaper *Morgenavisen Jyllands-Posten* (27 October 1991). In 1992 and 1993 AIM collected the data for the referendum study (Siune, Svensson & Tonsgaard 1992, 124f). The 1994 figures are from the Danish Election Survey (Borre & Goul Andersen 1997), with the data collected by AIM. This also applies to a study following the May 1998 referendum on the Amsterdam Treaty. Finally, the December 1998 figures are from a Sonar opinion poll published in *Morgenavisen Jyllands-Posten* (30 December 1998).

References

Barber, Benjamin (1984). *Strong Democracy*, Berkeley: University of California Press.
Borre, Ole & Jørgen Goul Andersen (1997). *Voting and Political Attitudes in Denmark. A Study of the 1994 Election*, Århus: Aarhus University Press.
Dahl, Robert A. (1989). *Democracy and Its Critics*, New Haven: Yale University Press.

Damgaard, Erik (ed.) (1980). *Folkets veje i dansk politik*, Copenhagen: Schultz.

Duncan, Graeme & Steven Lukes (1963). »The New Democracy«, *Political Studies*, Vol. 11, here »Democracy Restated«, pp. 188–213, in Henry S. Kariel (ed.) (1970), *Frontiers of Democracy*, New York: Random House.

Elklit, Jørgen & Ole Tonsgaard (eds.) (1989). *To folketingsvalg. Vælgerholdninger og vælgeradfærd i 1987 og 1988*, Aarhus: Forlaget Politica.

Højlund, Niels (1993). *Folkeafstemninger En trussel mod demokratiet!*, Copenhagen: Gyldendal.

Holden, Barry (1974). *The Nature of Democracy*, London: Nelson.

Inglehart, Ronald (1990). *Culture Shift in Advanced Industrial Society*, Princeton: Princeton University Press.

Kariel, Henry S. (ed.) (1970). *Frontiers of Democracy*, New York: Random House.

Martinussen, Willy (1973). *Fjerndemokratiet. Sosial ulikhed, politiske ressurser og politisk mobilisering i Norge*, Oslo: Gyldendal Norsk Forlag.

Milbrath, Lester W. & M. L. Goel (1977). *Political Participation: How and Why Do People Get Involved in Politics?* (2nd ed.), Chicago: Rand McNally.

Petersen, Niels Helveg (ed.) (1992). *På sporet af den nye grundlov*, Copenhagen: Gyldendal.

Petersen, Nikolaj (1999). »The Danish Referendum on the Treaty of Amsterdam«, pp. 101-122, in *Danish Foreign Policy Yearbook,* Copenhagen: DUPI.

Ross, Alf (1953). »Memorandum om folkeafstemning, væsentlig på grundlag af to svenske betænkninger«, pp. 157–187, in *Betænkning afgivet af Forfatningskommissionen af 1946*, Copenhagen: Schultz.

Schumpeter, Joseph A. (1976). *Capitalism, Socialism and Democracy*, London: George Allen & Unwin (5th ed., orig. publ. 1942).

Siune, Karen, Palle Svensson & Ole Tonsgaard (1992). *Det blev et nej*, Aarhus: Forlaget Politica.

Siune, Karen & Palle Svensson (1993). »The Danes and the Maastricht Treaty: The Danish EC Referendum of June 1992«, *Electoral Studies*, vol. 12, No. 2, pp. 99–111.

Siune, Karen, Palle Svensson & Ole Tonsgaard (1994). *Fra et nej til et ja*, Aarhus: Forlaget Politica.

Svensson, Palle (1993). »The Development of Danish Polyarchy – Or How Liberalization also Preceded Inclusiveness in Denmark«, pp. 169–189, in Tom Bryder (ed.), *Party Systems, Party Behaviour and Democracy. Scripta in honorem professoris Gunnar Sjöblom sexagesimum annum complentis*, Copenhagen: Copenhagen Political Studies Press.

Svensson, Palle (1996). »Denmark. The referendum as minority protection«, pp. 33-51, in Michael Gallagher and Pier Vincenzo Uleri (eds.), *The Referendum Experience in Europe*, London: Macmillan.

Sørensen, Max (1969). *Statsforfatningsret*, Copenhagen: Juristforbundets Forlag.

Togeby, Lise (1989). *Ens og forskellig. Græsrodsdeltagelse i Norden*, Aarhus: Forlaget Politica.

Zahle, Henrik (1996). *Regering, forvaltning og dom,* Copenhagen: Christian Ejlers Forlag.

The European Participation Crisis: The Problem of Democracy

Curt Sørensen

Abstract

The chapter examines how different social classes reacted to the »entry of masses into politics«-crisis (or »participation«-crisis) in Europe. In explaining the reactions of social classes to this crisis, the chapter also pays attention to different patterns of cleavages, sequences and alliances which again determined different »trajectories« in different regions of Europe. The general conclusion is that democracy, where it was established, succeeded as a result of the weakening of the agrarian upper classes, the protracted struggle of a strong labour movement for universal suffrage and civil rights, the development, in some parts of Europe, of alliances favourable to democracy and, last but not least, because the very content of the concept »democracy« was changed, making it more acceptable to ruling elites and dominant classes.

Economic Development and Political Change

During the last decade, research and debates on political development and regime transformations have been strongly influenced by an optimistic – and simplistic – view of the relationship between economic development and democracy: According to this view, capitalist economic development automatically produces both material affluence and democracy. This conception is evidently inherent in the »shock therapy« philosophy and strategy.[1] If we can just unleash capitalist economic development, affluence and democracy will automatically follow. Austerity programmes and suffering in the present will be rewarded by a happy life in the future.[2] In more sophisticated form, scholars within this optimistic tradition postulate capitalist development as a necessary, but not sufficient, condition of democracy.[3]

We must remember, however, that capitalist economic development has not always led to democracy. In Germany and Japan and in many Latin American countries, for example, capitalist economic development was associated with authoritarian political structures and politics. Capitalist economies have supported authoritarian regimes for long periods and had World War II had a different outcome, we might today find examples of fascist dictatorships with well-functioning capitalist economies.

Capitalist economic development did not always produce democracy. But even where it did, the process was much more complicated than often assumed. As emphasized by Rueschemeyer *et al.*, democracy was always a product of long periods of social and political struggle. They further asserted that social classes played a special role in the processes of development of democracy. Democracy never came as an automatic consequence of capitalist development as such but developed as a product of class struggles unleashed by capitalist economic development.[4]

There is also the problem of time span. The predominant transition theory approach tends to downplay or even neglect the importance of historical conditions that predate the shorter timespan of the immediate »crisis and reequilibration.«[5] The absence of a longer time horizon in this approach implies a failure to adequately theorize the implications of different historical preconditions and the legacy of the past in contemporary decision-making. Furthermore, this approach tends to emphazise the role of key actors in the transition and consolidation processes, abstracting from the historical-structural conditions within which they operate. A further consequence of this emphasis on elites is the underestimation of the importance of popular social movements and social classes.[6]

The abstraction from historical preconditions, the structural limitations and the underlying dynamics of social forces and classes may also help explain why some early contributors to the transition literature were overly optimistic about the possibility of establishing and consolidating democratic regimes. Some scholars argued that a »window of opportunity« had opened, allowing us to create or »craft« democracy anywhere, regardless of circumstances. In a similar vein, some authors even argued that democracy produces its own »preconditions.«[7]

Following Rueschemeyer *et al.*, I shall argue that the relationship between economic development and political development and regime formation is far more complex than assumed by shock theraphy theorists, as well as by the transition approach theorists. Economic development profoundly impinges on social structures and processes, and it is changes in these structures and processes which are decisive for political development and the formation of different types of political regimes.[8]

Economic development never takes place in a pure form. It is never »economic development« as such. Rather it is always specific, conditioned and influenced by prevailing historical-cultural circumstances. This means, first, that economic, social and political processes are deeply interconnected and, second, that these combined and complex processes of development have been very different in different regions of Europe.

Why did the trajectories and the outcomes differ so greatly? Can we achieve a better understanding of these processes? Several sets of interconnected circumstances and processes are important in answering this question: the different general character of these societies, their different political systems, the character of the »crisis of participation«, the nature and strategy of their labour movements, reactions of ruling elites and vested interests, reactions of other social classes and entrenched political subcultures to increased mass participation and the specific configuration of cleavages and alliances.[9]

In what follows, I shall concentrate on the question of the role of social classes in the development of democracy, particularly on the more specific question of the reactions of different social classes to the crisis of participation, trying to map out various trajectories.

Following Rueschemeyer *et al.*, I define democracy as a political system characterized by »regular, free and fair elections of representatives with universal and equal suffrage, ...responsibility of the state apparatus to the elected parliament ... [and] the freedoms of expression and association as well as the protection of individual rights.«[10] Hence, development of democracy is that process which led to the establishment of political systems characterized in this way. In my conclusion I return to the question of definition, and how it entered the political process. Concepts are not politically innocent.

The Participation Crisis

A »developmental crisis« can be understood as a »serious threat« to an existing political system, as an important institutional change and as a basic problem which must be solved.[11] A »participation crisis« is such a developmental crisis. The coming of the era of mass politics in Europe produced an »entry of masses into politics« or »participation« crisis.[12] In some countries the crisis of participation was solved – at least apparently and for the moment – quickly and efficiently. The mobilization of masses and their subsequent entry into politics were channeled through democratic mass parties, and a democratic popular culture developed. In other countries, the crisis of participation remained protracted and deep.[13]

Social mobilization can be seen as a development from an original, amorphous, not yet articulated position to a high degree of organization and ideology.[14] A mobilizing social group will increasingly articulate interests and make demands on other groups in society or on the state apparatus. This entire process takes place as a consequence of increasing social and political participation. Participation has an educative function.[15] On the other hand, however, participation does not necessarily lead to the development of a democratic political culture.

We should distinguish between two basic kinds of participation: democratic, genuine on the one hand and non-democratic, pseudo-participation on the other. Crucial in this context is the goal which the social movement in question seeks to achieve, the character of the political culture it develops and the amount of influence it attains. Does a social movement promote and protect democracy, or does it try to prevent or destroy democracy? Does it develop within its organizational network a democratic, popular culture based on humanistic, rationalist values, or does it encourage and cultivate an anti-humanistic and anti-rationalist authoritarian culture? Finally, does the movement ensure and promote a participation which leads to popular influence on the political process, or is the resulting participation mechanism directed completely from above and without any influence for the mass of participants?

The possible trajectories of mass mobilization and participation crystallized in Central Europe around the turn of the century. In his celebrated work on politics and culture in fin-de-Siecle Vienna, Carl E. Schorske identifies several main »solutions« to the problem of mass participation in politics.[16] Generalizing Schorske's observations, we can distinguish between four main responses to the crisis of participation: traditional liberalism Christian social movements, nationalist movements, and social democratic labour movements.

The traditional continental European liberalist response to the crisis of participation was non-mobilization, i.e., the attempt to exclude the masses from political life and reserve politics for an educated elite. In the new era of mass politics, however, this traditional solution proved inadequate. It was confronted with and defeated by the three variants of the new mass politics, which constituted three different types of social mobilization and participation.

The kind of mobilization and participation promoted at the turn of the century by Karl Lueger's populist, authoritarian, and anti-semitic Christian Social movement in Vienna was un-democratic. It was a pseudo-participation. So was Georg von Schönerer's ultra-nationalist movement and subsequent fascist mobilization and participation. The social democratic mass mobilization and participation movements, on the other hand, were democratic and genuine.

Finally, communist mobilization and participation, constitute a further category of mass mobilization, not captured, of course, by Schorske's observations. Communist movements tried to establish a mass base, and their ideology lay within the rationalist tradition, but they differed from social democratic movements by their differing goals and type of organization. The early adoption of the goal, strategy and party model of the Russian Bolsheviks strongly determined the development of the policy and structure of the communist parties in the West.[17]

Political participation and mobilization in Hitler's Germany or Stalin's Russia are examples of un-democratic, pseudo-participation and mobilization.[18] In general, political participation and mobilization in democracies, while genuine have usually been very restricted. Mobilization and political participation of workers in the Scandinavian and in Central European labour movements were genuine and democratic, whereas fascist or Stalinist mobilizations were not. Labour mobilization was also broad, covering whole areas of life, whereas mobilization and participation in modern »polyarchies« are restricted, mainly to electoral participation.

The key issue centers around democratic mass participation. Is mass mobilization and participation on a rational and humanistic basis possible? The most serious and comprehensive attempt to accomplish this kind of mass mobilization in European history was the social democratic labour movement. However, this movement lost to fascism, which represented quite another type of mass mobilization: anti-rationalist, anti-humanistic.

Mass mobilization and participation can therefore take different directions. Instead of democratic participation and democratic popular culture, ultra-nationalist and fascist forms of participation and political culture may develop. As the communist type indicates, un-democratic mobilization can even develop on a rational ideological base.[19] Mass mobilization is risky seen from a democratic point of view. At the same time, however, mass mobilization and participation is also indispensable in any genuine process of democratization. »Democratization« without both mass participation and the development of popular democratic culture results not in democracy, but in a system of »competitive elitism«.[20]

The Force of Social Classes

Under what circumstances does the one or the other kind of participation develop? A preliminary answer could be that the type of mass participation which evolves in a European society in the period studied here, reflected the nature of the existing social order and political system, the character and the strategy of the labour movement, the reaction of vested interests and other threatened classes and political subcultures, and the underlying pattern of cleavages and alliances. The existing social order and political system can be seen as a system of structural conditions which restrict and enable social action. Previous and present cleavages and alliances form an important part of this always existing universe of structural conditions. The European labour movement, as it unfolded in the age of mass politics, can then be seen as an active new force impinging on the traditional European social and political order provoking different reactions from various groups of elites and social classes.

The main beneficiary of the European extension of »citizen rights« and the main force in promoting universal suffrage was the working class.[21] Working class action was also important for the character and development of the participation crisis and the subsequent development of different kinds of participation. However, what determined the character and strategy of the labour movement?

Economic and social factors have often been identified as especially important influences on the character of the labour movement. A classic explanation of working class radicalization has pointed to the impact of the timing, character and pace of industrialization. In 1922, for example, the Norwegian historian Edvard Bull published a famous paper on the differences in radicalization of the three Scandinavian labour movements.[22] Bull emphasized differences in the timing and speed of industrialization and in the size of industrial units in the three countries. The Bull thesis was later adopted by the labour relations researcher Walter Galenson and by political sociologist S.M. Lipset.[23] For many years the Bull-Galenson-Lipset thesis about a causal relationship between late and rapid industrialization, the creation of uprooted social groups and the formation of big industrial units on the one hand, and political radicalization on the other, was the conventional wisdom within the sociology of labour movements and industrial relations.

Recent research, however, has contested the Bull-Galenson-Lipset thesis. According to Lafferty, for example, political structures were more important in explaining the differences in ideology and politics among the Scandinavian labour movements.[24] The importance of the surrounding political system for the character of the labour movement has also been advanced as a general thesis by Dick Geary and S.M. Lipset.[25] In the present context, I find this thesis useful because it directs attention to the question of relations between labour movement and the surrounding political system, and to the political reactions of other social classes to the rise of organized labour.

The working class and the labour movement acted and reacted in different ways depending on the character of the political system and on the different actions and reactions of the other classes in the total social actor system. Yet the working class and the labour movement also influenced the surrounding political system and the other social classes, provoking different responses.

How did vested interests react when confronted with the challenge of mobilization and increasing participation of the subaltern classes? The way ruling classes and elites handled the problem of mass participation deeply influenced political development in each society.

The reaction to the advancement of the labour movement is illustrative here. In the Scandinavian countries, the traditional ruling elites and economically dominant classes eventually accepted the ascending political elite of the labour movement, establishing a sort of truce and mutual understanding between capital and labour; this truce eventually led to a corporatist system.[26]

In Austria, Italy and Spain, on the other hand, organized labour was kept out of politics, and the labour political elite were denied access to governmental power. The ruling classes and elites were even prepared to dismantle democratic institutions and accept a fascist dictatorship in order to protect their vested interests and crush the labour movement.[27]

The German case lies between these two extremes. Back in old Wilhelmine Germany, the social democratic labour movement had been discriminated against in several ways, and social democratic workers looked upon as outcasts (*Vaterlandslose Gesellen*).[28] This apparently changed with the arrival of Weimar democracy. During the first years of the Weimar Republic and again from 1928-30, the SPD participated in government coalitions at the level of the Reich. For a longer period, the SPD also governed at the state level, and notably its Prussian position was important here.[29] In the final phase of the Weimar Republic, however, the SPD became sidetracked, and a series of intrigues prepared the way for the Nazi take over on January 30, 1933.[30] At the bottom of Weimar society, social democratic workers remained almost as outcaste as they had been in pre-1914 Germany.[31]

This highlights the quite different reaction of the traditional ruling elites and classes to the fascist mass movement and the rising fascist elite. The main question here is that of moral and political support and a willingness to allow Nazi access to governmental power. More than financial support, it was the lack of democratic convictions and values and the general preference of the traditional elites and ruling classes for an authoritarian solution which paved the way for the Nazi take- over.[32] As Eberhard Kolb puts it: »The business world did not create Hitler's government... But by their opposition to parliamentary democracy and preference for an authoritarian system, the bosses had accelerated the break up of the Weimar Republic and played into the hands of a dictatorship.«[33]

Also important in the process of the Nazi ascendency to power was the role played by the agrarian upper class and by the Reichswehr-elite.[34]

Much energy has been spent discussing the question: »Who financed Hitler?«[35] Big industry certainly contributed financially to the Nazi movement[36] but as Turner convincingly shows, they also contributed to the conservative DNVP and to the DVP. The Norwegian political scientist Bernt Hagtvet is probably correct in characterizing the whole issue of financing as a »side issue«.[37]

Reinhard Kühnl suggests that we view the relationship between the traditional ruling classes and elites on the one hand, and the rising Nazi-elite on the other, as a sort of alliance.[38] The Nazi movement was not just an instrument of big capital. It was an independent force that increasingly gained access to the centers of power in Weimar society. Its path to power was mediated by bargains struck with the traditional elites and ruling classes, as was also the case in Italian fascism's rise to power.[39]

As Luebbert points out, however, there was a major difference between West European and East European fascist development.[40] East European societies were traditional societies with weak levels of social mobilization. In these societies, a traditional dictatorship was sufficient to subdue the subaltern classes and protect the vested interests of the traditional ruling classes and elites. There was no need here for any alliance with fascism or the establishment of a fascist dictatorship. On the contrary, in Eastern Europe a relationship of rivalry and contestation developed between the forces of the old order on the one hand, and the new fascist elites and movements on the other. Especially in Hungary and Romania, the struggle between »the old« and »the new« Right became a conspicuous feature of political life in the interwar period. In Romania this contest exploded into armed struggle.[41]

In Central and Southern Europe, however, the labour movements were strong and the social order characterized by high levels of social mobilization and social unrest. In Germany, Austria, Italy and Spain, the ruling classes and elites felt sufficiently threatened to actively and forcibly repress the subaltern classes. Eventually an alliance between the forces of the old order and fascism crystallized, and a fascist dictatorship was established.[42]

The differing reactions of the ruling classes and elites to increasing mass participation of the subaltern classes thus produced different alliances and strategies in the various regions of Europe. Yet it would be a mistake to consider only the reactions of the ruling classes and elites. The reactions of the urban middle class and the peasantry were also important.

The reaction of these classes to the increasing participation of the subaltern classes in politics has often been described and explained in terms of the »middle class panic« thesis: Due to their exposed position between capital and labour, their economic marginality and the threat of »proletarianization« the lower sections of these classes panicked and moved toward extremist positions: extremist nationalism at the end of the nineteenth century and fascism in the twentieth century.[43]

Lipset's theory on »middle class extremism« rests on this broader »panic« thesis. According to Lipset, middle class extremism developed in countries characterized by both large scale capitalism and a strong labour movement. Squeezed between big capital and labour, the middle class often turned to fascism. Lipset spoke here of an »extremism of the middle« clearly distinguishable from traditional right-wing authoritarianism.[44]

Both the broader thesis on the panic of the lower layers of the middle class and Lipset's more specific thesis on position and movement of the German middle class can be criticized.[45] As demonstrated by Hamilton, not only the lower middle class but also, and to an even higher degree, the upper middle class and the upper classes increasingly voted for the NSDAP.[46] The scope of the thesis must be extended. It was not only a great part of the lower middle class, but the entire middle class and the bourgeoisie who panicked and turned to fascism.[47]

Secondly, what was at stake was not primarily material interests, but a clash of values. The Central European middle class as well as the peasantry and the bourgeoisie were frightened and aggressive because they perceived the labour movement as a threat to their basic cultural values and way of life.[48] This point, made by Bernt Hagtvet, is supported by local community studies such as those of William Sheridan Allen and Jeremy Noakes.[49] Like Hagtvet, they stress the strong class polarization within the Weimar society, the ideological-cultural dimension of this basic conflict and the strategic exploitation of this situation by the Nazi movement. Hence

> the most important factor in the victory of Nazism was the active division of the town along class lines...The victory of Nazism can be explained to a large extent by the desire on the part of Thalburg's

The European Participation Crisis

middle class to suppress the lower class and especially its political representative, the Social Democratic party.[50]

In the countryside, as well, the German and Austrian peasantry reacted violently against what they viewed as the threat from the labour movement. Especially in Austria, a country without the large bourgeoisie comparable to the Rhine bourgeoisie or Prussian Junker class, the main dimension of conflict emerged between the socialist labour movement of the towns and industrial areas and the authoritarian, Catholic peasants of the countryside. This class conflict was also mainly an ideological-cultural conflict.[51]

In the towns of Central Europe and almost everywhere in the countryside, an overwhelming alliance rose up against working class parties. Almost everywhere a bloc of parties from the right to the center formed a »citizen alliance« (*Bürgerblock*) or »camp« (*Lager*) to fight the labour movement and to keep it from political influence.[52] In Germany, the Nazi movement ultimately took the lead in these alliances, in many places swallowing the whole electoral basis of the citizen alliances.[53] The bourgeois and petty bourgeois masses were integrated into the Nazi movement:

> With its vicious attacks on the »Marxists«, the NSDAP actively took the lead in the class conflict at the local level, a conflict which was being intensified by the depression. With this tactic the NSDAP won over a large number of the middle class who no longer felt capable of mastering the situation and feared the coming of Bolshevism.[54]

The situation in Austria was in one respect more complicated due to the existence of different variants of fascism.[55] In another respect, the Austrian case was more polarized because the complicating element of two rival labour parties was absent.

We can now draw some provisional conclusions concerning the role of different social classes in the historical process of development of democracy in Europe. Scholars tend to point to the bourgeoisie as the main social agent for democracy. »No bourgeoisie, no democracy«, as Barrington Moore put it.[56] A similar view has been articulated by Seymour Martin Lipset and Robert A. Dahl.[57] This thesis has had a strong resurgence in the prevailing political and ideological climate following the breakdown of the former Soviet Union and the communist regimes in Eastern Europe. In current public debates, the market, bourgeoisie and liberalism have nearly been synonymous with democracy.[58]

Rueschemeyer *et al.,* on the other hand, emphasize the role played by the European working class in the actual historical process of democratization:

> democratization was both resisted and pushed forward by class interest. It was the subordinate classes that fought for democracy. By contrast, the classes that benefitted from the status quo nearly without exception resisted democracy. The bourgeoisie wrested its share of political participation from royal autocracy and aristocratic oligarchy, but it rarely fought for further extensions once its own place was secured... the working class was the most consistently pro-democratic force.[59]

This thesis, that the working class is »the most consistently pro-democratic force« seems to be confirmed by historical facts. In Germany and Austria, the working class was almost the only force pushing for democratization. In the Scandinavian countries, labour movements have been a major force in the development of democracy, albeit not the only one.

The agrarian upper class, especially in Germany, Hungary, Italy, Spain and Sweden and to a certain extent Denmark, was the main social force opposing democratization. But other forces were at work, too. In Norway, Sweden and Germany, the bureaucratic elite, for example, also resisted democracy, while the fatal role played by the Reichswehr elite in German development is well known.

In Germany and Austria, the peasants and the petty bourgeoisie in the towns long resisted democracy and in the late 1920s and the 1930s, they supported fascism. In Denmark and Sweden, however, and to a certain extent Norway, part of the middle class and the peasantry turned instead to democracy, and the Scandinavian countries took the social democratic road. The bourgeoisie wavered, fighting against the old monarchy for constitutional government and legal rights, but generally resisting an extension of suffrage to the lower classes. In the inter-war period, Europe's bourgeois classes were generally sceptical about democracy. In Central Europe especially, sentiments for an authoritarian »solution« grew strong in the late 1920s.

In the Weimar Republic and the First Austrian Republic, a substantial part of these classes turned to fascism, and it was left to the workers to sustain political democracy. This was reflected in the strength of political parties, too. In Germany, the Liberal Party (Deutsche Demokratische Partei) almost vanished by the end of the Weimar period, and in the Austrian Republic a liberal party was totally absent from the political scene.[60] The social democratic labour movement was the only strong and visible force sustaining democracy and fighting fascism.

We must therefore question the assertion advanced by Barrington Moore, S.M. Lipset and Robert A. Dahl that a strong bourgeoisie and a strong middle class are essential for political democracy. The Moore-Lipset-Dahl thesis must be rejected, or at least modified, and the Rueschemeyer *et al.* thesis seems confirmed. However, it needs some further clarification and modification. First, the working class movement need not be defeated, as were the German and Austrian labour movements in 1933/34, in order for democracy to succeed. Second, Rueschemeyer et al. do not pay sufficient attention to the importance of developing a strong democratic political culture based on popular movements. The development of such movements was essential for the development of democracy in the Scandinavian countries. The development of similar popular cultures within the organizational networks of the Central European labour movements, however, did not ensure democratic political systems in this region of Europe. Here the »environment«, including oppositional traditional elites and ruling classes plus the rising fascist movements, forced political developments in quite another direction. Third, although Rueschemeyer, *et al.* note the importance of alliances, this element should be stressed much more. The alliance established between peasants and workers in the Scandinavian countries during the 1930s constitutes one of the decisive differences between Scandinavian and Central European developments. Finally, workers did not everywhere and always fight for democracy. In Germany, communist workers certainly fought against fascism, but they did not fight for democracy. Working class support for the »Arrow Cross« movement in Hungary in the 1930s and the Peronist movement in Argentina in the 1950s are further examples of deviations from the general rule.

This again underlines the importance of the development of democratic traditions and of popular democratic culture. As noted by S.M. Lipset, organization and political culture are crucial. According to Lipset, the »raw« working class is not especially democratic; on the contrary, unmobilized and unorganized workers often display what he called »working class authoritarianism.«[61] But on the other hand, Lipset recognized that in Europe, the organized labour movement, not liberalism, has been the main force pushing for democracy.[62] This emphasis on organization and ideology, of course, has been a consistent part of the socialist tradition.[63]

The Importance of Cleavages, Sequences and Alliances

But the very fact that some social classes promoted democracy and other classes resisted it, is not in itself sufficient to explain the stability or instability of social orders, the different trajectories of European societies and the very different outcomes. We must explore the deeper configurations of socioeconomic, political and ideological cleavages and the resulting patterns of alliances and confrontations.

This has been recognized by several scholars within this field. In his classic explanation of the German *Sonderweg*, Lipset points to the importance of the character of earlier cleavages and the way they were handled as profoundly affecting subsequent development.[64] Especially important here is the sequence of crises and the phenomenon of crises accumulation:

> Were these issues dealt with one by one, with each more or less solved before the next arose; or did the problems accumulate, so that traditional sources of cleavage mixed with newer ones? Resolving tensions one at a time contributes to a stable political system; carrying over issues from one historical period to another makes for a political atmosphere characterized by bitterness and frustration rather than tolerance and compromise. Men and parties come to differ with each other, not simply on ways of settling current problems, but on fundamental and opposed outlooks.[65]

In his recent work on social classes and the origins of different political regimes in interwar Europe, Gregory M. Luebbert further develops the Lipset-Rokkan thesis on the importance of earlier cleavages and the phenomenon of crisis accumulation.[66] Luebbert points to the existence before 1914 of two different types of regimes in Europe: countries with liberal hegemony (e.g., Britain, France and Switzerland) and countries without liberal hegemony (e.g., Germany, Italy, Spain, Sweden, Norway and Denmark). In the liberal hegemony systems, liberalism could afford to make concessions to the working-class movements, which in turn became moderate. This resulted in the development of a kind of »alliance« or »compromise«, »Lib-Labism«, as Luebbert calls it.[67]

In countries where liberalism was weak, the attitude towards workers' movements and demands was hard and unsympathetic. Consequently, the labour movements in these countries developed in sharp opposition to liberalism and to the existing social order in general. In a manner reminiscent of Lafferty's explanation of the differences among the three Scandinavian labour movements and Geary's general account of the different trajectories of European labour, Luebbert thus explains the different character and development of the European labour movements by invoking the different character of the surrounding political systems, emphasizing especially the importance of the strength and character of liberalism in the respective countries.[68]

Yet why was liberalism strong in some countries and weak in others?

Adhering to the Lipset-Rokkan thesis, Luebbert explains the weakness of liberalism in Germany, Italy, Spain, Sweden and Norway by pointing to divisions within the middle class and liberalism, divisions rooted in cleavages of the pre-industrial period. Conversely, where the old cleavages and problems of the pre-industrial period were overcome before the emergence of new cleavages caused by industrialization and the rise of new social classes, liberalism remained united and therefore strong. This was the case in Britain, for example.[69]

After World War I, the Lib-Lab systems collapsed as class struggles intensified. Due to the successful integration of the working class in the pre-1914 Lib-Lab systems, however, these countries remained stabledespite the aggravated social and economic circumstances and the increasing conflicts of the interwar period.[70]

In countries where liberalism was weak before 1914 and where working class opposition was strong, attempts after the war to form coalitions based on the Lib-Lab model were short-lived and unsuccessful. Two different »solutions« occurred: either the peasants aligned themselves with the urban middle class against the workers, or they aligned themselves with the urban workers against the urban middle class and the bourgeoisie. The first type of coalition led to fascism and authoritarian corporatism, as in Germany and Italy. The second type of coalition led to social democratic hegemony and a democratic variant of corporatism. This was the Scandinavian solution.[71]

Luebbert convincingly demonstrates the effects of cleavages and alliances, but his analysis contains several debatable points. First, Luebbert is not sufficiently clear about the particular social class base of liberalism. Did the entire middle class support liberalism? What was the role of the bourgeoisie? Luebbert does not seem to distinguish between bourgeoisie and middle class.[72] Second, his classification of countries according to the strength of liberalism is debatable. Is it true, for example, that liberalism in pre-1914 Germany was as weak as he assumes?[73] Third, was strong liberalism always conciliatory toward the labour movement, and weak liberalism always intransigent and hostile toward working class demands? Luebbert's thesis concerning the relationship between liberalism and labour movement must be carefully examined in light of the historical record in each of the countries under study.

Luebbert's emphasis on liberalism as a political force and the middle class as its social basis leads him to ignore or minimize the role of conservative forces and the agrarian aristocracy in the different countries. He totally denies, for example, the role of the agrarian upper class as an anti-democratic force in Germany's political development. He argues that the economic power of the Weimar Junker class did not translate into political power.[74] Barrington

Moore, Hans-Ulrich Wehler, Ralf Dahrendorf, Alexander Gerschenkron and others take a more sophisticated approach, however.[75] They do not claim that the members of the agrarian upper class were politically active all the time, constantly seeking to transform their economic power into political power. Rather, the predominant position of the agrarian upper class from early on time in German history produced the specific social and political order of Wilhelmine Germany, an order which, despite the interruption of war and revolution, determined the basic character of the subsequent Weimar Republic.[76] Furthermore, actors with an origin in the Junker class actually played an important role in the decisive, final process of intrigues and struggles which led to the collapse of the Weimar Republic.[77]

Finally, Luebbert's analysis suffers from a generalized super-structuralism.[78] He seems to deny completely the importance of political action: »One of the cardinal lessons of the story I have told is that leadership and meaningful choice played no role in the outcome.«[79]

Luebbert thus pays little attention to the importance of political action and cultural struggle. However, even if historical and structural circumstances conditioned different trajectories in Northern and Central Europe, the outcome was never preordained. Political struggle in which some lost and some won determined the outcome. Different historical prerequisites and structural circumstances explain a great deal. But the actions of the actors involved were crucial, too. Neither social democratic rule in Northern Europe nor fascist dictatorship in Central Europe was predestined.

Different Trajectories

What kind of social order prevailed in Europe during the fateful period from the 1860s to the end of World War II?

This period saw the formation of a number of important nation-states, the entry of the masses into politics, the development of the European labour movement and of socialist and internationalist ideas, but also the rise of extreme nationalism and later fascism. It was the period of two world wars and repeated economic and political crises, a period of the birth as well as the breakdown of democracies.

In his provocative work, *The Persistence of the Old Regime*, Arno Mayer has questioned a number of dominant views on the character of this period and its social order.[80] Mayer challenges the prevailing view that the main feature of this period was capitalist development and modernization. On the contrary, he claims, the period was first and foremost characterized by the persistence of the old order. According to Mayer, this predominance of the old order is the main cause of the turbulent, explosive character of the whole period. In the end, the persistence of the old order produced what he calls »the European 30 years war« from 1914 to 1945. The savage struggle of traditional elites and ruling classes to preserve by any means necessary the old order and their privileged positions within this same order propelled European societies into first World War I, then fascism and subsequently World War II:

> the Great War of 1914, or the first and protogenic phase of this general crisis, was an outgrowth of the latter-day remobilization of the European anciens régimes. Though losing ground to the forces of industrial capitalism, the forces of the old order were still sufficiently willful and powerful to resist and slow down the course of history, if necessary by recourse to violence. The Great War was an expression of the decline and fall of the old order fighting to prolong its life rather than of the explosive rise of industrial capitalism bent on its primacy...after 1918-19 the forces of perseverance recovered sufficiently to aggravate Europe's general crisis, sponsor fascism, and contribute to the resumption of total war in 1939.[81]

Mayer has been accused of failing to appreciate the force of capitalist development in this period and the endemic contradictions and conflicts in capitalism. He thus acquits capitalism of any responsibility »for the horrors of the first half of the century.«[82] This criticism, advanced by Callinicos, resembles the critique of Blackburn and Eley against Hans-Ulrich Wehler, Dahrendorf and others on the character of Imperial Germany.[83] What is at stake here, however, is not the moral question of guilt or innocence. The question raised by Arno Mayer is the question of the main character of the European social order in the whole period from about 1860 to 1945. It is a question of recognizing the very complexity of European societies in this period and of different trajectories in different regions of Europe.

The key point is to recognize the penetration of industrial capitalism into the old order, the struggle between old and new, and the ensuing complicated patterns of cleavages and conflicts. Even Callinicos recognizes the complex and »mixed« character of societies in this period of European history due to the survival of elements and relations from the old agrarian order. He also emphasizes a decisive difference here between Britain and East and Central Europe:

> Explaining the eruption of military and social conflict after 1900 in terms of contradictions internal to the capitalist mode of production does not imply that the survivals of the old order on which Mayer concentrates can be ignored... Britain by the late nineteenth century did not offer the sharp contrast between old and new provided by the comparatively sudden onset of industrial capitalism in genuinely ancien régime orders such as Prussia, Russia and Austria-Hungary.[84]

The Central European societies, especially Germany and Austria, were to an exceptional degree »mixed« societies characterized by the clash between and the violent penetration of two competing social orders.[85] The sudden intrusion of industrial capitalism into the old order, intermingling old and new, produced an accumulation of many different cleavages. Reinforcing each other, they created explosive developments.

It is possible, then, to discern several trajectories in European political development: Central European societies, in the period from 1860 to 1945, due to their explosive mixture of new and old, had an unusually troublesome and conflict ridden political development. These societies saw the development of strong, radicalized labour movements. Not only did the traditional ruling elites and big capital resent the labour movement, so did the middle classes. Under the impact of successive economic and political crises, large sections of the middle classes eventually turned to fascism. The peasants, too, reacted violently against what they perceived to be a deadly threat to their entrenched subculture and traditional way of life. Furthermore, an alliance between, on the one hand, the traditional ruling elites and classes on the one hand and the rising fascist elite, on the other, crystallized, paving the way for a fascist take-over.

The trajectory of Scandinavian development was closer to the British path. The Scandinavian countries were in the fortunate situation that most of the old cleavages had been overcome before the development of new cleavages rooted in industrial capitalism. Thus, the Scandinavian social order was less explosive than the Central European social order. In the Scandinavian countries, both liberalism and the labour movement became moderate and conciliatory. Moreover, the key alliance between workers and peasants succeeded laying the foundation for the peaceful ascent of the labour movement to political power, the rescue of democracy in the turmoil of the 1930s and the construction of the Scandinavian welfare state model.

In Eastern and Central-Eastern Europe, the general development of society lagged behind Central European development (except in Bohemia). East European societies were more traditional and less mixed than the Central European societies. The subaltern classes were completely subjugated and displayed a very low degree of mobilization and participation. In times of crisis, therefore, a traditional dictatorship was content to repress them and ensure the privileged position of the ruling classes and elites. These countries saw no need for any alliance between fascism and the forces of the old order. Consequently, a situation of contest and struggle developed between »the Old« and »the New Right«.

The Russian trajectory, finally, was in certain respects similar to the East European, but due to the country's status as an »underdeveloped Great Power« and the attempt from the 1890's onwards to carry out a rapid industrialization initiated from above, the Russian trajectory resembled the German.[86] The combination of accumulated internal cleavages and pressures along with defeat in war produced the revolutions of 1905 and of February and October 1917. After the Bolshevik takeover, the new elite resumed Sergei Witte's old policy of rapid modernization directed from above, albeit on an enlarged scale. After Stalin's victory at the end of the 1920s, industrialization progressed at rapid speed, displaying what Alec Nove has called »excessive excesses.«[87] In this process of rapid and forced modernization, the ideology, created by Stalin and Bukharin in the 1920s, of »socialism in one country«, came to function as the Russian equivalent of »the Protestant Ethic« in the West.[88]

Summary and Conclusions

Class analysis seems to be a valuable, even indispensable, tool in long-term analyses of political development and regime formation, including the development of democracy. It is also possible to discern some main trajectories in European political development, trajectories which to a great extent have been determined by various patterns of class conflicts and alliances, underlying patterns of cleavage and in the developmental sequences.

However, class analysis must be applied cautiously and carefully. The relationships among social classes, political ideas and organizations are highly complex. S. M. Lipset's famous three- part division of social classes, political ideas and forces is rudimentary, catching only some of the main tendencies and trends.[89] The relations are complex because class interests are not directly and automatically translated into political ideas and organizations and because political ideas and organizations have been determined not only by class interests but by other factors as well. On the other hand, it would be impossible to explain long-term political development in Europe, the formation of different types of regimes, the crystallization of the maintrajectories, the strengths and weaknesses of major political movements and ideas etc., without heavy reliance on a theory of social classes. Class theory does not explain everything, but it explains a great deal.[90]

Social classes do not emerge instantly and automatically from an objective base. Class formation is a long, complicated process.[91] Furthermore, social classes must not be conceptualized as pure economic categories. Not only economic, but also political and ideological factors play a part in processes of class formation. Class interests are determined not only by economic position, but by politics and ideology as well. Class interests include values and norms as well as material demands. Class domination also involves political and ideological relations as well as purely economic relations.[92]

The previous argument also stresses the importance not only of class conflicts but also of class alliances. Patterns of class conflicts and class alliances are again influenced by previous cleavages and sequences in the development of such cleavages, cleavages often of a non-economic nature.

Finally, class analysis cannot stand alone: it must be completed by an analysis of elites, that is elaborated theoretically and investigated empirically.[93]

Economic development influences existing relations of interests and power. This is why the concept of »social class« is so crucial for our understanding of political development and regime formations. However, »social class« should be conceived not in the restricted Weberian sense as mere economic groups with similar chances in a market situation, but in the Marxian sense as categories and groups placed in different positions within the hierarchies of power, hierarchies and positions which are constantly crystallizing within the sphere of production.[94]

In European political development, the reaction of different social classes was a crucial factor during the emergence and unfolding of mass politics. As ruling classes and governing elites came to see the mobilization and increasing participation of subaltern classes as a threat to their positions and vested interests, they reacted strongly. In such situations came the risk of a counter-democratic backlash. Depending on the general character of the social order, a breakdown of democracy and the establishment of a dictatorship could take place. The reaction of the town middle classes and the peasants also influenced events. In cases where they reacted violently against threats to their culture and traditional way of life, the road to a fascist dictatorship was cleared.

European economic, social and political development in general and democracy development in particular has certainly not been a smooth, evolutionary process. On the contrary, it was a turbulent process with acute clashes of interests and struggles for power and influence. The conventional picture given by scholars as T.H. Marshall and Reinhard Bendix, as well as the prevailing conception articulated in recent debates is therefore quite misleading.[95]

We may also conclude that the thesis promoted by numerous scholars, e.g., Barrington Moore, Robert A. Dahl and S.M. Lipset, that the bourgeoisie or the middle class[96] has been the strongest force for democracy is not historically correct. In actual European development it was the organized working class – or more precisely: the social democratic labour movement – which was the main social and political force in the development of democracy.[97]

This observation and conclusion is also a main point in Rueschemeyer, Stephens and Stephens' seminal work on the relationship between social classes and democratic development,[98] although they fail to pay sufficient attention to the importance of the development of a popular democratic culture. The development of democratic popular participation and a democratic popular culture – the behavioural and normative dimensions of democracy – was rooted in the activism within the organizational network of European labour.[99] It was motivated and encouraged by a great vision.

In its genesis and development in the West, socialism was a vision nurtured within the labour movement and among groups of intellectuals. The vision embraced a continued extension of political democracy, universal suffrage, the involvment of the masses in politics, the breakdown of barriers between rulers and the ruled, the extension of democracy into the realm of economic life, the end of exploitation and oppression, democratic control and planning and the free and versatile realization of human potential.[100]

There is also the question of alliances. Rueschemeyer et al. take note of the importance of alliances but fail to elaborate this whole question in a more systematic way. This is the main task of Gregory Luebbert in his important study on the relationship between alliances and types of political regimes in interwar Europe.[101] The problem with Luebbert, however, as mentioned, is his super-structuralism. Moreover, Luebbert seems to deny the role of the agrarian upper class as a conservative, in some countries even reactionary, force in European democracy development.

Most important, however: Rueschemeyer et al. as well as Luebbert, Lipset and Moore completely fail to reflect on the very concept of democracy and how different conceptions of democracy have entered the political process itself. Democracy was originally about popular participation and influence. Anthony Arblaster very acutely captures the essential meaning of democracy as it has been understood in most of historic time when he writes:

> It is only in the twentieth century that theorists have attempted to

produce a version of democracy in which popular participation is threatened with suspicion, if not regarded as positively undesirable. This represents a fundamental departure from the traditional understanding of what democracy is, or was. Whether it was approved or not – and usually it was not – it was understood on all sides that democracy meant, to a lesser or greater degree, popular power, popular sovereignty, popular participation.[102]

It was precisely because democracy threatened or seemed to threaten vested interests and dominant power structures that it was conceived as a *problem*. Ruling classes and elites feared, and for a long time resisted, democracy because democracy entailed a dangerous increase in the power and influence of subaltern classes and groups. And if this no longer seems to be the case, it is perhaps due to the fact that the theory and practice of democracy has been emptied of its subversive content. In real European history, democracy was seen as a challenge and a problem. The entry of masses into politics launched a deep-going crisis in the European social order.

The crisis provoked by the entry of the masses into politics was in some parts of Europe solved by the development of democratic mass participation and popular democratic culture, both of which were essential and indispensable for the development of stable democracies. At the same time, however, the concept as well as the practice of democracy underwent a profound transformation.

Equally crucial for the development and acceptance of democracy was the restriction of democracy to elite competition and the concomitant transformation of the leaders of the labour movement from popular tribunes to professional politicians.[103] Joseph Schumpeter's famous re-definition of democracy as elite-competition has proven correct, not as a statement on the »real meaning of democracy« or as an assertion of what democracy should be, but as a prediction of what »democracy« would become as it developed in the real world of European politics.[104] In the Scandinavian countries, for example, the former labour leaders were transformed into professional political elites who were coopted, so to say, into the prevailing power system of ruling elites.

At the bottom of European societies, the labour movement continued to undergo a process of de-radicalization. Several events and processes contributed to this process: the collapse of international labour solidarity in 1914, the derailment of the Russian Revolution and the consolidation of Stalinism in Russia and subsequently in Eastern Europe, the historical defeat, in the interwar period, of European labour to fascism and the development, after the end of World War II, of the Cold War. Important, too, was the long period of economic progress, consumer expansion and social welfare construction from ca. 1950-1973, the period often called »the Golden Age«.[105]

The combined effect of all these developments produced a new kind of democracy which was acceptable for ruling elites and classes, all those social and political forces who previously had so savagely and so persistently resisted any attempts to develop democracy in its original and genuine sense.

Yet there has also been another solution to the crisis of participation. It is evident from the European experience that the particular form and ideology of the mass mobilization and mass participation of the European labour movement was not the only possible one. As demonstrated by fascism and extreme nationalism, mobilization and participation could and can take quite different directions and assume different forms and goals.

Fascist mass mobilization and mass movements in certain regions of Europe produced new fascist elites who in Italy, Germany and Austria succeeded in coming to power through a kind of mutual understanding or tacit alliance with the traditional ruling elites and classes. This solution to the crisis of participation became possible because dominant social and political forces in these countries, for one reason or another, ceased to conceive fascism as a threat to their vested interests, instead viewing it as a possible ally. The choice between the pluralist or fascist solution to the crisis of participation was hardly voluntary, however. It was conditoned by deeper historical-structural conditions and processes.

In general, the relationship between the old European order and rising industrial capitalism which gradually penetrated this order played a crucial role in European political development. Seen in the context of the development of democracy, the most »dangerous« types of societies and periods were those which were extraordinarily »mixed« due to the relatively sudden, rapid and massive penetration of rising industrial capitalism into the existing old order. This produced a very complex interplay of relations between traditional elites and ruling classes, peasants and the old petty bourgeoisie on the one hand and industrial capitalists, workers and the new middle class on the other. It was also an interplay between the political ideologies and movements of conservatism, fascism, liberalism, socialism and democracy. In these cases, the accumulation of mutually reinforcing cleavages and conflicts produced a highly turbulent path of political development.

If it is true that the period from about 1860 to 1945 can be seen as a sort of transition period during which industrial capitalism on the European continent penetrated the previous existing social order, then capitalism is still young and not at all »spät« or »post.« Capitalism in Central Europe was then only fully established as late as 1945. What we are now witnessing is capitalism triumphantly spreading to the last of the areas of the world which were still outside its orbit. Whether this new world will be peaceful and democratic, whether it will be without serious problems and deep cleavages - the proclaimed end of history remains to be seen.[106]

It also remains to be seen whether the challenge which once emanated from the entry of the masses into politics, from democratic mass politics and the European labour movement in particular – all that which used to be called »socialism« – can ever be revived. Perhaps in a distant future, when capitalism has run its course and all its possibilities have been exhausted, the time will come for democracy as it was always understood before its concept and reality was so profoundly transformed. In the meantime, we may conclude that the problem of democracy was »solved« either by a process of devaluation and restriction or, for certain periods and in certain countries, by the fascist solution. As to the crisis of participation, it was never solved.[107]

Notes

1. See Jeffrey Sachs, »What is to be Done?«, *The Economist*, 13 January 1990, and Sachs, *Poland's Jump to the Market Economy*, Cambridge Mass., 1993. For a critique see Alice Amsden, Jacek Kochanowicz & Lance Taylor, *The Market Meets its Match*, Princeton, 1994; Laszlo Andor & Martin Summers, *Market Failure. Eastern Europe's 'Economic Miracle'*, London: Pluto Press, 1998, and Peter Gowan, »Neo-LiberalTheory and Practice for Eastern Europe«, *New Left Review*, No. 213, 1995, p.p. 3-60. For the general problematic see also, Michel Chossudowsky, *The Globalization of Poverty. Impacts of IMF and World Bank Reforms*, London & New York: Zed Books, 1998; William Greider: *One World, Ready Or Not*, London: Penguin, 1997, and Hans-Peter Martin & Harald Schumann, *Die Globalisierungsfalle. Der Angriff auf Demokratie und Wohlstand*, Hamburg: Rowohlt Verlag, 1996.

2. For a revealing survey of poverty, malnutrition and health crisis produced by the shock therapy style of economic policy in Eastern Europe and the former Soviet Union see *UNICEF, Economies in Transition Studies, Regional and Monitoring Report, 1994. Crisis in Mortality, Health and Nutrition*, Florence, 1994. According to UNICEF »excess mortality« in Russia, Ukraine, Bulgaria, Hungay and Poland between 1989 and 1993 was 800,000.

   This projection of asserted positive effects of present policy into an indeterminate distant future very much resembles the Stalinist logic of sacrificing the present to »History«. Often the very same people who yesterday lauded the blessings of »socialist development of productive forces« today applaud the unrestricted »development of market forces« as the universal road to affluence and democracy.

3. Cf., for example, S.M. Lipset, »Some social requisites of democracy: economic development and political legitimacy,« *American Political Science Review*, Vol.

53, 1959; Philips Cutwright & James Wiley, »Modernization and politicalrepresentation: 1927-1966,« *Studies in Comparative International Development*, 1969, and Janos Kornai, *The Road to a Free Economy*, New York & London, 1990.
4. Dietrich Rueschemeyer, Evelyne H. Stephens & John D. Stephens, *Capitalist Development and Democracy*, Chicago: University of Chicago Press, 1992, p. 7.
5. Cf. Guillermo O'Donnell & Philipe C. Schmitter, *Tentative Conclusions about Uncertain Democracies*, Baltimore & London, 1991; Guillermo O'Donnell, Philippe C. Schmitter & Laurence Whitehead, *Transitions from Authoritharian Rule. Southern Europe*, Baltimore & London, 1986; Philippe C. Schmitter, *The Consolidation of Democracy and the Choice of Institutions*, paper, Stanford University, 1991, and *The Consolidation of Political Democracies: Processes, Rhythms, Sequences and Types*, manus., Stanford University, 1991; John Herz (ed.), *From Dictatorship to Democracy: Coping with the Legacies of Authoritharianism and Totalitarianism*, London,1989.
6. See also the penetrating analysis and criticism of this approach in Lene Bøgh Sørensen, *Political Development and Regime Transformations: The Hungarian Case*, Ph.D. dissertation, Aarhus: Institute of Political Science, University of Aarhus, 1995.
7. See for example Terry Karl, »Dilemmas of Democratization in Latin America,« *Comparative Politics*, October 1990, and Guiseppe di Palma, *To Craft Democracies, An Essay on Democratic Transitions*, Berkeley: University of California Press, 1990, and for a criticism Lene Bøgh Sørensen, *op.cit.*, pp. 142ff.
8. On the concept of »political regime« and a typology see Juan Linz, »Totalitarian and Authoritarian Regimes,« in Fred Greenstein & Nelson Polsby (eds.), *Macropolitical Theory, A Handbook of Political Science*, Vol. 3, 1975.
9. On the concepts of »participation crisis« (Grew) and »entry into politics crisis (Lipset),Raymond Grew (ed.), *Crises of Political Development in Europe and the United States*, Princeton: Princeton University Press, 1978, p. 7ff. and p. 21ff., and S.M. Lipset, *Political Man*, London: 1963, p. 79ff. On the concept of «cleavage» see S.M. Lipset & Stein Rokkan, «Cleavage Structures, Party Systems and Voter Alignments: An Introduction,» pp. 1-64, in S.M. Lipset & Stein Rokkan (eds.), *Party Systems and Voter Alignments: Cross-National Perspectives*, New York, 1967.
10. Rueschemeyer et al., *op.cit.*, p. 43.
11. Cf. the discussion in Grew, *op.cit.*, p. 10ff. and p. 21ff.
12. See note 13, and Grew, *op.cit.*, Lipset, *op.cit.*, and Hobsbawm, *op.cit.* See also E.J. Hobsbawm, *Nations and Nationalisms Since 1780*, Cambridge: Cambridge University Press, 1992, Chapter 4.
13. Cf. in addition to Grew, *op.cit.*, and Hobsbawm *op.cit.*, Dick Geary, *European Labour Protest 1848-1939*, London: Methuen, 1984, Robert Gildea, *Barricades and Borders. Europe 1800-1914*, Oxford University Press, 1987; Theodore Hamerow, *The Birth of a New Europe: State and Society in the Nineteenth Century*, Chapel Hill, N.C.: University of North Carolina Press, 1983; Harvey Mitchell & Peter N. Stearns, *Workers and Protest: The European Labor Movement, the Working Classes and the Origins of Social Democracy, 1890-1914*, Ithaca Ill., 1971; Peter N. Stearns, *European Society in Upheaval. Social History Since 1800*, New York & London, 1967; Norman Stone, *Europe Transformed 1878-1919*, London, 1983, and Charles Tilly, Louise Tilly & Richard Tilly: *The Rebellious Century 1830-1930*, London, 1975.

14. See Charles Tilly, *From Mobilization to Revolution*, New York, 1978.
15. Cf. for this argument Graeme Duncan, *Marx and Mill*, Cambridge: Cambridge University Press, 1973, and Norman Geras, *The Legacy of Rosa Luxemburg*, London, 1976.
16. Carl E. Schorske, *Fin-de-Siecle Vienna: Politics and Culture*, New York, 1980.
17. It also means that it is necessary to distinguish between endogenous developed features and »imported« features, and between the Stalinist leadership and the mass base of the Western communist parties. See for example Ossip K. Flechtheim, *Die KPD in der Weimarer Republik*, Frankfurt a.M., 1969, and Herman Weber, *Die Wandlung des deutschen Kommunismus. Die Stalinisierung der KPD in der Weimarer Republik*, Vols. 1-2, Frankfurt a.M., 1969.
18. An important difference between communism and fascism was the different content of the two ideologies. Communism, after all, was within the rationalist tradition with roots in the Enlightenment whereas fascism was anti-rationalist. In communism there was a discrepancy between theory and practice; in fascism, on the contrary, practice was in full accordance with ideology.
19. On differences between communism and fascism see note 17 and 18.
20. For this concept and the theory on competitive elitism, see David Held, *Models of Democracy*, Cambridge: Polity Press, 1987, Chapter 5.
21. See Reinhard Bendix, *Nation Building and Citizenship*, Berkeley: University of California Press, 1977, and T.H. Marshall, *Citizenship and Social Class*, Cambridge: Cambridge University Press, 1950.
22. Edvard Bull, »Arbeiderbevegelsens stilling i de tre nordiske lande 1914-1920«, (orig. publ. 1922), reprinted in *Tidsskrift for arbeiderbevegelsens historie*, 1, 1976, pp. 3-28.
23. Walter Galenson (ed.), *Comparative Labor Movements*, New York, 1952. Cf. also Niels Elvander, *Skandinavisk arbetarrörelse*, Stockholm: Liber-Förlag, 1980, pp. 47-48, and S.M. Lipset, *Political Man*, London: Mercury, 1963.
24. W.M. Lafferty, *Economic Development and the Response of Labor in Scandinavia: A Multi-Level Analysis*, Oslo, 1971.
25. Dick Geary, *European Labour Protest 1848-1939*, London: Methuen, 1984, and S.M. Lipset, »Radicalism or Reformism: The Sources of Working-Class Politics,« pp. 219-251, in S.M. Lipset (ed.), *Consensus and Conflict: Essays in Political Sociology*, New Brunswick & Oxford, 1985. To the thesis on the importance of the general political system Lipset adds a further thesis on the importance of the presence or absence of a feudal system in the pre-industrial capitalist period.
26. Walter Korpi, *The Working Class in Welfare Capitalism*, London: Routledge & Kegan Paul, 1978, and *The Democratic Class Struggle*, London: Routledge & Kegan Paul, 1983; John D. Stephens, *The Transition from Capitalism to Socialism*, Chicago: University of Illinois Press, 1986; Nils Elvander, *Skandinavisk arbetarrörelse*, Stockholm: Liber-Förlag, 1980, and Gregory M. Luebbert, *Liberalism, Fascism or Social Democracy: Social Classes and the Political Origins of Regimes in Interwar Europe*, Oxford: Oxford University Press, 1991, p. 121ff and p. 267ff.
27. Charles A. Gulick, *Austria: From Habsburg to Hitler*, Vols. 1-2, Berkeley, 1948; Gerald Brenan, *The Spanish Labyrinth*, Cambridge: Cambridge University Press, 1960; Hugh Seton-Watson, *Italy from Liberalism to Fascism*, Cambridge Mass.,

1963. For comparative analyses see Dick Geary, *European Labour Protest 1848-1939*, London: Methuen, 1984, and Luebbert, *op.cit.*

28. See Dieter Groh, *Negative Integration und revolutionärer Attentismus. Die deutsche Sozialdemokratie am Vorabend des Ersten Weltkrieges,* Frankfurt a.M.: Ullstein, 1973; Vernon L. Lidtke, *The Outlawed Party. Social Democracy in Germany 1878-1890*, Princeton N.J.: Princeton University Press, 1966; Günther Roth, *The Social Democracy in Imperial Germany*, Totowa N.J.: Bedminster, 1963, and Carl E. Schorske, *German Social Democracy 1905-1917*, New York: Wiley & Sons, 1965.

29. Hagen Schulze, *Otto Braun oder Preussens demokratische Sendung*, Berlin, 1977, and in general W.L. Guttsmann, *The German Social Democratic Party 1875-1933*, London, 1981, and Georg Fülberth & Jürgen Harrer, *Die deutsche Sozialdemokratie 1890-1933*, Darmstadt & Neuwied, 1977.

30. See Karl Dietrich Bracher, *Die Auflösung der Weimarer Republik*, Villingen, 1955, and Hans Mommsen, *Die verspielte Freiheit. Der Weg der Republik von Weimar in den Untergang 1918 bis 1933*, Berlin, 1989.

31. Guttsmann, *op.cit.* See also William Sheridan Allen, *The Nazi Seizure of Power. The Experience of a Single German Town*, London, 1966.

32. I agree with Bernt Hagtvet, *op.cit.*, p. 114, and Eberhard Kolb, *op.cit.*., p. 193. H.A. Turner focuses much too narrowly on the question of financing.

33. Eberhard Kolb *op.cit.*, p. 193.

34. Bracher, *op.cit.*; Mommsen, *op.cit.*; Kolb *op.cit.*, Chapter 6; Kühnl, *op.cit.*; and F.L. Carsten, *The Reichswehr and Politics 1918-1933*, Oxford, 1966.

35. Cf. for a survey of the discussion, Eberhard Kolb, *The Weimar Republic*, London, 1988, p. 191ff.

36. Cf. Eberhard Czichon, *Wer verhalf Hitler zur Macht?*, Köln, 1967, Dick Geary, »The Industrial Elite and the Nazis in the Weimar Republic« in Peter Stachura (ed.), *The Nazi Machtergreifung*, London, 1983; George W.F. Hallgarten & Joachim Radkau, *Deutsche Industrie und Politik von Bismarck bis heute*, Frankfurt a.M., 1974, pp. 195ff, and D. Stegmann, »Zum Verhältnis von Grossindustrie und Nationalsozialismus 1930-1933«, pp. 399-482, in *Archiv für Sozialgeschichte*, Vol. 13, 1973. For another view, see H.A. Turner, *German Big Business and the Rise of Hitler*, New York & Oxford, 1985. It is worth noting, however, that big industry never dreamt of supporting the SPD, let alone the KPD. In this respect, class interests certainly set some limits!

37. Bernt Hagtvet, »The Theory of Mass Society and the Collapse of the Weimar Republic: A Re-Examination«, in Stein Ugelvik Larsen, et al., *op.cit.*, p. 114.

38. Kühnl, *op.cit.*

39. Lyttelton, *op.cit.*; Seton-Watson, *op.cit.*; and Tasca, *op.cit.*

40. Luebbert, *op.cit.*, pp. 258-266.

41. See F.L. Carsten, *The Rise of Fascism*, Berkeley: University of California Press, 1980, Chapter 5; Andrew Janos, *The Politics of Backwardness in Hungary 1825-1945*, Princeton: Princeton University Press, 1982, Chapters V and VI; and Joseph Rothschild, *East Central Europe between the Two World Wars*, Seattle: University of Washington Press, 1974.

42. Cf. in general F.L. Carsten, *op.cit.*, and Gregory M. Luebbert, *op.cit.* For Germany,

Bracher, *op.cit.*, Mommsen *op.cit.*, Kolb *op.cit.*, and Reinhard Kühnl, »Pre-Conditions for the Rise and Victory of Fascism in Germany,« pp. 118-130, in Stein Ugelvik Larsen et al., *Who Were the Fascists?*, Bergen-Oslo-Tromsø, 1980. For Austria, Charles A. Gulick, *op.cit.*, Gerhard Botz, »Introduction« and »The Changing Patterns of Social Support for Austrian National Socialism (1918-1945),« pp. 192-201 and pp. 202-225, in Ugelvik Larsen et al., *op.cit.*, and Bruce F. Pauley, »Nazis and Heimwehr Fascists: The Struggle for Supremacy in Austria, 1918-1938,« pp. 226-238, in Ugelvik Larsen et al., *op.cit.* For Italy, Adrian Lyttelton, *The Seizure of Power. Fascism in Italy 1919-1929*, London, 1973, Seton-Watson, *op.cit.*, and Angelo Tasca, *Glauben, Gehorchen, Kämpfen. Aufstieg des Faschismus*, (1938), Wien, 1969, and for Spain, Paul Preston, *The Coming of the Spanish Civil War*, London, 1983.

43. For the middle class panic thesis, see for example Theodor Geiger, *Die soziale Schichtung des deutschen Volkes: Soziographischer Versuch auf statistischer Grundlage*, Stuttgart: Enker Verlag, 1932, pp. 109-122; William Kornhauser, *The Politics of Mass Society*, Glencoe: The Free Press, 1959; Harold Laswell, »The Psychology of Hitlerism«, *Political Quarterly*, Vol. 4, 1933, pp. 373-384; S.M. Lipset, »Fascism – Left, Right and Center,« pp. 131-176, in S.M. Lipset: *Political Man*, London: Mercury, 1963; Sigmund Neumann, »Germany: Changing Patterns and Lasting Problems,« pp. 354-392, in Sigmund Neumann (ed.), *Modern Political Parties: Approaches to Comparative Politics*, Chicago: University of Chicago Press, 1956; For a critique of the thesis see Richard F. Hamilton, *Who Voted for Hitler?*, Princeton: Princeton University Press, 1982, Chapter 2.

44. S.M. Lipset, »'Fascism'-Left, Right and Center,« pp. 131-176, in S.M. Lipset, *Political Man*, London: Mercury, 1963.

45. See Richard Hamilton, *op.cit.*, and the criticism advanced by Hagtvet and Kühnl - Bernt Hagtvet & Reinhard Kühnl, »Contemporary Approaches to Fascism: A Survey of Paradigms,« pp. 26-51, esp. pp. 29-31, in Ugelvik Larsen et al., *op.cit.*

46. Hamilton *op.cit.*

47. Hagtvet's comment on Hamilton's results is worth citing here: »in essence what he has done is to replace the traditional argument that the social specificity of Nazi support may be identified with the lower middle classes with the view that this specificity must be extended to include higher echelons of society,« Bernt Hagtvet, »The Theory of Mass Society and the Collapse of the Weimar Republic: A Re-Examination«, in Ugelvik Larsen, et al., *op.cit.*, p. 110.

48. Ibid.

49. William Sheridan Allen, *The Nazi Seizure of Power: The Experience of a Single German Town*, London, 1966, and Jeremy Noakes, *The Nazi Party in Lower Saxony, 1921-1933*, Oxford: Oxford University Press, 1971.

50. W.S. Allen, *op.cit.*, p. 274.

51. See Gerhard Botz, *Krisenzonen einer Demokratie. Gewalt, Streik und Konfliktunterdrückung in Österreich seit 1918*, Frankfurt & New York: Campus, 1987; Charles A. Gulick, *Austria from Habsburg to Hitler*, Vols. 1-2, Berkeley, 1948; Anson Rabinbach, *The Crisis of Austrian Socialism. From Red Vienna to Civil War 1927-34*, Chicago: University of Chicago Press, 1983; Curt Sørensen, *Mellem Demokrati og Diktatur*, Vols. 1-2, Ph.D. dissertation, Aarhus: Institute of Political Science, Aarhus University, 1992, and Adam Wandruszka, »Österreichs politische

Struktur. Die Entwicklung der Parteien und politischen Bewegungen,« pp. 289-485, in Heinrich Benedikt (ed.), *Geschichte der Republik Österreich*, München, 1954.

52. Cf. William Sheridan Allen, *The Nazi Seizure of Power: The Experience of a Single German Town*, London, 1966, and Jeremy Noakes, *The Nazi Party in Lower Saxony 1921-1933*, Oxford: Oxford University Press, 1971.
53. A long and comprehensive discussion about the electoral support for Nazism continues today. Neither the Bendix thesis focusing on the previous non-voters as the basis for the Nazi upsurge at the general elections in 1930, nor the Lipset thesis, pointing to the radicalization of the middle class as the main explanation for the Nazi victory in 1930 fully explains their support. The pre-1930 Nazi movement can perhaps be characterized as predominantly a petty bourgeois movement. After 1930, the movement increasingly gained support from other sectors of the population, including, as Hamilton demonstrates, the upper and upper middle classes. In general, social democratic and communist voters and voters for the Zentrum were resistant to the Nazi appeal. Electoral research thus confirms evidence produced by community studies such as those of W.S. Allen and Jeremy Noakes. See Thomas Childers, *The Nazi Voter: The Social Foundation of Fascism in Germany, 1919-1933*, Chapel Hill, N.C.: University of North Carolina Press; Jürgen W. Falter, *Hitlers Wähler*, München, 1991; and Richard F. Hamilton, *Who Voted for Hitler?*, Princeton: Princeton University Press, 1982.
54. Jeremy Noakes, *op.cit.*, p. 136.
55. See Gerhard Botz, »Introduction,« pp. 192-201, in Ugelvik Larsen, et al., *op.cit.*
56. Barrington Moore, *Social Origins of Dictatorship and Democracy: Lord and Peasant in the Making of the Modern World*, London: Penguin Press, 1969, p. 418.
57. S.M. Lipset, »The Conditions of the Democratic Order,« Part I in S.M. Lipset, *Political Man*, London: Methuen, 1963, and Robert A. Dahl, *Polyarchy*, New Haven, Conn.: Yale University Press, 1971, Chapter 3.
58. For a theoretical critique of this now so dominant conception, see Anthony Arblaster, *The Rise and Decline of Western Liberalism*, Oxford: Blackwell, 1984, and *Democracy*, Buckingham: Open University Press, 1994; Emily Hauptmann, *Putting Choice before Democracy*, Albany: State University of New York Press, 1996; John Hoffman, *State, Power and Democracy*, Sussex: Wheatsheaf, 1988; C.B. Machpherson, *The Life and Times of Liberal Democracy*, Oxford: Oxford University Press, 1977, and *Democratic Theory: Essays in Retrival*, Oxford: Clarendon, 1973; Ellen Meiksins Wood, *Democracy Against Capitalism*, Cambridge: Cambridge University Press, 1995, and Maureen Ramsay, *What's Wrong with Liberalism? A Radical Critique of Liberal Political Philosphy*, London & Washington: Leicester University Press, 1997. Referring to the level of political practice, it can be argued that liberalism existed for centuries before it became democratic and that liberalism in real history often resisted the process of democratization, opposing, for example, extensions of suffrage, see Arblaster *op.cit.*, Luebbert, *op.cit.*, and Ruschemeyer, et al., *op.cit.*
59. Rueschemeyer, et al., *op.cit.*, p. 46 and p. 8.
60. On Germany see Thomas T. Mackie & Richard Rose, *The International Almanac of Electoral History*, London, 1982, pp. 154-155.
61. S.M. Lipset, *Political Man*, London: Methuen, 1963, Chapter IV.

62. S.M. Lipset, *op.cit.*, p. 128.
63. A main point made by theorists otherwise as different as Karl Kautsky, Rosa Luxemburg and Otto Bauer.
64. S.M. Lipset, »Social Conflict, Legitimacy, and Democracy«, Chapter III in *Political Man, op.cit.*, cf. especially pp. 83ff.
65. Lipset *op.cit.*, p. 83.
66. Gregory M. Luebbert, *Liberalism, Fascism or Social Democracy. Social Classes and the Political Origins of Regimes in Interwar Europe*, Oxford: Oxford University Press, 1991. Compare also Luebbert's explicit reference to S.M. Lipset & Stein Rokkan, »Cleavage Structures, Party Systems and Voter Alignments: An Introduction,« pp. 1-64, in S.M. Lipset & Stein Rokkan (eds.), *Party Systems and Voter Alignments: Cross-National Perspectives*, New York: Collier-Macmillan, 1967, in Luebbert, *op.cit.*, p. 327, note 24.
67. Luebbert, *op.cit.*, Ch. 2.
68. On Scandinavia see W.M. Lafferty, *Economic Development and the Response of Labor in Scandinavia: a Multi-Level Analysis*, Oslo, 1971. On Europe, see Dick Geary, *European Labour Protest 1848-1939*, London: Methuen, 1984; Luebbert, *op.cit.*, Chapter 2, 3, 4 and 5.
69. Ibid.
70. Ibid., Ch. 6.
71. Ibid., Ch. 7 and 8.
72. The bourgeoisie is the class of big and medium capitalists, the middle class consists of two categories: the »old middle class« of small artisans, shopkeepers and retailers and the »new middle class« of white collar workers and civil servants.
73. See the discussion in David Blackburn & Geoff Eley, *The Peculiarities of German History*, Oxford: Oxford University Press, 1984.
74. Luebbert, *op.cit.*, p. 309.
75. Barrington Moore, *Social Origins of Dictatorship and Democracy: Lord and Peasant in the Making of the Mordern World*, London: Penguin Press, 1969; Hans-Ulrich Wehler, *The German Empire*, Hamburg-New York, 1985; Ralf Dahrendorf, *Gesellschaft und Demokratie in Deutschland*, München: Piper, 1968; Alexander Gerschenkron, *Bread and Democracy in Germany*, Berkeley: University of California Press, 1943; For another interpretation see David Blackbourn & Geoff Eley, *The Peculiarities of German History*, Oxford: Oxford University Press, 1984.
76. For a similar criticism of Luebbert see Lene Bøgh Sørensen, *Political Development and Regime Transformations: The Hungarian Case*, Ph.D. Dissertation, Aarhus: Institute of Political Science, University of Aarhus, 1995, pp. 101-102.
77. See Bracher, *op.cit.*, Mommsen, *op.cit.*, and Carsten *op.cit.*
78. Cf. again for a similar criticism, Lene Bøgh Sørensen, *op.cit.*, pp. 101-102.
79. Luebbert, *op.cit.*, p. 306.
80. Arno J. Mayer, *The Persistence of the Old Regime*, London: Croom Helm, 1981.
81. Arno Mayer, *op.cit.*, p. 4.
82. Alex Callinicos, *Against Postmodernism*, New York, 1990, p. 43.
83. See note 75.
84. Callinicos, *op.cit.*, pp. 43-44.

85. I use the term »Central Europe« in three senses. In the narrowest sense it covers Germany and Austria, in a second sense it covers the core area of the former Dual Monarchy, i.e., Austria, Hungary and Czechoslovakia. In the broadest sense it designates this core area plus Germany. This simultaneous use of three concepts reflects the general confusion and disagreement on the delimitation of the Central European region.
86. For a characterization of Russia as underdeveloped Great Power, see Theda Skocpol, *States and Social Revolutions*, pp. 81ff. See also Theodore H. Von Laue, *Sergei Witte and the Industrialization of Russia*, New York & London: Columbia University Press, 1963, and *Why Lenin? Why Stalin?*, London: Weidenfeld & Nicholson, 1966.
87. Alec Nove (ed.), *The Stalin Phenomenon*, London, 1993, p. 28.
88. This interpretation of Russian development and of Stalinism as modernization strategy and policy has been inspired by the works of John H. Kautsky. See his *Communism and the Politics of Development: Persistent Myths and Changing Behavior*, New York: Wiley & Sons, 1968, *The Political Consequences of Modernization*, New York: Wiley & Sons, 1972, *Patterns of Modernizing Revolutions: Mexico and the Soviet Union*, Beverley Hills & London: Sage, 1975. See also Theodore von Laue, *Sergei Witte and the Industrialization of Russia*, New York & London: Columbia University Press, 1965, and *Why Lenin?, Why Stalin?*, London: Weidenfeld & Nicholson, 1966; Moshe Lewin, *Russian Peasants and Soviet Power*, London: Allen & Unwin 1962, *The Making of the Soviet System*, London: Methuen 1985, and *Russia/USSR/Russia*, New York: The New Press 1995; Barrington Moore, *Social Origins of Dictatorship and Democracy: Lord and Peasant in the Making of the Modern World*, London: Penguin Press, 1969; Alec Nove, *The Stalin Phenomenon*, London, 1993, and *Was Stalin Really Necessary?*, London: Allen & Unwin, 1964; A.F.K. Organski, *The Stages of Political Development*, New York: Alfred Knopf, 1965; Teodor Shanin, *Russia as a 'Developing Society'. The Roots of Otherness: Russia's Turn of Century*, London: Macmillan 1985, and Theda Skocpol, *op.cit.*
89. Right wing and conservative parties are associated with the upper classes, the Left and socialist parties with the lower classes and the liberalist center parties with the middle classes. See S.M. Lipset, *Political Man*, London: Mercury, 1963, Chapters 7 and 8.
90. For a survey of concepts and debates, see Anthony Giddens & David Held (eds.), *Classes, Power and Conflict. Classical and Contemporary Debates*, London: Macmillan, 1982, and Stephen Edgell, *Class*, London & New York: Routledge, 1993. My own conception has been much influenced by Erik Olin Wright. See his *Class, Crisis and the State*, London: NLB, 1978, and *Classes*, London: Verso, 1985; Ellen Meiksins Wood, *The Retreat from Class*, London: Verso, 1986; Ira Katznelson & Aristide R. Zolberg (eds.), *Working-Class Formation*, Princeton: Princeton University Press, 1986; E.P. Thompson, *The Making of the English Working Class*, London: Penguin, 1968, and D. Rueschemeyer, et al., *op.cit.*
91. See Ira Katznelson & Aristide Zollberg (eds.), *Working Class Formation*, Princeton: Princeton University Press, 1986.
92. The power of the nomenclatura in the former Soviet Union, for example, was exercised primarily by political and ideological means. In this respect, the

nomenclatura rule was more like the rule of the feudal ruling class of the past than the domination of the capitalist class in modern societies.

93. Elites are small groups of especially powerful persons such as members of the government, the top bureaucracy, military leaders, the cultural and mass media elite etc. See T.B. Bottomore, *Elites and Society*, London & New York: Routledge, 1993. Whereas social classes are constituted by their relationship – economic as well as political and ideological – to the means of production and investment policy, elites are constituted by their control over resources not directly involving control over the means of production and investment policy. Elites are powerful due to other resources and relations than ruling classes. Both elites and ruling classes are very important in any process of political development and regime formation. For empirical analyses of elites and discussions see T.B. Bottomore, *op.cit.*, T.B. Bottomore & Robert J. Brym (eds.), *The Capitalist Class: An International Study*, London: Harvester Wheatsheaf, 1989; Steward Clegg, et al., *Class, politics and the economy*, London: Routledge & Kegan Paul, 1986; G. William Domhoff, *The Power Elite and the State. How Policy is Made in America*, New York: de Gruyter, 1990; John Scott, *Who Rules Britain?*, Cambridge: Polity Press, 1991, and *Corporations, Classes and Capitalism*, London: Hutchinson, 1979, and Maurice Zeitlin, *The Large Corporations and Contemporary Classes*, Cambridge: Polity Press, 1989.

94. On Weber's conception of »class« see Max Weber, *Wirtschaft und Gesellschaft*, (1922), Johannes Winkelmann (Hrsg.), Tübingen: J.C.B. Mohr, 1985, pp. 531ff. For a survey of class theories see note 8.

95. Reinhard Bendix, *Nation Building and Citizenship*, Berkeley: University of California Press, 1977 [1964]; T.H.Marshall, *Citizenship and Social Class*, Cambridge: Cambridge University Press, 1950.

96. Barrington Moore *op.cit.*, p. 418; S.M. Lipset: »The Condition of the Democratic Order«, Part I in S.M.Lipset: *Political Man*, London: Methuen, 1963, and Robert A. Dahl, *Polyarchy*, New Haven, Conn.: Yale University Press 1971, Chapter 3. Scholars have unfortunately not always been very precise in their terms. Often the expressions »middle class« and »bourgeoisie« seem to be used almost indiscriminately.

97. See the references given in note 13.

98. Rueschemeyer et al., *op.cit.*.

99. On the cultural activities of for example the Austrian labour movement see Julius Deutsch, *Unter Roten Fahnen. Vom Rekord zum Massensport*, Wien, 1931; Brigitte Emig, *Die Veredelung des Arbeiters. Sozialdemokratie als Kulturbewegung*, Frankfurt a.M., 1980; Alfred Georg Frei, *Rotes Wien. Austromarxismus und Arbeiterkultur. Sozialdemokratische Wohnungs- und Kommunalpolitik 1919-1934*, Berlin, 1984; Helmut Gruber, *Red Vienna. Experiment in Working Class Culture 1919-1934*, Oxford: Oxford University Press, 1991; Hans Hautmann & Rudolf Hautmann, *Die Gemeindebauten des Roten Wien 1919 bis 1934*, Wien, 1980; Reinhard Kanonier, *Zwischen Beethoven und Eisler. Zur Arbeitermusikbewegung in Österreich*, Wien, 1981; Helene Maimann (Hrsg.), *Mit uns zieht die neue Zeit. Arbeiterkultur in Österreich 1918-34*, Wien, 1981; Wolfgang Neugebauer, *Bauvolk der kommenden Welt. Geschichte der sozialistischen Jugendbewegung in Österreich 1919 bis 1934*, Wien, 1975, and Joseph Weidenholzer, *Auf dem Weg zum 'Neuen*

Menschen'. Bildungs- und Kulturarbeit der österreichischen Sozialdemokratie in der ersten Republik, Wien, 1981.

100. Cf. Wolfgang Abenroth, *Sozialgeschichte der europäischen Arbeiterbewegung*, Frankfurt a.M: Suhrkamp, 1965; Julius Braunthal, *History of the International*, Vol. 1, *1864-1914*, London: Nelson & Sons, 1966, *History of the International*, Vol. 2, *1914-1943*, London: Nelson & Sons, 1967, and *Geschichte der Internationale*, Vol. 3, Hannover: Dietz, 1971; David Caute, *The Left in Europe since 1789*, London: Weidenfeld and Nicolson, 1966; G.D.H. Cole, *A History of Socialist Thought*, Vols. I-V, London: Macmillan, 1959-60; Dick Geary, *European Labour Protest 1848-1939*, London: Methuen, 1984; Dick Geary (ed.), *Labour and Socialist Movements in Europe Before 1914*, Oxford, New York & Munich: Berg, 1989; Michael Harrington, *Socialism*, New York: Saturday Review Press, 1972; George Lichtheim, *A Short History of Socialism*, London: Weidenfeld & Nicolson, 1970, and Adolf Sturmthal, *The Tragedy of European Labour 1918-1939*, London: Victor Gollancz, 1944. On Marx's conception see Shlomo Avineri, *The Social and Political Thought of Karl Marx*, Cambridge: Cambridge University Press, 1968; Hal Draper, *Karl Marx's Theory of Revolution*, Vols. I-IV, New York & London: Monthly Review, 1977-1990; Alan Gilbert, *Marx's Politics*, Oxford: Martin Robertson, 1981; Richard N. Hunt, *The Political Ideas of Marx and Engels*, Vols. I-II, London: Macmillan, 1974, and University of Pittsburgh Press, 1984, and David McLellan, *The Thought of Karl Marx*, London: Macmillan, 1971.

101. Luebbert, *op.cit.*

102. Anthony Arblaster, *Democracy*, Buckingham: Open University Press, 1994, p. 61. See also Jens A. Christophersen, »An historical outlook on the different usages of the term 'democracy',« pp. 77-138, in Arne Naess et al., *Democracy, Ideology and Objectivity*, Oslo: Oslo University Press, 1956, and Arthur Rosenberg, *Demokratie und Sozialismus*, [1937], Frankfurt a.M.: Europäische Verlagsanstalt, 1962.

103. On the classical elaboration of this thesis see Robert Michels, *Zur Soziologie des Parteiwesens in der modernen Demokratie*, [1911], Stuttgart: Kröner Verlag, 1925 and Max Weber, *Politik als Beruf*, [1919], Johannes Winckelmann (Hrsg.), *Max Weber. Gesammelte Politische Schriften*, Tübingen: J.C.B. Mohr, 1988, pp. 505-560.

104. Joseph Schumpeter, *Capitalism, Socialism and Democracy*, [1942] New York: Harper & Row, 1975, p. 269.

105. For an eminent analysis of this period, see Eric Hobsbawm, *Age of Extremes. The Short Twentieth Century 1914-1991*, London: Michael Joseph 1994, Part Two.

106. Francis Fukuyama, *The End of History and the Last Man*, New York, 1992. For quite another perspective on capitalist development and history, see Karl Polanyi, *The Great Transformation*, [1944], Boston: Beacon, 1957, and the works of Eric Hobsbawm, *The Age of Revolution 1789-1848*, New York: Mentor, 1962, *The Age of Capital 1848-1875*, London: Weidenfeld & Nicholson, 1995, *The Age of Empire 1875-1914*, London: Abacus, 1994, and *Age of Extremes: The Short Twentieth Century History 1914-1991*, London: Penguin, 1994.

107. For a similar argument though within the framework of a much longer historical perspective see Ellen Meiksins Wood, *Democracy Against Capitalism*, Cambridge: Cambridge University Press, 1995 .1995.

Immigrants at the Polls: Immigrant and Refugee Participation in Danish Local Elections[1]

Lise Togeby

Abstract

Starting from the fact that voter turnout among immigrants in Denmark is higher than in other countries where immigrants are eligible to vote in local elections, this article argues that the main explanation is that the Danish local election system, with its rules for voting for individual candidates, contains greater incentives to collective mobilization than the election rules in, e.g., Sweden. In some Danish towns, certain ethnic groups are mobilizing collectively, which is expressed in very high voter turnout. As a result, among Turks in Århus, for example, the voter turnout is as high as the turnout among native Danes, regardless of Danish or Turkish citizenship and regardless of gender.

Introduction

When democratic constitutions were first written in Europe, there was no doubt that only a country's citizens should be eligible to vote, and it was probable that nobody felt differently when servants and women eventually got the right to vote. After World War II, the influx of foreign workers to Western Europe changed this state of affairs. Due to the new wave of immigration, more and more people became permanent residents in Western European countries without having any influence on decisions that affected their daily lives or on general political decisions. The fact that naturalization was a long and complicated process increased the problem, since many immigrants did not have the right to vote.

This situation led to a debate, about the conditions for obtaining citizenship and about giving resident aliens the right to vote in their respective countries of residence. In 1963, Ireland became the first country to allow immigrants to vote in local elections; Sweden followed suit in 1976, Denmark in 1981, Norway in 1982, and Holland in 1986. Sweden has even discussed allowing immigrants to vote in national elections, but popular resistance has been so great that the idea died down (Hammar 1990).

When immigrants became eligible to vote in the Scandinavian countries, it was not a result of pressure from immigrant groups. It was a generous gesture from the political elite – in Denmark inspired by Sweden's example. Therefore, it seems reasonable to ask whether immigrants are actually utilising the right they have been given. Do they actually turn out at the polls?

The general conclusion is that immigrant participation in elections is relatively low in all countries, but information about voter turnout is rather haphazard and scattered (Hammar 1990). Compared to other countries, Sweden has the most information about this issue, but the results are far from encouraging: immigrant participation has declined gradually since the first immigrant election in 1976, when turnout among immigrants was 60 per cent. In the 1985 election, 48 percent voted and in 1998, 38 per cent. This should be compared to a turnout among Swedish citizens in the same elections of just under 90 percent.

Surprisingly, voter turnout among immigrants seems to be higher in Denmark than in Sweden. For the first two elections in Denmark with immigrant participation, total immigrant participation was calculated, but it has not been done since. During the 1981 election, 61 percent voted; in 1985 it was 53 percent. This should be compared with a general voter turnout of approximately 70 percent in Danish local elections. A voter registration-based study from the 1997 local elections further indicates that immigrant turnout has declined only slightly since the 1980s. Thus, there is hardly any doubt that immigrant turnout is higher in Denmark than in Sweden. The turnout in Denmark also seems to be higher than in Norway[2] and the Netherlands.[3]

This is surprising, especially in view of the fact that Sweden has in most areas gone much further than Denmark in creating a multicultural society. Sweden makes a much larger effort to inform immigrants about elections in their own languages, and comparative studies indicate that ethnic tolerance is generally greater in Sweden than in Denmark (Togeby 1997). Still, immigrants use their right to vote less in Sweden than in Denmark.

This raises questions of what factors influence voter turnout among immigrants, why voter turnout is greater in some societies than others, and why some groups of voters use their right to vote more often than others.

This article addresses these questions on the basis of an analysis of voter turnout in the Danish local elections in 1997, focusing particularly on Turks and Lebanese.[4] These two groups have been chosen because we have information about them from two different studies: a register-based study from the two largest municipalities in the country, Århus and Copenhagen, and a study among selected ethnic minorities in Denmark. Because of the special data from Århus and Copenhagen, the conditions in these two cities will have a key position in the discussion. Finally, a comparison, to the extent possible, with Sweden will enable us to vary both the national and local context for voter participation.

Theories of Voter Turnout

For many years, European research on voter turnout has been very limited. In most European countries, most citizens vote in parliamentary elections, and we know that they do this primarily because they perceive voting as a civic duty. Variations in voter participation are thus rather limited, since those who abstain from voting tend to be the socially marginalized. Low voter turnout in a group may be an indication of weak social integration (Blondel, Sinnott & Svensson 1998).

However, when we view the development of democracy from a long-term perspective, voter participation becomes more interesting. Extending the right to vote to all citizens regardless of wealth, profession and gender is seen as the decisive formal criterion for establishing a political democracy, and high voter turnout is seen as an indication that democracy is also working (cf. Rokkan 1970). When the majority of the population has not only been given the right to participate in decisions through general elections, but actually uses this right, the democratization process is seen as having come far. This democratic perspective makes it relevant to examine voter turnout in trying to understand how immigrants relate themselves to their new country.

At the same time, in seeking to analyze immigrants' voter participation we must return to the theories that were developed in connection with analyses of the establishment of democracy in Europe. This again means that the central question must be how to mobilize social groups that have not previously participated in the democratic process.

In *Participation and Political Equality* (1978), Verba, Nie & Kim developed the distinction between individual political mobilization and group-based political mobilization. Individual mobilization is issue neutral. Its purpose is not to take care of particular interests, but to live up to the role as the good citizen, and it is based on a belief that »I can make a contribution.« Individual mobilization is based on individual resources such as time, education, prestige, experiences (1978, 11ff.). Today voter participation demands so few resources that most people who simply live up to the norm about voting also use their right to vote. Thus, in contrast to other forms of political participation, voting is only loosely connected to individual resources (cf. Verba, Schlozman & Brady 1995).

Group-based or collective political mobilization is determined by interests. It is expressed through a high degree of group consciousness and is usually sustained through strong organizations. Collective mobilization depends on lively interaction among people with similar abilities and interests and on stable and lasting patterns of interaction. Collective mobilization explains why some groups, despite few individual resources, manage to achieve high levels of participation. The classical example of collective mobilization is the European working class at the turn of the century, but there are other examples, such as the American civil rights mobilization in the 1960s or the feminist mobilization in the 1970s.

If we transfer this idea to the immigrants' situation in Western Europe today, the first question is whether we find among immigrants any signs of collective mobilization directed towards voter participation. The next question is whether the differences between Denmark and Sweden can be explained by differences in the collective mobilization of ethnic minorities. If a collective mobilization is taking place, some ethnic groups will participate more than would be expected on the basis of their individual resources.

Collective mobilization of a group, e.g., of one or more ethnic minorities, will depend on group characteristics, but also on the conditions in the society the minority lives in. It will depend on what the literature on social movements calls *the political opportunity structure* (Eisinger 1973; Kitschelt 1986), i.e., the electoral system, other electoral arrangements, party system, and the indigenous population's attitudes towards ethnic minorities. The question then becomes: how open are the receiving country's institutions and culture to including ethnic minorities in the political process?

Most of our information about immigrant voter turnout comes from Sweden. Hence, it is appropriate to briefly recount the most important results from the Swedish studies. In a thorough analysis of the first immigrant election in 1976, Tomas Hammar (1979; cf. 1990) lists five factors that explain the low voter turnout among Sweden's immigrants: 1) the majority of the immigrants have the same characteristics that lead to low voter turnout in the native Swedish population, e.g., weak social integration; 2) many immigrants, because of language problems and isolation from Swedish society, know very little about the election and its alternatives; 3) the election has less importance for immigrants, either because they plan to return to their home countries, or because they perceive the electoral issues as irrelevant; 4) many immigrants have weak relations to the political system, which means that very few of them see voting as a social norm; 5) many immigrants experience counter-pressure as a result of different values and behaviour at home and in the receiving country. In a more recent analysis, Hammar (1990) focuses on the differences between immigrant voter turnout in Sweden and Denmark. His explanation for the difference is that the Danish electoral system, with its provisions for personal voting for individual candidates, is more conducive to a mobilization of immigrant groups.

Roth & Nordlöf (1978; cf. Hammar 1979) have performed ecological analyses based on the same 1976 voting data as used by Hammar. They conclude that the following five factors - here listed according to significance - can explain variations in voter turnout in Swedish municipalities: 1) general voter turnout in the municipality; 2) number of immigrant candidates; 3) size of municipal budget for immigrant purposes; 4) degree of industrialization in the municipality; and 5) number of immigrant organizations in the municipality.

Finally, Bäck & Soininen's (1994; 1998) analysis of local elections in Sweden in 1994 points out that low voter turnout is based on two major factors: 1) poor economic and social integration into Swedish society; and 2) a fatalistic outlook. As indications of integration, they cite long residence in Sweden, Swedish citizenship, membership in Swedish associations, and use of Swedish media.

Combining these results from the Swedish studies with the more general considerations about individual and collective mobilization allows us to construct an overall explanatory model. Traditionally, research on voter participation distinguishes between contextual and individual factors (Blondel, Sinnott & Svensson 1998). In the case of immigrant voter participation, a third factor could be added: group characteristics. Individual characteristics, the first factor, can explain why some persons in an ethnic group vote more than other persons in the group. Characteristics of the specific ethnic groups can explain why some ethnic groups vote more than other groups. Finally, characteristics of social context can explain why voter turnout in some towns is greater than in other towns and why voter turnout is greater in some countries than in others. The contextual factors can also help explain differences between ethnic groups, because the context can be more conducive or less conducive to collective mobilization. Contextual factors can also help explain differences between individuals, for instance, context can increase or decrease social inequality. An outline of possible explanations is shown in Table 1.

Table 1. Possible explanations for variations in voter turnout.

Contextual characteristics: Country and/or county	Characteristics of ethnic group	Individual characteristics
1. *Economic/social processes* A. Unemployment B. Welfare state regime C. The state's integration policy 2. *The political opportunity structure* A. Electoral system B. Party system C. What issues do the local councils deal with? 3. *Cultural factors*	A. Hostility towards foreigners 1. *Immigrant history in Denmark* A. Time of arrival B. Size of group C. Immigrants/refugees 2. *Organization in Denmark* A. Settlement patterns B. Organization formations 3. *Imported cultural characteristics* A. Gender roles B. Democratic experiences C. "Social capital" D. Cultural distance to Danish way of life 4. *Collective mobilization*	1. *General integration factors* A. Age, marital status, cash benefits B. Length of stay in municipality 2. *Specific integration factors for ethnic minorities* A. Day-to-day practical integration: work, union membership, children in school, time of arrival in Denmark, Danish education B. Cultural integration: Danish citizenship, Danish skills, follows Danish news, Danish friends, attachment to Denmark 3. *Double integration:* immigrant density in neighbourhood, membership of ethnic associations, length of stay in municipality 4. *Cultural factors* A. Gender B. Attitudes: e.g., trust in other people, attitude towards authorities, fatalism 5. *Experienced hostility from Danish society*

Concretization of the Explanatory Model

Starting with the *contextual factors*, we distinguish between economic, political and cultural factors. Of special interest in explaining differences between Sweden and Denmark is the political opportunity structure.

First, local elections have a greater saliency in Denmark than in Sweden. In Sweden, local and national elections take place on the same day, which means that the local elections are overshadowed in the media by the national election. And immigrants can only vote in local elections. In addition, more issues are decided on the local level in Denmark than in most other countries. Second, both countries use proportional representation, but in Denmark the seat allocation system is combined with rules about voting for specific candidates. Candidates who are placed low on the party list are sometimes elected instead of candidates who are placed higher, and it may be the case that not many votes are needed to get a candidate elected. In Sweden, it was not possible to vote for a person but only for a list until the last election. It is still difficult to evaluate the effect of the new rules about personal votes. In Denmark, however, immigrants have several years' experience in voting for their own candidates, where the odds that he or she will be elected are good. The Danish political opportunity structure is thus much more open to new groups than the Swedish.

Moving on to the second main category of explanatory factors, *characteristics of an ethnic group*, I will mainly comment on characteristics of the Turkish and the Lebanese groups. Turks (i.e., Turkish citizens including Turkish and Kurdish populations) constitute the largest immigrant group in Denmark and the one that has been here the longest. The first Turks came to Denmark as labour migrants in the late 1960s, and the group has continued to grow due to a policy of family reunification. Almost all Turkish immigrants come from villages in central Turkey. People from the same region have followed each other to Denmark, where they are concentrated in a few urban neighbourhoods. The largest concentration of Turks is in Copenhagen's southwest suburbs of Ishøj, Albertslund, Høje Tåstrup and Brøndbyerne. In absolute numbers, Copenhagen and Århus municipalities have the largest number of Turkish immigrants. Ghetto formation is stronger in Århus than in Copenhagen, as Turks are concentrated in a limited number of residential zones in Århus. They are also more organized in Århus than in Copenhagen. Compared to other immigrant groups, the Turks have higher levels of employment frequency and also a higher degree of unionization. These two factors are also true for women. All the same, Turks have been reluctant to apply for Danish citizenship.

Refugees from Lebanon, who came to Denmark in the mid-1980s, consist of persons with Lebanese citizenship and a large number of stateless Palestinians. Compared with other refugee groups, the Lebanese have been in Denmark a relatively long time though, but still considerably less than the Turks. The Lebanese constitute the third largest group of ethnic minorities in Denmark after Turks and Yugoslavs. The Lebanese live mostly outside the capital. In relative numbers, there are most Lebanese in Karlebo, Korsør, Århus, Slagelse, Sønderborg, and Odense. In absolute numbers, most of the Lebanese are found in Århus, Copenhagen and Odense. They live close together, especially in Århus, with 75 per cent in the Gellerup area. In Copenhagen, the largest concentration of Lebanese is in Nørrebro. The employment level among Lebanese is relatively low, especially among Lebanese women. However, more Lebanese than Turks apply for and obtain Danish citizenship.

The two groups are similar in several respects. Both come from the Middle East, their skin is darker than the average Dane's, they are Muslims, and their gender role patterns differ significantly from the Danish norm. The two groups also exhibit major differences: the Turks immigrated primarily as foreign workers, while the Lebanese are refugees; the Turks came to Denmark before the Lebanese; the Turks have adapted better to the Danish labour market than the Lebanese and except for the many Lebanese in Gellerup, the Turks tend to live in more compact settlements than the Lebanese.

Whether a collective mobilization is taking place among Turks and Lebanese residents will be concluded on the basis of the main results of the empirical analysis. Still, here it is possible to state whether the conditions for collective mobilization exist. I will argue that such conditions exist to a much higher extent for the Turks than for the Lebanese, and to a higher extent for ethnic minorities in Århus than in Copenhagen. The Turkish social network is stronger than that of the Lebanese. The Turks came to Denmark through voluntary chain immigration, they live rather concentrated in selected urban areas, and they organize much more than the Lebanese. Furthermore, the conditions for collective mobilization are better in Århus than in Copenhagen due to the low geographic concentration in Copenhagen compared to Århus. In Århus, 75 per cent of the Lebanese live in the same neighbourhood and school district, Gellerup. The Turks, too, live relatively concentrated in a strip stretching from west to northwest Århus in four adjoining school districts. Political organization among Turks is also higher in Århus than in Copenhagen.

In addition, candidates with Turkish backgrounds ran and were elected in local elections in 1997 in both Århus and Copenhagen, in both cities on the Social Democratic list. No candidates with Lebanese backgrounds were elected in either city, but Lebanese or Palestinians ran in both cities on small local lists. The Århus city council currently has two immigrant representatives out of 31 seats: one from Turkey and one from Pakistan. In Copenhagen's city council there are currently seven immigrant representatives out of 55 seats: two from Pakistan, one from Turkey, two from Morocco, one from Syria, and one from Chile. In both cities, it was thus possible to mobilize around immigrant candidates with realistic chances of being elected in the 1997 elections.

Finally, we will examine *individual characteristics*, which can be divided into at least five different types. Here, I will comment only on the three forms of integration variables. First are the general integration factors that cover the majority population and presumably also immigrants. We expect that the middle-aged vote more often than the young and the old, that married people vote more often than singles and divorcees, and that recipients of welfare benefits vote less than people who are working. Furthermore, it is expected that persons who have lived in a municipality for a long time vote more often than those who have lived there only for a short period.

Second, certain more specific integration factors must be assumed to have a special significance for immigrants. One aspect is day-to-day and practical integration, such as having a job, being member of a union, having children in a Danish school, obtaining a Danish education and having resided for a prolonged period in the country. The other aspect of integration is cultural and is indicated by good Danish language skills, following Danish news in newspapers and on TV, having Danish friends, feeling an attachment to Denmark, and having Danish citizenship. All these integration factors are assumed to increase voter participation.

The third factor is »double integration«, i.e., that immigrants and refugees integrate easier into their new country if they are well integrated into their ethnic group. Indications of double integration are, membership in ethnic associations, immigrant density in one's neighbourhood, especially the presence of many people from one's own ethnic group, and - once more - how long one has lived in the locality. In other words, the hypothesis is that living in an ethnic community, especially for a long period, increases the chances of double integration and, hence, consequently of voting in local elections.

The Data

These hypotheses will be tested by means of two sets of data concerning local elections in Denmark in November 1997. The first data set consists of register-based information about all eligible voters in the municipalities of Copenhagen and Århus. Eligible voters include all persons with Danish citizenship and foreign nationals who for at least three years have had a permanent residence permit in Denmark. Citizens from the Nordic countries and the EU, however, are allowed to vote in local elections as soon as they take up permanent residence in Denmark. The total number of cases in this study is approximately 620,000, of which 74,000 persons have either foreign citizenship or are Danish citizens, born outside Denmark. This sample comprises roughly one-third of all eligible voters in Denmark with a foreign background. In addition to information about voter participation, we also have data on citizenship, place of birth, polling district, age, gender, marital status, period of residence in the municipality, receipt of public assistance, and we have been able to calculate relatively detailed information about immigrant density in the local areas. The study is a collaborative effort by researchers at the University of Aarhus and the municipalities of

Århus and Copenhagen[5]. Most of the analyses in the article are based on these unique data.

We also have data from a study from November 1998 of four ethnic minorities in Denmark: Turkish immigrants and Lebanese, Somali and Bosnian refugees. This 1998 study focused on ethnic discrimination and was financed by the Board for Ethnic Equality in Denmark, but the survey also included a question concerning voter participation. The survey gathered information about a number of other individual characteristics besides those found in public registers, such as Danish skills, media consumption, association activities and experienced discrimination. The survey is therefore a useful supplement to register data.[6]

As mentioned earlier, we will focus especially on the Lebanese and the Turks. The register-based study includes 3,548 Lebanese and 5,190 Turks. The survey includes 264 Lebanese and 273 Turks. The register information covers only Århus and Copenhagen, while the survey is based on a representative sample of all Turks and Lebanese who had been living in Denmark at least three years at the time of the survey.

The Big Picture: All Ethnic Groups

Let us begin the empirical analysis by examining voter turnout in Århus and Copenhagen in all larger ethnic groups in the two cities. The purpose of this analysis is to carry out preliminary assessments of possible explanations as to why some groups would turn out to vote more than others. The primary purpose is to identify signs of collective mobilization.

There are two reasons why Table 2 shows voter turnout for Copenhagen and Århus municipalities separately: first, general voter turnout in the two municipalities differs significantly, and we have to assume that the general factors that condition the low voter turnout in Copenhagen have approximately the same influence on immigrants as on the indigenous Danish population (cf. results from the Swedish studies of the 1976 election). Voter turnout in Århus at the 1997 local elections was 71 per cent, corresponding to the national average, but turnout in Copenhagen was only 58 per cent. Second, an ethnic group may be mobilized in one city, but not in the other.

We will search for three indicators of political mobilization. The most important indicator of ethnic mobilization in a particular ethnic group will be a surprisingly high voter turnout, for example, as high as the indigenous Danish population. Another indicator will be that if collective mobilization has occurred only in one city and not in the other, the gap between the group's voter turnout in the two cities will either be larger than expected or smaller than expected, based on the general turnout. Finally, in all likelihood, it is an indicator of collective mobilization if citizenship does not play a significant role in voter turnout. Based on resource/integration considerations, it is to be expected that persons with Danish citizenship have a higher turnout than persons from the same ethnic group who have maintained their original citizenship (Bäck & Soininen 1998). If this difference is not present, it is probably a sign that collective mobilization is stronger than individual mobilization. In order to simplify, the table presents only one figure for each ethnic group. The asterisk indicates that citizenship has only little influence on turnout.

Table 2. Voter turnout among ethnic minorities from third countries and among Danish-born Danish citizens. Danish Local elections 1997. Per cent.

Country	In Copenhagen	In Århus	Difference Århus-Copenhagen
Denmark	**61**	**72**	11
Pakistan	**61***	(73*)	
Czechoslovakia	48		
Turkey	**47**	**73***	26
Ghana	46*		
Algeria	45*		
Brazil	44*		
India	43		
Chili	43		
Hungary	43		
Soviet Union	43		
Iran	**42**	**47**	5
Poland	**41**	46	5
Iraq	**40***	43*	3
Morocco	**39**		
Ethiopia	39		
Philippines	36		
Jordan	31		
Ex-Yugoslavia	**30**		
Somalia	28	54*	26
Egypt	26		
Lebanon	**25**	**44***	19
Vietnam	25	**43***	18
Thailand	23		
China	21		
Tunisia	20		
All third countries	35	50	15
Total	58	71	13

Note: The countries are listed according to voter turnout in Copenhagen. Only turnout for groups of at least 200 persons is listed, except for the group of Pakistanis in Århus of only 86 persons. Groups of more than 1000 persons are in bold type. The asterisks indicate approximately the same turnout among those with and those without Danish citizenship. The table includes the larger national groups from all so-called third countries except Israel and South Korea.

The table shows, first, an even greater difference between voter turnout of ethnic minorities in Copenhagen and Århus than between the voter turnout of indigenous Danes. Second, it shows great differences in voter turnout among ethnic groups in both Copenhagen and Århus. In Copenhagen, turnout varies from 61 per cent among Pakistanis to 20 per cent among Tunisians. In Århus, the turnout varies from 73 per cent among Turks and Pakistanis to 43 per cent among Vietnamese and Iraqis.[7]

The most interesting groups for this study are (1) the Pakistanis in Copenhagen who vote as much as indigenous Danes in Copenhagen and (2) Pakistanis and Turks in Århus who vote as much as indigenous Danes in Århus. At the same time, citizenship appears to have no influence on turnout for these three groups. In addition, all three groups had candidates elected on the Social Democrats' or/and on the Socialist People's Party's lists. A Turkish representative was also elected in Copenhagen, but here the Turkish immigrant group does not show the same signs of mobilization as the three other groups. In comparison, the Turkish turnout in the Swedish elections in 1994 was 47 per cent, the same as the relatively low figure for Copenhagen municipality, which would indicate that collective mobilization of Turkish immigrants in Sweden has not taken place.

Other groups also show signs of mobilization, although not as strongly as the Turks and the Pakistanis. In Copenhagen these other groups include immigrants and refugees from Ghana, Algeria, Brazil and Iraq and in Århus they are refugees from Somalia, Lebanon and Vietnam. It is not clear what explains the relatively high voter turnout among groups in Copenhagen, whereas one obvious explanation for mobilization of the three groups in Århus is settlement patterns. As mentioned, three out of four Lebanese in Århus live in the Gellerup area. A fourth of the Somali live in Gellerup, while another fourth live in the nearby Frydenlund. Finally, the Vietnamese are gathered in the four adjacent neighbourhoods Gellerup, Frydenlund, Hasle and Tilst. All three groups are relative large. In Copenhagen, the ethnic minorities are generally more dispersed than in Århus. It is easier to establish and maintain close social relations in Århus than in Copenhagen, which means that collective mobilization is also easier.

We can only guess at the explanations for the other differences between voter turnout among ethnic minorities. Perhaps there is a pattern of higher voter turnout in groups that have lived in Denmark for a long time compared to those who have been here shorter, but this pattern is weak. Nor are there any clear indications that immigrants from one part of the world vote more than immigrants from other parts. The only obvious indication of this kind is the very low turnout among all groups from Southeast and East Asia. It seems that these groups bring with them cultural values and norms that discourage them from participating in the Danish representative democracy.

All in all, the only convincing explanation for the differences in voter turnout demonstrated in Table 2 is that some minority groups have mobilized collectively while others have not.

Turks and Lebanese

The next question concerns variations in voter turnout within ethnic groups, and here we will focus on immigrants from Turkey and refugees from Lebanon. The first analyses will be based on the register data. Each group will be analyzed separately, and focus will be on the differences between Århus and Copenhagen, because the question is whether individual and collective mobilization factors play different roles in the two cities and for the two ethnic groups.

Only the results from the multivariate analysis will be presented. In addition to information about voting, the register-based data set includes information about sex, age, marital status, citizenship, length of stay in the municipality, recipients of welfare benefits and density of the different immigrant groups in the local neighbourhood. The calculations are performed by means of logistic regression, as the voter turnout to be explained is a dichotomous variable. The results are shown, first, in the outline in Table 3 and, second, for the most important results, in Figures 1-4. Only Figures 1-4 will be commented upon.

Starting with the Lebanese, Figure 1 shows the interaction between municipality, gender, age and voter turnout. We observe the same curvilinear relation with age in all groups, and municipality of residence appears to be more significant than gender. In both municipalities, women have a slightly lower turnout than men, but the difference is small.

Figure 2 keeps age and municipality constant, skips gender, but adds Lebanese density in local area and citizenship[8]. The figure illustrates that municipality of residence is involved in some very characteristic interactions. In Århus, Lebanese density is significant and citizenship insignificant, while in Copenhagen it is the reverse. The lowest turnout is found among Lebanese in Copenhagen without Danish citizenship, and the highest among Lebanese in Århus who live in the high-density Gellerup area. The middle section of the figure shows that people from Copenhagen with Danish citizenship have a slightly higher turnout than people from Århus who live in areas with low Lebanese density.

Table 3. Outline of the multivariate analyses of voter turnout: Danish local Elections 1997. Register data.

Lebanese	Turks
Municipality: Highest turnout in Århus *Gender:* Highest turnout among men	*Municipality:* Highest turnout in Århus *Gender:* Interaction with age: young women vote more than young men, while older men vote more than older women
Age: Curvilinear: Highest turnout among the middle-aged	*Age:* Curvilinear: highest turnout among the middle-aged
Marital status: Highest turnout among married persons	*Marital status:* Not significant
Citizenship with interaction with municipality: Voter turnout among Danish citizens highest: Only significant in Copenhagen	*Citizenship with interaction with municipality:* In Copenhagen, the voter turnout is highest among those with Danish citizenship. No significant relationship in Århus.
Length of stay in municipality with interaction with municipality: Highest turnout among those with long stay: Only significant in Århus	*Length of stay in municipality:* Highest among those with long stay
Share of Lebanese in neighbourhood with interaction with municipality: The higher the immigrant density, the higher the voter turnout: Only significant in Århus	*Share of Turks in neighbourhood:* The higher the immigrant density, the higher the voter turnout
Recipients of cash benefits: Not significant	*Recipient of cash benefits:* Not significant
N: 3548	N: 5190

Note: The analyses are performed by means of a logistic regression. Although we are using population data, a significance level of 0.01 is used as criterion for accepting the relations.

An obvious interpretation of these results is that the high turnout in Århus is a consequence of a collective mobilization of the Lebanese group, while voter turnout in Copenhagen is a result of individual mobilization based on individual resources. These more detailed analyses further support the interpretation already formulated in connection with Table 2.

For the Turks, Figure 3 shows the result of an analysis that includes municipality, gender, age and voter turnout. This time, the curves for the four groups are not similar, as they were for the Lebanese. However, we may note that among Turks, young women vote more than young men, while older Turkish women have an especially low voter turnout. In fact, the curves for the Turks are very much like the curves produced in calculations for Danish-born Danes. Young Turkish women from Århus actually have a slightly higher turnout than young Danish-born men and women from Århus.

Figure 1. Turnout among Lebanese by age, gender and municipality. Danish lokal election 1997. Register data. Predictet probabilities of voting

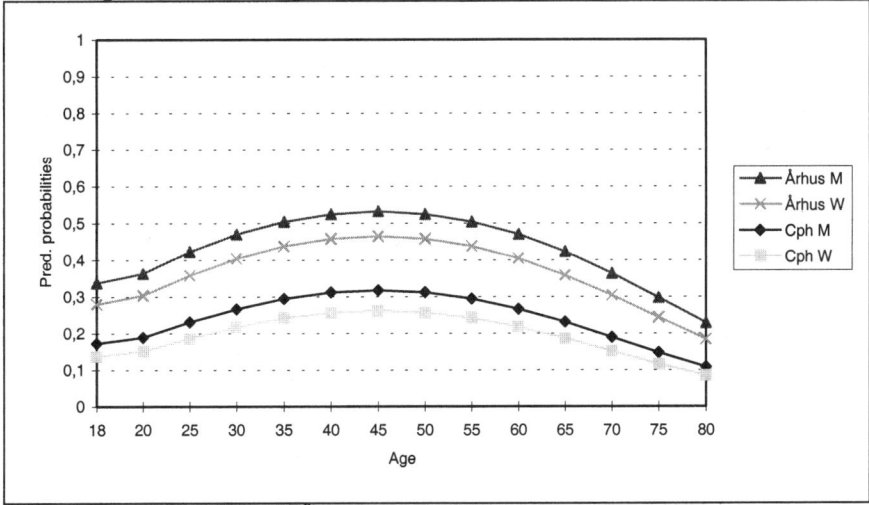

L = -2,37+ 0,099*age -0,0011*age^2+ 0,27*sex -0,8911*municipality
Cph: Copenhagen; M: men; W: women.

Figure 2. Turnout among Lebanese by gender, municipality, immigrant density and citizenship. Danish lokal elections 1997. Register data. Predictet probabilities of voting

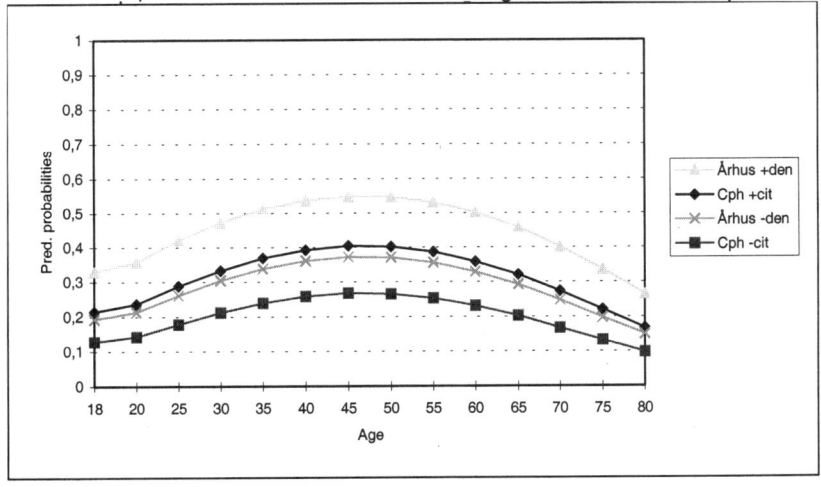

L = -3,0637+ 0,1028*age -0,0011*age^2 -0,342*municipality +0,1827*citizenship +0,4363*citizenship*municipality +0,1433*density -0,1251*density*municipality
+den: high density of lebanese; -den: low density of Lebanese; +cit: Danish citizenship; -cit: no Danish citizenship.

Immigrants at the Polls

Figure 4 again leaves out the gender variable and includes instead three other variables, i.e., density of Turks in the local area, attainment of Danish citizenship and length of stay in the area. Since it would take 12 lines to show all combinations of the significant variables, which would make it difficult to distinguish all of them, I have chosen to show only six lines, among these the combination of characteristics resulting in the lowest and highest voter turnout in each municipality. The highest voter turnout is found among Turks who live in Århus, have lived there for many years, and who live in areas with a high density of Turks. The lowest voter turnout is found among Turks who live in areas of Copenhagen with few immigrants, who have lived in Copenhagen for only a short period, and who have maintained their Turkish citizenship. In this group of Turks, voter turnout decreases to the level of the Lebanese turnout. The figure clearly indicates that density of Turks is significant in both Copenhagen and Århus, while citizenship is significant only in Copenhagen. The lack of association between citizenship and turnout for both Lebanese and Turks living in Århus should be seen in comparison with Swedish and Norwegian studies showing that immigrants with Swedish or Norwegian citizenship vote significantly more than non-citizens (Bäck & Soininen 1998; Kval & Bjørklund 1996).

For the Turks, the conclusion is that the strongest mobilization characteristics are found in Århus, but that there are also signs of mobilization in Copenhagen. In fact, voter turnout is surprisingly high among middle-aged Turks who have lived for a long period in Copenhagen and who have Dan-

Figure 3. Turnout among Turks by age, gender and municipality. Danish lokal elections 1997. Register data. Predictet probabilities of voting

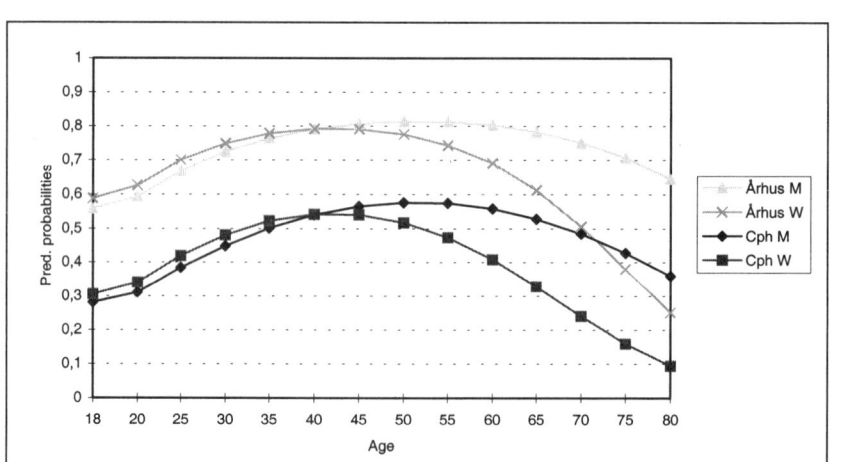

L = -1,6762 +0,1433*age -0,0017*age^2 +0,2211*sex -0,0297*sex*age +0,0006*sex*age^2 -1,1697*municipality
Cph: Copenhagen; M: men; W: women.

Figure 4. Turnout among Turks by age, gender, immigrant density, lenght og stay in the municipality, citizenship and municipality. Danish lokal elections 1997. Register data. Predictet probabilities of voting

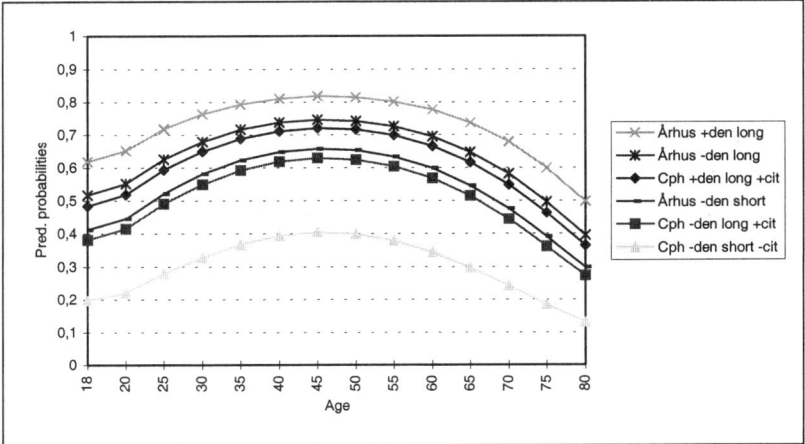

L = -2,1695 +0,1194*age -0,0013*age² -1,044*municipality+ 0,084*density +0,4246*length of stay +0,0741*citizenship +0,4186*citizenship*municipality
+den: high density of Turks; -den: low density of Turks; +cit: Danish citizenship; -cit: no Danish citizenship; long: lived more than 5 years in the municipality; short: lived less than 5 years in municipality.

Figure 5. Turnout among Lebanese by media consumption, having children in Danish schools, having a Danish education and membership of an ethnic organization. Danish local elections 1997. Survey data. Predictet probabilities of voting

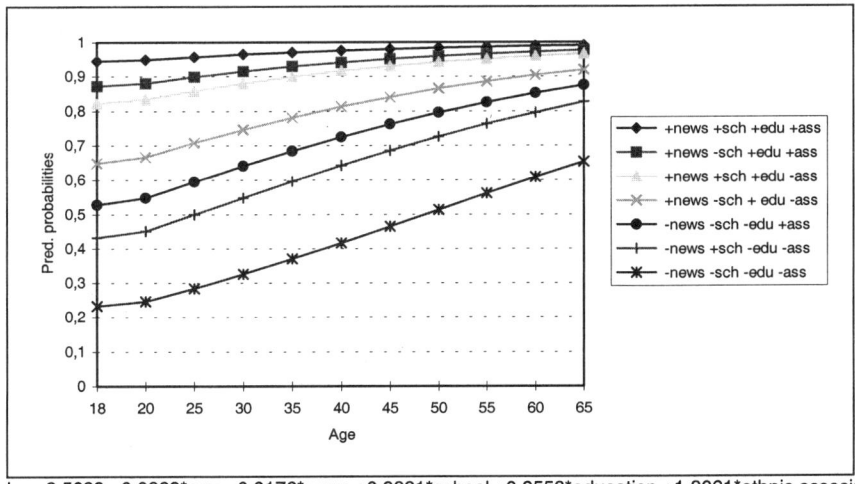

L = -2,5639 +0,0389*age +0,0176*news +0,9221*school +0,8553*education +1,3061*ethnic association
+news: high consumption af Danish media; -news: low consumption of Danish media; +sch: children in Danish schools; -sch: no children in Danish schools; +edu: completed Danish education; -edu: no Danish education; +ass: member of ethnic organizations; 'ass: not member of ethnic associations.

Immigrants at the Polls

ish citizenship. In Copenhagen, there are signs of both collective and individual mobilization, while collective mobilization dominates completely in Århus.

Register data from Århus and Copenhagen municipalities gives data only about the significance of demographic and socio-economic factors. Using data from the discrimination study allows us to analyze the effects of a number of other factors, including other integration factors, attitude variables and perceived discrimination. As age has a significant influence on other variables and can easily cause spurious relations, the relations were controlled for age and gender. Table 4 shows the results of these analyses, which are again performed by means of logistic regression. The table uses significance levels to indicate the strength of the relation between the different variables and voter turnout. As the groups are relatively small, relations up to and including the 0.1 significance level are shown. Fortunately, the results from the two studies support each other.

Starting again with the Lebanese, the table shows that besides age and gender, the following factors are significant when controlled for age and gender: marital status, Danish education, children in a Danish school, union membership, length of stay in Denmark, Danish citizenship, membership of an ethnic association and experienced discrimination. The major emphasis seems to be on the factors classified above as the practical, day-to-day integration, but also cultural integration is obviously important.

In the final multivariate analysis, only those factors significant at the 0.05 level were included. Figure 5 shows the total effect of age, education, children in Danish school, keeping up with Danish news, and membership of an ethnic association. The change in the level of voter turnout is explained by the change from register data to survey data, which always exaggerates voter turnout. Apart from that, the figure illustrates how one integration factor can be added to the next and each time increase voter turnout. The higher the total integration in Danish society, the higher the voter turnout. Notable here is that membership of an ethnic association also has a positive influence on voter turnout for Lebanese.

In general, for the Lebanese, individual integration in Danish society is most significant, but there are also traces of the significance of double integration in the form of membership of ethnic associations.

The Turks present us with more complicated and unexpected relations. The surprising element is the interaction between gender and integration variables: for women, the integration variables and, especially, the cultural integration variables are significant. The highest voter turnout among women is found among those who have jobs, Danish citizenship, good Danish language skills, and who can formulate a complaint if they feel they are treated

Table 4. Outline of the explanatory variables for voter turnout. Danish local elections 1997. Survey data. Significance level (p-values) after control for age and gender.

Variables	Lebanese	Turks
Demographic variables		
Age	0.000 (curvilinear)	0.000
Gender	0.02	n.s. (but interaction)
Marital status	interaction with gender: 0.04	n.s.
Practical day-to-day integration		
Occupation	n.s	interaction with gender: 0.09
Danish education	0.001	n.s
Children in Danish school	0.01	n.s.
Union member	0.1	0.02
Arrival in Denmark	interaction with gender: 0,06	n.s.
Cultural integration		
Danish citizenship	0.1	interaction with gender: 0.02
Danish language skills	n.s.	interaction with gender: 0.001
Can formulate a complaint	n.s.	interaciton with gender: 0.1
Follows Danish news	0.001	0.05
Has Danish friends	0.1	n.s.
Feels attachment to Denmark	0.08	n.s.
Double integration		
Municipality with many Turks or Lebanese	n.s.	n.s.
High immigrant density in neighbourhood	n.s.	0.03
Member of ethnic association	0.04	0.09
Cultural factors		
Trust in other people	n.s.	n.s.
Practicing religion	n.s.	n.s.
Experienced hostility		
Experienced discrimination	0.08	n.s.
Experienced hostility	n.s.	n.s.
Confidence in Danish authorities	n.s.	n.s.
N	274	273

Note: The analysis is performed by means of logistic regression. n.s. means that the relation is not significant at min. 0.1 level.

badly. For Turkish women, then, cultural integration in Danish society creates high voter turnout. The same factors are not found among the men; in fact there are weak associations that point in the opposite direction. However, immigrant density in the neighbourhood and membership of ethnic associations are significant for voter turnout among both women and men. It should also be mentioned that age as well as following Danish news and union membership are significant among Turks.[9]

Figure 6. Turnout among Turks by gender, density og Turks and language skills. Danish lokal elections 1997. Survey data. Predictet probalities of voting

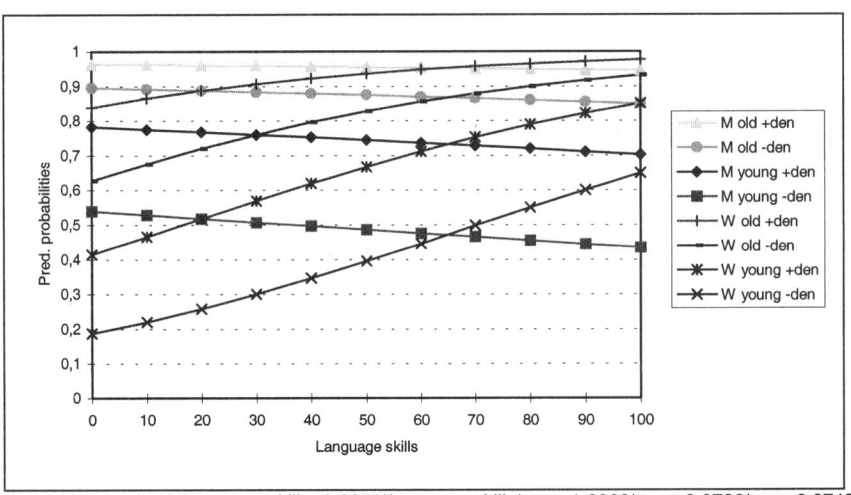

L = -1,9684 +0,0209*language skills -0,0251*language skills*sex +1,6263*sex +0,0798*age -0,3743*density
M: men; W: women; young: 25 years; old: 50 years; +den: high density of Turks; -den: low density of Turks.

The somewhat surprising connections are illustrated in Figure 6, which shows the results of a logistic regression including – besides voter turnout – gender, age, immigrant density[10] and Danish language skills.[11] The figure shows, first, that the curves (i.e., relation with Danish skills) go in opposite directions for men and women. For the women, voter turnout increases relatively strongly with increasing Danish skills, while it declines slightly for men. The two bottom lines in the figure represent, respectively, young women and young men who live in neighbourhoods with low immigrant density. The lowest voter turnout is found among young women with poor Danish skills, who live in neighbourhoods with few other immigrants. The two upper lines represent middle-aged men and women who live in neighbourhoods with a very high immigrant density. The highest voter turnout is found among middle-aged men who live in areas with a high density of Turks, regardless of their Danish language skills, and among women with the same characteristics *if* they have good Danish skills.

The conclusion for the Turks is that collective mobilization is significant for both men and women, but that women, are also influenced by their cultural integration into Danish society. Among women, there are examples of both individual and collective mobilization, while the men demonstrate collective mobilization only. It would hardly be an exaggeration to say that voter turnout among Turkish women exhibits strong signs of individual female emancipation, for the men it is their double integration that makes collective mobilization most significant for them.

Conclusion

The analyses clearly demonstrate the effects of individual mobilization based on individual integration resources as well as the effects of collective mobilization based on the community within ethnic groups. Obviously, collective mobilization has been significantly stronger among Turks than among Lebanese, although there are also clear indications of collective mobilization among Lebanese in Århus. Among Turks, the collective mobilization in Århus is stronger than in Copenhagen and, generally, there are very few traces of mobilization based on individual integration factors among Turkish men. The opposite is true for Turkish women, where high voter turnout is a sign of not only collective mobilization, but also an expression of individual emancipation.

As predicted, we found more signs of mobilization among Turks than among Lebanese, and we found more signs of mobilization among Lebanese and Turks in Århus than in Copenhagen. However, we did not predict differences between Turkish men and women.

There can be no doubt that the relatively high voter turnout among some ethnic minorities in Denmark is a result of a collective mobilization of certain groups in certain cities. The Danish local election system is exceptionally conducive to collective mobilization. The proportional election system combined with the possibility to vote for individual candidates and special rules for seat allocation mean that, in the big cities, on the big parties' lists, some low-ranking candidates will almost always be elected instead of higher-ranking candidates. For the big parties, the lowest ranking candidate is usually very »cheap« in terms of personal votes. Therefore, the chances of winning are good if small groups collectively aim at getting single candidates elected. One example is the social democratic list in Århus Municipality in 1993: the Social Democrats received 67,021 votes, had 15 candidates elected, and the last seat cost only 426 votes (cf. Elklit 1997 29ff). Such good odds create a good basis for mobilization, something which the large minority groups understand.

In addition, the characteristic conditions of each ethnic group in the municipality determine the extent of the group's mobilization. If we take the results from Århus and Copenhagen, mobilization has occurred primarily among the established groups of foreign worker immigrants, i.e., Turks and Pakistanis, while there seems to be no significant mobilization among the older refugee groups (cf. Table 2). Perhaps this is because these groups are generally too small and too scattered.

One of the more surprising results of this analysis is that a high density of immigrants in some parts of Danish cities seems to have at least a moderate positive effect on voter turnout. The probable reason is that there are usually social networks in areas with a high density of certain immigrant groups, which contributes to collective mobilization. Although this corresponds well with what we know about integration and mobilization of immigrant groups in the US (Wolfinger 1965), the result still seems surprising. Studies in Sweden indicate that voter turnout among immigrant groups decreases as immigrant density increases. Or, as Swedish researchers prefer to put it, turnout decreases along with the absence of contacts to the Swedish majority society (Jonsson 1999). Apparently, immigrant concentrations have different consequences for voter turnout in Denmark and Sweden.

The largest difference between Denmark and Sweden is that voter turnout among certain immigrant groups in Denmark is high, even as high as among Danish-born Danes, while all immigrant groups in Sweden have a rather low voter turnout. It is also remarkable that citizenship is not significant for those groups in Denmark with a very high voter turnout. The explanation for these differences seems to be that mobilization in Sweden is based exclusively on individual characteristics, while mobilization of ethnic minorities in Denmark is also collective. Collective mobilization is probably facilitated by a strong concentration of immigrants in the local area, while individually-based mobilization is weakened by it. Ghetto-like communities may create both collective mobilization and collective demobilization, and it is this latter phenomenon that Sweden is now experiencing.

To conclude, the main explanations for differences in voter turnout among immigrants in Denmark and Sweden seem to be the differences in the political opportunity structure. The Danish local government electoral system creates far better opportunities for collective mobilization than the Swedish system.

Notes

Another version of the article is printed in *Journal of Ethnic and Migration Studies,* vol. 25, No. 4. 1999.

1. An earlier version of the article was presented in *Journal of Ethnic and Migration Studies,* vol. 25, No. 4. 1999. Birgit Møller has assisted with the statistical analyses and Annette Andersèn with proofreading and editing.
2. In 1983, during the first election in Norway with immigrant participation, 46 per cent of immigrant voters voted declining to 39 per cent in 1995 (Kval & Bjørklund, 1996: 21)
3. During the municipal elections in Amsterdam in 1998, 39 per cent of the Turks, 23 per cent of the Moroccans, and 21 per cent of the Surinamese voted. In the municipal

elections in 1994, voter turnout in all groups had been higher than in 1998 (Fennema & Tillie, 1999).
4. Most of the refugees from Lebanon are stateless Palestinians.
5. The other participants in the project are Jørgen Elklit, Birgit Møller and Palle Svensson.
6. The data collection, carried out by Statistics Denmark in November 1998, was primarily administered over the telephone by bilingual interviewers, supplemented with questionnaires mailed to those interviewees whose telephone numbers were not available. The survey was based on a representative sample of all persons with a Lebanese, Turkish, Bosnian or Somali background who had lived in Denmark for at least three years at the time of the survey. Despite a considerable effort to reach the respondents, only 47 per cent of the Lebanese and 48 per cent of the Turks responded. The low response rate was due to difficulties in establishing contact with the immigrants, not because they refused to participate (Møller & Togeby, 1999).
7. In Sweden in 1994, turnout for the comparable groups were: Chile: 59 per cent; Turkey: 47 per cent, Iraq: 42 per cent; Iran: 41 per cent; Ethiopia: 34 per cent; Poland: 32 per cent, ex-Yugoslavia: 27 per cent (Bäck & Soininen, 1998). In Norway in 1995, turnout was: Pakistan: 48 per cent; Vietnam: 46 per cent; Turkey: 39 per cent; Iran: 36 per cent; Chile: 35 per cent; Philippines: 34 per cent; Iraq: 32 per cent; Somalia: 31 per cent; Morocco: 27 per cent; Poland: 22 per cent; ex-Yugoslavia: 19 per cent; Ethiopia: 19 per cent; China: 16 per cent (Bäck & Soininen, 1998).
8. Based on a variable measuring the density of Lebanese in the smallest geographic units that the available data allows us to work with. These geographic units are a little smaller in Copenhagen than in Århus; hence, measurements are also more valid in Copenhagen. The highest category includes areas where six per cent or more of the eligible voters come from the Lebanese group. The figure shows the lines for Lebanese living in areas with the lowest and the highest Lebanese density. A similar procedure is applied to the Turkish data.
9. When the relation with age does not appear as curvilinear in this study, it is primarily because the study is limited to the 18-65 age group, which means that the oldest people in the study are still in the labour active age.
10. Immigrant density is determined by asking the respondents to evaluate the number of immigrants in the neighbourhood.
11. Danish language skills are measured by an index from 0 to 100, constructed as a combination of the respondents' own assessment of their language skills, and of the interview language.

References

Blondel, Jean, Richard Sinnott & Palle Svensson (1998). *People and Parliament in The European Union*, Oxford: Clarendon Press.
Bäck, Henry & Maritta Soininen (1994). »Invandrarnas valdeltagande«, in Henry Bäck and Anders Håkansson (eds.), *Väljare i kommunalvalet*, Stockholm: SNS Förlag.
Bäck, Henry & Maritta Soininen (1998). »Immigrants in the Political Process«, *Scandinavian Political Studies*, Vol. 21, pp. 29-50.

Eisinger, Peter K. (1973). »The Conditions of Protest Behavior in American Cities«, *American Political Science Review*, Vol. 67, pp.11-28.

Elklit, Jørgen (1997). »Valgsystemet: teori og praksis«, in Jørgen Elklit and Roger Buch Jensen (eds.), *Kommunalvalg*, Odense: Odense Universitetsforlag.

Fennema, Meindert & Jean Tillie (1999). *Civic Communities in a Multicultural Society. Ethnic Networks in Amsterdam*, paper presented at the 1999 ECPR Joint Session of Workshops, Mannheim.

Hammar, Tomas (1979). *Det första invandrarvalet*, Stockholm: Liber Förlag.

Hammar, Tomas (1990). *Democracy and the Nation State*, Aldershot: Avebury.

Jonsson, Christer (1999). *Valdeltagandet bland röstberättigade utländska medborgare i tolv valdistrikt i Göteborg*, Göteborg: Invandrarförvaltningen, Stencils.

Kitschelt, Herbert P. (1986). »Political Opportunity Structures and Political Protest: Anti-Nuclear Movements in Four Democracies«, *British Journal of Political Science,* Vol. 16, pp. 57-89.

Kval, Karl-Eirik & Tor Bjørklund (1996). *Valgdeltagelse og partistemmegivning blandt utenlandske statsborgere ved kommunevalgene fra 1987 til 1995*, Oslo: Institutt for samfundsforskning.

Møller, Birgit & Lise Togeby (1999). *Oplevet diskrimination. En undersøgelse blandt etniske minoriteter*, Copenhagen: Nævnet for Etnisk Ligestilling.

Rokkan, Stein (1970). *Citizens, Elections, Parties*, Oslo: Universitetsforlaget.

Roth, Per-Anders & Hans Nordlöf (1978). *Immigrant Vote in the Swedish Election of 1976*, Stencils, Gothenburg: Department of Political Science, University of Gothenburg, Sweden.

Togeby, Lise (1997). *Fremmedhed og fremmedhad i Danmark*, Copenhagen: Columbus.

Verba, Sidney, Norman H. Nie & Jae-on Kim (1978*). Participation and Political Equality*, Cambridge: Cambridge University Press.

Verba, Sidney, Kay Lehman Schlozman & Henry E. Brady (1995*). Voice and Equality*, Cambridge, MA.: Harvard University Press.

Wolfinger, Raymond E. (1965) »The Development and Persistence of Ethnic Voting«, *American Political Science Review*, Vol. 59, pp. 896-908.

Elites and the Management of Ethnoterritorial Conflict in Western Democracies

Derek W. Urwin

Abstract

Elites in Western democracies have had the choice of three broad strategic approaches to how they seek to resolve ethnonational disputes through territorial management. Containment and control is rarely sustainable in a pluralist democracy, while redistribution often fails to address the essential grievances. Western elites have been obliged to consider a strategy of positive discrimination. The particular strategy selected, and its ability successfully to address ethnonational concerns will depend upon several factors that arise from the ethnonational group or groups and the historical structure and style of territorial management of the state.

As their societies have become internally more complex and more exposed to the vicissitudes of international political and economic currents, so have modern democratic governments been increasingly buffeted by demands – and demands that are often confusing and contradictory – for action and a distribution or redistribution of public goods from what seems like an ever increasing host of organisations and groups. No matter what the nature of the supplicant or the specific content of the demand, organisations and groups normally seek legislation or other forms of government action that will be applied unreservedly across the whole territory of the state and binding upon everyone who lives there. The major exception to this politics of universalism, to a desired conformity across state territory, arises from the politicisation of indigenous cultural groups which, on the basis of a number of recognisable stigmata, claim an identity distinctive from that of the rest of the state population. On the basis of that distinctiveness, they argue that they merit special treatment. Because »those who share a place share an identity« (Mackenzie 1976, 130), geography emerges as the factor which distinguishes this kind of political agitation from that pursued by all other bodies which seek to influence government. Geography is the priest that marries community to territory, imbuing them almost with the Biblical connotations of the chosen people and the promised land (Doob 1976, 24-30; Sachs 1992, 111).

Ethnonational demands therefore draw attention to, and are based on, »the politics of difference« (Taylor 1992, 38-43). They project a territorial element – what Feagin and Capek (1991, 34) have called »the social control of space« - that is largely absent from all other demands and issues that confront national elites. That geographical ingredient is integral to the agenda of politicised ethnonational minorities, an agenda that possesses three broad constituent elements: rectification of a perceived absence of an equality of citizenship, positive discrimination to secure and strengthen cultural rights, and institutional political recognition, through some form of autonomy, of the uniqueness of the group as a collectivity.

The essential consequence of this stance is that political ethnonationalism lays claims upon states and elites on behalf of both communities and territories. Not only may these not be congruent with state populations or boundaries; they may not be congruent with each other. Typically, the ethnonational demand is for an adjustment to the management structures and styles of a specific territory within the existing state, with the implication that the desired new pattern of territorial management will shape the lives of all who live there no matter what their cultural identity or political wish. The symbiotic link between territory and community may well push the latter into sharp opposition to prime objectives of any state and its elite. These include the desire to preserve the integrity of the state territory, and to ensure within these geographical confines the legitimacy of its existence, a legitimacy that rests upon popular support for, and acquiescence to, its political authority.

With the advent of mass politics in the nineteenth century, the Western liberal democratic state became more firmly rooted in the principle of a universal citizenship itself built upon the twin foundations of an equalisation of rights and obligations for all individuals within its territorial borders, and the notion of a homogeneous nation-state. Ethnonational discontent, even where the community already has been granted some greater or lesser decentralisation, merely serves to undermine these twin foundations, and stresses the difficulties elites may face in seeking to guarantee both the integrity of state territory and complete political legitimacy. Traditionally, the typical elite response in earlier decades to ethnonational discontent was one of »studied neglect« (Esman 1977, 381). While their presence elsewhere in the world might seriously disrupt the tenor of government and the stability of the state, in the West ethnonational minorities, according to the liberal democratic canon, could be dismissed as little more than negligible and doomed survivors of a world long gone. Conventional wisdom accepted that processes of historical and socio-economic change would, sooner or later, bring their existence to an end. Elites, therefore, did not need to concern themselves greatly with indigenous minorities. At best, such attitudes led to a benign tolerance or indifference, at worst to centralising policies intended to hasten the end of ethnonational distinctiveness.

That studied indifference proved unsustainable in the second half of the twentieth century with the emergence of a new politics. The appearance, or in some instances a revival, of ethnonational movements was part of this new wave, challenging the centralising nature of state politics. In Quebec, the so-called Celtic fringe of the United Kingdom and France, Catalonia and the Basque provinces, the Swiss Jura, the Alto Adige, and Flanders, rejuvenated political movements that claimed to represent ethnonational concerns juxtaposed themselves against the state, obliging national elites to look again at their traditions and styles of territorial management. The possible dismemberment of a state was never part of an elite agenda. Most regimes, however, were prepared at the least to consider how some of the more specific complaints of ethnonational minorities might be addressed. A few proved willing to go further, to accept some territorial restructuring within existing boundaries.

The full gamut of elite managerial responses to ethnonational demands can range from total resistance to total acquiescence. Neither extreme has been seriously or willingly considered by modern elites. All have opted to respond positively with some form of concession. The possible options available to elites can be categorised under three broad headings.

Containment and Control

Elites seek to stabilise the state and society, and/or to eliminate the issue by one of two means. First, they can choose to ignore the problem, attempting to pursue a policy of studied neglect by, for instance, insisting that because the ethnonational community is already a full and equal partner in society, no further reform is necessary. Alternatively, elites can opt for a more repressive and coercive thrust that effectively centralises policy direction with the objective of either hastening the assimilation of minorities into the mainstream or constructing and maintaining a kind of ethnonational apartheid as the best means of securing societal stability. This broad option insists upon the integrity of territory and standardisation of its management.

Redistribution

Elites seek to buy peace through the provision of public largesse. They use money to distribute public goods and benefits for cultural as well as economic purposes, most typically through some form of regional economic policy. Whilst ostensibly recognising that there are specific ethnonational needs, this broad strategy is also designed to maintain central control and integrity of territory.

Positive Discrimination

Elites accept the legitimacy of at least some ethnonational claims and seek to develop a political response that recognises that some groups and territories, because they are different, merit special political treatment. The elites then have the choice of opting for accommodation through territorial or group concessions, or indeed some combination of the two. Territorial accommodation involves grants of power being ceded to geographical regions, that is some form of devolution, with full-scale federalisation being the ultimate territorial step. By contrast, group accommodation only indirectly involves geographical devolution. It is more appropriate to regard it as a kind of consociational approach that through an application of some form of proportionality involves a sharing or duplication of public goods among distinctive or conflicting ethnonational groups. Again, whether they select either a group or a territorial strategy, elites may also have to consider whether to impose a standard formula across the whole of the state territory, making it applicable to all groups and communities within the state, or to offer preferential or distinctive treatment to only some regions or some groups, leaving the prevailing structures and styles of territorial management untouched in the remainder of the state.

The most coherent arguments for an elite strategy of containment and control, perhaps, are those advanced by Lustick (1979). Because he regards ethnonational identities as terminal, unchangeable and inherently conflictual, he argues that any kind of »melting pot« strategy that assumes the ultimate triumph of acculturation and assimilation will be doomed to failure. The state can survive only if the elite adopts and rigorously maintains a control system where penetrative linkages guarantee the predominance of the central elite and its state ideology.

Control systems have a long historical degree in the Western experience, but in contemporary times have been restricted to a relatively small number of coercive measures and examples. Even so, they have been quite prominent in a few policy areas, notably that of language planning and rights (Weinstein 1991), something which can strike at the heart of minority ethnonationalism. One difficulty with this option, however, is that it presupposes relatively unsophisticated political systems and societies. Modern democracies are highly complex and complicated organisms, where at best ethnonational concerns find it difficult to monopolise the political agenda. Moreover, contemporary democracies are too open and too pluralist for elites to be able to develop or sustain this kind of directive repression for any length of time.

Indeed, the more probable outcome in modern democracies to a policy of containment and control is an intensified resentment and unrest among the minority community. This was the consequence, for example, in the Alto Adige to the Italian elite's decision to circumvent the 1946 Paris Agreement between Italy and Austria which had provided for substantial autonomy for the region. The problematic nature of this kind of elite policy is merely underlined by the experiences of the Basque provinces and Northern Ireland. The more Spanish governments under and after Franco attempted to »control« the Basques, the more it seemed to fuel a broad Basque dissatisfaction. On the democratic control system employed by the Protestant/Loyalist majority in Northern Ireland after 1921, and the post-1972 efforts of British governments under direct rule of the province, one major study (McGarry and O'Leary 1990, 269) concluded that »the quality of majority control democracy is dubious«, and that »Majoritarian democracy only works well when key conditions are present: when the exclusion of the minority is temporary, and when the issues dividing the majority from the minority are not fundamental«.

The point is that politicised ethnonationalism is rarely, if ever, not fundamental. The politics of identity easily lends itself to zero-sum competition. Hence, it is almost impossible for containment and control to be adopted by elites as a temporary device. In the long run, containment and control might allow elites to maintain territorial integrity, but probably at the price of full political legitimacy. Whether they can then afford to ignore the negative costs to democratic principles and practices is a moot question. Elites in a modern pluralist democracy will almost certainly find that they cannot implement sufficiently repressive or cost-effective control policies that prohibit ethnonational political mobilisation and organisation, while simultaneously denying to the associated communities any possibility of participating in and seeking a share of political influence and power.

Contemporary elites, therefore, have chosen not to resist totally, to reject containment and control for some kind of compromise. On occasions these might be highly limited and ad hoc in nature, merely seeking, as British governments traditionally did in response to Welsh linguistic and cultural demands, to satisfy a very specific complaint (for example, a desire for bilingual road signs) without any acceptance of the general principles of ethnonational rights that bound all the areas and subjects of complaint together. More typically, however, elites have been obliged to seek and develop a more systematic approach to ethnonational concerns, to accept that a more positive response was more likely to guarantee the continuity of state imperatives.

The modern Western democracy is a welfare state, to which the principle of redistribution, almost invariably measured and assessed in economic and monetary terms, is integral. With the upsurge in ethnonational concerns after the late 1950s, elites found it easier, in wishing to respond positively to these concerns, to consider extending redistributive policies from the level of individuals and social classes to that of cultural communities and the regions they inhabited. In most countries, however, economic responses were merely part of broader elite designs to improve the economic lot of the state as a whole. The favoured responses were regional economic policies, but these, in other words, tended to be acceptable to elites usually only if it could be argued that they would benefit the whole state economy. It was almost as if any allayment of ethnonational discontent that came in their wake was viewed as a bonus rather than a primary objective.

This perspective was particularly prominent where regional economic policy was specifically linked to institutional decentralisation, as in France where the primary objective of the new regional units was the implementation of a national economic plan which itself was intended to modernise and rationalise the French state and economy. The French model was repeated to some extent in Italy. In both instances an adequate regional redistribution did not occur, while the impact of the regions upon the national picture was weak (Loughlin & Mazey 1994). Not only did existing disparities persist; they tended to become wider and the regulatory power of the central elites was heightened. While regional policy may have been seen by elites as a decentralising process, they were significantly less likely to see in it a place for decentralised politics.

There are several reasons why redistribution has in general proved not to be a successful formula for the resolution of the politics of difference. It is invariably almost impossible to separate out a regional policy from all other state policies that might have a regional impact. At the least, this makes it very difficult to evaluate the impact of a regional policy with any great precision. Second, it was fallacious to believe that money and redistribution could be used to resolve all ethnonational complaints. In the 1960s, for example, Belgian elites willingly committed themselves to huge financial outlays, unjustifiably so by any strict accountancy criteria, in an effort to resolve the dispute between Flanders and Wallonia, but to no avail (Heisler & Peters 1983). Like control policies, regional policies run the risk of fuelling ethnonational agitation further, or even creating a fruitful climate for it where none had previously existed (see Newman 1994; Watson 1978). Poorer ethnonational regions could take a policy as an elite admission that injustices did, in fact, exist, while economically advantaged regions feared that internally generated resources and benefits could be diverted elsewhere by the state.

Above all, there are at the end of the day things that money cannot buy. Economic demands or complaints rarely, in fact, have been the full content of or even central to ethnonational concerns. These are invariably driven by a much broader conception of cultural and territorial justice. It is that broader concern that made the elite essays into redistribution almost irrelevant. It demanded, if elites were serious in considering the politics of difference, a political response. Sooner or later, therefore, elites in modern democracies have been obliged to respond politically, to consider measures and strategies that amounted to positive discrimination in favour of the ethnonational community.

The recent record of elite forays into territorial management is both extensive and informative. While it illustrates that elites have opted for either the territorial or the group route towards political accommodation, it also indicates that the range of choices available to elites is, in any one situation, circumscribed by several factors, including the historic relationship between the ethnonational community and the centralising state, the geopolitical environment, and both the specific structure of the state itself and its traditions and conceptions of how territory ought to be managed. In Switzerland the Jura dispute was eventually resolved by the creation of a new canton, an option possible under Swiss constitutional federalism. Equally, federalism has provided a framework within which Canadian elites have sought to accommodate the demands of Quebec. The Canadian experience, however, also illustrates that while federal structures may on the surface facilitate accommodation, they may, because central elites are not constitutionally in complete control of the situation, equally inhibit the emergence of a solution fully acceptable to all, no matter how willing the national elite may be.

At the other extreme, the so-called *Proporzpaket* of 1969 and 1972 introduced by Italy to resolve the discontent in the Alto Adige is often held up as the major example of a successful group approach.

The long search from 1958 to 1994 in Belgium for a resolution of conflicting regional and linguistic demands ultimately embraced a marriage of territorial and group perspectives. While territoriality could be applied with few complications to Flanders and Wallonia, both elites and ethnonational groups had to accept a group or power-sharing principle for bilingual Brussels, something which continued after the final transformation of the country into a federal state in 1994 to modify the territorial principle. The United Kingdom and Spain are two further states which, like Belgium, faced pressure from more than one ethnonational front. Unlike the Belgian elites, however, who sought a solution that would be consistently applicable to the whole state, their British and Spanish counterparts, products of states with a history of differential regional relationships with the centre, accepted the possibility of territorial options that would permit the application of different structures and outcomes for different regions or communities within the state. Not since the 1880s and the Home Rule all round promise of a Liberal government has there been an attempt in the United Kingdom to find a single devolved structure for the British state. The reforms for Scotland and Wales advanced by the 1997 Labour government, along with the Good Friday agreement on the future of Northern Ireland, merely continue this variegated approach towards the three territories. In Spain, while decentralisation was part of the 1978 Constitution, the devolution of power to Catalonia and the Basque country was substantially more extensive than that offered to other regions, including the ethnonationally distinctive but politically quiescent periphery of Galicia.

While Western elites have therefore demonstrated the possibilities of both territorial and group strategies of accommodation, the record of recent decades suggests that the former has been the more popular alternative. Certainly, it is the more logical, since ethnonational communities invariably identify strongly with a territory and the political claims they lodge before the state tend to be on behalf of both community and region. However, there are at least two problems that elites may subsequently face if they opt for a territorial approach. The first is that any concession to ethnonational aspirations, no matter how minimal, may stimulate a ratchet effect, raising minority expectations even further – or even creating expectations where none previously existed. The latter seems to have been the outcome of the French regionalisation programme, which arguably assisted the generation of an interest that earlier had not been present. In the French case, however, the potential ratchet effect did not materialise because of the powerful disinclination of the central elites to go beyond what had been introduced.

In most instances, however, territorial accommodation, while admittedly meeting some ethnonational aspirations, may merely create a new and more potent stage upon which further concessions can be sought. In Belgium the willingness of the elites to seek an accommodation acceptable to all regional-linguistic interests merely served to fuel a momentum that carried the country forward to the full federalisation of the state. Even so, Flemish interests since 1994 do not see the story as having come to a fairy tale ending. They look forward to a future where the Belgian state is diminished even further, where an even more autonomous Flanders will exist within a broader European integrative framework. Equally, in the United Kingdom, the commitment of the Labour government to Scottish and Welsh devolution after 1997 radically changed the nature of expectations. The debate in Scotland, for example, about what will or should happen once the new Scottish Parliament is in place in 1999 covers scenarios which most observers agree go far beyond what the government originally had in mind when it introduced the legislation in the House of Commons. The thin end of the wedge is an ever present danger where elites seek to defuse discontent through a territorial strategy.

The second major problem with a territorial strategy is that it cannot be immediately applicable in all ethnonational situations. Underlying any territorial devolution is the assumption that congruence exists between community and region, and on that basis the grant of authority and autonomy is geographical: it does not explicitly relate to an ethnonational community. The fact that there is not always congruence between group and territory limits the likelihood of success for a territorial strategy, for what has been called ethnoregional federalism (Laponce 1987). The most awkward ethnoterritorial problems that elites have been called upon to resolve are those where a single territory is inhabited by and claimed as its own by more than one ethnonational community. If, where this is the case, an elite applies a territorial option, it could be accused of effectively washing its hands of the affair, of inviting the rival claimants to continue their arguments at the regional level, with victory going to the stronger or larger of the claimants. At some point, an elite faced with this kind of scenario will inevitably be pushed towards considering some kind of group solution that invites the rival communities to share power in a proportional manner that nevertheless guarantees the rights and distinctive character of the smaller ethnonational group or groups. The model which it has often been suggested that elites in this position should consider is that of consociational democracy.

How far the consociational model can be applied uncritically to situations where the fundamental differences derive from the politics of identity, however, has been a matter of some debate, with many critics arguing that, in fact, it is of little value unless very specific conditions prevail. Among others, for example, Barry (1991, 100-135) argues that in ethnic disputes there is a much lower level of tolerance and degree of empathy than where economic or religious cleavages predominate. The key difference again relates to territory: a central question is not so much how territory is managed but who controls it. Indeed, the reputed success of the settlement in the Alto Adige which, despite several strains and alarms, has survived for almost three decades, may be less typical of such situations than the dilemma of Northern Ireland where since the early 1970s British governments, with the later assistance of Irish governments in Dublin, have attempted to persuade both the Loyalist and Nationalist communities to accept a settlement that, whatever the particular details of the various schemes advanced over the years, firmly represents a group approach.

The fact that these various initiatives in Northern Ireland were rejected by one or the other community, and that considerable scepticism still prevails in many quarters about the likely success of the 1998 Good Friday agreement simply underlines the fact that in such circumstances elites can rarely be masters of their own fate. For a group strategy to work, all the elites can do is to encourage and to be willing to delegate to the communities as much as possible; the key condition would seem to be the willingness of the competing ethnonational communities to accept accommodation and compromise, and to appreciate the concerns and fears of the other side. Even so, where ethnonational communities both reside in and claim the disputed territory, a group strategy would seem to be the only option for possible success, and Western elites have ultimately had to accept this conclusion in situations where an uncomplicated territorial devolution cannot eradicate the roots of unrest.

The context, therefore, in which demands are raised and concessions offered is important. This makes it difficult for any standard recipe to be developed. The alternatives available to elites are almost always circumscribed by the historical and institutional pattern of centralising politics. It is this pattern which has played such an important role in helping to shape the perceptions and ambitions of ethnonational communities. While many elites seem to have been prepared to expend large amounts of money and energy to ethnoterritorial problems in order to maintain territorial integrity and control, there is a limit to how much can be expended and how much in the way of success may be achieved. At the end of the day local factors can be at least as important as national ones, and that, as Mitchell (1996, 33) has stated, implies that »accommodation policies are not always within the gift of the centre«.

Both the way in which Western elites have approached ethnoterritorial disputes and the fetters which have hampered their freedom of action have been further determined by some basic principles of Western democratic life. These include an effective institutional structure for representation and debate, a broad acceptance of a pluralist society with its consequence of difference, and tolerance as an essential component of democratic behaviour. And quite often elite willingness to seek solutions may have been driven not only by a sense of justice or acceptance of ethnonational rights, but simply as part of everyday pluralist life where political parties and their elites compete against each for political advantage. These factors have constrained not only the elites but also the ethnonational political movements which may have gained important concessions, but these have more often been rather minimalist, far from the far-reaching dreams of secession or independence.

In the next century elites will probably continue to respond positively to ethnonational concerns when they deem some action is necessary. Equally, processes of socioeconomic change and accommodationist policies may continue the slow process of ethnonational absorption which has always been present in the past. However, a changing environment may place elites in a very different arena. It is commonplace now to read that the phenomenon of globalisation, along with the ending of the Cold War, will increasingly squeeze the role of the state, and by implication of its elites (see Cerny 1995; Porter 1990): one end scenario has been the re-emphasis of more localised particularism and collective identities. In Europe the potential impact of the European Union upon the relationship between the state and indigenous ethnonationalism is still perhaps to be realised. Regions are already catered for within the formal EU institutional structure, and ethnonational movements and organisations have already begun to look equally towards Brussels as to national elites for the realisation of their objectives. It may well be the case that »the possibility of regional empowerment in Europe has influenced culturally distinctive regional movements away from the demand of full independence towards the demand for greater autonomy within the context of the European Union« (Marks & McAdam 1996, 266). But even this, if it is true, represents a challenge to elites and their imperatives of territorial integrity and legitimacy. It would seem that the last chapter on ethnonational politics in Western democracies is yet to be written, and hence that in countries with distinctive cultural communities, elites will still be required to ponder on and seek to resolve the politics of territorial difference.

References

Barry, B. (1991). *Democracy and Power: Essays in Political Theory*, Oxford: Oxford University Press.

Cerny, P. (1995). »Globalization and the Changing Logic of Collective Action«, *International Organization*, Vol. 49, pp. 595-625.

Doob, L.W. (1976). *Patriotism and Nationalism: Their Psychological Foundations*, Westport: Greenwood Press.

Esman, M.J. (ed.) (1977). *Ethnic Conflict in the Western World*, Ithaca: Cornell University Press.

Feagin, J.S. & S. Capek (1991). »Grassroots Movements in a Class Perspective«, *Research in Political Sociology*, Vol. 5, pp. 27-53.

Heisler, M.O. & B.G. Peters (1983). »Scarcity and the Management of Conflict in Multicultural Polities«, *International Political Science Review*, Vol. 4, pp. 327-44.

Laponce, J. (1987). *Languages and their Territories*, Toronto: University of Toronto Press.

Loughlin, J. & S. Mazey (eds.) (1994). »The End of the French Unitary State: Ten Years of Regionalization in France«, special issue of *Regional Policy and Politics*, Vol. 4, No. 3.

Lustick, I. (1979). »Stability in Deeply Divided Societies: Consociationalism versus Control«, *World Politics*, Vol. 31, pp. 325-44.

Mackenzie, W.J.M. (1976). *Political Identity*, London: Penguin.

Marks, G. and McAdam, D. (1996). »Social Movements and the Changing Structure of Political Opportunity in the European Union«, *West European Politics*, vol. 19, pp. 249-278.

McGarry, J. & B. O'Leary (eds.) (1990). *The Future of Northern Ireland*, Oxford: Clarendon Press.

Mitchell, J. (1996). »Conservatives and the Changing Meaning of Union«, *Regional and Federal Studies*, Vol. 6, pp. 30-44.

Newman, S. (1994). »Ethnoregional Parties: A Comparative Perspective«. *Regional Politics and Policy*, Vol. 4, pp. 28-66.

Porter, M. (1990). *The Comparative Advantages of Nations*, London: Macmillan.

Sachs, W. (1992). *The Development Dictionary: A Guide to Knowledge as Power*, London: Zed Books.

Watson, M. (1978). »A Critique of Development from Above: The Lessons of French and Dutch Experiences of Nationally-Defined Regional Policy«, *Public Administration*, Vol. 56, pp. 457-81.

Weinstein, B. (1991). »Language Planning as an Aid and a Barrier to Irredentism«, pp. 111-38, in N.Chazan (ed.), *Irredentism and International Politics*, London: Adamantine Press.

Mogens N. Pedersen's Bibliography

1 »Kvindernes mobilisering i dansk politik«, *Danske økonomer*, 1965, pp. 531-39. Also printed in *Kvinden og Samfundet*, 1966, pp. 40-47.
2 »Preferential voting in Denmark: The Voter's Influence on the Election of Folketing Candidates«, *Scandinavian Political Studies*, Vol. 1, 1966, pp. 167-87.
3 »Partiernes holdning ved vedtagelsen af regeringens lovforslag 1945-66«, *Historie*, 1967, pp. 404-35.
4 »Consensus and Conflict in the Danish Folketing 1945-65, *Scandinavian Political Studies*, Vol. 2, 1967, pp. 143-66.
5 »Valgforklaringer«, *Historie*, 1967, pp. 595-614.
6 »Lovgivningsprocessen«, *Dansk Historielærerforening*, 1968, pp. 110-18.
7 »Politik og dens udformning«, pp. 109-69, in K. Helweg Petersen (ed.), *Borger i Danmark, I,* Copenhagen, 1969.
8 (With Erik Damgaard and P. Nannestad Olsen) »Party Distances in the Danish Folketing«, *Scandinavian Political Studies*, Vol. 6, 1971, pp. 87-106.
9 »Lawyers in Politics: The Danish Folketing and American Legislatures«, pp. 25-63, in Samuel C. Patterson & John C. Wahlke (eds.), *Comparative Legislative Behavior: Frontiers of Research*, 1972, New York: John Wiley and Sons, Inc.
10 »Nogle forskningspolitiske fodnoter til beretning om behavioralismens gennembrud i amerikansk statskundskab«, *politica*, Vol. 5, No. 2, 1972, pp. 13-33.
11 *Danske Politiker-Arkiver: En oversigt over dataarkiver indeholdende oplysninger om danske politikere 1848-1971*, Aarhus: Institute of Political Science, 1972, 121 pp.

12 »Den problemfyldte samtidsorientering«, *Historie og Samtidsorientering*, Vol. 13, 1974, pp. 445-50.
13 »The Geographical Matrix of Parliamentary Representation: A Spatial Model of Political Recruitment«, *European Journal of Political Research*, Vol. 3, 1975, pp. 1-19.
14 (with Poul Rasmussen) »Tidsforbruget ved studienævnsarbejde: Bemærkninger om nogle konsekvenser af gennemførelsen af universitetsstyrelsesloven«, *Økonomi og Politik*, Vol. 49, 1975, pp. 219-28.
15 »Interlocking Crises. State and University in Denmark«, *Wetenschap en Democratie*, Vol. 2, 1976, pp. 145-59.
16 *Political Development and Elite Transformation in Denmark*, London/Beverly Hills, California: Sage Publications, 1976, (*Sage Research Papers in political sociology 06-018*), 61 pp.
17 »Om den rette brug af historiske materialer i statskundskaben: Nogle didaktiske overvejelser«, pp. 235-71, in *Festskrift til Erik Rasmussen*, Aarhus: Politicas Forlag, 1977.
18 »Norsk Presseforskning«, *Pressens Årbog 1977*, Copenhagen: C.A. Reitzel, 1977, pp. 188-91.
19 »The Personal Circulation of a Legislature: The Danish Folketing, 1849-1968«, pp. 63-101, in William O. Aydelotte (ed.), *The History of Parliamentary Behavior*, Princeton: Princeton University Press, 1977.
20 »Om voteringsanalysens muligheder og begrænsninger – bemærkninger til en anakronistisk debat om brugen af kvantitative metoder«, *Statsvetenskaplig Tidsskrift*, 1977, No, 4, pp. 259-63.
21 »The Danish University between the Millstones«, *Minerva. A Review of Science, Learning and Policy*, Vol. XV, 1977, pp. 335-76, & appendix pp. 377-86.
22 (with Kjell Eliassen) »Professionalization of Legislatures: Long Term Change in Political Recruitment in Denmark and Norway«, *Comparative Studies in Society and History*, Vol. 20, No. 2, 1978, pp. 286-318.
23 »La mizurazione del mutamento nei sistemi partitici: una critica«, *Rivista Italiana de Scienza Politica*, No. 2, 1978, pp. 243-61.
24 »The Dynamics of European Party Systems: Changing Patterns of Electoral Volatility«, *European Journal Political Research*, Vol. 7, 1979, pp. 1-26.
25 Eds., »Dansk Politik i 1970'erne. Studier og Arbejdspapirer«, Copenhagen: Samfundsvidenskabeligt Forlag, 1979, 319 pp.
26 »La Transformación de las Universidades Escandinavas: experimentos de participación, politización y otras discontinuidades«, *Revista de Estudios Politicos*, No. 11, Nueva Epoca, 1979, pp. 63-84.
27 »On Measuring Party System Change: A Methodological Critique and

a Suggestion«, *Comparative Political Studies*, Vol. 12, 1980, pp. 387-403.

28 (with Howard O. Hunter) *Recent Reforms in Swedish Higer Education*, Stockholm: Ratio, 1980, 65 pp.

29 (with Howard O. Hunter) »Recent Reforms in Swedish Higher Education«, *Minerva: A Review of Science, Learning, and Policy*, Vol. XVIII, No. 2, 1980, pp. 324-51.

30 »Sverige: Universitetsreformen i nordisk perspektiv«, *Uddannelse*, No. 2, 1981, pp. 57-68.

31 »Towards a New Typology of Party Lifespans and Minor Parties«, *Scandinavian Political Studies*, Vol. 5, New Series, No. 1, 1982, pp. 1-16.

32 »The Political Parties in Denmark«, *Factsheet Denmark*, published by the Ministry of Foreign Affairs, 1982, 4 pp. Also in French and German.

33 »Denmark: state and university – from coexistence to collision«, pp. 233-74, in Hans Daalder og Edward Shils (eds.), *Universities, Politicians and Bureaucrats – Europe and the United States*, Cambridge: Cambridge University Press, 1982.

34 »Changing patterns of Electoral Volatility in European Party Systems 1948-1977: Explorations in Explanation«, pp. 29-66, in Hans Daalder & Peter Mair (eds.), *Western European Party Systems – Continuity and Change,* London: Sage Publications Ltd., 1983.

35 »A John Berrigan on Realignment in Denmark: A Critical Comment«, *Scandinavian Political Studies*, Vol. 6, New Series, No. 1, 1983, pp. 99-103.

36 »The Political Parties in Denmark«. *Factsheet Denmark*, published by the Ministry of Foreign Affairs, 2nd Rev. ed., 1983, 4 pp.

37 »Why, Who and How? – Normative Problems of Co-determination in the Public Sector, Illustrated by University Reforms in Denmark and Sweden«, *Statsvetenskaplig Tidskrift*, No. 4, 1983, pp. 315-30.

38 (with Kjell A. Eliassen) »Några Reflektioner om Svensk Statsvetenskap«, *Politologen*, Vol. 13, No. 1, 1984, pp. 9-15.

39 »Vælgerbevægelighed og politisk rekruttering: Nogle spekulationer og nogle foreløbige resultater«, pp. 60-85, in Ole Berg & Arlid Underdal (eds.), *Fra Valg til Vedtak*, Oslo: Aschehoug, 1984.

40 (with Kjell A. Eliassen) *Organisering og Styring av den Offentlige Sektor i de Skandinaviske Lande*, Slutrapport, Oslo: Bedriftsøkonomisk Institutt, 1984, 169 pp.

41 (with Kjell A. Eliassen) *Svensk Samhällsorganisation och Förvaltning. En Inventering av Svensk Forskning*, Oslo: Norwegian School of

Management, 1984, 185 pp. Published also by HSFR (Brytpunktserien), Stockholm, 1984, 138 pp.

42 »Electing the Folketing«, *Factsheet Denmark*, published by the Ministry of Foreign Affairs, 1984, 8 pp. Also in Danish, German and French.

43 »Forming a Government in Denmark«, *Factsheet Denmark*, published by the Ministry of Foreign Affairs, 1984, 8 pp. Also in Danish, German and French.

44 »Research on European Parliaments: A Review Article on Scholarly and Institutional Variety«, *Legislative Studies Quarterly*, Vol. IX, No. 3, 1984, pp. 505-29.

45 »Demokratiseringen af universiteterne – hvad har den ført til?«, pp. 42-56, in *Report from IX Nordic Seminar for University Administrators*, Aarhus: Academia Færoensis, 24-28 June, 1984.

46 (with Kjell A. Eliassen) »Omkring studiet af nogle centrale politiske institutioner i Danmark: Et skandinavisk perspektiv«, *politica*, Vol. 16, 1984, pp. 298-325.

47 (with Kjell A. Eliassen) *Skandinaviske Politiske Institutioner og Politisk Adfærd 1970-84. En kommenteret bibliografi, [Scandinavian Political Institutions and Political Behavior 1970-84. An Annotated Bibliography]*, Odense: Odense University Press, 1985, 158 pp.

48 (with Kjell A. Eliassen) *Nordiske Politiske Fakta, [Nordic Political Facts]*, Oslo: Tiden Norsk Forlag, 1985, 194 pp.

49 (with Kjell A. Eliassen) » Political Science in Sweden: A Critique«, *Politologen*, Vol. 15, 1986, pp. 11-14.

50 »The Danish 'Working Multiparty System': Breakdown or Adaption?«, pp. 1-60, in Hans Daalder (ed.), *Party Systems In Denmark, Austria, Switzerland, The Netherlands, and Belgium*, London: Francis Pinter Publishers, 1987.

51 »Skyggebilleder? - Nogle kommentarer til validitetsdiskussionen omkring Søren Risbjerg Thomsens metode til økologisk inferens«, *politica*, Vol. 19, No. 3, 1987, pp. 333-42.

52 »Er partisystemet på vej ind i alderdommen?«, in *De politiske partiapparaters rolle i fremtiden*, Roligheds hæfte, No. 2, 1988, pp. 7-26.

53 »Lyngsie som taktiker. – Allerupsagen og fagbevægelsens strukturproblemer før første verdenskrig«, pp. 223-44, in H. C. Johansen, M.N. Pedersen & J. Thomsen (eds.), *Om Danmarks Historie 1900-1920. – Festskrift til Tage Kaarsted*, Odense: Odense University Press, 1988.

54 »The Defeat of All Parties. The Danish Folketing Election 1973«, pp. 257-81, in Kay Lawson & Peter H. Merkl (eds.), *When Parties Fail -*

Emerging Alternative Organizations, Princeton: Princeton University Press, 1988.

55 »The Irreversible Process of University 'Democratization': The Danish Case«, *International Journal of Institutional Management in Higher Education*, Vol. 12, 1988, pp. 115-28.

56 »Partierne mellem det 19. og det 21. århundrede», *Vartovbogen,* 1989, pp. 71-89.

57 »En kortfattet oversigt over det danske partisystems udvikling», *politica*, No. 3, 1989, pp. 265-78.

58 »Højre, Venstre – og Revolutionen«, in special edition of *NYT fra Odense Universitet*, September, 1989, 17 pp.

59 »EDB og ophavsret – praktiske problemer og politiske udviklinger«, *DDA Nyt*, No. 54, 1990, pp. 5-11.

60 »Hvordan tegner fremtiden sig for de politiske partier?«, pp. 78-84, in J. Elklit (ed.), *De politiske partier – nu og i fremtiden*, Copenhagen: Lintas/GR, 1990.

61 »Electoral Volatility in Western Europe 1948-77«, pp. 195-207, in Peter Mair (ed.), *The West European Party System*, Oxford: Oxford University Press, 1990.

62 »Politologen som konsulent - tanker om en rolle under udvikling«, *Statsvetenskaplig Tidskrift*, Vol. 93, No. 4, 1990, pp. 317-28.

63 »The Birth, Life, and Death of Small Parties in Danish Politics«, pp. 95-114, in Ferdinand Müller-Rommel & Geoffrey Pridham (eds.), *Small Parties in Western Europe – Comparative and National Perspectives,* London: Sage Publications, 1991.

64 »Folketingets eget – slet ikke så helt lille – bureaukrati«, *Administrativ Debat*, No. 1, 1991, pp. 1-4.

65 (with Lars Bille) »Public Financing and Public Control of Political Parties in Denmark«, pp. 147-72, in Matti Wiberg (ed.), *The Public Purse and Political Parties – Public Financing of Political Parties in Nordic Countries,* Jyväskylä: The Finnish Political Science Assocition, 1991.

66 »Klarer han pynten? - Logit-metoden mellem forenklingens Scylla og realiteternes Charybdis«, *politica*, No. 23, 1991, pp. 440-43.

67 »Magtudredningens 'Missing Link' - eller : Hvor er den social-demokratiske magtelite blevet af?«, *Statsvetenskaplig Tidskrift*, No. 4, 1991, pp. 305-12.

68 (with Poul Meyer) *Nederlag - Politiske Erindringer 1932-1947*, Odense: Odense University Press, 1992, 119 pp.

69 »Fremtidens politiker - hvordan ser hun ud?«, pp. 27-31, in D. Bouchet

& Kurt K. Klausen (eds.), *Temaer i den samfundsvidenskabelige debat*, Odense: Odense University Press, 1992.

70 »Eine kurzgefasste Übersicht über die Entwicklung des dänischen Parteiensystems«, pp. 91-108, in Franz Urban Pappi & Hermann Schmitt (eds.), *Parteien, Parlamente und Wahlen in Skandinavien*, Frankfurt/New York: Campus Verlag, 1994.

71 *En decentral forskningsdatabase - et pilotprojekt ved Odense Universitet*, Beretning afgivet til Undervisningsministeriet, Odense: Odense Universitet, 1994, 53 pp. + appendiks.

72 »Incumbency Success and Defeat in Times of Electoral Turbulences: Patterns of Legislative Recruitment in Denmark 1945-1990«, pp. 218-50, in Albert Somit, Rudolf Wildenmann, Bernard Boll & Andrea Römmele (eds.), *The Victorious Incumbent: A Threat to Democracy?*, Aldershot: Dartmouth, 1994.

73 »Nékteré Rysy: Danské Politické Kultury, [Certain Features of Danish Political Culture]«, in Karel Lrárky (ed.), *Dué dánské prednásky*, Prague: Institute of International Relations, Paper No. 2, 1994, 5 pp.

74 »Reflections on the Danish Party Systems in the 1990s: New Challenges in New Electoral Arenas«, pp. 178-83, in Council of Europe (ed.), *Disillusionment with democracy: political parties, participation and non-participation in democratic institutions in Europe*, Strasbourg: Council of Europe Press, 1994.

75 (ed. with J. Elklit) *Kampen om kommunen. Ni fortællinger fra kommunalvalget i 1993*, Odense: Odense University Press, 1995, 238 pp.

76 »Blaabjerg: Når fortid, nutid og fremtid mødes i en vestjysk valgkamp«, pp. 57-80, in M.N. Pedersen & J. Elklit, *Kampen om kommunen. Ni fortællinger fra kommunalvalget i 1993*, Odense: Odense University Press, 1995.

77 (with J. Elklit) »Om 'Kampen om kommunen'«, pp. 9-14, in M.N. Pedersen & J. Elklit, *Kampen om kommunen. Ni fortællinger fra kommunalvalget i 1993*, Odense: Odense University Press, 1995.

78 (with J. Elklit) »Kommunalvalget 16. november 1993: Hvad er konklusionen«, pp. 214-38, in M.N. Pedersen & J. Elklit, *Kampen om kommunen. Ni fortællinger fra kommunalvalget i 1993*, Odense: Odense University Press, 1995.

79 »Sagkyndigudtalelse ved besættelsen af August Röhss professur ved Göteborgs Universitet«, *Statsvetenskaplig Tidskrift*, Vol. 98, 1995, pp. 71-83.

80 »Jens Otto Krag«, pp. 253-59, in David Wilsford (ed.), *Political Leaders of Contemporary Europe. A Biographical Dictionary*, Westport, Conn.: Greenwood Press, 1995.

81 »Euro-parties and European Parties: New Arenas, New Challenges and New Strategies«, pp. 15-39, in Svein S. Andersen & Kjell A. Eliassen (eds.), *The European Union: How Democratic Is It?*, London: Sage Publications, 1995.

82 »Young Man in a Hurry: Recollections of a Soldier of Fortune«, *Scandinavian Political Studies*, Vol. 19, 1996, pp. 181-204.

83 »Present at the Creation«, pp. 253-97, in Hans Daalder (ed.), *Comparative European Politics: The Story of a Profession*, London: Pinter, 1997.

84 »A Catalyst for Discussion«, *European Journal of Political Research*, Vol. 31, 1997, pp. 93-97.

85 »Left-Right Political Scales: 'Some Expert Judgments'«, *European Journal of Political Research*, Vol. 31, 1997, pp. 147-50.

86 »De, der selv siger stop«, pp. 62-73, in J. Elklit & R. Buch Jensen (eds.), *Kommunalvalg*, Odense: Odense University Press, 1997.

87 »Vælgermøderne - et møde med vælgerne?«, pp. 142-53, in J. Elklit & R. Buch Jensen (eds.), *Kommunalvalg*, Odense: Odense University Press, 1997.

88 »Når kagen skal deles: Konstitueringens politik«, pp. 309-26, in J. Elklit & R. Buch Jensen (eds.), *Kommunalvalg*, Odense: Odense University Press, 1997,

89 (with Kjell Goldman & Øyvind Østerud eds.) *Leksikon i statskundskab*, Copenhagen: Akademisk Forlag, 1997, 264 pp. Also published in a Swedish and Norwegian version (Stockholm & Oslo: Universitetsforlaget, 1997)

90 (with Lene Anderson) »Rekrutteringen af kommunale chefer. En administrativ elite under forandring«, *politica*, Vol. 30, No. 3, 1998, pp. 298-308.

The bibliography was prepared by Kasper Møller Hansen, with the annual reports from SDU - Odense University and Aarhus University as main sources.

NB: Mogens N. Pedersen is editor of several journals. These are, however, not included nor are internal papers, book reviews, newspaper articles and publications less than 2-3 pages.

Contributors

Gunnar Sjöblom, Copenhagen University
Dag Anckar, Åbo Academy
Erik Damgaard, Aarhus University
Kjell A. Eliassen and Catherine Børve Monsen, The Norwegian School of Management
Jørgen Elklit, Aarhus University
Heinz Eulau, Stanford University
Michael Goldsmith, Salford University
Roger Buch Jensen, University of Southern Denmark - Odense University
Ulrik Kjær, University of Southern Denmark - Odense University
Michael Laver, Dublin Trinity College
Leif Lewin, Uppsala Universitet
Arend Lijphart, University of California, San Diego, and Peter J. Bowman, Mira Costa College
Peter Mair, University of Leiden
Jørn Henrik Petersen, University of Southern Denmark - Odense University
Palle Svensson, Copenhagen Business School
Curt Sørensen, Aarhus University
Lise Togeby, Aarhus University
Derek W. Urwin, Aberdeen University